T0309443

Human Factors for Informatics Usability

Developed with the sponsorship of SERC and CREST

Human Factors for Informatics Usability

Edited by

B. SHACKEL
Professor, HUSAT Research Institute and Department of Human Sciences, Loughborough University of Technology

S.J. RICHARDSON
Principal Project Officer, HUSAT Research Institute, Loughborough University of Technology

CAMBRIDGE UNIVERSITY PRESS
Cambridge
New York Port Chester
Melbourne Sydney

Published by the Press Syndicate of the University of Cambridge
The Pitt Building, Trumpington Street, Cambridge CB2 1RP
40 West 20th Street, New York, NY10011, USA
10, Stamford Road, Oakleigh, Melbourne 3166, Australia

British Library cataloguing in publication data available

Library of Congress cataloging in publication data available

ISBN 0 521 36570 8

Transferred to digital printing 2004

CONTENTS

PREFACE

For most ordinary users and even for some computer professionals the human-computer interface is still more of a space frontier and a time barrier than an open door to communication. As Sir John Fairclough (Chief Scientific Adviser to the UK Cabinet Office) has said, at the time when he was Chairman of the IBM UK Laboratories, "Human Factors is the Nº 1 issue today".

The computer and informatics industry is beginning to realise the need to change from the domination of technology-oriented goals to achieve balanced solutions truly proven to match the expectations, needs, capabilities and satisfaction of the users. The problem is that it is much harder to design for what real users really want. The aim of this book is to show how the knowledge and methods from the discipline of Ergonomics/Human Factors can help to improve Informatics Usability for real people.

The computer and now the informatics industry has grown amazingly during its first 35 years, without much formal attention to Human-Computer Interaction (HCI). Does it really need to be concerned about the user? The answer comes from some leaders of the industry itself. "People costs are already very much greater than machine costs for over 95% of the human-machine interactions. Actions to reduce the human costs and simplify the human interface to computers will have the greatest impact on growth".

So the industry is changing orientation, and may be expected to spend much more effort and resources on 'computer ergonomics' or 'computer human factors' to improve the usability, efficiency and quality of the HCI.

This book has been developed from the review papers presented by invited speakers at an Advanced Study Course held at Loughborough University 14–19 December 1986. The Course was sponsored by the European Science and Technology Research Committee of the Commission of the European Communities

(CREST) and by the Science and Engineering Research Council (SERC) of the United Kingdom. It had three objectives:

1. to review the knowledge and methods available from the field of human factors to help improve the usability of informatics systems;
2. to present recent theoretical and methodological developments in this field; and
3. to stimulate increased application of this knowledge and these methods and developments.

On completion of the course, students were expected to have gained an advanced overview of the theory and practice presented and to be able to start applying at least some of the knowledge gained.

To achieve these objectives some of the leading international authorities on human factors presented review papers, attended panel sessions, provided demonstrations and answered the many questions one would expect from advanced academic, industrial and commercial students. The speakers presented a rich and stimulating mixture of research and practice, built up from many years of experience in this complex field.

All the chapters in this volume are based upon their contributions, but they have been substantially revised and expanded to present a comprehensive review. They have been grouped together in five parts, as indicated in the list of contents, and the scope of the book is outlined in the latter part of Chapter 1.

The material in this book is as timely today as when presented; it is not out of date. Indeed in many respects it is more timely, because the industry is now recognising the need to heed the users. Computer designers are becoming receptive to the importance of the human factors aspects. I am very grateful to the contributors for their tolerance of the interchanges and delays inherent in editing and revision, including delays due to my eye operations, and I wish to thank them for their forebearance and above all for the quality of their contributions.

This book is not intended primarily for professionals or experts in human factors or human-computer interaction, although they may well find substantial new material here. Its principal target audience comprises the very many designers, software and hardware engineers, system design managers, management services managers and user managers who are now becoming aware of the importance of usability. The book is intended to provide for them not only a comprehensive introduction and a thorough overview but also some substantial first guidance about what they can do and how they can approach the problems of informatics usability.

The book is also intended to serve as an introductory text for postgraduate conversion courses and for undergraduate courses in computing and information technology, and for short advanced courses in informatics. Many courses are now being developed and established; this overview and primer on usability and human-computer interaction should provide a good foundation for them. Further, it will serve its purpose even more fully if it helps not only to structure and stimulate this field of research and application but also to increase the interaction between readers and writers. The addresses of all the contributors are given in the next section. The intensity of involvement of all at the course and subsequently during editing has been such that probably every author will welcome communication from any reader.

Looking to the immediate future of HCI, it seems likely that there will be considerable development in two distinct directions. In research and system development, the study of new HCI possibilities will probably accelerate, in such areas for example as speech systems, natural language systems and storage structures using different approaches. In application and system design, there will probably be a marked growth of attention to formal methods of designing for human use. Some research will also be needed to improve and generalise these methods, particularly the approach of user-centred design; but in the main the concentration needs to be upon disseminating and applying the knowledge and techniques already available from the human sciences.

It will be evident to the reader, from the way in which different chapters deal with different issues from different orientations, that the subject of HCI is still developing, with much to be done and with many interesting challenges. For the researcher, in both computing and human sciences there is still much to learn about people and the possibilities which computer technology may bring for human development. For the computer professional and designer, the challenge is to learn new skills and facts about people, to accept new methods and advisers, and especially to work with users. As a result, computers and informatics systems with good usability may gradually evolve to a new status as useful, symbiotic, servants and partners of society.

Brian Shackel
Quorn, June 1990.

[illegible]

CONTRIBUTORS

Professor B. Shackel,
HUSAT Research Institute and Department of Human Sciences,
Loughborough University of Technology,
Loughborough, Leicestershire, LE11 3TU. (UK)

Mr. S.J. Richardson,
HUSAT Research Institute,
Loughborough University of Technology,
The Elms, Elms Grove,
Loughborough, Leicestershire, LE11 1RG. (UK)

Dr. P. Barnard,
MRC Applied Psychology Unit,
15 Chaucer Road, Cambridge, CB2 2EF. (UK)

Professor A. Chapanis,
Industrial and Human Factors Consultancy Services,
Suite 210 Ruxton Towers,
8415 Bellona Lane,
Baltimore, Maryland 21204. (USA)

Ms. L. Damodaran,
HUSAT Research Institute,
Loughborough University of Technology,
The Elms, Elms Grove,
Loughborough, Leicestershire, LE11 1RG. (UK)

Professor K.D. Eason and Mrs. S.D.P. Harker,
Department of Human Sciences,
Loughborough University of Technology,
Loughborough, Leicestershire, LE11 3TU. (UK)

Professor B.R. Gaines,
Department of Computer Science,
University of Calgary,
Alberta, T2N 1N4 (CAN)

Mr. A. Gardner,
HUSAT Research Institute,
Loughborough University of Technology,
The Elms, Elms Grove,
Loughborough, Leicestershire, LE11 1RG. (UK)

Professor S. Greif,
Fachbereich Psychologie,
University of Osnabrück,
45 Osnabrück,
Postfach 4469. (FRG)

Professor E. Mumford,
Manchester Business School,
Booth Street West, Manchester, M15 6PB. (UK)

Dr. W. Newman,
Rank Xerox EuroPARC,
61 Regent Street, Cambridge, CB2 1AB. (UK)

Professor B. Shneiderman,
Department of Computer Science,
University of Maryland,
College Park, Maryland 20742. (USA)

Mr. T.F.M. Stewart,
Systems Concepts,
Museum House, Museum Street,
London, WC1A 1JT. (UK)

Dr. P. Wright,
MRC Applied Psychology Unit,
15 Chaucer Road, Cambridge, CB2 2EF. (UK)

Ir. J. Ziegler and Professor H.-J. Bullinger,
Fraunhofer Institut für Arbeitswissenschaft und Organisation (IAO),
Holzgartenstraße 17,
D-7000 Stuttgart 1. (GDR)

ACKNOWLEDGEMENTS

The Editors would like to acknowledge the contributions of all who assisted with the planning, administration and running of the course and all those who have contributed to the preparation of this book.

Our thanks are specifically directed to the sponsors (CREST and SERC) for their generosity, to staff at the HUSAT Research Institute and the Support Team from HUSAT and Bell-Howe Conferences for their dedication and enthusiastic support for this venture, our authors for their valued contribution and the students for their participation and new found enthusiasm for the subject.

We should also mention, by name, Denise and Cliff McKnight, Linda Deal and Helen Savage for their part in production and Cambridge University Press for their patience and guidance.

Finally, a special thanks to our partners, friends and close colleagues for their unquestioning tolerance and support, without whose aid we might still be writing.

Part 1

Informatics Usability — Introduction, Scope and Importance

CHAPTER ONE

HUMAN FACTORS FOR INFORMATICS USABILITY — BACKGROUND AND OVERVIEW

BRIAN SHACKEL AND SIMON RICHARDSON

1. Introduction

The purpose of this chapter is to provide the general background and context for human factors and usability, to present a brief historical outline, and to give an overview of the contents of the book.

Informatics usability is one of the major technical areas within the field of Human-Computer Interaction (HCI). HCI deals with all aspects of the human use of computers, usually in the context of interactive Informatics systems. Informatics is used in this book as equivalent to the term Information Technology, and both terms will often be abbreviated as IT.

Human-Computer Interaction (HCI) is a major part of the larger subject termed Human-System Interaction (HSI) and HSI is a large part of the applied side of the discipline known as Ergonomics or Human Factors — see Figure 1.

So Human Factors for Informatics Usability involves a consideration of all the possible contributions which could be made from anywhere in the discipline of Human Factors (HF) to improve the usability of IT systems. Further, since Informatics Usability is obviously an inter-disciplinary applied field, a proper treatment of this subject must include reference to and relevant inputs from the closely related areas such as software system design and cognitive psychology. Therefore, the contents of this book range from computer-human interface design to organisational issues, from formal models in HCI and designing expert systems to the contributions of cognitive psychology, and from HF strategy and the design process to evaluating usability.

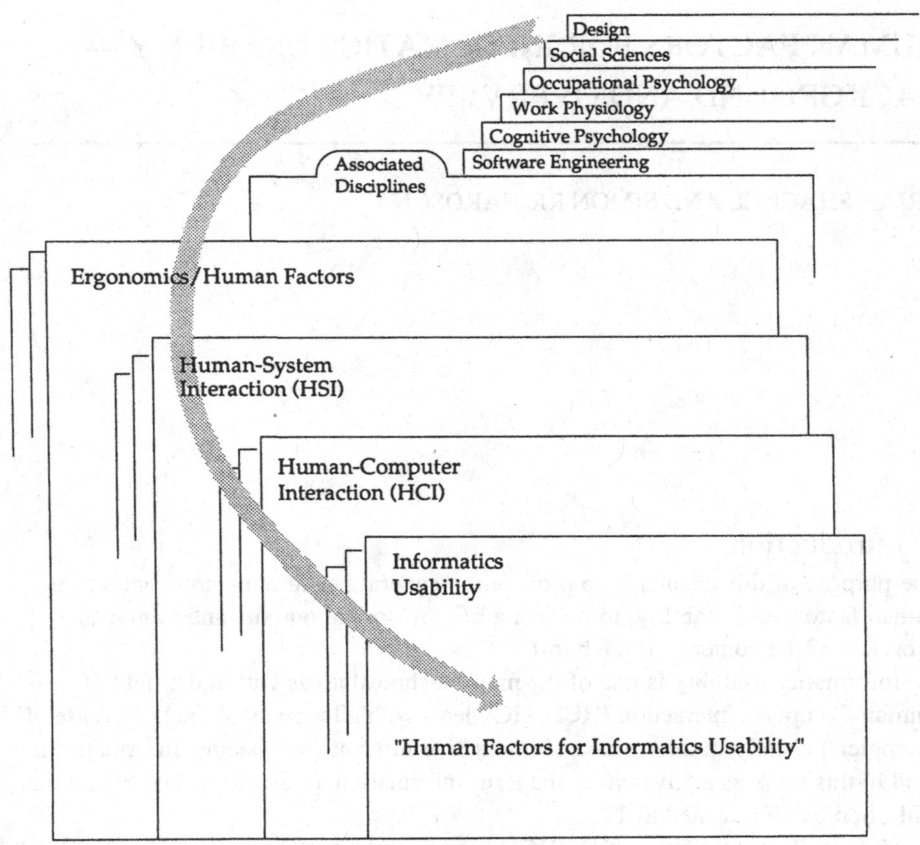

Figure 1: The context of this book and the associated disciplines.

To present the background and overview, we shall proceed from the general to the particular. So, the growth of Ergonomics/Human Factors will first be summarised; then Human-System Interaction (HSI) and the growth of Human-Computer Interaction (HCI) will be outlined; the importance of Human Factors and Usability will next be discussed; and finally the scope and contents of this book will be reviewed.

1.1 *The growth of Ergonomics/Human Factors*

In Great Britain, what is now called ergonomics had its beginning in the scientific study of human problems in ordnance factories during World War 1. This kind of work continued under the Industrial Health Research Board between the wars.

World War 2 led to greater emphasis not merely on matching men to machines by selection and training, but also, much more than previously, to the designing of equipment so that its operation was within the capacities of most normal people. This fitting the job to the man increased considerably the collaboration of engineers in certain fields with the biological scientists. This collaboration, beginning primarily with military problems, because it was there particularly that operators were pushed to their limits, continued after the war and led to the formation in 1949 of the Ergonomics Research Society.

Similar developments occurred in other countries, leading in the USA to the formation of the Human Factors Society in 1954. On the international scene, the formation meeting which accepted the first constitution and rules of the International Ergonomics Association was held during the Annual Conference of the Ergonomics Research Society in Oxford in 1959; the first international conference of the IEA was held in Stockholm in 1961. The IEA now has 16 member societies in nations around the world.

1.2 *Ergonomics/Human Factors — scope and definition*

The principal purpose or philosophy of Ergonomics is not primarily to improve productivity or output or human methods of doing work; these are quite properly the main aims of other disciplines. The prime purpose of Ergonomics is to study and understand the situation of people at work and play, and thus to be able to improve the whole situation for the people. Of course this knowledge may also be used to assist with productivity, and at times managers may need to be persuaded to use Ergonomics by the expectation of some such benefit, but the main thrust of Ergonomics remains always user-centred.

Therefore, Ergonomics is defined as the study of the relation between man and his occupation, equipment and environment, and particularly the application of anatomical, physiological and psychological knowledge to the problems arising therefrom. This definition is in two parts and clearly describes both a science and a technology.

Thus, the scope of work in Ergonomics must clearly embrace both research and practical application. Research is essential to increase our knowledge about how people behave in total situations, how they are similar to and different from engineering components, and how they respond to and are influenced by their task and environment.

In the study and treatment of practical situations, Ergonomics (or Human Factors — the equivalent name used in the USA) places major emphasis upon efficiency in the operation of the equipment as measured by the human performance of actual users. Allied with efficiency are the safety, comfort and satisfaction of the operator. Because the aim is to optimise the human-machine and human-environment combinations by improving the system and the environment, this aspect has also been termed 'Fitting the System to the User'. Equally important are the personnel factors such as selection, training, and adaptation to environmental and working conditions. These are studied both as part of ergonomics and as separate topics under the headings of Work Physiology and Occupational Psychology. From this knowledge people can be helped to alter themselves, within limits, to improve the human-machine partnership; this personnel aspect has also been termed 'Fitting the User to the System'.

1.3 *Why is Ergonomics/Human Factors essential?*

There are three basic reasons why Ergonomics is essential for modern industry, especially in relation to product and system design.

First the complexity and sophistication of modern industrial technology sets continually higher demands upon the human operatives and controllers; but complexity also causes designers to need too long a training and to be too busy with technical problems either to deal with the human factors properly or to learn enough about how to deal with them.

Second, there is a time and space barrier. The complexity of modern technology also separates designer and user, and thus usually prevents effective feedback from the user to improve the design. Therefore the ergonomist is an essential link who operates as a sort of preventive and predictive feedback channel.

Third, there is the separation of responsibilities and of the cost consequences. A further problem which follows from the complexity is that often the designer, manufacturer/marketer, buyer and user are separate. They may well be in separate organisations and certainly will have separate aims and criteria. The designer (and engineer) will aim for a good machine solution, and will expect to spend all his budget costs on technical machine factors; the manufacturer/marketer will aim to cut the capital cost (but not necessarily the running costs); the buyer will aim to pay a low price and will expect savings to come from the purchase (perhaps by staff reductions); the user will aim to minimise his personal loss (of skill, earnings, etc.) due to the new machine or method of working. Therefore, the separation between them may often cause each of these four people not to use ergonomics, because they cannot see the cost justification within their own cost limits. Only the manager in charge of the user sees the final result, where the true cost of the extra training, and of the inefficiency and losses if the design is not ergonomic, can exceed any savings in purchase cost.

Because each sector of responsibility is separate, as noted above, the cost-benefit evaluation of ergonomics can often be difficult to prove (but for references and examples see Beevis and Slade, 1970; Corlett and Coates, 1976; Shackel, 1987; and Corlett, 1988). Therefore, a recent new concept may be helpful. Organisations using new systems (i.e., the 'buyers') are beginning to realise that the running and repair costs (including selection, training, maintenance, and labour turnover) may far exceed the capital costs. Some are beginning to ask the manufacturer/marketer not only to give a standard purchase warranty, but also to guarantee the total running costs not to exceed some annual value over an agreed 'life' usage. This is called total 'life-cycle' or 'system-life' costing and should be strongly supported by ergonomists, because it helps to show more clearly the cost-benefit value of ergonomics.

2. Human-Systems Interaction (HSI)

When Human Factors/Ergonomics knowledge and methods are applied to the problems of human-computer interaction, in the context of interactive IT systems, the aim must be to harness all the relevant approaches used to deal with human and organisational problems in all areas of Human-Systems Interaction (HSI). The field of HSI can be characterised as follows.

HSI is concerned with methods, media and mechanisms for enhancing cooperation between people and systems in an interactive organisational environment. This field comprises:

(1) the definition of the organisation and job contexts for the users in and of a system and the consequential job and task situations and needs,

(2) the design of the organisation, of the jobs and of the tasks as an integrated whole socio-technical system,

(3) the design of the human interfaces based upon the organisation, job and task demands and upon the physical and cognitive characteristics and needs of the users, and

(4) the formulation of tools and techniques for designing, constructing, evaluating and monitoring both the organisation of and the individual human user parts of interactive human-machine systems.

In addition to the human-system contact points, HSI includes the study of those aspects of the humans, the organisation, the job, the tasks, the machines, and the environment which directly influence the effectiveness and acceptability of systems for the user.

The term HSI itself requires a brief comment. In order to improve the design of the interfaces between people and systems one must study the requirements of particular users doing particular tasks, i.e., the human-system interaction. Often, such studies of functional interaction must come before the new physical interface can be produced. In accordance with current practice, therefore, the term HSI is used to mean both the human-machine processes and functions (HS Interaction) and the hardware and software components which facilitate these interactions (i.e., the HS Interface).

Finally, we must remember that we are concerned with human-machine systems rather than humans or machines separately. That is to say, human and machine form a 'socio-technical system' in which they must be complementary components working to a common goal. HSI is not just concerned with the displays and controls that an operator uses to interact with a machine — essential though these are. True socio-technical systems are designed to serve a purpose and that purpose is provided by people. On the one hand, inside the system, the people may be system specifiers, designers, constructors, purchasers, managers, supervisors, operators or maintainers. On the other hand, in the wider context of those served by the system, the people are the users of the products or services provided. HSI is concerned with each and every aspect of these various human interactions with machines. All advanced IT systems, therefore, have an HSI dimension.

3. Historical changes and their consequences for usability

3.1 *Growth of and changes in computing*

There have been rapid growths and changes in computing which have fundamentally altered the predominant type of users and their expectations so that the user population is no longer homogeneous. For a fuller review see Gaines (1985), and for useful references see Burch (1984) and Shackel (1985).

At the beginning of the digital computer era, the designers of computers were specialists and the users of computers had to become computer specialists. The potential power of this new machine and the speed of computation was so useful for certain scientific disciplines that some scientists found it worth the cost of time and effort to learn how to use it.

In the late 1950s the potential for the computer in industry and commerce was recognised, and the first serious business machines were developed; again, they were designed by computer specialists for use by data processing professionals. From the mid 1960s the minicomputer and remote terminal access to the time-sharing mainframe brought computer usage nearer to the layman. However, already the difficulties for the non-specialist and the problems of human-computer interaction were recognised (Nickerson, 1969; Shackel, 1969; Sackman, 1970).

The advent of the microcomputer in 1978, in widespread use from 1980, caused much growth in the use of computers for many different purposes by non-specialists of all types — from bank clerk to business executive, from librarian to life insurance salesman, and from secretary to stockbroker and space traveller. This rapid growth in computing, leading to widespread usability problems, is summarised in Figure 2.

The result of this rapid growth is that both the market for the IT industry and the users of IT equipment have changed significantly. The market has become much more selective, partly through experiences of poor usability. The users are no longer mainly computer professionals, but are mostly discretionary users (Bennett, 1979). As a result, the designers are no longer typical of or equivalent to users; but the designers may not realise how unique and therefore how unrepresentative they are.

Moreover, with the growth of IT, the many new users bring different needs to be satisfied. Earlier users were committed to using computers because of personal interest or job requirements. But the potential new users are such people as managers, physicians, lawyers and scientists who are committed to their tasks but not at all to the computer. They have choice and will only use computers if they are appropriate, useful and usable. So the market now contains important new categories of users. Moreover, some predict that these end users will be the primary decision makers in the future about acquiring equipment. Thus to be

Computer Type	Approx. Growth Era	Main Users	User Issues
Research machines	1950s	Mathematicians Scientists	Machine reliability; users must learn to do all the programming
Mainframes	1960s & 1970s	Data-processing professionals supplying a service	Users of the output (business managers) grow disenchanted with delays, costs, lack of flexibility
Minicomputers	1970s	Engineering and other non-computer professionals	Users must still do much programming; usability becomes a problem
Microcomputers (plus applications packages)	1980s	Almost anyone	Therefore usability is the major problem

Figure 2: Growth of digital computers and user issues.

successful, the IT industry must improve the usability of interactive systems, and to do so the understandable orientation of designers in the early years must now be completely reversed; designing must start with the end users and be user-centred around them. Therefore the human factors aspects become paramount.

3.2 *Human-Computer Interaction and usability aspects*

However, the growth of attention to the consequential human factors and usability aspects was slow to develop (see Figure 3). Some attention was being given to the ergonomics aspects of computers as early as the late 1950s, although this was primarily involved with military systems. However, some work was being done on the ergonomic design of commercial computers by 1960 (Shackel, 1959 and 1962), and the possible vision for the future of close-coupled symbiosis, which may be near to being realised today in 1990, was proposed by Licklider (1960). Through the 1960s such work as existed was scattered and mostly, in the USA especially, was still related to military systems. Attention at that time was mainly focussed upon hardware issues, large systems and process control rather than on office and business systems.

The first international meeting was held in 1969 in Cambridge UK (International Symposium on Man-Machine Systems), and the first journal for the area was established in the same year (International Journal of Man-Machine Studies). The first research group to be established with its main focus upon this subject started in 1970 (HUSAT at Loughborough University, UK). Through the 1970s significant work developed though still largely in small, somewhat isolated groups. The first specialised workshop meeting was held in 1976 as a NATO Advanced Study Institute on Man-Computer Interaction. Considerably greater attention to ergonomics and usability issues was stimulated by the arrival of the micro-computer in 1978. Thereafter, there was rapid growth in work on the human factors of computer systems for office, business and commercial use.

In 1980 the recent considerable growth was crystallised in four books (one from a conference), to be followed by several books each year thereafter, by a second main journal in 1982 and by seven major conferences in 1982–84 (see Figure 3). The first international conference on Human-Computer Interaction was sponsored by IFIP as INTERACT '84 (held in London in September 1984) and the second, INTERACT '87, was held in Stuttgart; the third, INTERACT '90, will be held in Cambridge UK, and INTERACT '93 is already being planned.

Another sign of growth in any field is the appearance of interest groups and scientific societies. National groups have now developed in a number of countries, for example: the Computer-Human Interaction Special Interest Group of the Association for Computing Machinery (ACM SIGCHI); the Human-Computer

1959	First recorded paper in the literature (Shackel, 1959) as reported by Gaines (1984)
1960	Seminal paper by Licklider (1960) on 'Man-Computer Symbiosis'
1969	First major conference ('International Symposium on Man-Machine Systems')
1969	*International Journal of Man-Machine Studies* started
1970	Foundation of HUSAT Research Centre, Loughborough University
1970-73	Four seminal books published (Sackman, 1970; Weinberg, 1971; Winograd, 1972; Martin, 1973)
1976	NATO Advanced Study Institute on 'Man-Computer Interaction'
1980	Conference and book on 'Ergonomics Aspects of Visual Display Terminals' (Grandjean and Vigliani, 1980)
	Three other books (Cakir, Hart and Stewart; Damodaran, Simpson and Wilson; Smith and Green (eds.))
1982	Journal *Behaviour and Information Technology* started
1982-84	Seven major conferences held in USA, UK and Europe with attendances ranging from 180 to over 1000 with an average of nearly 500
1983	European ESPRIT and British Alvey programmes begin
1985	Journal *Human-Computer Interaction* started
1985	ESPRIT HUFIT Project No. 385 begins 1st December
1985	From 1985 the conferences of national societies ACM and BCS, on CHI and HCI respectively, become annual
1986	Three HCI Centres launched in the UK under the Alvey initiative
1987	Second IFIP INTERACT International Conference on HCI
1988	Major Handbook on HCI published (M. Helander (ed.))
1989	IFIP establishes Technical Committee on HCI (IFIP TC 13)
1990	Third IFIP INTERACT International Conference on HCI

Figure 3: Growth of Attention to Ergonomic Aspects of Human-Computer Interaction (see Gaines, 1985, for a review of early development).

Interaction Specialist Group of the British Computer Society (BCS HCI SG); the Fachausschuss Software Ergonomie of the Gesellschaft für Informatik (GI FSE); the joint Man-Machine Interaction group of the Dutch Computer and Dutch Ergonomics Societies (NGI and NVvE MMI); and the IT Special Interest Group of The Ergonomics Society (ES ITSIG). Some further details of the growth and scope of HCI, to supplement this brief outline, are given by Gaines (1984), Shackel (1985) and Bullinger *et al.* (1987).

3.3 *Recent and current research initiatives*

The rapid growth of IT since 1982 was particularly assisted by the major funding programmes for research and development. These programmes did give more attention and support to human issues than any hitherto. For example, the Japanese Fifth Generation Conference Report (Moto-Oka, 1982) states: "Human beings communicate using a wide variety of forms: natural language, both spoken and written, pictures, images, documents, and the like. It is not easy for current computers to respond to them intelligently since they are not equipped with intelligent man-machine interfaces". Similarly, the report of the Alvey Committee (Alvey, 1982) states: "Information technology helps man handle and use information, and the system designer's aim is to produce a machine that matches, complements, and extends man's capability".

At the same time as the Japanese and British programmes were being developed, an even larger initiative was developed within the European Community under the ESPRIT programme (European Strategic Programme for Research in Information Technology), starting with pilot projects in 1983. The progress of ESPRIT has been recorded in successive annual conference Proceedings (ESPRIT '84 to ESPRIT '89 so far) published by North-Holland.

Within the UK Alvey initiative, costing over £300 million, the so-called Man-Machine Interface programme enabled over £10 million to be allocated to various projects broadly covering HCI topics. One example of the growth achieved is the inauguration of three centres of HCI excellence to try to assist the British IT industry; these three centres, two in England and one in Scotland, brought together leading research groups. In Scotland, for example, expertise at the Heriot-Watt and Strathclyde Universities was linked in the Scottish HCI Centre, and in London the Alvey funding similarly enabled University College and Queen Mary College to collaborate and establish the London HCI Centre. At Loughborough extensive research programmes already existed in HUSAT (Human Sciences and Advanced Technology Research Centre) within the Department of Human Sciences and in LUTCHI (Loughborough University of Technology Computer-Human Interface Research Centre) within the Department of Computer Studies; therefore, these linked their expertise to form the 'HCI Service at Loughborough University' to provide an integrated support service for industry from a human factors perspective.

Within Britain, the five-year Alvey programme has not been followed by a similar one with the same scale of funding. The two programmes which are relevant for HCI are: on the one hand the more industry-oriented 'Information Engineering Advanced Technology Programme', administered through the Department of Trade and Industry, within which all projects must be 50% funded by industry, and on the other hand the Joint Research Councils' (ESRC, MRC and SERC) Initiative in Cognitive Science/Human-Computer Interaction.

By contrast the ESPRIT programme has been succeeded by several programmes which involve human factors to some extent, and the funding for the R & D programmes through the Commission of the European Communities has certainly been increased. The previous work has now been expanded into ESPRIT II, RACE, DRIVE, DELTA and others under the large FRAMEWORK Plan.

From the above it is evident that 'classical' ergonomics/human factors has developed successfully over the past 20 years to deal primarily with the design of the hardware interface. But in the IT systems of the future, more and more it is the software and the software interface (Shackel, 1969) which will determine the usability and 'friendliness' of the system for the user. As a result, alongside physical ergonomics we need to see major growth in what has come to be called 'Cognitive Ergonomics'.

Cognitive Ergonomics is concerned with the study, measurement, analysis and modelling of human cognitive behaviour in relation to advanced technology systems. The range of variability involved must be even larger than in physical ergonomics, with the wide ranging differences between system users in intelligence, experience, memory and motivation. Therefore, major research programmes are needed "To enhance our understanding of the general computational principles underlying natural and artificial forms of intelligence, and their application in the design of systems involving human-computer interaction" (as is stated in the British programme plan for the research initiative in Cognitive Science/Human-Computer Interaction).

However, it should be noted that almost all the human factors research and application work fostered by these initiatives has been focussed upon the model of the single individual working with his/her computer, usually in an office environment. Very little has been concerned with the wider issues of human-system interaction and organisational factors.

Nevertheless, these initiatives, coupled with the development of special interest groups within the various scientific/professional organisations (as noted above) and along with an increase in research output, in publications and in conferences, are most encouraging. On the European front, the promise of wide collaboration between industry and research institutions and the value of a European wide dissemination of technical information from human factors research is beginning to bear fruit. Given the nature of the IT market, the promise of an increase in global communications and the rise of fourth and fifth generation technologies, this is not a moment too soon.

4. The importance of human factors and usability

There is now no doubt about the importance of human factors in the eyes of the computer industry in the USA, where there is greater development of human factors in industry than in Europe. This is particularly evident in the large numbers of human factors professionals and others from industry at the regular ACM CHI

(Computer Human Interaction) conferences; the total attendances in 1983, '85, '87, '89 and '90 have been 1000, 1200, 1400, 1700 and 2300, and the percentage from industry has been 70% to 80% each time. Ironically, this rapid growth in attention to human factors in the US industry is attributable, at least in part, to a European ergonomic standard, namely the German DIN standard for keyboard height to be not more than 30 mm. The realisation that an ergonomic standard could override all other aspects in the marketplace came as a big surprise and had a powerful effect on quite a number of US companies.

To illustrate this changed situation one merely has to note the marked change of emphasis upon human factors in IBM which was handed down from the very top (Shackel, 1986). As a result, special conferences were held, a worldwide programme of short courses for IBM engineers was instituted, and usability became of equal importance with functionality.

The following excerpt is typical of the writings of quite a number of the ergonomists in this field some years ago, but it is taken directly from a lecture by the IBM Vice President and Chief Scientist (Branscomb, 1983).

> "All that has changed. No longer the exclusive tool of specialists, computers have become both commonplace and indispensible. Yet they remain harder to use than they should be. It should be no more necessary to read a 300 page book of instructions before using a computer than before driving an unfamiliar automobile. But much more research in both cognitive and computer science will be required to learn how to build computers that are that easy to use. That is why our industry is paying increasing attention to the field of applied psychology called human factors, or ergonomics...Equally neglected has been human factors at the level of systems design. We know that system architecture has significant and widespread implications for user friendliness, but we know next to nothing about how to make fundamental architectural decisions differently, in the interest of good human factors...Thus the effort to design for ease of use could benefit enormously from basic research, not only in adaptive systems and computational linguistics, but above all in terms of controlled experiments involving actual use by representative end users — for you can't evaluate ease of use without use."

Finally, in Britain one of the earliest presentations of the importance of human factors in IT was published in an authoritative and well-illustrated report by the National Electronics Council (1983), in which several case studies are described to emphasise the need to design for people and build in usability from the start.

5. The scope of this book

The philosophy of 'Human Factors' and 'Ergonomics' is concerned with ensuring a good match of the equipment, workplace, environment and organisation to the people therein so as to promote comfort, convenience, efficiency, health and job satisfaction; it does not have productivity as its principal goal. But one must always recognise that managers and designers often need to see a potential advantage in productivity or economy to be persuaded to use ergonomics; therefore, the importance of this work can best be shown by examples of direct benefits, converted into cash terms if possible. Yet, for many users the benefits of the computer in an informatics system may be remote and hidden; the terminal or workstation is effectively the computer as they see it. It is essential then that the interface from the computer must be made to match well the needs and characteristics of the human user, if good usability is to be achieved.

This book is designed to meet part of that need. We have drawn together a collection of papers, written by an internationally recognised group of experts, which examine the conceptual, theoretical and empirical basis of usability. In addition, the authors have drawn out a number of the components of usability and subjected them to close scrutiny, at the same time highlighting the implications of their work for professional practice. Thus, the book is a rich mixture of theory and practice as well as academic debate and pragmatic prescription which will benefit from study at a number of levels.

Our focus of attention has been on the usability of systems from a cognitive, psychological and organisational perspective and the consequent effect of these considerations on 'how' systems might be designed. As such, it will be noted that few papers specifically refer to the physical attributes either of human users (physiology, anthropometry, anatomy, etc.), or the physical environment (illuminance, temperature, humidity, etc.) in which computers and people come together. This seemingly important omission, on our part, is not intended to deny the value of these factors or remove them from the 'how' question domain. It is rather a recognition that 'physical' factors have long been the subject of study, are already well documented, have been widely disseminated and would place such demands on the size of this book that it would extend to several volumes. The same cannot be said of the subjects reviewed here; we are still learning, as will be seen by the reader when the texts are examined. But even now the study of usability from cognitive, psychological and organisation perspectives has something very definite to offer designers with a strong promise of more in the future.

The book is divided into five parts. In Part 1, after this introductory chapter, we present an overview of the subject of usability; we focus on the concept and definition of usability and its relationship to the design process. The importance of this whole subject is then explained and illustrated by a 'business case' which shows how usability has some very practical implications for user-system efficiency and effectiveness.

Part 2 begins with a review of how and where human factors can contribute to the process of design. This analysis is then balanced by the practical experiences of two individuals who look at human factors from the perspective of a human factors practitioner and a technical designer. Both illustrate the problems they have and the difficulties in application which can be experienced. The concluding chapter introduces some more formalised methods for bringing human factors knowledge into the system design process.

In Part 3 some more specialised issues are addressed. We begin by examining the contribution of cognitive psychology to HCI and then we consider how far formal models and techniques can yet be used in human factors design. A detailed exposition with specific recommendations on designing expert systems concludes this part.

The three chapters in Part 4 present approaches at both strategic and tactical levels to deal with organisational and human factors design issues, especially in large systems and with user-participation methods.

Part 5 contains further practical guidance. Taxonomies and rules for dialogue style are offered; the design and evaluation of documentation are described. Finally, methods and 'rules' are presented in detail by which to evaluate usability.

6. Synopsis

6.1 *Part 1. Informatics Usability — Introduction, Scope and Importance*

In Chapter 2, Shackel outlines first the context of usability in terms of the acceptability equation, that is the factors which contribute to the acceptability of the system to the user. Next the framework of usability is noted, in terms of the four principal components of the user-system situation. Then a formal definition of usability is presented and developed into an operational form; using this operational definition the procedure for setting usability goals is illustrated. Five fundamental features of design for usability are then reviewed, and the actions needed during the design process to provide better usability of interface and system are summarised. Finally, some principles and procedures for evaluating the human factors aspects of the interface are outlined.

Chapanis, in Chapter 3, directly tackles this issue by making a strong business case for human factors. Whilst he clearly stresses the difficulties of making this case he offers persuasive evidence at a variety of levels, and with reference to different interface factors to re-affirm the claim that in product design and in implementation the discipline has much to contribute. The evidence is drawn not only from laboratory and case studies but also from his own experience and involvement in IT with a leading supplier; moreover, for some of his examples he is able to present the financial benefits achieved. Despite the difficulties reported in the later chapters by Stewart and Newman we are left with the feeling that the risks of not using human factors expertise, i.e., rejection of a system, inappropriate use, poor market penetration, etc., more than justify the extra training required for designers or even the deployment of human factors personnel and consultants.

6.2 *Part 2. System Design — Orientation and Approaches*

In Chapter 4, Eason and Harker develop the theme of meeting the needs of heterogeneous users by discussing the systematic application of knowledge about user needs, motives and tasks. They briefly examine the nature of the design process as it has emerged from Alvey research, and the rôle of human factors within it. They discuss the market for human factors information as defined by a study of designers needs and relate this, and the design process itself, to available sources of human factors information and expertise. They conclude that the medium by which the message is transmitted to designers is important and stress that human factors is not merely an 'add-on' to design but a vital part of it. There are problems though in turning the information into a form which is effective, valid and usable.

This latter issue is taken up by Stewart in Chapter 5 and Newman in Chapter 6. In these two papers we see the problems of trying to disseminate and use human factors information being described firstly by a leading human factors consultant and secondly by an interactive system designer. Stewart's paper, particularly, is a candid and sometimes amusing account which not only illustrates the value of deploying human factors expertise but also stresses something of the political and social climate of the consultant's role. Newman, on the other hand, appeals to the human factors discipline to provide more normative and prescriptive information to assist the interface designer especially in the provision of more usable models and representations.

In Chapter 7, Gardner describes one approach towards formulating a 'User-Centred Design' methodology which also provides a framework for a selective review of existing advice on human factors in Requirements Specification and the design of Users' Facilities. It is argued that different advice is needed at different stages in the System Life Cycle and suggestions are made for using the existing sources of advice to greatest effect.

Eason and Harker, Stewart, Newman and Gardner all have a common theme in their papers. They all describe some aspect of what it is really like, 'out there', in the 'real world' environment of informatics design. Their papers contrast very sharply with some of the academic and theoretical treatments of these issues in other sources. Perhaps the most striking theme is that they challenge the popular notion of a segmental linear design process and therefore raise such issues as where best to deploy human factors expertise, and when and in what form can the human factors knowledge best be transferred.

A second theme is that there is still an assumption in some quarters that human factors is simply a cosmetic addition to technical solutions which serves to make a more aesthetically pleasant interface. Whilst such a view is mistaken and is vanishing rapidly in some places (e.g., IBM, cf. Shackel, 1986), the attitude in parts of the European IT industry is still too backward.

6.3 *Part 3. Special Topics in Depth*

In Part 3 of the book we move into a selection of review papers which address particular facets in the study of usability, moving through a number of levels of analysis from cognitive psychology through to formal models and then to the design of expert systems.

In Chapter 8, Barnard focuses on the dialogue which occurs between the two information processors at the interface, i.e., the human and the technical parts of the system. He analyses this from the perspective of knowledge requirements and cognitive activities in human computer interaction. In doing so, he explicitly examines the contribution that cognitive psychology is making to the study of usability and its limitations. The analysis stresses that whilst human cognition is complex, and that our understanding of the processes is still considerably deficient, there are already some findings and some theories of value.

Clearly one benefit from the study of cognitive processes is that they provide the basis for the development of formal, mathematical models. In Chapter 9, Ziegler and Bullinger describe models and formal descriptions of the user interface which are gaining increasing attention in the field of human-computer interaction because of their value for analytic and constructive purposes.

They stress that different types of models can be distinguished in this context:

- structural descriptions of the system and interface architecture
- formal notations for 'dialogue processors' which are used for the specification and automatic generation of interfaces
- cognitive models of the task and the user knowledge which are used for analysing and predicting usability characteristics of an interface.

Their paper presents a survey of the more frequently used modelling techniques and formal notations with example applications. It focuses on cognitive modelling techniques but also briefly addresses formalisms which are used for interface implementation. The application of the methods for different purposes is discussed. Three major classes of formalisms — state-transition networks, grammars and production systems — are presented. Each of the methods has its strengths and weaknesses with respect to the particular application purposes which are being reviewed in order to provide general guidelines for using such techniques.

The principles which underlie Shneiderman's prescriptions (Chapter 14) are equally evident in Chapter 10, where Gaines moves the topic into the complex domain of expert systems. He surveys the human factors problems of using expert systems technology including both knowledge acquisition and application. The variety of dialogue styles in expert systems is illustrated and analysed. The basic paradigm shifts brought about by developments in knowledge-based systems in information technology are described. The applicability of existing human factors guidelines for human-computer interaction is discussed. Problems in knowledge acquisition for expert systems are reviewed and some of the techniques for automating the knowledge engineering process are described. The usability problems of expert systems are seen as a superset of those for earlier generations of informatic systems, involving new levels of complexity as human-computer interaction takes place at the level of knowledge processes, and requiring major interdisciplinary study.

6.4 *Part 4. Organisational Aspects and Design in Large Systems*

In Chapters 11, 12 and 13, the level of analysis of usability issues changes to an examination of organisational questions with Greif's analysis of implementation issues, organisation tasks, and task analysis. Thereafter Mumford offers a different perspective on the design process, reviewing the merits of user-participation and presenting her well-developed ETHICS method for involving users in design. Damodaran then approaches the issue of usability from a strategic level, illustrating her prescriptions from the perspective of experience with a major consultancy programme.

More specifically, Greif in Chapter 11 describes how allocation of tasks between humans and technology within many organisations seems to depend more on the qualities of increasingly sophisticated informatics systems than on the qualities of the human user. He notes that rarely does an organisation achieve an appropriate balance between the two. Whatever the balance there will be implications for organisational structure, particularly in such aspects as the division of labour within it, the structure and arrangement of tasks, and the structure and arrangement of communication networks. Unfortunately the reciprocal and interactive effects which exist between organisational design and informatics design are often overlooked. Greif suggests that a promising approach to resolve some of these problems is by the use of a particular form of task analysis, developed at the University of Osnabrück.

One aspect, highlighted by Gardner in Chapter 7, is further developed by Mumford in Chapter 12. Gardner emphasises the need for an appropriate definition of user requirements — an important point which is given fuller consideration by Mumford who stresses the use of participation as a facilitating process in the design of total work systems. She demonstrates how some of the valuable lessons from research and from her experience as a consultant can be developed into a methodology, which integrates business and organisational needs, to arrive at appropriate human and technical solutions. The methodology, ETHICS (Effective Technical and Human Implementation of Computer-based Systems), seeks to ensure that any technology which is introduced is humanistic, liberating and assists personal development. The methodology is reviewed from the point of view of its theoretical basis and examples are given of its practical value in a number of settings.

Damodaran, in Chapter 13, confronts the same problem but from a set of constraints imposed by the client environment. She describes some of the problems encountered, and solutions implemented, of trying to tie good human factors practice into a structured design methodology. Like Stewart's paper in Part 2, we see some of the real political issues associated with the rôle of the human factors practitioner and some of the technical challenges that the client environment imposes. She concludes her analysis with a series of prescriptions about the need for, and content of, a human factors strategy to complement strategies for technological design.

6.5 *Part 5. Design and Evaluation — Some Specific Methods*

This concluding part contains discussions and specific advice on interface dialogue styles and on documentation, and ends with a paper presenting various methods and a set of guidance 'rules' for usability evaluation.

In Shneiderman's Chapter 14 we see the translation of many research findings of the type described by Barnard into some prescriptions on interface design. Shneiderman's review focuses on five primary interaction styles: menu selection, form fill-in, command language, natural language interaction, and direct manipulation. Each style is described, some guidelines are offered, and an airlines reservations example is shown in all five styles. Then a set of IF-THEN rules are offered to help in decision making during design. This is a first attempt that is meant to provoke discussion and encourage others to offer an extended, refined, and validated set of rules.

The application focus of many chapters in this book is on the usability of software, but usability issues are of course also important in the design and use of the documentation. In Chapter 15, Wright emphasises that there are many kinds of computer documentation but the focus of her paper is on producing adequate support for "end-users" of software applications (rather than programmers, product developers or maintenance engineers). Approaches to document design which emphasise the range of information which writers need are endorsed and help is offered for writers to specify the information needs for a particular documentation task, such as providing reference material. After considering some of the consequences of, and reasons for, badly written documents, a framework is proposed which outlines how readers interact with documentation. The design implications of this framework are discussed with reference to both online and hard copy documents.

The book concludes with a valuable paper by Chapanis on usability evaluation, in which he describes a number of different approaches ranging from field studies to various designs for laboratory based studies and to evaluation by experts. He first discusses some basic issues of theory, measurement and procedure; he then offers guidance on improving an existing product, on comparing two or more products, and on evaluating computers against a standard; finally he presents a general evaluation strategy.

His conclusion is a warning but also optimistic, and applies equally to design as well as to evaluation —

> "It's hard to measure usability and do it well but it can be done."

The rest of the book aims to introduce and explain why and how usability can be designed and implemented well in informatics systems.

need to provide diagnostic information [illegible] are presented [illegible] and validated [illegible].

CHAPTER TWO

USABILITY — CONTEXT, FRAMEWORK, DEFINITION, DESIGN AND EVALUATION

BRIAN SHACKEL

1. Introduction

For many users the informatics system is essentially the terminal or workstation which they are using, and that is the central computer as they see it. But only too often these users are seen as 'end-users' by designers — and this name may well betray an attitude which causes some of the bad design for users and failures in usability. Designers must see the user as the centre of the computer system instead of as a mere peripheral. This simple concept, easy to state but harder to achieve, is often expounded by ergonomists and human factors specialists. It has been emphasised by Nicholls (1979):

> "In spite of changes in the nature of computing, remnants of old thinking remain with us. In former days, when the CPU was at the heart of a system, designers naturally talked of 'terminals' and 'peripherals'. I suspect it was in this period that people began to use the term 'end user'. The unconscious symbolism is both a symptom and a cause; the 'end' user at the 'terminal' was often the last person to be considered in the design of the system. It is important to develop a new view of computing systems, and to look at the user in a different light ... taking this view of computing, the centre of a system is the user."

So, if we are to improve the usability of interactive computer systems, then the former orientation of designers must be completely reversed.

2. Usability context — the acceptability equation

When users and purchasers make decisions about systems, their decision depends not only upon usability but upon an assessment balancing various factors; they probably consider also how useful the system will be, whether they feel it is suitable and they would like to use it, and how much it will cost, both financially and in terms of the personal, social and organisational consequences. Without being able as yet to define a mathematically precise relationship between these terms, it is suggested that the relevant factors are associated in some form of trade-off paradigm such as that in Figure 1. This paradigm suggests that whether I accept something depends upon whether I consider it sufficiently useful, usable and likeable in relation to what it costs me. If I do not accept something, then the combination of utility, usability and likeability are not sufficient for it to satisfy my wants in relation to human and financial costs.

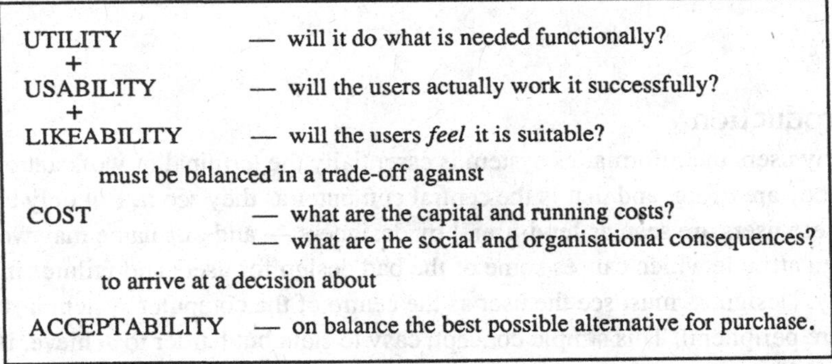

UTILITY — will it do what is needed functionally?
+
USABILITY — will the users actually work it successfully?
+
LIKEABILITY — will the users *feel* it is suitable?
must be balanced in a trade-off against
COST — what are the capital and running costs?
— what are the social and organisational consequences?
to arrive at a decision about
ACCEPTABILITY — on balance the best possible alternative for purchase.

Figure 1: The paradigm of usability and related concepts

Thus, this paradigm helps to place usability in its balanced position with functionality; as computers become cheaper and more powerful, it seems certain that usability factors will become more and more dominant in the acceptability decisions made by users and purchasers.

3. Usability framework and criteria

Successful system design for usability requires much attention to various aspects of the user. However, the user must not be considered in isolation from other aspects of the situation; that would only be perpetuating in reverse the all too common fault in the past of considering the technological tool in isolation from the user. Good system design depends upon solving the dynamic interacting needs of the four principal components of any user-system situation: user, task, tool and environment.

Likewise usability, an important goal for good system design, depends upon the dynamic interplay of these four components (this framework is based upon earlier similar approaches by Bennett, 1972, 1979, and Eason, 1981) — see Figures 2 and 3.

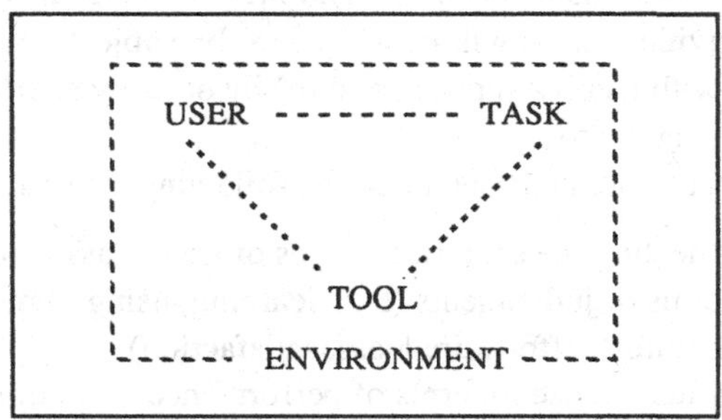

Figure 2: The four principal components in a human-machine system.

Figure 3: These joint authors as *Users* are revising a paper (*Task*) for an electronic journal using a computer and VDT (*Tool*) in the *Environment* of a research centre.

With the framework of the four principal components in mind, we can now turn to the meaning of usability. Usability depends (a) upon the design of the tool (the VDT and the computer system) in relation to the users, the tasks and the environments, and (b) upon the success of the user support provided (training, manuals, and other job aids such as on-line and off-line 'help' facilities). We consider that usability for individual users will be judged (a) by subjective assessment of ease of use of the design with its user support, and (b) by objective performance measures of effectiveness in using the tool.

Evaluation will therefore be based upon the following criteria:

- success rate in meeting the specified ranges of users, tasks and environments
- ease of use in terms of judgements (e.g., learning, using, remembering, convenience, comfort, effort, tiredness, satisfaction)
- effectiveness of human use in terms of performance (e.g., time, errors, number and sequence of activities, etc.) in learning, relearning and carrying out a representative range of operations.

4. Usability definition

From the above suggestions, it is evident that usability considered in this way is not only conceived of as *ease of use* but also equally involves *efficacy* i.e., effectiveness in terms of measures of (human) performance. Therefore, the formal definition proposed for the usability of a system or equipment is:

> 'the capability in human functional terms to be used easily and effectively by the specified range of users, given specified training and user support, to fulfil the specified range of tasks, within the specified range of environmental scenarios'.

A convenient shortened form for the definition of usability might be 'the capability to be used by humans easily and effectively', where:

easily	=	to a specified level of subjective assessment
effectively	=	to a specified level of (human) performance.

The definition of usability was probably first attempted by Miller (1971) in terms of measures for 'ease of use', and these were developed further by Bennett (1979) to describe usability. The concept of usability was first fully discussed and a detailed formal definition, as above, was attempted by Shackel (1981), and Bennett (1984) modified and developed the definition.

The problem with these definitions is that they are conceptually satisfactory but still only generalised in form; they do not specify what is usability in quantifiable or measurable terms. Therefore, I have integrated and developed further these

Proposed Operational Definition of Usability

Usability can be specified and measured by means of the operational criteria defined below. The terms should be given numerical values when the usability goals are set during the design stage of 'requirements specification'.

For a system to be usable the following must be achieved:

Effectiveness

- The required range of tasks must be accomplished at better than some required level of performance (e.g., in terms of speed and errors)
- by some required percentage of the specified target range of users
- within some required proportion of the range of usage environments

Learnability

- within some specified time from commissioning and start of user training
- based upon some specified amount of training and user support
- and within some specified relearning time each time for intermittent users

Flexibility

- with flexibility allowing adaptation to some specified percentage variation in tasks and/or environments beyond those first specified

Attitude

- and within acceptable levels of human cost in terms of tiredness, discomfort, frustration and personal effort
- so that satisfaction causes continued and enhanced usage of the system.

Figure 4: Definition of Usability proposed in terms of goals and operationalised criteria which can have numerical values specified and measured.

approaches, and now propose an operationalised definition of usability in Figure 4.

This definition has been formulated so that numerical values can be specified during the design stage of user requirements specification. In that stage of the design process, various system requirements are specified and the usability requirements should be specified in just as much detail as any other aspect of the intended system.

4.1. *Setting usability goals*

To illustrate this definition, and to demonstrate how it should be used during the design stage of requirements specification to set usability goals, the following example has been prepared.

Let us suppose that a design team is writing the specification for a software package by which either microcomputers or 'dumb' terminals on a large system may be used to dial up and login to a remote host computer, so that the user can join in a computer conference or deal with electronic mail. The required range of user tasks might be specified by the team, with the help of an ergonomist adviser, in the form shown in Figure 5. Then, using the definition of usability given in Figure 4, the desired usability goals may be set in terms of testable numerical values as shown in Figure 6.

User Requirements Specification for Electronic Mail Software Package

The required range of user tasks shall be:

1. Set parameters for 2 terminals (ADM3/VT100)
2. Set up auto-dial and auto-login

3. Initiate dial up and login
4. Start on-line usage
5. Send and receive a file
6. Set auto-record of the communication to file on/off
7. Set slave printer on/off
8. End on-line usage

9. Set up preset unattended dial up/login/file transfer
10. Read auto-recorded file
11. Read received file
12. Leave the system

Tasks 3 - 8 shall each be done by a maximum of two keystrokes.

Figure 5: Illustrative specification of user tasks as basis for Figure 6.

Thus, perhaps the most important feature of this process is that the usability goals thus set become criteria by which to test the design as it evolves and to improve it by iterative redesign. Such tests are embodied first in trials of early versions of the design and later in formal evaluations of prototypes. The bases of evaluation are discussed and some of the relevant procedures are outlined in the final sections of this paper below.

4.2 *Specifying usability attributes*

Having set usability goals at the more global level, it will usually be necessary to specify in more detail the usability attributes desired for various features of the system or aspects of its operation. A useful procedure for this process of attribute

Illustration of Defining Usability Goals

To achieve the target usability, tasks 3 - 8 shall be done:

Effectiveness

- at better than 2 seconds for each task with no more than one error per 50 attempts
- by 90% of the target range of managers, secretaries and professionals
- in any office situation which complies with the offices, shops and factories acts and which does not seriously contravene the workstation and environment specifications recommended in the V.D.T. Manual (Cakir, Hart and Stewart, 1980) or in Designing Systems for People (Damodaran, Simpson and Wilson, 1980)

Learnability

- either within 2 hours of starting use via learning with the manual and help system or within 1 hour of starting use via the training course
- based upon the 'getting started' manual to be provided or upon the 2 hour training course to be prepared
- within half-hour relearning time for users who have (1) completed the learning defined above, (2) done all the tasks once per week in half-hour sessions for 3 further weeks, and (3) then not done the tasks for an interval of 4 weeks

Flexibility

- with the task flexibility requirement only to apply to tasks 1, 2 and 9, but with the environment flexibility requirement to apply to tasks 3 - 8 that user performance shall not deteriorate more than 10% in warm conditions up to 95° F and 95% R.H.

Attitude

- and with attitude questionnaire results on 5-point scales ('very good' to 'very bad') to be at least 80% in 'good' or better and only 2% below 'neutral'
- so that questionnaire results also give at least 90% 'yes' answers to the question: "Imagine you must use this system 5 times per day every day — would you be satisfied to continue using it, and if not please comment why not?"

Figure 6: Setting usability goals via the definition of usability

specification was developed in 1978 by Gilb in his "design by objectives" methodology (later published in Gilb, 1988).

This procedure has been adapted by Bennett (1984), whence the following example and explanation are taken — see Figure 7.

"Attributes are given brief descriptions and then further defined by a series of parameter categories across the top of the table. Each attribute takes on real meaning only when we specify how we will measure it in the 'Unit of Measure' column. In the example in Figure 7, the Unit-of-Measure (hours) is chosen to be long enough to give an idea of steady-state user performance, yet short enough for feasible testing. The rest of the Parameter Categories in the sample table are used to specify values that establish various levels of performance. The figure for the Planned Value indicates a satisfactory performance for the final user of the system, and it should be consistent with the Planned Values for all other system attributes. The Worst Case Value marks the borderline between a tolerable and an intolerable system. If the observed value for any one attribute goes beyond the assigned Worst Case level for that attribute, then the system as a whole may be formally unacceptable. While the system may not be 'worthless', it has not met the goals. An explicit Current Value provides a basis for comparisons. For example, management may be prepared to accept a lower-than-currently-available level for user performance for part of a system if the overall level of system performance, as measured by other high-priority attributes, is greater for the new system. The Remarks column may contain a reference to source information or to additional details listed in another table containing an expansion for this attribute.

In Figure 7, Attribute *a* relates to learnability. Project team members specify that the 'easy to learn' attribute will be measured by five people using a prototype mockup to perform a sample teleconferencing task. For a particular scenario, the estimated Planned Value is four hours. A refined measure would give an estimate of expected deviation. The Worst Case Level provides an upper bound value; all agree that something is seriously wrong if, on the average, it takes the user more than six hours to learn the task and perform to the standard. The basis for this measure is not given here, but of course it would have to be available. The table shows that there is no Current Value data available to show the time for learning comparable performance skills with an alternative conferencing tool.

Attributes *b*, *c*, and *d* focus on throughput. Attribute *e* addresses one measure of flexibility as the new teleconferencing function is integrated into people's work patterns. Attribute *f* shows how attitude will be measured. Note that this table only gives an overview at a glance. The details for Attributes and for Parameter Categories must be contained in supporting documents."

This method raises three questions.

First, how do we set the values shown in each parameter category? At this stage in the development of these concepts, most requirements people are not accustomed to supplying goals specific enough to make careful trade-offs. In addition, development people are not accustomed to receiving such goals. For these reasons,

Development Goals for Usability of a System

PARAMETER CATEGORIES

Attributes	Means Used to Measure	Unit of Measure	Planned Value	Worst Case Value	Current Value	Remarks
a. Basic Conf. tool must be easy to learn	test sample of 5 people using proto-type	hours, score	4	6	no data	must be able to learn
b. Conf. tool leads to results comparable to face-face	sample task suitable for tele-conf.	hours to complete structured interview	2	4	4	a key selling point
c. Relation of errors in Conf. use to errors in other parts	kind and rate of errors	count of errors due to confusion about design	1/hr	5/hr	?	must fit existing style of system use
d. Recovery from errors (system or user)	observe log of user reactions	count of errors requiring > 30 sec.	hold to 2/hr	more than 7/hr	1/hr in current system	field reps say is of key import
e. Smooth transitions from menus to commands in use of new function	task set requiring use of new and old function	count actions, time, to make transitions	less than 1/10 overall time	1/3	1/10 time is currently spent overall moving between current system parts	
f. Attitude toward continued use	interview after question-naire	score	80%	50%	current system score 80%	word-of-mouth is key for referral selling

Format adapted from Gilb (1988)

Figure 7: A sample attribute specification table showing parameters for usability attributes. Each objective is established by the values chosen for that parameter category. (Quoted with permission from Bennett, 1984.)

values must be arrived at through iteration and negotiation. At the least, this method places important values "on the record", and thus avoids unpleasant surprises — such as requirements people envisioning an on-the-job training time of three hours and development people assuming that users will attend a 30-hour class.

Second, how do developers make trade-offs intended to meet goals? Again, there is no magic process, but both the target values and the trade-offs made are explicit in this approach. In a private communication, Stuart Card has pointed out that making trade-off points explicit can have a beneficial effect on use of system resources. For example, it may be very expensive to achieve three-second response time for a particular kind of information retrieval request. If an analysis of goals with respect to work patterns reveals that such a request comes at a natural closure point for users, then the response time can be reasonably adjusted upward for that requirement without damaging the overall usability of the system. If target values and trade-off points are explicit, then there is hope for tracing results observed in the field back to specific design decisions so that we can learn from experience.

Third, how often must progress be monitored? The scope and frequency of monitoring the process is a business decision. For example, a minor new release of standard technology for an existing product intended for training specialists is usually less tricky than introducing a product intended for a new user group.

Among other issues which may be raised is the suggestion that parts of this process are impossible; for example, some attributes may be considered "unmeasurable". But, as Gilb states, if the existence of a quality can be determined, then it is measurable — if only at the level of "present" or "absent". It is better to have some measure for an important system quality (even if the method to measure it is weak) than to have no measure whatsoever. No measure means no hope of control over that particular quality. If there is no convenient objective measure, then we can make use of sampling and statistical methods from the social sciences in order to quantify opinion.

Finally, there is the question of who should be directly involved with setting goals and specifying attributes. Too easily this may be seen solely as the work of the designers (not users) and of the technologists (not managers). On the contrary, to achieve usability in the ultimate design it is essential that users and managers are fully involved in this specification process (as is discussed in the next section of this chapter). Gilb reports that one top manager's initial reaction to an Attribute Specification Table was, "That's for the technical people." Gilb countered with, "No, the set of tables is your primary instrument of control." It is not good sense to launch a costly project without getting all members of the team to reach a clear agreement about what they are trying to accomplish.

5. Usability design – process and precepts

The place of human factors in relation to various stages of the design process, and the best procedures for assisting designers to achieve good usability design, have been studied intuitively and empirically for many years. Meister and Farr (1967) showed some of the problems designers have in utilising human factors information; various handbooks and textbooks have been produced with a focus on general ergonomics in relation to general systems (McCormick, 1976, 1982; Van Cott and Kincade, 1972), and more recently some handbooks on the human factors of computer systems have appeared (notably Shneiderman, 1987, and Helander, 1988). However, relatively few attempts have been made to give prescriptive advice on how to bring ergonomics into the design process (cf. Christensen, 1971; Shackel, 1971, 1974 Chapter 2); moreover, it is only recently that an attempt has been made to do this in relation to the design of computer systems (cf. Damodaran *et al.*, 1980 and the chapters by Damodaran, Eason and Harker, and Gardner in this book).

However, in the last few years two strands of development appear to be converging towards a common set of precepts. Based upon a wide range of research and design experience at the HUSAT Research Centre, Eason (1982, 1983) described various issues involved in the process of introducing information technology, and proposed an evolutionary system development process; this includes various ways of involving examples of the users, pilot systems, trials and experiments, progressive implementation of facilities, evaluation of users, user support and assistance to help the learning by the organisation. Some of these procedures are reported by Miller and Pew (1981) as being used by them in the course of a large system development study. Moreover, Gould and Lewis (1983) have similarly devised a methodology from their experience and have proposed four precepts for design for usability which in essence are very similar; they also give examples of the use of simulation and prototyping as part of the usability development process.

From these various approaches, one can synthesise and propose a set of fundamental features which will probably find widespread acceptance by experienced human factors specialists as key precepts for the process of design for usability. These are listed in Figure 8 below. The essentials of these fundamental features are as follows:

User-Centred Design – designers must understand who the users will be and what tasks they will do. This requires direct contact with users at their place of work. If possible, designers should learn to do some or all of the users' tasks. Such studies of the users must take place before the system design work starts, and design for usability must start by creating a usability specification. (See also Norman and Draper, 1986).

Participative Design – a panel of expected users (e.g., secretaries, managers) should work closely with the design team, especially during the early formulation stages and especially when creating the usability specification. To enable these users to make useful contributions, they will need to be shown a range of possibilities and alternatives by means of mock-ups and simulations. A valuable procedure, although not easy, is to write the parts of the operating manual describing the interface and how to use it; then user tests of a drawing of the interface with this draft manual can reveal potential problems before they have been embedded into the design.

Experimental Design – early in the development process the expected users should do pilot trials and then subsequently use the simulations, and later the prototypes, to do real work. Whenever possible alternative versions of important features and interfaces should be simulated or prototyped for evaluation by comparative testing. These studies should be formal and empirical, with measures of the performance and the subjective reactions of the users. Thus, ease of learning and ease of use can be assessed and difficulties revealed.

Iterative Design – the difficulties revealed in user tests must be remedied by re-design, so the cycle — design, test and measure, re-design — must be repeated as often as is necessary until the usability specification is satisfied.

User Supportive Design – this area is often left until a very late stage in the design process, and then some documentation and 'help' screens are written in a hurry at the last minute; the other aspects of user support are usually left to others by the designers, who are often unaware of their relevance and importance. Careful attention to all these support facilities can significantly assist usability (cf. Damodaran, 1986).

Relating these key precepts to the typical stages of the system design process can

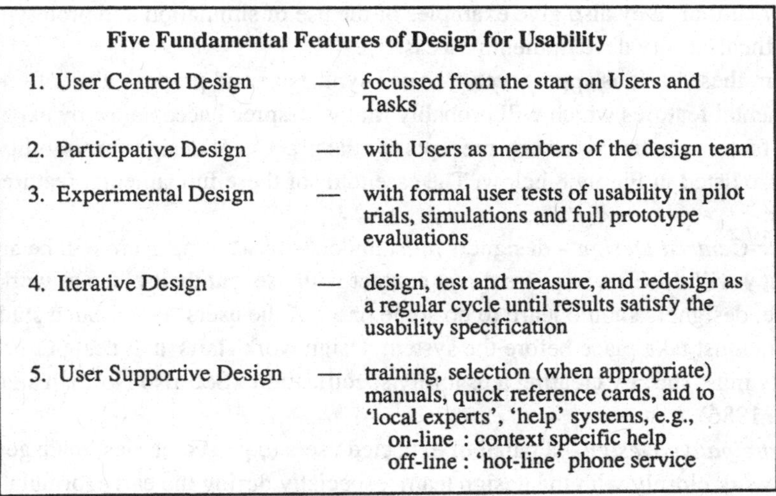

Five Fundamental Features of Design for Usability

1. User Centred Design	—	focussed from the start on Users and Tasks
2. Participative Design	—	with Users as members of the design team
3. Experimental Design	—	with formal user tests of usability in pilot trials, simulations and full prototype evaluations
4. Iterative Design	—	design, test and measure, and redesign as a regular cycle until results satisfy the usability specification
5. User Supportive Design	—	training, selection (when appropriate) manuals, quick reference cards, aid to 'local experts', 'help' systems, e.g., on-line : context specific help off-line : 'hot-line' phone service

Figure 8: To be successful, Design for Usability must be based upon these Five Fundamental Features.

provide both a first level of elaboration of the precepts and a reminder of the action programmes required. An outline of the usability actions appropriate to the system design stages is given in Figure 9.

It should be noted that these precepts (Figure 8) are derived from separate groups, one at a university research centre and the other at the largest computer corporation.

Usability Actions in the Stages of System Design

System Design Stage	**Usability Actions**
Feasibility	*Define* range of *Users*, *Tasks* and *Environments* to be covered. Do the proposals match the needs? Preliminary functions and operations analyses. Preliminary allocation of functions. *Participative Design* – panel of users in the design team. Create and formalise the *Usability Specification* by defining *user requirements* and setting *usability goals*.
Research	*Studies*, often experimental, of *human capabilities* re system operational concepts. Use *pilot studies* in the field to explore *users' operational needs* and to study possible effects upon *organisational and social structure*.
Development	*Detailed analyses* of all functions, tasks and operations involving or affecting humans. *Design* all human factors aspects of equipment and workplaces. *Specify* all environmental issues. Use guidelines to assist as design ideas are developing. *Check* design ideas against available human dimension, behaviour and performance data. *Test* subsystem sections in initial *evaluation trials* with samples of likely users. *Iterative Design* – use test results as basis for redesign, and test again. Propose *selection* criteria (if relevant); develop *training* scheme; provide for other forms of *User Support* needed.
Prototype	Extensive *laboratory evaluation* with samples of likely users. *Full field trials* with representative actual users in proper working environment. *Iterative design.*
Regular Operation	Provide for *User Support* – provide training, encourage and aid 'local experts', arrange 'hot-line' for help, etc. Gather extensive evaluation data (both objective performance data and subjective attitude data); *feed back* the evaluation data as check on decisions and predictions made during design; learn from the data – *modify the design databases, models and methods* for future use.

Figure 9: A synopsis of the various activities needed in the successive stages of system design to improve usability.

The various precepts have been recommended separately by many human factors specialists but none before have integrated them in this way and shown their value as a totality from practical examples.

Further, three studies reported at the CHI '85 conference all add illustrative support to the usability specification process and design procedures outlined above. Wilson and Whiteside (1985) show the practicality and advantage of specifying usability metrics and formally defining usability goals. Olson (1985) illustrates the benefit of deliberately designing alternative versions for each part of the user interface aspects of a first prototype. Butler (1985) presents a case study to emphasise the value of setting usability goals and measures at the requirements stage, and he also describes the process as 'evolutionary design'.

6. Usability evaluation

6.1 *Evaluation bases*

Evaluation is an important topic. Chapanis (1981) has reviewed the needs and basic procedures. Hirsch (1981) described the work and procedures of the IBM San Jose human factors centre, which does many evaluation studies. Neal and Simons (1983) described a very useful recording and playback facility used at that same centre. Grudin and MacLean (1984) described various methods for measuring performance and preference, Helmreich (1984) presented the results of user acceptance research and Raveden and Johnson (1989) have proposed a substantive checklist approach to evaluation. In his chapter on 'Evaluating Usability' in this book Chapanis brings together many of the relevant issues.

In previous sections usability has been discussed in terms of its four major components (user, task, tool and environment), and has been shown to depend upon the interaction of these four major components of the system situation. This leads to the question: is it possible, reasonable and measurable to relate the concept of usability to, for example, a specified population being able to achieve some specified performance level? This, it will be remembered, was part of the definition proposed.

The first answer must be to pose a counter question — how else can the product be designed for a market with some reliable and rational (i.e., scientifically based) assurance of success? The second answer is that this has already been done, and if the problem can be solved for one type of product then surely it can be solved for others. As an example consider the US legislation (Federal Register, 1971) and the British Standard (1975) on childproof medicine containers, both of which are essentially concerned with performance and not material or dimensional issues; they specify that at least 85% of a test panel of children shall be unable to open the containers before a demonstration, 80% still unable after a demonstration, and at least 90% of a panel of adults shall be able to open and properly reclose them following written instructions only.

There are three general types of measurement available for evaluation: dimension, performance and attitude — see Figure 10. *Dimensional criteria* are the most familiar and simplest, relying on physical measurement; the same procedures are involved for human usability, but primarily in relation to human body size. The problem with analytic dimensional criteria is that they do not enable judgement that something is more useful simply because it is 2" higher, etc.; ultimately dimensions must be related to other criteria based upon human performance or attitude if any scale is to be derived. In summary, dimensional criteria only allow pass/fail judgements; satisfying them may be a necessary but not a sufficient measure of usability.

Performance criteria involve an objective statement of some achievement, often in terms of time and errors, against which human performance can then be measured. Although the interpretation of performance criteria for evaluation purposes is often also in terms of pass or fail, the measurements obtained for comparison with the criterion give some indication of the degree of usability achieved.

Attitude criteria can be defined with the same precision and operational form as performance criteria. There has been much research in psychology on controlled methods of gathering subjective data from humans, and various forms of scaling technique are now well developed and proven.

It must be emphasised that these three types of criteria and measurement should not be regarded as alternatives, but as complementary, with regard to the assessment of usability. This is perhaps evident from the fact that different types of measurement are involved, which clearly will assess different characteristics of the tool, along with the task and environment, in relation to the user.

Dimensions will be primarily relevant to the size, shape and other characteristics of the tool in relation to human size and related requirements. *Performance* will assess the operational capability which can be achieved by the human user, but of course will not assess the cost or difficulty for the user. The *attitude* measures assess the user's view of the cost and relative difficulty in achieving the performance. We should note that attitude criteria are no less valid than any other; indeed in many respects they are more valid with regard to usability, because ultimately it is the human user who must express the judgement of this characteristic. Performance measures cannot be the sole criterion, because the human may readily achieve a given performance, but still not prefer to do the task or use the tool because it is very inconvenient and awkward, so that he may well prefer (i.e., find more usable) another similar tool which gives less speed or more errors but is easier or more convenient.

Criteria	Types of Measurement
Dimension (analytic)	physical; anthropometric
Performance ('objective')	physiological; operational; experimental; functional
Attitude ('subjective')	psychological, e.g., by controlled scaling techniques

Figure 10. The general types of criteria and measurement available for evaluation.

6.2 *Evaluation procedures*

The above discussion attempts to provide a simple analytical framework for the issues of criteria and measurement in relation to usability. The procedures involved in system evaluations during design and after installation both include and re-orient the above into appropriate operational and time-scheduled processes. In many respects, the processes used for the human factors evaluation of system usability are similar to those used for engineering evaluation of system utility. Some brief comments only will be made on a few points of relevance.

There are three principal evaluation procedures used in human factors:

1. *Expert Review*: appraisals by human factors specialists, using the measures of dimensions (and other analytic comparison data), and of attitude (by 'expert opinion').
2. *Simulation Trials*: experiments with mock-ups and prototypes, with limited number of subjects but essentially equivalent to ultimate users, using measures of performance and attitude.
3. *User Performance Tests*: full experimental studies of final equipment with samples of actual users, using measures of dimensions, performance and attitude.

For guidance on principles and procedures, see Chapanis (1959), Meister and Rabideau (1965), Parsons (1972), Chapanis (1981) and the chapter by Chapanis in this book. While these are invaluable reference sources, we should note that on the one hand they expound basic methodology, which is very necessary, but on the other hand that their applications frame of reference mainly relates to larger military systems; there is still much to be done in modifying, developing and testing usability evaluation procedures for human-computer interaction in non-military systems. For the present, we shall recommend only one precept, which is well founded on considerable experience: attitude assessments are most reliable when users have actual 'hands-on' experience in the situation concerned, so that adequate experience (often accompanied by appropriate performance tests) is the essential pre-requisite for valid attitude measurement.

7. Conclusion

From this discussion it is evident that neither the specification of usability nor its evaluation are sufficient on their own; both must be done thoroughly and skillfully if good design for usability is to be achieved. Only in that way will the interfaces become not bottlenecks but gateways, through which the informatics system successfully interacts with and serves the user.

CHAPTER THREE

THE BUSINESS CASE FOR HUMAN FACTORS[1] IN INFORMATICS

ALPHONSE CHAPANIS

1. Introduction

Despite all the good things you have heard, or read, about human factors, applying it has one very serious drawback: it costs money. The manufacturer who has human factors professionals on his staff, or who hires human factors consultants, has to pay their salaries or fees, and, in America at least, that is no small matter. In addition, if the human factors professional wants to carry out any experiments, tests, or evaluations, as he almost certainly will want to do, that costs money too.

In a cost-conscious, or price-competitive economy, engineers, designers and managers are reluctant to allocate development resources to activities that do not provide benefits that exceed their costs. Moreover, the benefits, whatever their nature, must be measurable. So those of us who are intimately associated with the development process are constantly being confronted with, "Is it worth it? Prove to me that human factors will yield benefits that make it worthwhile."

The need to justify oneself in the market place is not unique to human factors. Other engineering specialties, such as safety engineering, industrial design, and maintainability engineering, have at one time or another had to face the same challenges, and have successfully responded to them. Although their acceptance has often been grudging, most engineering specialities are now regarded as essential partners on product development teams. The situation with regard to human factors is not that good for at least four reasons:

---

[1] In this article I shall not try to make subtle distinctions among the terms *human factors*, *human engineering*, and *ergonomics*, but shall treat them as synonymous.

1. Human factors is still relatively new. I keep finding an astonishing number of engineers and designers who have never heard of it, or if they have heard of it, have serious misconceptions about it.
2. Since many engineers and designers feel that human factors is nothing more than common sense, they feel that they, being human themselves, are quite capable of designing for human use.
3. Most human factors scientists, especially those in universities and laboratories, seem to be unaware of the necessity for demonstrating the economic significance of their work (see, for example, Berns, 1984).
4. Many manufacturers, engineers, and marketeers think that usability and ease of use have no market value. They feel that people base their buying decisions more on cost and appearance than on usability.

So many other people have written about the first two of these points that it would be redundant for me to do so. I shall address the fourth, and, in so doing, I hope that I may alert more human factors professionals to the importance of the third. To use terms that one generally hears in corporate boardrooms, I shall try to make a business case for human factors.

2. Some methodological considerations

Proving the worth of human factors is not an easy task for several reasons. The first has to do with where and how it is practised.

2.1 *Identifying the human factors contribution*

Human factors, as those of us in the profession always stress, needs to be used from the very beginning of any development project, and it needs to be applied throughout the entire development cycle. We also argue that human factors professionals need to be made members of any design team. In the beginning of any development project, human factors can help in the identification of users, their needs, and their characteristics. These are then used in the specification of product requirements — how the product must look and what it must do to meet user requirements. The human factors professional can help in preparing functional specifications, in conducting task analyses, and in providing the data that are needed for trade-off studies when concepts are being explored and tested. All this and more has already been so thoroughly discussed by other contributors in this book and in other places that I do not need to elaborate on them any further.

The difficulty from a methodological standpoint, however, is that when human factors is so thoroughly integrated into the development cycle, you cannot identify with certainty exactly what or how much human factors contributed to the final product. Abrahamsen (1984), for example, has discussed the design of the Burroughs ET 1100 computer workstation, Kelley (1984) the design of NCR's Skylink self-service ticketing terminal, and Peterson and Botterill (1982) the design of the IBM System/38 computer. All three describe a number of features that are useful and sound from a human factors standpoint. The difficulty, however, is that we cannot extract from these accounts exactly what human factors contributed. Or, to put it in other terms, how much less usable would these products have been if there had been no human factors involvement in their development? This is an important question because if we are to prove the value of human factors, we have to be able to show that human factors contributes something that would not have been there if the product had been designed solely on the basis of common sense, intuition, past experience, or conventional practices.

A closely related problem concerns costs. When human factors is part of a design team, it is sometimes difficult to put a precise dollar value on what it costs. Often those costs are buried in generalised personnel or development costs that cannot be allocated to specific projects.

2.2 *An ideal scenario*

Given these difficulties, what kind of evidence would we need to provide a strong business case for human factors? Because of the thorough involvement of human factors in the design process, we should ideally find two similar systems one of which was designed and developed without any human factors contributions, the other with such contributions. The two systems should then have been marketed under similar conditions and the subsequent sales figures compared. Alternatively, the two systems should have been placed in comparable application environments and their effects on productivity, worker satisfaction, and cost savings should have been assessed. At a minimum, the evaluation should:

- involve at least two products, one of which is a genuine product[1] developed and marketed without any human factors involvement, the other of which was developed or modified according to human factors principles
- be conducted under conditions that allow us to conclude with reasonable

[1] In specifying that the evaluation should involve a genuine product, I mean to exclude laboratory studies that use artificial products and tasks and that are aimed at the discovery of general principles. However persuasive and appealing such studies may be to the scientist or scientist-practitioner, it is generally difficult or impossible to extrapolate from them to real work situations. For that reason they seldom make a convincing business case.

certainty that whatever differences appeared could be attributed to the human factors contributions

- allow us to make some estimate of the monetary benefits that result from whatever increases are observed
- allow us to make some estimate of the cost of the application of human factors to the development of the modified product.

3. Some human factors "success" stories

3.1 *Meeting success criteria*

It's difficult to find studies that satisfy those requirements. Harris's (1984) presidential address to the Human Factors Society contained abstracts of 25 human factors success stories, only three of which appear to involve computers or computer systems. While the reputed gains are impressive, none of the three stories involving computers, and few of the others, translated gains into monetary terms; none of the 25 provided an estimate of the costs of the human factors studies that were involved in the development of the product or system, and none provided information on the procedures that were used to substantiate that the gains could be legitimately attributed to human factors. By these comments, I don't mean to question the validity of the success stories that Harris cites, but rather to show how difficult it is to prove their validity.

As another example, Karlin (1977) cited three projects that, he claimed, resulted in large financial payoffs. One was a study conducted by Ellis showing that the so-called "hands on" portion of DIMENSION® PBX customer training sessions could be left out with a resultant saving of service advisers' time estimated by AT & T at $2.5 million in 1977. In Ellis's (1977) own description of his study in the same proceedings, however, there is no mention of dollar savings attributable to his findings. Once again, I do not dispute Karlin's statement, but rather point out that it is not substantiated.

Thompson, McEvers and Olson (1986), on the other hand, convincingly translated the productivity gains they found into dollar savings. Their study concerned data entry operators who processed customers' cheques received by the Pacific Gas and Electric Company. Before they made certain changes, there was an average backlog of $415 million in cheques waiting one or more days for deposit. After they made their changes, the backlog decreased to $169 million. The difference of $246 million accumulated interest in the bank for an extra day or two at a rate of about $40,000 per day. They (a) changed the job, (b) redesigned the layout of the workplace, (c) instituted two five-minute exercise periods during the work day, and

(d) changed from payment on an hourly basis, regardless of quantity of output, to a straight piece work incentive plan. Since these four variables are completely confounded, it is impossible to know with any degree of certainty what was responsible for the productivity gains that were reported.

This is not a unique state of affairs. Most studies that claim to show productivity enhancements, from whatever source, fail to meet the rigorous methodological requirements of valid scientific evidence. It's easy enough to measure productivity gains, or cost savings. What is hard is to prove with certainty what was responsible for those gains and savings. In this connection, I quote from Kariya (1984) in an article on so-called "ergonomic chairs".

> "The arguments presented to support a cost-justification are classic examples of slick financial analysis surrounding a core of educated guesses. Armed with typical office-worker salary and benefit figures, 'average' operating efficiencies, and 'conclusive results' from various European, NIOSH, and independent tests, a smart salesperson can easily show how such a purchase will pay for itself in less than 10 months and perhaps be the best investment the office manager ever made.
>
> If it were possible to prove beyond a shadow of a doubt that a product would increase worker productivity by just 1%, virtually any capital investment of $500 per worker could be justified. With chairs, the only direct and incontrovertible result is improved comfort that may translate into better performance. But this causal relationship is vague at best. Unlike factory conditions, where performance can be measured in quantifiable units, the office worker typically is evaluated in qualitative terms. Industrial engineers, if they are to demonstrate increased productivity in the office as they did on the assembly line, will have to define new standards that will permit objective evaluation of ergonomic products." (pp. 147-148).

3.2 *A convincing human factors success story*

To offset all those discouraging comments, I want to cite a study that comes close to being ideal in proving the benefits of human factors. It is Malone's (1986) account of the development of the centred, high-mounted brake light on automobiles, a feature that is now required by law on all new cars sold in the United States. Based on some prior research, Kirkpatrick and Malone directed a large-scale human factors field assessment of several brake-light configurations. Three experimental groups and one control group of 525 taxicabs each in Washington, D.C., were monitored over a one-year period during which data on rear-end collisions, other collisions, and mileage were recorded. Drivers in the four groups had been matched for age, sex, and prior accident history. The vehicles accumulated nearly 60 million vehicle miles under a wide variety of weather and road conditions.

The results in Figure 1 show that cabs equipped with a centred, high-mounted brake light experienced a rear-end accident rate 54% lower than that for the control vehicles. Neither of the other two configurations differed significantly from the control group, although both showed slightly lower accident rates. That these findings could not be attributed to differences in general safety performance is shown by the data for non rear-end accidents. They were essentially the same for all groups. Not only did the centred, high-mounted brake light result in fewer rear-end collisions, but it also reduced by 38% the severity of the damage to vehicles that were involved in rear-end collisions. Although the study could not explain why this occurred, a reasonable hypothesis is that drivers in a vehicle following one with a high-mounted brake light apply their brakes faster resulting in a slower speed and so less damage to both vehicles.

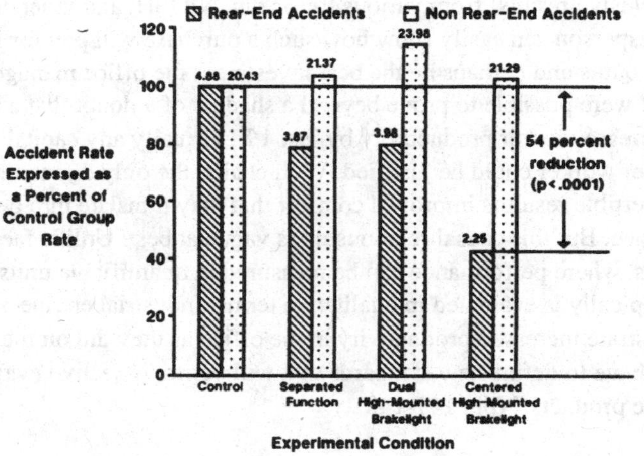

Figure 1: Accident rates for four groups of vehicles in a field test of brake light configurations. The numbers above the bars are numbers of accidents per million vehicle miles (after Malone, 1986).

These findings were cross-validated several years later in two other, independently conducted studies, one on 5400 Bell Telephone System company vehicles, the other on 900 New York City taxicabs. Accident reductions of 53% and 50% were found in those two studies, thus duplicating almost exactly the original findings by Kirkpatrick and Malone.

The National Highway Traffic Safety Administration then used vehicle damage costs to calculate the cost-benefit ratio, or return on investment, for the centred, high-mounted brake light. There were about 3.2 million accidents in 1977 that could have been affected by the new light. If the new light had been installed, this figure would have been reduced by 54%, thereby preventing 1.7 million accidents. Since the average cost of repair of the control vehicles was $317, the cost saving would be $317 x 2 x 1.7 million, or $1.096 billion. For those vehicles with the high-mounted lights that still suffered an accident, the cost of repair was only $194, resulting in a saving of $123 per vehicle. The total saving for 1.5 million vehicles came to $369 million, for a combined estimated saving for all vehicles of $1.465 billion. These figures are conservative because they do not include medical, legal, and out-of-work costs.

Although we are told that the cost of installing a light in 1977 was about $4.00 per vehicle, the one thing this report does not give us is the cost of conducting the several human factors studies. However, even if we were to assume that the studies cost as much as $1 million, these costs would be less than 0.1% of the projected savings for one year alone.

4. The value of human factors in computer systems

I have not been able to find a study with computer systems that matches this one in its methodological thoroughness, with controls and cross validation, with the findings translated into monetary gains, and with estimates of the costs of the human factors studies. Still, I don't think the situation is hopeless. There is a considerable amount of evidence, more or less indirect, that supports the value of human factors in informatics. I shall start with the weakest kind of evidence and progress to stronger ones as I continue, from indirect evidence to experimental studies and then to results of both costs and benefits from operating situations. Although the first one sounds trivial, I don't think we can dismiss it cavalierly.

4.1 *Advertising value*

Ease of use, human factors and ergonomics have advertising value. Figure 2 is an example of one of many advertisements these days that stresses ease of use. Some advertisements, and Figure 3 is an example, specifically mention human factors or human engineering. Others (Figure 4) use the word ergonomics. To be sure, saying so doesn't make it so. The point I do want to make, however, is that ease of use, human factors and ergonomics apparently have some advertising value. If they did not, I'm sure advertisers would not be highlighting them.

More convincing are advertisements that make comparisons between the advertiser's product and some other. For example, in the May 1984 issue of *United Magazine* TeleVideo Personal Computers boasted:

The Source Is Friendly.
Many online information services claim to be "user friendly." But only one really lives up to that promise.
The Source.
You see, The Source is specifically designed to save you time online. With new, shorter menus. Simpler commands. And a user's manual so well-written and easy to understand, it's setting an industry standard.
The Source is also the only service that gives you introductory lessons and assistance, free of online charges.
So you get up-to-speed on our dime, not yours.
You get to the information you need in record time, without frustration. Everything from the hour's headlines to travel reservations. From special interest groups to online stock trading. So you don't waste your valuable time. Or money.
Call 1-800-336-3366, send the coupon, or visit your nearest computer dealer.
And make friends with America's friendliest online information network.

Figure 2: Part of an advertisement that stresses user friendliness and ease of use (*Personal Computing*, August 1986).

> "Note that TeleVideo's ergonomic superiority over IBM extends from fully sculpted keys and a comfortable palm rest to a 14-inch, no glare screen that tilts at a touch."

Figure 5 shows another advertisement from *The Wall Street Journal* in which Texas Instruments invited prospective customers to make side-by-side comparisons between its personal computer and IBM's. Figure 6 is part of another advertisement in which Decision Data Corporation compares its display station with IBM's. I think it's unlikely that either of these two corporations would dare to print such advertisements if they were not confident of their validity. While I can't put a dollar figure on the value of such advertisements, there surely must be some.

Incidentally, I'm not entirely sure what to make of the fact that in all the advertisements I've been able to find in which such comparisons are made, one of the products has always been an IBM product. It might mean that IBM products are not very good, or alternatively it might mean that IBM products are the standards that everyone else strives to match and to surpass.

ave made
in electron-
itations
g and selling
them for that.
mation, are
a name for
only state-
e ovens, radio
lectronics
ve the kind
ill make our
ell as quality.
bination of

our inspired engineering and up to the minute production techniques.

The kind you would expect from a 7.5 billion dollar company.

And we'll also use some of the most remarkable human engineering found anywhere. (Our management team is young, aggressive and creative.)

We've already begun the work at our recently expanded plant in Huntsville, Alabama where we expect to produce hundreds of thousands of color TV's and microwave ovens annually.

And we'll continue it in the future with the introduction of some of the most innovative electronics products you could imagine.

We'll do it because we're commit-

ted to do whate
the American n
We're alre
national marke
Needless t
we'll succeed.
After all,
willing to spenc
So they should
spend less.
And as fo
Hitachi, Sharp,
Mitsubishi, Zer
Fisher, Magnav
Amana, Maran
Well, we'r
out about our p
didn't want then

Expensive electronics. Without the expense.

Figure 3: Part of an advertisement highlighting the words "human engineering". (*The New York Times*, September 17, 1984).

Figure 4: Part of an advertising brochure from Wyse Technology, Incorporated, highlighting the words "ergonomically engineered".

"Dare to Compare."

When choosing a computer, there are two important things to look for. Who runs the best software— and who runs the software best! That's why we're staging a dramatic country-wide side-by-side comparison against IBM™ called "Dare to Compare."

Come to a participating dealer. Take the "Dare to Compare" challenge. And this is what you'll see.

TI makes software faster to use.

Take a closer look at the picture on the right. See how we give you more information on-screen than the IBM PC? That way you'll spend less time looking for data, and more time using it. We also give you 12 function keys, while they give you 10. Unlike IBM, we give you a separate numeric keypad and cursor controls. And that saves you both keystrokes and time. We also isolated the edit/delete keys to reduce the chance of making mistakes.

TI makes software easier to use.

TI gives you up to 8 colors on-screen simultaneously, which makes separating the data a lot easier. IBM displays only 4. Our graphics are also sharper. And easier on the eyes.

And TI makes it easier to get your data on-screen. Our keyboard is simpler— more like the familiar IBM Selectric™ typewriter than the IBM PC keyboard is.

TI lets you see for yourself.

Right now, you can "Dare to Compare" for yourself at participating TI dealers all over the country. Stop in, present your business card, put both machines through their paces using the same software titles, and see the difference for yourself. We'll give you a TI solar powered calculator free, just for taking our challenge*.

Figure 5: Part of an advertisement in which Texas Instruments invites comparison between its Professional Computer and IBM's Personal Computer (*The Wall Street Journal*, May 10, 1984).

4.2 *The costs of lawsuits*

That's all very well, you might say, but what is there to keep ad men honest? After all, it's easy enough to claim that your product is human factored even though you might not have any human factors professionals on your staff or might not even have used a human factors consultant. As a matter of fact, there is one thing that is beginning to restrain advertisers from making extravagant claims about ease of use, and that is the threat of a lawsuit. Lawsuits involving computers are by no means as common as general product liability lawsuits, but they do happen. The October 26,

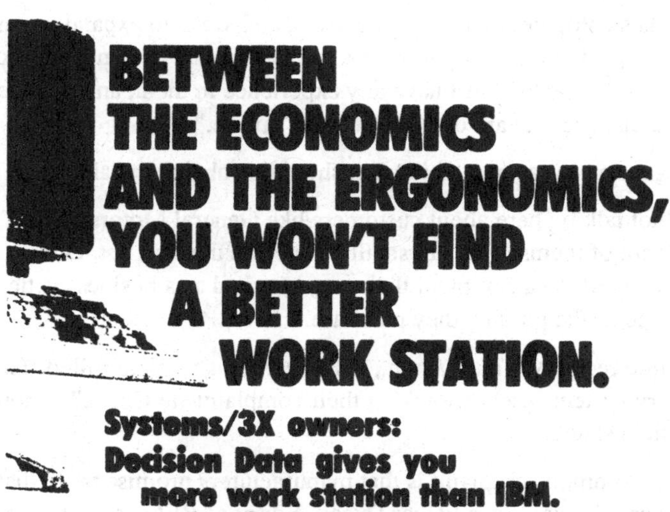

BETWEEN
THE ECONOMICS
AND THE ERGONOMICS,
YOU WON'T FIND
A BETTER
WORK STATION.
Systems/3X owners:
Decision Data gives you
more work station than IBM.
For less money.

Figure 6: Part of an advertisement in which Decision Data Computer Corporation invites comparison of its display station with IBM's (*Datamation*, October 1, 1985).

1981 issue of the *International Herald Tribune*, for example, carried an article titled "Computer Boom's Flip Side: Frustrated Users". Among other things, the article said that:

> "More and more small-business men are buying computer systems only to find that they do not work as expected 'Fully half, if not more, of all computer users suffer some frustrated expectations,' said Thomas K. Christo, a North Hampton, N. H., lawyer who represents computer users in suits against vendors. Computer manufacturers say the percentage of dissatisfied users is far smaller but acknowledge that the problem exists."

Robert P. Bigelow, an attorney in Massachusetts, wrote in the November 1981 issue of *Infosystems* about two lawsuits involving computers. In one of them a jury awarded a company $286,000 in regular and consequential damages and $2,000,000 in punitive damages because a computer system didn't perform as expected. In rendering his opinion substantiating the award, the presiding judge said:

> "It's a particularly serious problem it seems to me (*and the problem he was referring to is a computer system that didn't perform as had been claimed by the manufacturer*) in the computer industry particularly in that part of the industry

> which makes computers for first-time users, and seeks to expand the use of computers by...targeting as purchasers businesses that have never used computers before, who don't have any experience in them, and who don't know what the consequences are of a defect and a failure."

His opinion goes on to say something that should be obvious to all of us:

> "We are not talking here about customers like General Motors and AT & T who can take care of themselves, but small businesses that can not. Once such a business converts to a computer their very survival as a business is tied to the performance of the product they purchase."

Somewhat more recently, *Time* (Anon., 1983) carried an article called "Getting rid of the bugs: angry systems users are taking their complaints to Court." Among other things the article stated:

> "The most common complaint is that manufacturers promise more than their machines can deliver. Says Esther Dyson, Editor of *RELease 1.0*, an electronics newsletter: The industry is raising false hopes. Computers are not user friendly. In fact, they are a pain to operate."

In 1985 Dunlop said that there had been a dramatic increase in litigation and arbitration because of the increase in problems attributable to systems failing to perform as anticipated. Although I can't assess the impact of such lawsuits on the computer industry, I suspect that they must exert at least a moderating influence on the kind of advertising computer manufacturers publish. If nothing else, such lawsuits must at least alert computer manufacturers to the importance of usability considerations, and, hopefully, to the contributions human factors can make to usability. Human factors can't guarantee that a product will never be challenged in a court of law because of its user-friendliness, but I feel confident that it can help to make such lawsuits less likely.

4.3 *Endorsements from independent raters*

One step better than mere advertisements are endorsements, or their converse, condemnations, from independent raters. Some years ago I did some work for the Rolm Corporation in the development of their Phonemail™ system. Specifically, I helped to develop the decision tree, the dialogs and prompts, and labels for keys, and the wording used in this system. This is the case in which I can assert confidently, even if immodestly, that human factors made a substantial contribution to the final product. My appearance on the scene was responsible for a complete change in design philosophy aimed at making the product usable. It could very well be that the reason I was able to contribute so much was that I had no experience with the system, or anything like it, before I went out to California. I approached the prototype as a truly naïve, first-time user.

In any case, after the product had been put on the market, the December 1982 issue of *Datamation* (Tyler, 1982) carried an article from which I quote the following:

> "I have concluded that the Rolm product is likely to be superior in functionality to any other voice mail system currently available, says Bruce Hasenyager, a vice president of Kidder, Peabody & Co., who has followed the voice mail market for some time. They've done a good job designing the product from a human factors standpoint." (p. 54).

This is another case in which I can't put a dollar figure on the value of such an endorsement, but it must be substantial, especially since it comes from an independent person who is presumably knowledgeable about such matters. I suspect, but can't prove, that the marketing value of such an endorsement is considerably greater than the consulting fees I earned from my work on that project.

Within recent years, there have been several systematic efforts to rate computers and computer programs on criteria such as "ease of learning", "ease of use", "versatility", and "flexibility". For example, Consumers Union, an independent organisation in the United States that tests and evaluates consumer products, published a set of three articles late in 1983 and early in 1984 rating some 20 models of computers for both home and small-business use. Additional articles have appeared periodically since then. Willis and Miller (1984) published a buyer's guide with ratings on 144 computers, one of Software Digest's rating books (1984) compares 30 word-processing programs, and a *1987 Computer Buying Guide* (Fry, Hughes, and Mansfield, 1986) rates computers, peripherals, modems, monitors, printers, and software. Even as I was writing this article, the scholarly journal *Science* announced in its 28 November 1986 issue that it was initiating a new feature called Software Reviews.

It's difficult to judge the impact of these ratings, of course, but when Consumers Union rates the print quality of the Commodore VIC-1525 and Radio Shack DMP-100 as poor, and the print quality for the Atari 1027 as excellent, it must certainly have some sales value. Similarly, I'm sure that a statement such as:

> 'Excellent manual written in clear, concise language. Good on-screen tutorial. No complex codes or commands to remember.'

must have some substantial value over a statement such as this one:

> 'Manual is poor and does not explain basic principles of the program.'

Ratings such as these are too late for designers because they appear after a computer has been manufactured and put on the market. Nonetheless, at least some manufacturers regard these ratings seriously and take measures to try to correct deficiencies when they are pointed out. For consumers, such ratings are useful because they provide at least some guidance in a marketplace that offers a confusing variety of devices with extravagant claims. There is also evidence that consumers do pay attention to these ratings. In writing about the penetration of computers into colleges and universities, Fiske (1984), for example, said that by the fall of 1984 Dartmouth University was to have wired every dormitory room for computers and that while the school did not intend to require students to purchase a computer, it would urge students to do so. Moreover, the school intended to recommend that students choose the Apple Macintosh "for its user friendliness, graphics and word processing" (p. 90).

As we see more and more ratings of computers and computer programs, ease of learning, ease of use, versatility and flexibility are certain to become increasingly important. Computers that are consistently rated poorly on usability features will undoubtedly suffer in the marketplace.

5. Experimental studies on computer design

Although the human factors literature contains hundreds of laboratory and experimental studies that have tested various kinds of hardware and software alternatives, such as one kind of error message versus another, or black letters on white versus white letters on black, for a number of reasons most of these studies do not provide convincing support for a business case. All too often these studies have compared theoretical alternatives, not genuine products, and it is hard to evaluate the contribution of the theoretical findings to marketable products. The subjects for the experiments are often college students who may, or may not, be representative of typical users. The tasks performed in the studies are often unrealistic or artificial ones devised only for purposes of the tests. And, most important of all, the conclusions of the studies hinge on the statistical significance of differences observed. Rarely are those differences translated into terms, for example, of dollar savings or productivity improvements, that businessmen are interested in.

Despite these drawbacks, I don't think all experiments should be summarily dismissed as having no relevance to the business case. Following are three examples that illustrate why.

5.1 *Improving a text editor manual*

Sullivan and I (1983) took an existing product, a text editor manual, about which we had heard numerous complaints, rewrote it, and then compared the rewritten with the original manual. The manual was an IBM text editor and computer operations/ description manual #SH20-1089-1. The text editor, IBM Program #5796-PAC (1973), was implemented on an IBM 3277 terminal. Our article describes in detail the procedures we went through in rewriting the manual. Since those procedures are not particularly germane to the point I want to make here, I shall not elaborate on them. Suffice it to say that, having rewritten the manual, we engaged the services of 12 secretaries who were recruited through a newspaper advertisement. Subjects were randomly assigned to work with either the original or rewritten versions of the manual. Except for being assigned to different manuals, the two groups were treated identically.

On the first day subjects familiarised themselves with the computer by going through an interactive keyboard learning program. On the second day the subjects were given one of the two manuals for the first time and a letter task that consisted of a typed but unformatted letter. Instructions on how to format it were handwritten in the left-hand margin. The letter was about 200 words long. Subjects had to type the letter into the computer, deciding what format codes to use. The task required them to single-, double-, and triple-space selected portions of the letter; use the tab codes; make paragraphs; use an address format; and change the left- and right-hand margins.

After working on the letter for 2.5 hours, subjects were given a rest and asked to work on a chapter-editing task for another hour. This task consisted of an eight-page chapter of a book containing deliberate errors that had been previously stored in the computer. Each subject was given a printed copy of the uncorrected chapter with editing changes marked on it in red. The changes included substituting words, inserting letters, erasing a paragraph, splitting a paragraph into two, and combining two paragraphs into one.

One measure of performance was an index of quality consisting of points for each correct use of a formatting code in the letter task and for each correction made in the chapter-editing task. The results in Figure 7 speak for themselves. Performance on both tasks was substantially better for the subjects who worked with the new manual. Figure 8 shows some data on the average numbers of commands used successfully and the average numbers of questions that were addressed to the experimenter by the two groups of subjects. Once again, the results are large and clear-cut. Subjects who used the revised manual were obviously more proficient and less confused than those who used the old one.

5.2 *Improving commands for a text editor*

The second experiment I want to discuss is by Ledgard, Singer and Whiteside (1981) who worked with a commercially available editor, Control Data Corporation's NOS

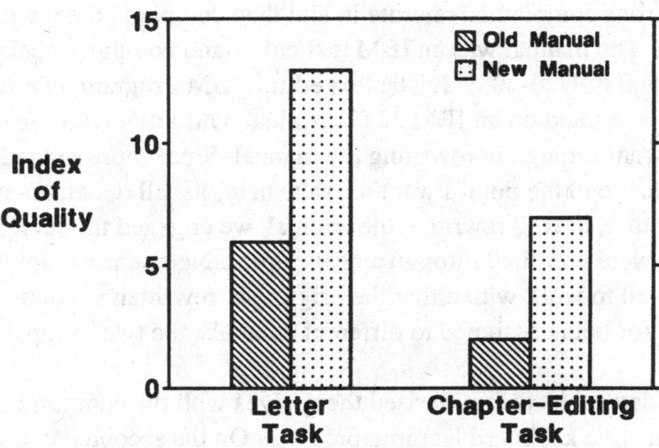

Figure 7: Measures of the quality of two tasks by subjects who worked with either an original or revised text editor manual (after Sullivan and Chapanis, 1983).

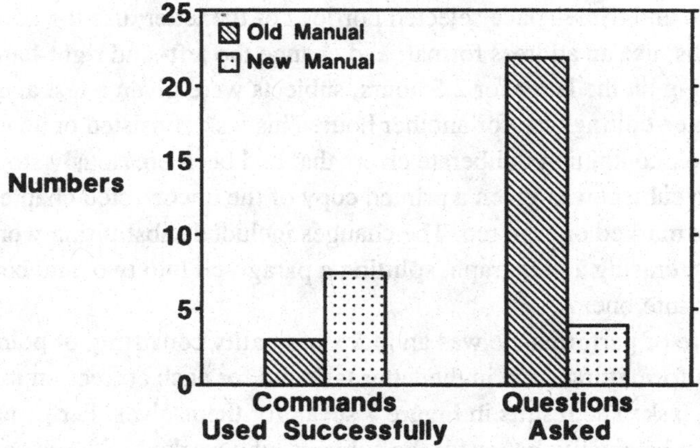

Figure 8: Average numbers of commands used successfully and average numbers of questions asked by subjects who used either an original or revised text editor manual (after Chapanis and Sullivan, 1983).

Version 1 Text Editor. Examples of the notational commands used by this system are in Table 1. Also in Table 1 are the corresponding more English-like commands prepared and tested by these investigators.

The subjects for this study were 24 paid volunteers consisting of eight *inexperienced users* (individuals who claimed less than 10 hours of experience with

Function	Notational editor	English editor
Current line moves back to the nearest line containing TOOTH	FIND: /TOOTH/ ;1	BACKWARD TO "TOOTH"
Erases 7 lines starting with the current line. Next line becomes the current line.	DELETE; 7	DELETE 7 LINES
Displays all lines from current line to the last line of text. The current line becomes the last line displayed.	LIST; *	LIST ALL LINES
Changes every instance of KO to OK in the current and all subsequent lines. The current line becomes the last line to be changed.	RS: /KO/ ,OK/ ;*	CHANGE ALL "KO" TO "OK"

Table 1: Examples of functions as expressed by the notational editor and English editor tested by Ledgard, Singer and Whiteside (1981).

computer terminals), eight *familiar users* (individuals who claimed between 11 and 100 hours of experience with computer terminals), and eight *experienced users* (people who claimed over 100 hours of terminal use). Half of each of these three groups of subjects was given a manual and a table containing either the notational or experimental version of the commands. They were allowed to study these materials as long as they liked, the experimenters answered any questions they had, and the subjects were encouraged to practise using the editor until he or she felt comfortable with it. When a subject felt ready, he or she was given a set of editing tasks to perform.

After completing the first set of tasks, each subject then went through the same procedure with the editor he or she had not used previously.

The results are striking. Figure 9 shows the average percentages of the tasks completed by all groups for the two kinds of editors. As might be expected, there is a direct relationship between the amount of work done and prior computer experience. But notice that all groups completed more of the tasks with the English editor than with the notational editor.

Even more impressive results were obtained with the error data (Figure 10). Once again the percentage of errors was directly related to prior computer experience: the more experience, the fewer errors. But notice, once again, the large differences for all groups between the numbers of errors committed with the notational and English editors.

The familiar and experienced subjects were given a preference questionnaire

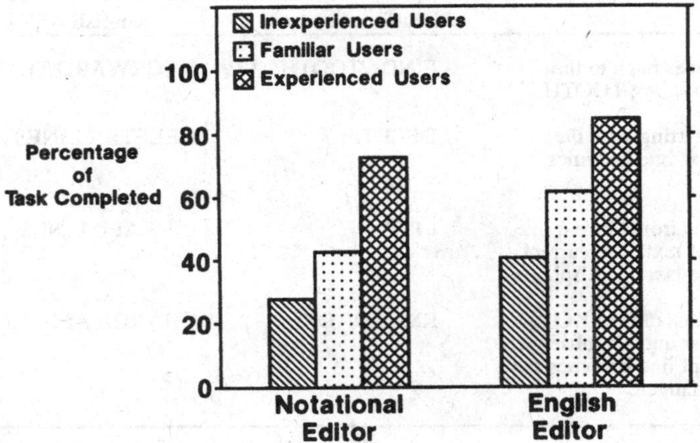

Figure 9: Average percentages of tasks completed by three groups of subjects using either a notational or more English-like editor (after Ledgard, Singer and Whiteside, 1981).

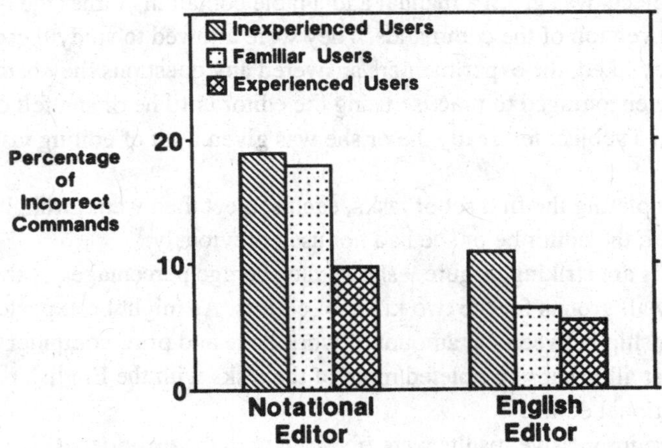

Figure 10: Average percentages of incorrect commands made by three groups of subjects using either a notational or more English-like editor (after Ledgard, Singer and Whiteside, 1981).

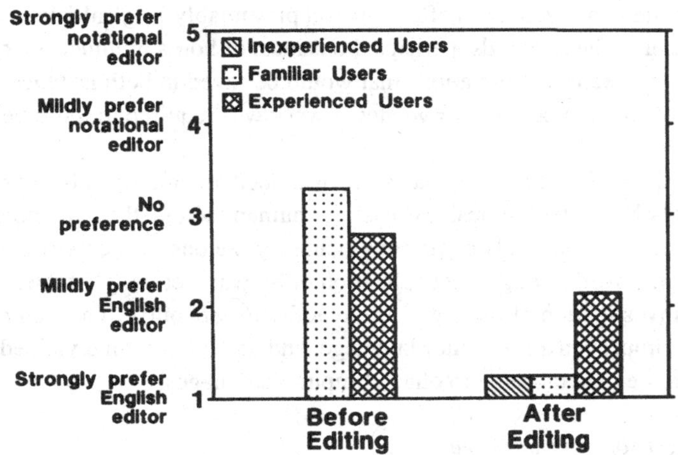

Figure 11: Attitudes towards a notational and more English-like editor expressed by three groups of subjects (after Ledgard, Singer and Whiteside, 1981).

before and after using the editors. The inexperienced subjects were given the questionnaire only after using the editors. The results in Figure 11 show a clear shift in preference toward the English editor for both of the more experienced groups. The inexperienced subjects also strongly preferred the English editor. These results support the conclusion that careful attention to the surface syntax of commands can greatly improve performance even for experienced persons.

5.3 *The relevance of such studies to the business case*

In view of what I said earlier about most laboratory studies, you might well wonder how the foregoing two contribute to the business case for human factors. There are, it seems to me, two important characteristics of these studies that are relevant. First, both studies were done with existing products. The manual that Sullivan and I worked with and the text editor language that Ledgard *et al.* studied were both products that had been produced by the computer industry. They were on the market and were not hypothetical or theoretical products devised for purposes of an experiment. Second, since both were already existing products, you can identify the human factors contributions without ambiguity. An additional consideration is that Sullivan and I used subjects who were representative of the user population. Although neither did, both sets of investigators presumably could also have a put a dollar value on the cost of the respective experiments. What we don't know, of course, is the commercial value of the improvements that were made in both products. We can feel confident, however, that the benefits of both efforts would presumably be available to a large audience of users. The hundreds, perhaps thousands, of hours of unnecessary work, untold errors and needless frustrations that would be saved in both instances must certainly more than compensate for whatever work was required to improve both systems.

Although the two studies that I have just described are not the only ones in the literature that help bolster the business case for human factors, they are, nonetheless, in the minority. Experiments become convincing for the business case when existing products are improved through the application of human factors. That does not preclude the investigation of more general hypotheses, of course. The study by Ledgard *et al.* improved a text editor language, and at the same time yielded principles that are generalisable to other computer languages.

5.4 *Improving a software package*

The third study goes quite a bit further than the preceding two in providing more substantial evidence for the benefits that come from the application of human factors principles to software design. Keister and Gallaway (1983) started with an NCR software package that was already being used with reasonable success by some 500 customers. Following a series of interviews and detailed analyses involving typical users, they decided to modify two out of the 125 programs in the application. The two programs they picked were those involving heavy user-system interactions. The modifications they made fall into eight major categories and include such things as changes in screen formatting, screen content, abbreviations, and error correction and feedback messages.

To compare performance on the two versions of the program twenty subjects were employed for one day. The subjects were all good typists and had had prior data entry experience. The subjects were first given an opportunity to learn both systems and then were assigned to sets of 60 transactions with only one of them. Halfway through the day, they switched. Subjects who had initially worked with the modified program switched to the original one. Those who had initially worked with the original program switched to the modified one.

From the several sets of data these authors use to describe their findings I have extracted only two to talk about here. Figure 12 shows the learning curves for subjects who worked with both kinds of programs. Although performance improves for both, the most impressive feature of the data is the large and consistent differences between the two. Since both curves seem to be leveling off it seems reasonable to assume that the difference in performance would persist over longer periods of time.

The second set of data (Figure 13) shows the average errors in sets of 60 transactions. Initially, errors were much fewer with the modified program. Much

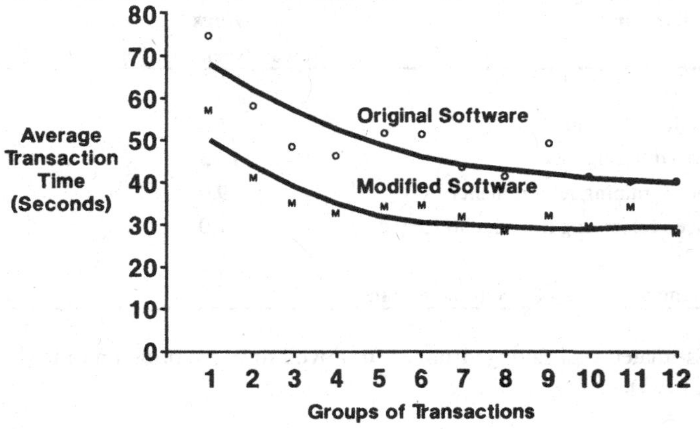

Figure 12: Learning curves for subjects who used either the original or the modified software program (from Keister and Gallaway, 1983).

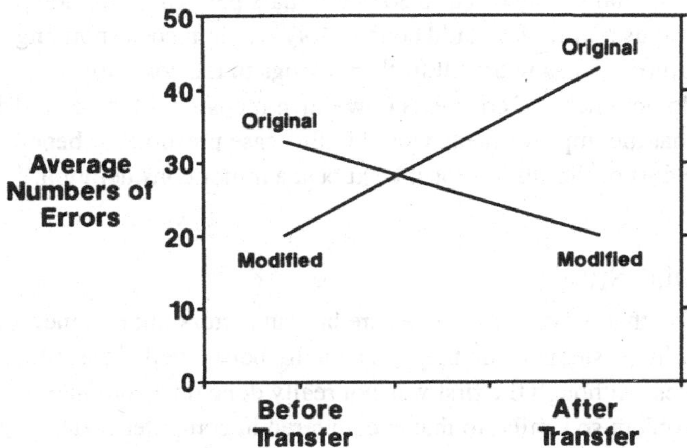

Figure 13: Average numbers of errors made by subjects who used either the original or the modified software program (after Keister and Gallaway, 1983).

more impressive, however, is what happened after the subjects switched. Subjects who had initially worked with the modified program committed nearly 90% more errors when they switched to the original program. On the other hand, subjects who had initially worked with the original program made nearly 40% fewer errors when they switched to the modified one.

Source of Savings	Savings (in man-weeks per year)
1. Reduction of errors	1.6
2. Improved throughput	13.5
3. Reduced training requirements	9.0*
4. Reduced relearning time due to forgetting	1.0

* Assuming a 50% employee turnover rate.

Table 2: Estimated cost savings from an improved software program (after Keister and Gallaway, 1983).

From these and other data, Keister and Gallaway then made some estimates of potential cost savings to a customer at a typical application site. These are shown in Table 2. Altogether they estimate that a company using the improved programs would find that the work previously done by three data entry operators could be done by two, for a potential saving of 20 to 30,000 dollars per year. Additional improvements in user attitudes could conceivably result in corresponding reductions in employee turnover rates with still further savings to the company.

What we do not know, of course, is how much it cost to do these studies. Still, if you consider that the improvements would in this case presumably benefit 500 customers, the cost of the studies must be at best a minor consideration.

6. Operational Studies

More impressive than laboratory studies are human factors improvements that are made on operating systems while they are actually being used. I describe briefly two such case studies. Although the first was not really done on a computer system, it deals with a problem so similar to that encountered in computer systems that it is worth more than passing mention.

6.1 *Improvement of international telephone dialling*

Clegg (1985) describes a series of studies that were undertaken to improve international telephone dialling. One of them was particularly impressive because it was done in two countries, the USA and Japan. The change involved the interception of erroneous calls to any one of six destination countries and the delivery of a spoken error message. Trials in the US extended over nearly a two-year period, during which incorrect outgoing calls were reduced from about 3% to less than 1%. Similar results were found in Japan. Although this might appear to be a trivial improvement, it is put into proper perspective when we consider the millions of such calls that are made in a single year. Unfortunately, we have no estimates of the costs of the study or of the monetary impact of the change.

6.2 *Improving system messages for JCL*

More complete data came from unpublished studies by Mosteller and Rooney (1982) on errors made by programmers in a data processing organisation. Briefly, these authors report that about 1.7% of all jobs fail with job control language (JCL) errors. Although that might not seem like a large figure, as we shall see, it turns out to be important when it is considered in the total context of this organisation's work.

When a programmer makes an error he gets a message. An analysis of over 3000 JCL errors showed that about 85% of them were accounted for by nine common error messages. One of them, message Number IEF657, says simply "Symbol not defined in procedure". Further study of the data showed that when an operator received such a message he or she very often resubmitted the job without change. This resubmission could not be traced to inexperienced or unskilled users. Retries rather reflected the behaviour of users who were unable to take any corrective action using the error message provided. There are two problems with this particular message: First, it does not identify the undefined symbol so that the user has to guess which one is causing trouble; second, it does not say in what statement the undefined symbol appears. Because of this two-fold lack of specificity, correcting the error can be very difficult, especially on large jobs.

Mosteller and Rooney wrote a new error message that was subsequently installed on a system at the Lockheed California Company. The upper part of Figure 14 shows the sources of over 3000 errors before the new message was used. Message Number IEF657 accounted for about 9.8% of all those recorded. Incidentally, percentages of 8.6% were recorded at the Boeing Computer Group and 9.4% at the Canada Systems Group, giving an average of about 9.3% for three different installations. The data for one week after the new message had been installed at Lockheed are shown in the bottom part of Figure 14. In that one week, only seven IEF657 error messages were recorded, or only 1.7% of the total. The decrease of 8.1% is over 2.5 times the next largest change in error frequencies and it seems to be clearly attributable to the improved wording of the message.

Although these percentages may seem small, they have to be considered in the context of an organisation employing nearly 300 programmer analysts. On the average, each programmer spends about 3 hours a week correcting errors. Mosteller estimates that improved error messages would reduce that time by over 60%. Assuming a base salary cost of $35,000 per year, the net savings would amount to

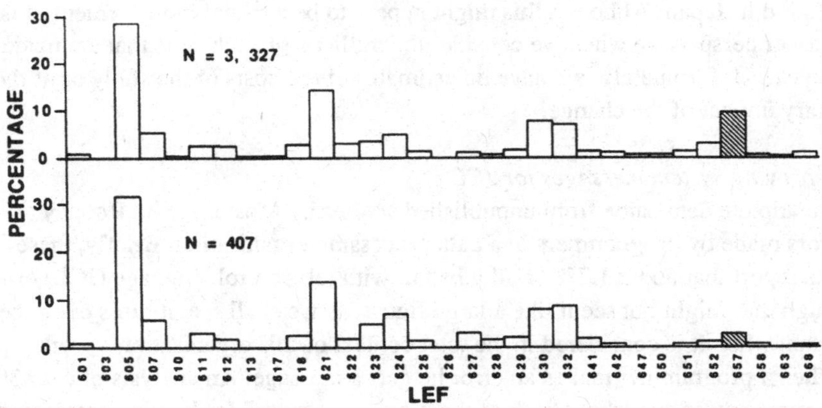

Figure 14: Distribution of programmer errors with an original help message (above), and the distribution of errors during one week after the incorporation of an improved error message (below) (unpublished data from Mosteller, 1983).

about $521,051 per year. Once again, unfortunately, we do not have data on the costs of collecting the data and making this improvement. Since the JCL system has been in operation for about 20 years and is likely to continue to be used for another 10 at least, the savings over the next decade would perhaps be on the order of $5,000,000. That would support a very great deal of human factors effort!

7. The cost of ignoring human factors

Another way of building a business case for human factors is to look at instances in which computer systems that were poorly designed from a human factors standpoint have been manufactured, put on the market, and have subsequently resulted in costs to the manufacturer, either directly in reduced sales, or indirectly in increased customer dissatisfaction and tarnished corporate image. Although complaints about poor design are common, it's hard to document what those poor designs cost. Occasionally, however, it is possible to find instances in which the failure to consider good design has resulted in substantial costs to manufacturers. Two such examples follow.

7.1 *Lost sales due to poor user manuals*

In 1984 Greenwald reported in the weekly magazine *Time* that Coleco had lost $35 million in the last quarter of 1983 because of a flood of returns by customers of the first version of Coleco's Adam computer. In a statement to shareholders, management blamed much of the customer dissatisfaction on "Manuals which did not offer the first-time user adequate assistance". Coleco subsequently reintroduced the Adam computer with a new instruction manual.

This experience is supported, though not quantitatively, by Joseph Sugarman, president of J S & A, a mail-order house in the US that specializes in high-tech merchandise. Sugarman was quoted as saying, "Very often, items with the highest rate of return are those where customers are frustrated with the instructions."

The converse of these experiences is reported by W.T. Collins, a vice president for consumer affairs at RCA. RCA's instructions were formerly written by design engineers, but they are now prepared by technical personnel who train distributors in how to operate and service RCA products. The reason, according to Collins, is that "We realised that engineers have a tendency to make the content of a manual a bit too technical". The result of this change, Collins adds, is that during the following year it reduced to a mere trickle the number of complaints RCA had received from customers about difficulties they have had understanding RCA's user manuals.

Although these examples do not provide sufficient information to make an incontestable case for human factors, I think they are sufficiently compelling to be believable. Indeed, I think I can assert with confidence that the time, effort, and cost of writing a good user's manual will be repaid many times over in sales, customer satisfaction, and corporate image.

7.2 *A recall due to poor keyboard design*

Quite a different kind of example concerns the keyboard on IBM's PCjr. Late in 1983 IBM announced its newest entry into the small computer market with a great deal of fanfare because the PCjr was expected to set a new standard for the home computer market. But almost from the very beginning, the PCjr was the object of widespread and vociferous complaints. Most of the complaints were directed at the computer's socalled "chiclet" keyboard with its small keys that were at best awkward to use. I am told by colleagues within IBM that the choice to go with this kind of keyboard was made by marketing against human factors recommendations. Whatever the true reason, it was a poor choice. Suffice it to say, in July 1984 IBM announced that it was replacing the original keyboard with a full typewriter-style keyboard as standard equipment. Moreover, in a move that I believe is unprecedented in the computer industry and reminiscent of the many expensive automobile recall programs we have seen in recent years, IBM offered to exchange old keyboards for new ones, at no cost to current owners. We can only speculate on what that recall cost IBM. At the very least it must be in the millions of dollars, and that, by any standard, is an expensive object lesson about the costs of ignoring good human factors design.

8. A case study of installability

Although they are somewhat different from the kinds of things that are usually associated with computers, problems of computer installation are of concern both to computer manufacturers and customers. And, it so happens, I have a good case study supporting the use of human factors in such an application. But first let me say a few words about why this is a matter of some importance.

8.1 *The installation process*

When a large computer or computer system has been manufactured, shipped out to a customer's shop, and delivered onto his loading platform, what happens? Obviously, it has to be installed. Boxes or crates have to be moved into the customer's facility; they have to be uncrated; the equipment has to be fitted into the space the customer has; it has to be assembled and attached to auxiliary systems, such as power and water if required; and finally the entire system must be connected together and tested as a whole.

In the case of large systems, installation is normally planned for long in advance. A year or more before actual delivery, the manufacturer's sales representatives, customer engineers, and systems engineers have been visiting the customer's shop, advising the customer and guiding him to a smooth and timely installation. How well all that planning works out in reality affects the manufacturer's costs and image, and the customer's productivity, profitability and satisfaction.

Look at it from the customer's standpoint. He's already been shown and told what the computer system can do. But when that equipment arrives on his platform, there are some additional human elements in the picture. Remember that the customer has had the equipment on order for several months, maybe even a year or more. Now he's got it, he's going to be using it, he's anxious to see it set up and running, and he may even be a little apprehensive about whether he will be able to use it properly and effectively. Moreover, getting equipment set up and running always disrupts the customer's own activities to some extent. The sooner and the easier installers can get equipment working, the better.

8.2 *The background*

The study I want to talk about shows how human factors improved the installation process for large computers resulting in substantial savings to the manufacturer, IBM in this case. The work was done by R. E. Granda and A. Silvestro, two human factors specialists at IBM Poughkeepsie in 1977 and 1978. What led to the study were some serious concerns management had about the installability of the IBM system 370, model 168s and the 3000 series of computers. These concerns centred around the large amounts of time required to install the 168s, the large expenditures of manpower required for installation, and the much faster installation times achieved by some of IBM's competitors who had roughly comparable systems.

To take just one area of corporate concern, the greatest part of installability costs — up to 90% of them — are manpower costs. As you know, manpower costs are increasing, while hardware costs are decreasing. Because installation is such a labour-intensive activity, the more reductions that can be made in manpower costs, the greater the cost savings and other benefits to the manufacturer.

8.3 *The study procedure*

A task force was set up to investigate these problems and Granda and Silvestro worked closely with that task force. Although the task force studied many aspects of the installation process, I shall confine myself to only the human factors part of the work. First Granda and Silvestro studied current practices. From that study they defined and identified problem areas, after which they devised and made recommendations for improving the operation. Finally, the recommendations were tried out on a test installation of the 168 to check their feasibility before they were actually put into practice.

8.4 *Areas of human factors improvements*

Human factors improvements were made in ten major areas:

- Frame Covers
- Frame alignment
- Console assembly
- Cables
- Pre-installation planning
- Tail gate connections
- Logic and installation manuals
- Small parts
- Tool Kit
- Outriggers

It would take quite a bit of time to explain what all these improvements were. Since their exact nature is irrelevant to the main thread of my story, I shall digress only enough to describe two of them.

The installation of a mainframe computer requires a large number of cables and during the first stages of installation installers have a lot of different kinds of cables to contend with. For example, there are DC bulk cables and I/O cables, a distinction that is very important because these cables are of different sizes and serve different functions. A shipment might contain as many as 15 to 20 crates of cables for only a CPU and 40 to 50 crates of cables for an entire system. Before Granda and Silvestro did their study, cables were crated in no particular order. When cables arrived at a customer's location they were typically dumped out, disentangled, sorted and matched against an available document. The cables were then labeled, routed, identified, and connected. All of that involved a considerable amount of work.

The solution Granda and Silvestro arrived at was a simple one. They had cables presorted prior to shipment. The cables are put into crates in the order in which they have to be installed. Checks for proper labeling and mechanical condition are made at the place from which they are shipped. When the crates arrive at the customer's site, they can either be laid out for inspection if space is available, or the cables can be kept in their boxes until they are needed in the installation sequence. This solution is so simple one might well wonder why it had not been thought of before. I have no answer to that question. All I can say is that is was apparently not thought of until these human factors specialists had studied the problem.

Not all the installation problems were solved as simply as the one involving cables. In the case of the tail gate connections, for example, Granda and Silvestro tried a couple of solutions, both essentially designed to organise the way in which tail frames were connected. Eventually, they ended up with a vertical bar going down the entire length of a frame. This bar was loosely connected to the frame with all the wires and connectors attached and the bar was simply moved over as a unit to the next frame to which it was to be connected.

8.5 *The costs and the benefits*

Without elaborating any more on the exact nature of the human factors improvements, what was the bottom line? It is shown in Table 3. Installation savings were computed first for the 270 IBM 3033s that had been shipped to January 15, 1979. The net savings attributable to human factors changes, after deducting the cost of the study, amount to nearly a quarter of a million dollars. Extrapolating to installations that were planned for delivery up to the end of that year yielded net savings of over a half million dollars. Actually, the savings are even greater than that because the lessons learned and the practices instituted because of this study have been applied to the installation of newer systems that are the successors to the 3033s. Taken together, these savings are significant even for a company as large as IBM!

To summarize, this is a success story relating to an often unrecognised aspect of large computer systems. A professional human factors team working in a field situation was able to make significant contributions to an important part of the company's business. These savings resulted in a reduced number of hours required for installation with consequent savings in dollars. What these figures do not include

Number of 3033s shipped	270
Total number of installation hours saved	40,770
Total savings due to reduction in installation time	$1,630,800
Savings attributable to human factors changes	$244,620
Net savings attributable to human factors changes (after deducting the costs of the study and of implementing the changes)	$219,620
Net savings attributable to human factors changes (extrapolated to the end of 1979)	$554,840

Table 3: Installation savings on IBM 3033s actually shipped to January 15, 1979, and extrapolated to December 31, 1979.

is the increased productivity and satisfaction that customers must certainly feel because computers are now installed faster and with less disruption to their own business activities. Still another unmeasured ingredient is the increased satisfaction that customer engineers feel because of the reduction of the hard labour and physical tasks that they have to be involved in. Customer engineers now experience fewer frustrations and get home earlier. Though we cannot measure those things, they must surely be important and should not be ignored.

9. Cost avoidance through human factors — an example

My final example is, in my opinion, the most impressive one. It forecasts the amounts of money that could be saved if human factors were used to simplify the operation of a specific computer system. The calculations are for two kinds of savings: (1) those resulting from a reduction in the training requirements for operators of the system, and (2) those resulting from a reduction in the number of telephone requests for assistance from operators who have difficulties using the system. Since my informant never identified the system, I shall refer it to as System X.

Based on sales predictions, a computer manufacturer arrived at the projected numbers of these systems that would be in use over a ten-year period (Column 2 of Table 4). As you may infer from the numbers, sales start out modestly, build up to a peak about five years later, after which the numbers decline as they have to compete with newer, more advanced systems that are certain to appear on the market. There is,

Year	Anticipated numbers of systems in use	Operators to be trained	Seminars required	Trainers required
(1)	(2)	(3)	(4)	(5)
1985	28,000	47,600	4,760	96
1986	108,500	184,450	18,445	369
1987	219,000	372,300	37,230	745
1988	336,250	571,625	57,163	1,144
1989	450,500	765,850	76,585	1,532
1990	477,750	812,175	81,218	1,625
1991	395,000	671,500	67,150	1,343
1992	280,000	476,000	47,600	952
1993	165,000	280,500	28,050	561
1994	55,000	93,500	9,350	187
		4,275,500	427,551	

Table 4: Estimates of training requirements.

of course, some margin of error in these estimates, but, as I shall show later, even if the estimates are off by a very considerable amount, it would not substantially affect the conclusion reached in this case.

This manufacturer's past experience with related kinds of systems has shown that, due to turnover, 1.7 operators have to be trained each year for each system. So the numbers of operators that have to be trained in Column 3 of Table 4 are 1.7 times the numbers of systems in Column 2. Since 10 operators can be trained at a time, the numbers of training seminars in Column 4 is one-tenth the figures in Column 3. Finally, since it was estimated that one trainer could conduct 50 two-day seminars per year, we end up with the numbers of trainers in Column 5. I'm sure you will agree that the numbers in Table 3 add up to an impressive training program. What is even more impressive is the cost of that training program. It was computed at a staggering $1,186,939,000 over the ten-year period!

The second part of this story concerns the costs of telephone calls from operators who might have difficulties using the system. This manufacturer, like many others, has a so-called "hot-line", a toll-free telephone number that one can call with questions about the system. Since System X had not yet been built, the forecasters made use of data from two earlier products that were similar in certain respects to the projected new System X. Those earlier data showed that operators of the two existing systems made on the average 5.6 calls per year. These, incidentally, were calls from experienced operators and were requests only for assistance with the operation of the system. They did not include calls with requests for information about such things as publications and applications.

The numbers of projected systems in use (Column 2 of Table 5) are the same as those in the corresponding column in Table 4. The estimated numbers of calls per year in Column 3 were obtained by multiplying the numbers in Column 2 by 5.6. On the assumption that a service representative can handle 3,250 calls per year, the numbers in Column 3 have been divided by 3,250 to get the numbers of representatives required in Column 4. The average cost per call in 1985 was estimated at $20 and that figure was expected to increase 8% per year. Appropriate arithmetic gives the costs of the calls in Column 5. These add up to a sizeable value of $407,958,284 over the ten-year period!

Year	Anticipated numbers of systems in use	Estimated number of calls	Representatives required	Cost of calls
(1)	(2)	(3)	(4)	(5)
1985	28,000	156,800	49	$ 3,136,000
1986	108,500	607,600	187	13,124,160
1987	219,000	1,226,400	387	28,609,458
1988	336,250	1,883,000	580	47,440,752
1989	450,500	2,522,800	777	67,556,438
1990	477,750	2,675,400	824	78,592,550
1991	395,000	2,212,000	681	70,178,088
1992	280,000	1,568,000	483	53,726,212
1993	165,000	924,000	285	34,192,896
1994	55,000	308,000	95	11,401,730
		14,084,000		$ 407,958,284

Table 5: Estimated costs of service calls.

If we add the cost of the training program to the cost of service calls we get $1,594,897,284 as the cost to the manufacturer of supporting this system over the ten-year period. That is an average of roughly $160 million per year.

Consultations with experts showed that it was entirely reasonable to expect that human factors improvements in the operation of the system could cut training requirements in half, and that those same human factors improvements could reasonably reduce the numbers of service calls by from 50 to 75%. These two sources of savings would amount to from $737,448,642 to $899,438,213. How much would it cost to get those human factors improvements made? I can't answer that, because I was never allowed to know the conclusion of the story. What I can say is that if only one-twentieth of one percent of the total estimated support costs were allocated to a human factors improvement program, it would have been one of the most generously funded human factors programs I have ever heard about and it would pay for itself something on the order of 100 times over. Perhaps you can see now why I said earlier that substantial errors in the initial assumptions would not seriously change the conclusion. Even if all the initial forecasts were so wrong that the projected costs were inflated by a whole order of magnitude, a program of human factors improvements would still pay for itself at least ten times over.

The final question, of course, is: Could a human factors program produce improvements of the kind that had been forecast? I can't answer that question. All I can say is that improvements of the magnitude predicted were, in my opinion, reasonably attainable. I wish I could finish the story for you, but I can't. What finally happened is buried in company archives to which I have never been privy.

10. Conclusions

So where do we stand? Is human factors worth its cost? It's difficult to prove conclusively, with scientifically defensible methodologies, that human factors involvement in the design of computer systems will pay for itself. That, however, is something that is true of all efforts to show productivity gains, or cost savings, from whatever kind of improvements one might make. As a result, we have to rely on more or less indirect forms of evidence. In the case of human factors these are several.

First, human factors has advertising value, particularly when the advertisements compare one product with another. Ease of learning and ease of use also figure prominently in ratings of computer systems and programs by independent testing organisations. Although the impact of such ratings cannot be assessed, they must have some value. More impressive are instances in which the failure to design products well has resulted in substantial losses to manufacturers, either through lawsuits or through reduced sales. Although no manufacturer likes to publicise such failures, enough of them do get into print to make telling stories. Those of us who have contact with designers, engineers, and businessmen occasionally hear about other such disasters. Unfortunately, we cannot talk about them because they are revealed to us under conditions of confidentiality, but they do happen more often than is supposed and they constitute painful lessons for everyone involved.

Although most laboratory studies suffer from too many technical drawbacks to make them acceptable evidence for the commercial value of human factors, some studies do make an effort to translate their findings into practical terms. Those suggest strongly that human factors improvements can yield substantial productivity gains, or cost savings. I don't think we can dismiss all such work as irrelevant.

Finally, the most conclusive kind of evidence comes from studies that have assessed directly the productivity gains or cost savings that result from human factors involvement. Such studies are hard to find because few people are willing to take the time and effort to do them. Those that I summarise show very large benefits from human factors.

Taking all these lines of evidence together, I think I can assert confidently that human factors does pay for itself and pay for itself handsomely. The reason it does is that in the final analysis computers exist for only one purpose, and that purpose is to serve mankind. Human factors is dedicated to the fulfilment of that purpose.

PART 2

System Design — Orientation and Approaches

CHAPTER FOUR

HUMAN FACTORS CONTRIBUTIONS TO THE DESIGN PROCESS

KEN EASON AND SUSAN HARKER

1. Introduction

It is widely agreed that we need to improve Information Technology products so that they are usable by and acceptable to a broader range of the population. Such a goal must depend upon the systematic application of knowledge about the characteristics, needs and motives of the people who will use these products and the tasks that they undertake. There is a large and growing body of information about human behaviour which could be used for these purposes. The question this review addresses does not concern the available knowledge but the way that it can be put to effective use within the design process.

There are two directions from which we can approach this review; we can examine the knowledge and organise it for application or we can examine the design process and try to specify the contributions that are required. In usability research the dominant message is to understand the user and the task in order to determine what will be usable. Applying the same edict we will approach this review by first examining the design process and then turn to the human factors contributions that are available and how they might fit into this process.

2. The nature of the design process

As part of the Alvey Programme of Information Technology Research we have been examining information technology design processes for the purposes of specifying human factor inputs (Harker and Eason, 1990). It is apparent that there are many varieties of design process and that they are undergoing rapid change. We cannot hope in a single paper to do justice to the variety we have found but in Figure 1 we

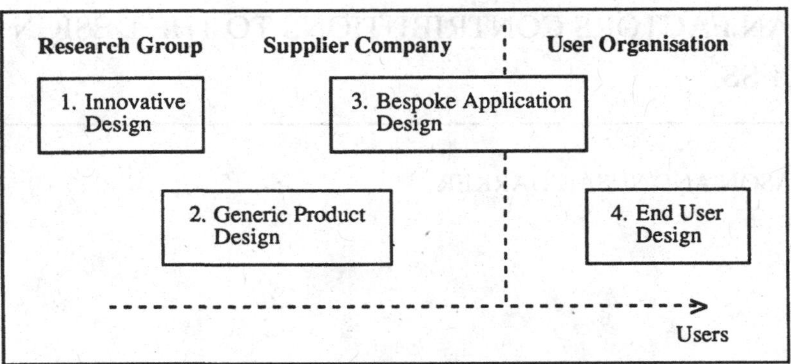

Figure l: Major forms of design process.

have tried to indicate the major types of design process that are relevant to the definition of human factor contributions and relate them to the organisational environments in which they are likely to occur.

The process by which the end user acquires a system can be seen as involving a number of separate but related design processes. The basic forms of equipment and software will have been created by a research and development process which turns advances in technology into the first examples of new types of application. Of particular relevance to human issues is the development of new forms of interface between the human and the machine. These new advances may result from design work in universities or in the research establishments of suppliers.

In many instances the next stage is for suppliers to take the new concepts and produce generic products which they will be able to sell to a variety of customers. An alternative is for basic tools to be used to create bespoke applications for specific customers. The bespoke development may be undertaken entirely by the user organisation or may involve a customer-contractor relationship with a supplier. Finally, there is an increasing array of options available to end users to 'design' the particular way they wish to employ the system.

This is a crude summary of a structure that shows many subtle varieties and relationships but serves to identify a number of factors which are crucial to the user. The early processes are a long way removed from the specific end user and, by the time the product reaches the end user, many design decisions will have been taken. This is more likely to be the case if the product rather than the bespoke route is taken to application design. Obviously the earlier design processes will need to operate on more generic knowledge about human behaviour than the later processes where the individual target user may well be involved in the design work.

We have access to several examples of each of these types of design process from our research studies. In analysing this data we are employing a socio-technical theoretical perspective because the design process has to be explained both as a technical process and as a social process in which people in interlocking work rôles coordinate their activities to produce the desired end product. The richness revealed by this perspective is not easily summarised but we can identify some major, perhaps obvious, features of these processes. We offer these below in order to build up a framework against which we can examine the characteristics of different types of human factors contributions. We will first report the state of the art and then identify some of the significant trends which are affecting the nature of the design process.

2.1 *The design cycle*

There are many variations in the phases of the design process but it is usually possible to distinguish a general movement from specification through design and build to implementation. This appears to be an 'invariant task structure' (Harker and Eason, 1980) in that it is inevitable that, in some form, it is first necessary to establish the objectives of design, then to envisage and create a solution and then to try it out. We employ this view of the design cycle below to examine some of the characteristics, problems and priorities of each design type.

2.2 *Specification*

In general the nearer the design process is to the end user the tighter is the specification. At the research end of the spectrum the process is by definition uncertain and the specification of the target system is fairly broad. The specification of the generic product is increasingly dominated by marketing considerations because the information technology industry is intensely competitive and very fast moving. The priorities of the market place have been price and functionality with each supplier intent upon offering at least as many if not more services or features than their competitors. The specification for the bespoke system is the subject of negotiation between customer and contractor. In the past the customer has been represented by senior management or technical specialists but increasingly end users are playing a direct rôle with the result that the specification may state detailed task and user requirements. Where there is flexibility for end user design, the specification may be a matter of individual needs and characteristics.

2.3 *Design and build*

Although there are hardware considerations in the design of systems, it is software design that dominates current concerns. It is often described as a black art engaged in by individual craftsmen and it is common for time and performance targets not to be met. A US General Accounting Office study (1985) found that in nine large projects, only about 52% of the functionality planned for systems reached the user. The rest was lost in 'designer drift' as the designers struggled to create workable systems within the constraints placed upon them.

The process varies a great deal across the different areas of design. At the innovative stage the design is usually the responsibility of a single person or a very small team with the main emphasis on creating a system with the desired performance characteristics. The teams creating generic products and bespoke systems may well be large with many specialised rôles which have to be coordinated. Damodaran (Chapter 13), for example, describes a very large system which is being designed by a number of teams of designers which requires an architecture team to lay down the standards within which other designers will work. In both generic and bespoke design the work is usually undertaken under considerable technical and time constraints as well as a tight specification for the system to be produced. In the generic case, for example, the designer has to fit his product into a consistent product range and run it on existing operating systems. Indeed we have found that most designers in the commercial environment are working to enhance existing products.

At the end user stage design is usually a matter of employing the flexibility and adaptability built into products and the evidence suggests that novice users do not make good use of this flexibility (Eason, 1984), whether it is to customise software to suit their task needs or to adjust their furniture to suit their physical characteristics. At this end of the process, and also within the bespoke systems development, a significant part of design relates to social structure change and the marriage of the social and the technical systems. There is little evidence that this is a systematic part of the design of many bespoke systems but design methodologies such as ETHICS (Mumford and Weir, 1979; see also Chapter 12) exist to correct this inadequacy.

2.4 *Implementation*

All design types end with some attempt to implement and test the system. Innovative design usually leads to a prototype product which can be tested within the development environment and usually against technical criteria. Generic product design leads to a product which is similarly tested in the development environment but may then be tested in a Beta Test field site before it is released. Bespoke applications and End User Designs proceed to full scale implementation with a consequent range of additional activities related to training, organisational change and user support.

2.5 *Design developments*

The nature of the design process is undergoing rapid change in which four trends may be particularly significant. First, the technologies upon which the new products are to be based are changing so that new interfaces will use speech, will involve mixed media and will have an expert system base. Second, the tools of the design trade are changing rapidly. The advent of fourth generation languages and prototyping tools means programmers can re-use code and can generate application prototypes rapidly. Thirdly, the process of managing design processes is now being formalised into Structured Design Methodologies (Burchett, 1985) so that the specification, documentation and design of large systems can be carefully controlled. The integration of the new design methods and the new tools into automated software design environments is a widely discussed consequence of these developments. Finally, the process is gradually moving from being technology led to being market and user led. For many the problem which now presents itself is not what could be produced but what is worth producing.

3. The market for human factor contributions

This description of design processes is little more than a thumbnail sketch but it does help us consider the nature of human factor inputs that will be required. We can ask two questions. What is needed and what form will it have to take to be usable? The answers are going to be different for each of the different design types.

The recognition that technical capability and cost are not the only considerations in the production of appropriate designs creates a potential market place for methods of handling human issues. If design is to embrace market and user considerations, there will be a need at all stages of design to define the relevant user and task considerations and create solutions to meet them. However, the nature of these considerations at the innovative design stage and in general product developments are different from bespoke and end user development. In the former case the specific user is, to a large extent, unknown and unavailable and some generalised version of needs, characteristics and requirements must be used. In the latter case where the specific users are known it is possible for them to be studied, consulted or to participate in the design process.

3.1 *Survey of designers re: 'Market Needs'*

There is then a market, albeit one that varies in its requirements. But what form would inputs have to take to be widely used? We conducted a small survey of designers to identify some of the critical issues. We questioned 63 designers of computer based systems who were attending a short course on human factors in computer systems (Eason, Harker and Poulson, 1986). These were people with some commitment to and experience of the use of human factors, and Table 1 summarises their views of the obstacles to the employment of human factors.

Availability	N	Fit With Existing Practice	N
Knowledge not available	35	Takes too long	38
Not available when needed	22	Not cost beneficial	31
Information not directly relevant	21	Opposition from others	29
		Would not fit design philosophy	19
[Sample = 63]		Other, e.g., technical design only	19

Table 1: Obstacles to employing human factors.

The respondents were primarily experienced in bespoke applications or generic product developments. They were asked to nominate up to three obstacles or to identify others not on the list provided. The obstacles fell into two categories, areas where information was needed but was not available at the point of need, and obstacles which derived from current practice and which would mean that, even if information was available, it could not be used. There was a fairly even spread of problems suggesting human factors inputs will have to satisfy a number of criteria.

The availability problem concerns non-existent information, information not being directly relevant to the design issue in question (being based, for example, on out-of-date technology), or not being available by the time it was needed. In many cases relevant information did exist and the problem is not that more research is needed but that it has to be available where and when it is needed. The form of delivery is crucial. Allen (1977) reports a number of studies of information utilisation in Research and Development Laboratories and concludes that designers rarely look beyond their 'local environment' for information. Given the time constraints under which most designers operate, Zipf's (1965) 'Principle of Least Effort' seems to apply and anything that requires effort to search and understand is likely to be ignored. Boff (1987) identifies seven 'choke points' which block the access of relevant information by designers which include both the non-existence of information and the tendency for designers to use 'valued information', i.e., that which fits their existing frame of reference and is easily available.

Given these characteristics it will be necessary, albeit difficult, to process primary information so that it can reach and be used by designers. The nature of the processed information will be different for the different design environments, i.e., generalised information about user behaviour must reach innovative designers and generic product designers but much more specific information is necessary when the design concerns identifiable groups of people.

Although availability is a significant issue, a more frequently cited problem is the degree to which human factors inputs would fit within the existing design process. Given the constraints of time and resources any extra effort devoted to issues not currently on the agenda is not welcome and there is the fear that it will 'take too long' and delay the design process. Although the problems users experience with unusable products are now well known there are still many design processes that are considered to be only about technical design, i.e., 'human issues are the responsibility of people during implementation', and there is the perennial problem of demonstrating that human factors contributions can be cost effective. One of the major problems is that the design method, which is now being formalised and automated, is seen by many as not providing the opportunity for human factors to be considered. A final problem is that even where there are people who want to deal with these issues, there may be active opposition from others in the design process. These may be people who do not want to complicate design further or who remain to be convinced about the cost-benefits of human factors. There is also the possibility that opposition is based upon feelings of interference from people who 'do not understand design' or a perceived threat that known ways of working may be changed. Whatever the reasons it seems likely that attempts to create inputs to the design process which do not consider the structure and dynamics of the process are likely to be rejected.

These issues again vary across the different design processes. The innovative design process may be fairly flexible but it is a long way from the users and, on our evidence, is a situation in which untested views about user characteristics and needs can thrive and alternative views may not be welcome. Both the generic product and bespoke application development tend to be heavily controlled, highly constrained processes and although user considerations are becoming more prevalent, time, resources, relevance and 'fit with practice' are major obstacles. User considerations naturally tend to dominate end user developments but why look for systematic evidence about user behaviour when implicit and unsystematic user views are instantly available? This takes us into the difficult area of whether people know what is good for them. These issues are further explored in the following analysis of human factors methods and information sources.

3.2 *Methods available to meet 'Market Needs'*

The available methods and sources of information can be conveniently described in three broad categories: Knowledge Based, Procedure Based, and Professional Based.

The first group of methods are knowledge based in that they attempt to provide designers with relevant knowledge about the needs, characteristics and requirements of users and their tasks. The second group we have called procedure based because they provide a set of techniques for dealing with human issues in the design process. Finally, there are professional based methods in which human factors specialists contribute directly to the design process and may be able to provide both direct access to relevant knowledge and employ appropriate procedures. In the sections below we will examine each group of contributions with a view to assessing how and where they could be of service within the design process and what will be necessary to render them usable and acceptable to designers.

4. Knowledge based contributions

The responses of the survey sample (referred to above) in relation to the knowledge based methods are set out in Table 2 below.

		Have Used	Would Use	Usability
Unprocessed				*Low*
	Primary Data Sources / Text Books	10	3	
	Bibliographic Systems	–	–	
	Guidelines / Checklists	20	16	
	User Models	–	–	
	Standards	19	15	
	Expert Systems	–	–	*High*
Processed				

Table 2: Knowledge based contributions.

The different methods are classified along a dimension from relatively primary or unprocessed sources of data to methods where there has been a considerable degree of processing in order to render the information in a form relevant to design decisions. In the survey of 63 designers cited earlier we also asked what human factor contributions the designers had experienced and found valuable, and what they had not experienced but thought might be of value. Although this survey did not cover all the methods listed in Table 2, we have included the results where they are available. The results suggest that whilst processed contributions such as standards and guidelines are widely valued, access to primary data sources and text books is not.

Most of the designers surveyed were not human factors specialists; so this suggests that processed contributions are much more usable than unprocessed contributions, which is in line with the 'least effort' view of information seeking behaviour.

4.1 *Primary sources and text books*

The literature on human behaviour with information technology systems is widely scattered, covering as it does many subjects from the cognitive psychology of man-computer dialogues to the physiology of seating comfort and eyestrain and to the social psychology of job design and organisational change. There is an increasing number of attempts to capture the theories and findings of this area in text books, e.g., Grandjean (1984), Card *et al.* (1983), Cakir *et al.* (1980), Shneiderman (1980), Oborne (1986), but most non-specialists would find it a difficult literature to search and to understand.

4.2 *Bibliographic searches*

One way of easing access to the literature is the creation of bibliographic search systems, such as *Ergonomics Abstracts* or the Human Factors Information Service at Loughborough University, which would enable the user by combinations of key words to access relevant primary sources. This will certainly make access less problematic but leaves the problem of digesting and integrating what may be fragmentary and conflicting information.

4.3 *Guidelines and checklists*

The most obvious way to process primary data is to summarise the data available on each subject into a series of guidelines which tell the designer what to do in specific circumstances. This was seen as a very useful approach by the designers in the survey. There are however a number of problems with this approach. First, the variety of users, tasks, technologies and applications is very large and the creators of guidelines can either issue very general guidelines which may not be very helpful or issue very large volumes of guidelines. The manual provided by Smith and Mosier (1984) contains, for example, over 600 guidelines. As Gaines and Shaw (1984) comment, when the number gets large, the guidelines themselves present a usability problem. A second problem is that, in the processing, the origins of data may be lost and the user may interpret it inappropriately, i.e., a guideline may have been based on the behaviour of a group of programmers but if the sample is forgotten the designer may think it will also apply to a group of inexperienced users. Any guideline has therefore to carry with it a statement of its domain of applicability. A further problem, as an analysis by Maguire (1982) has shown, is that many of the guidelines may be in conflict with one another. Whilst they are potentially useful, the designer may therefore have difficulty locating a relevant guideline and has to be careful that its advice is valid for his problem.

4.4 *User models*

In recognition of these problems, Lansdale (1985) and others advocate the integration of guidelines into user models. There are, as Young (1983) points out, many different kinds of model (the user's model of his task or of the system, the designer's model of the user, even the system's model of the user) and it is extremely important to be clear what is modelling what. One type of model which has the potential to be very helpful and usable is the user's model of his task world and the expectations and stereotypes the user has of the tools he uses in this task world. If the designer can model the user's view it may be possible to create new systems which are congruent with this model and are consequently easy for the user to understand and use. It is also likely that the integrative nature of the user/task/tool model will embody advice on many of the human factors issues.

Much of the early work in this area centred on identifying powerful metaphors that could provide a central source of advice to designers. The 'typewriter' metaphor, for example, underpins many word processor applications and the 'untidy desktop' metaphor has had a powerful influence on the development of the icons and windows form of interface. Metaphors of this kind constitute concise, usable and abstract, yet powerful models of the target but leave the designer to exercise creativity in meeting the target. The problems lie with the validity of the metaphor, the degree to which it can be implemented, and its relation to the representation that the designer already possesses.

The problem of validity is that any model is a simplification of reality and it may not capture many issues of importance to the user. A powerful but inappropriate model may be very dangerous. It is vital therefore that any user models are founded on empirical analysis of the user population in question. The problem of implementation is that a user's stereotypes and expectations of the task and tool world are based on what currently exists. The new system should change and enhance this in ways which go beyond these expectations. In a study to develop new telecommunication interfaces, Hannigan and Kerswell (1986) found that an interface based on existing expectations was immediately usable by subjects but limited the way new facilities could be offered. In contrast an interface created to provide a usable way of offering new facilities did not match existing stereotypes of a telephone and subjects found it initially difficult to 'model' the new system. The final problem is that all designers carry a more or less explicit and systematic representation of the world for which they are designing. They may have significant psychological investment in this representation; they believe in it much more than any alternative that is offered and may reject others or seek out those that are congruent with existing beliefs. User models are not fed into a vacuum and the process of matching them to existing concepts needs careful handling if threatening, foreign concepts are not to be rejected.

4.5 *Standards*

One way of ensuring due note is taken of important human factors findings, even in circumstances where they are not wanted, is to formulate them as standards that have some degree of sanction behind them. There are now national and international standards in existence or under development which cover both hardware and software subjects (see, for example, BSI, 1987; ISO, 1988; and DIN 66, 1981). Many organisations, both supplier and user organisations, have developed their own internal standards. These standards have two important functions. They serve to spread good practice on human factors issues and they also serve to provide consistency between products which, in itself, is an important human factors goal because it facilitates the transfer of training. Standards have, however, been slow to emerge because the variability of human characteristics and needs make it very difficult to formulate general, mandatory rules. We have discussed elsewhere (Harker and Eason, 1985) the problem of creating standards as a problem of defining the number of contingencies upon which good human factors solutions need to be based. There are a few in relation to some hardware topics because the extent of human variability, for example in visual perception and body size, is at least measurable, but software issues are subject to cognitive, task and contextual variables which make it difficult to be prescriptive. There are several ways of dealing with this problem. At an organisational level, one technique is to formulate standards which designers must follow unless they have authority to vary them when they can demonstrate that the standard does not fit the circumstance for which they are designing (Taylor and Harker, 1985). Another is to offer performance standards which specify what should be achieved but do not state how to achieve it. This is one way of avoiding the difficulty of tying standards to existing technology. Another technique which is gaining in popularity is to define procedural standards. These tell designers what steps to take to determine the relevant criteria for the specific product and should perhaps be considered as a procedural based approach. Gardner (see Chapter 7) describes a manual which is made up of a series of such procedural standards closely related to the stages of the design process.

4.6 *Expert systems*

If human factors knowledge is to reach designers in a usable form it has to be processed in some way and one approach which is being actively canvassed, although there are few working examples at present, is to develop expert systems for providing human factors advice. Russell (1986) outlines one possible system. The general principles underlying systems of this kind would enable designers to specify the user/task context and their requirements, and the system would provide the best human factors advice available. If this can be achieved it will provide a service covering most of the methods examined above. It remains to be seen, however, how much of available human factors knowledge can be processed in this way. There is also the danger that the system which provides this support may become complex to operate or its output difficult to interpret and so render it unusable by non-specialist designers.

4.7 *Knowledge based contributions and types of design process*

We have evaluated these methods in general but we can also examine them in respect of the different types of design discussed earlier in this paper. Methods that rely on relatively unprocessed primary data or on sorting complex guidelines will require time, effort and perhaps specialist knowledge from the designers who use them. This is unlikely to be the situation of the average designer in the large project teams to be found in bespoke applications design and may be too much to expect from 'end user' designers. Specialists are more likely to be found as part of central human factors teams or possibly as specialist designers of interfaces who may well have to be experts in human and technical disciplines in order to produce human-computer interfaces. This kind of specialist seems more likely to be found at the innovative end of the design spectrum. The concept of a generic user model seems likely to be more useful at the supplier end of the process. It is not clear that such models would add to the specific knowledge that can be obtained from the users themselves when the design is specific to a user organisation. Where there are large numbers of designers in a single team and they consider themselves primarily technical in orientation, the methods of standards and tailored guidelines offer the best hope of acceptability unless and until the promise of expert systems is fulfilled. One route which has yet to be explored which may be very effective is to build the relevant knowledge into the tools that application designers are beginning to use, i.e., if designers re-use code in designing new applications it is important that any code, for example that which defines screen layout, is based on good human factors practice.

5. Procedure based contributions

Table 3 below lists the different types of procedural contributions that can be made and again provides the results from the survey of 63 designers.

	Have Used	Would Use	Easy to Fit
Evaluation Methods	14	25	
Specification Methods Design Methods Implementation Methods	13	13	
General User Centred Design Methods	8	27	Difficult to Fit

Table 3: Procedure based contributions.

The most common kind of procedure used has been the human factors evaluation of systems and products followed closely by methods which support the specification and design of systems. It will be noted in Table 3 that respondents are particularly keen to see more use made of evaluation methods but even keener to see a broader form of user centred design employed, a type of design process most had not experienced. The figures for respondents seeking these types of contribution are higher than for any category of knowledge based contribution. This may be a recognition that the establishment of human factor properties of systems is not simply the application of existing knowledge but a process of arriving at a specific solution for a specific application. The order of presentation of these contributions in Table 3 is broadly in terms of how easy it is to fit these procedures into existing design processes. It is not too difficult to evaluate the quality of systems (although it may be more difficult to get attention paid to the results). It is more difficult to get human factors procedures into the specification and design processes because they have to match existing procedures. When all these human factors procedures are combined to give a user orientation to all stages of design, there may be severe problems in maintaining the existing design processes. The adoption of human factors procedures therefore tends to move from an additional element to what is potentially a major change in design philosophy.

5.1 *Evaluation contributions*

Testing whether a product or system does serve the needs of its chosen users and is usable by them is obviously important if design is to be more concerned with human issues. There exist many methods designed for this purpose which range from tests for time and error performance with human-computer interfaces to evaluation of the acceptability of systems in organisational settings.

It is, of course, common for products and systems to be tested before implementation. Typically each module is tested as it is built and the entire system may be subjected to pre-release trials. In most cases these evaluations are technical proving trials and do not pay specific attention to issues of usability. To be useful such tests must provide data which can be fed back into the design process. Early tests consist mostly of conceptual 'walk throughs' but, when a working system is available, full scale trials become possible.

It would seem, on the face of it, relatively straightforward to add usability evaluations to the different kinds of evaluation that are already undertaken. There are, however, significant problems. Testing products for usability, for example, depends on making assessments of how a given target group of users would respond to it. Ideally this is done by running real trials with real users. This can be expensive, time consuming and difficult to undertake. Frequently the substitute is to run experimental evaluations with subjects in the laboratory. Chapanis (Chapter 16) describes in more detail the principles of usability evaluation. The danger (Eason, 1984) is that the artificial conditions of the experiment may not be a reliable indication of what would happen in practice. For example, an experiment in which subjects are asked to try out a range of facilities on a product will show where errors are made, how long it takes, etc. But how will it show whether discretionary users will find the facilities sufficiently 'user friendly' to make any use of them in practice?

Another problem is that it is very difficult for would-be users to evaluate the adequacy of a system at the conceptual stage of design. They can make a much more realistic assessment when they have a working system to examine. Unfortunately, at this stage, it may be too late to make major changes in the design if problems are revealed. One of the most promising features of developments in tooling for design is the emergence of fourth generation languages which can be used for rapid prototyping of system interfaces very early in the design process. Our evidence suggests that most design teams that are building prototypes are not, at present, using them to evaluate usability. When they are shown to users they are usually used for demonstration purposes. As Harker (1986) points out, to make good and valid use of a prototype, users need to be given 'hands-on' experience of it for realistic tasks. The creation of techniques suitable for the human factors exploitation of prototyping could be a fruitful area for future developments.

5.2 *Specification contributions*

To be usable and acceptable a product must meet the task needs of users and match the characteristics of users. Since task and user needs are very variable each design process requires a human factors specification procedure. Existing specification processes highlight business, economic, market and technical criteria. Again there should be an opportunity to complement normal specification procedures with techniques designed to identify human requirements.

Within the bespoke and end user type of application the users themselves can play a rôle in specification. Users have difficulty in identifying their business requirements and also have problems specifying personal needs and characteristics. One of the problems is that, initially, they do not know how to judge what is possible and, when shown the options, how to judge the implications for themselves and their organisation. There is, therefore, a need to develop forms of task and user analysis which users can adopt or play a part in, while a design process is in its initial stages.

Supplier led design processes that are aimed at a wide market have no specific user population to participate in the specification process and, as we have considered before, there is a danger that the human factors needs that are considered are based on a 'model' or 'metaphor' of the user that the designers carry. If this is not well founded, the result may not be very successful. The need here is for a human factors specification process, such as is outlined by Shackel in Chapter 2, which will work alongside market and technical specification processes and be based on empirical evidence of user behaviour in the relevant market segment.

An important consideration in the application of these techniques is that the conclusion must be fed into the design process with the same weighting process as technical, economic and other criteria. Gilb (1988), in particular, has emphasised in his 'design by objectives' approach the need to specify human factor criteria in quantifiable and measurable forms if they are to be taken seriously in the design process.

5.3 *Design and implementation contributions*

The human factors contributions to design and implementation can be conveniently divided into technical system design and social system design. The contribution to technical systems design is the application of all the human factors knowledge discussed in Section 1 to meet the specification for a particular product or system. Some knowledge is universal and can be applied as a standard to every design. Most, however, is contingent on the user, task, application and context and requires the identification of specific solutions appropriate to the design process. Procedures are needed therefore to recruit relevant knowledge to the design process. There are two schools of thought about how this should be done. If expert systems, standards or the building of proven solutions into the tools of the trade become the dominant route, there is a feeling that it could improve the human factors quality of products and systems by removing it from the discretion of technical designers. The other school of thought is that, because design is and will remain a skilled process requiring many weightings and trade-offs between competing criteria, all designers must be trained in human factors procedures in order to be able to integrate human and technical concerns in their design work. This appears to be an argument about whether designers should be allowed to be creative. It is worth remembering that one of the job design criteria we would ask designers to use on behalf of users is the need to retain discretion and autonomy. The same must apply to technical designers. Any scheme to implement human factors by robbing technical designers of significant areas of autonomy is likely to meet resistance. Conversely, giving structure and support on detailed issues may be seen as providing more opportunity to concentrate on strategic topics. Whether technology controls or facilitates is as important for the job of designer as it is for the job of user. At the application end of the design spectrum, the design and implementation of the organisational change is often as important to the users as the technical change. Techniques are therefore needed for job design, training design, workstation and workplace layout design, etc., (see Damodaran *et al*., 1980, for example techniques). These topics need to be addressed in both bespoke systems design and end user design where there is a specific organisation undergoing change, as is discussed by Damodaran in Chapter 13. There are also consequences, as Bjørn-Andersen (1984) has shown, for the design of generic products. It may be, for example, that the design of a product supports a particular management style which may not be acceptable in some countries. Shop floor data collection terminals are not, for example, acceptable in some Nordic countries because they do not provide usable feedback to the person providing the input and this is a basic criterion in many job design approaches.

Where organisational change is planned there is the interesting question of who is doing the designing. If techniques are created to aid this process, to whom are they directed? In this paper it may have been presumed that the target for human factors advice is the technical designer. In this case, however, it will probably be users or specialist staff in personnel or administration. It is probably also the case in respect of the specification and evaluation techniques described earlier. In some respects one of the 'political' effects of developing techniques of this kind could be to provide tools for users to exercise their rights in systems design and thereby to exert greater influence over technical designers. It is important to note that in the political arena in which systems are introduced into organisations, the users do not necessarily speak with one voice. Different user departments may have different priorities and the management may have goals that conflict with the workforce and their representatives. One of the difficulties facing the implementation of human factor contributions is how to provide appropriate help to all the 'stakeholders' (Mitroff, 1980) in the process. Eason (1988) illustrates the ways in which methods and tools may be used by non-specialists to engage with information technology and organisational change as a socio-technical process.

5.4 *General user centred design*

Suppose all the techniques described above were to be utilised within the same design process. It would then include an analysis of user and task requirements, the inclusion of these factors in the formal specification, the use of human factors knowledge in technical design and in the design of organisational change, and regular evaluation against human factor criteria to establish whether progress towards usable and acceptable outcomes was being made. Such a combination may represent a fairly powerful orientation of design towards user issues and it is not easy to add this combination to the design processes described earlier in this paper. The individual procedures often create problems of fit with existing practice. In combination they will almost certainly demand changes of design philosophy.

The nature of the changes are fourfold; to broaden the agenda of design objectives from the technical to the socio-technical, to increase the range of people involved in taking design decisions to include users and their representatives, to increase the time devoted to specification and design (although perhaps with compensating gains in the time devoted to implementation) and to increase the number of design-evaluation iterations in the design process. These changes could create pressure to move from a linear 'one shot implementation' model of design to one which explicitly recognises its iterative, evolutionary character (Eason, 1982).

Such changes would obviously not be implemented lightly within design teams. Many of the concepts are foreign to designers trained for technical systems development. There is, however, quite a strong movement in this direction especially within bespoke application development. It is fuelled both by the realisation that more attention must be paid to usability and acceptability questions and by the appearance of technical tools to support this kind of design. Rapid prototyping tools, for example, mean that iterative design and evaluation cycles are a feasible basis for a design process. There are, however, what appear to be countervailing forces. If, for example, the attempts to introduce more discipline into systems development through Structured Design Methodologies lead to a clearer, linear, staged approach to design with major points of review and management authorisation, what is the rôle of iterative design and evaluation and to what extent can the specification be changed if evaluations show the earlier decisions were inadequate? However, it may be possible to use these methodologies and complement them with human factors procedures (see, for example, Damodaran, Chapter 13).

5.5 *Procedural contributions and types of design process*

The implications of procedural contributions for the design process are so evident that the preceding sections have listed many ways in which the different types of design process may be affected. This section will therefore be limited to a few observations. It is at the user organisation end of the design spectrum where these procedures have, so far, had most impact albeit in a fragmentary way. The range of concepts and techniques is already quite extensive. Hirschheim (1985), for example, provides a very comprehensive analysis of the extent to which a variety of design methodologies for office automation deal explicitly with user and organisational issues. The methods advanced for use in user organisations are all concerned, in one way or another, with the customer-contractor relationship and the way in which users can participate in or take control of some of the design procedures.

The equivalent procedural developments are not so evident in the innovative and generic product design environment. There is some evidence of a growth in interest in human factors evaluation procedures and in task and user analysis procedures but it is not on the same scale as within bespoke developments. It seems probable that the procedures necessary to serve the supplier-led design processes will have to be radically different from those employed in user organisations, if only because the target population is diffuse and distant from the design team. Running evaluation exercises with subjects playing the rôles of users is, for example, quite different from running evaluation exercises with people who expect to be the users. In the development of generic products the specification is often the responsibility of a marketeer rather than a user as would be the case for a bespoke application. Thus there is a need to develop specification techniques which will support the marketeer in adding the rôle of human factors to the requirements for the product. Whilst there may be general concepts that can be transferred from user-organisation design procedures there appears to be a considerable amount of work to be done to formulate similar procedures for the innovative and generic product design processes.

6. Professional based contributions

The final form of contribution to consider is that which can be provided by professional staff qualified in human factor disciplines.

If there is a need for human science knowledge to be applied in systems design an obvious route is to employ specialists in these disciplines to complement the work of existing professionals who are predominantly trained in technical subjects. Table 4 lists some of the potential rôles such human factors specialists might play. They are listed on a scale which reflects a range from direct involvement as a member of a design team, through operating as a central service, to providing a training service to enable designers to acquire the necessary skills and knowledge. The survey of 63 designers shows that, although relatively few had experienced direct working with human factor specialists, most felt this to be a desirable option. This could be a

	Have Used	Would Use	
			Direct
Involvement in Design by			
Human Factors Specialists Human Factors 'Gatekeepers' Central Human Factors Laboratories	11	29	
Training by Human Factors Specialists	7	31	
			Indirect

Table 4: Professional contributions.

recognition that human factor issues are difficult and require specialist treatment but we have to accept that the sample might be biased; designers attending a course on human factors might be expected to respond favourably to the idea of training given by human factors specialists.

6.1 *Involvement of human factors specialists in design*

The assignment of a human factors specialist to each design team is one way of ensuring specialist knowledge is available and the team has the ability to conduct the appropriate human factor procedures. If widely adopted this approach would rapidly outstrip the supply of qualified human factors staff. Where it is adopted it raises questions about the kind of rôle such specialists could and should play. There are beginning to emerge people with qualifications in the technical and the human disciplines who can play a full rôle in technical design and bring the requisite human factors knowledge into the team. People with this kind of background seem particularly interested in working on interface design solutions. Whilst a contribution of this kind is desirable it is doubtful whether any one person can maintain and develop expertise across the full range of technical and human subjects that may be necessary in design. This cannot therefore be regarded as the complete solution.

There may also be good structural reasons for maintaining the human factors rôle as complementary to but separate from that of the technical designers. The rôle of the human factors specialist may be to help establish the specification, to provide design standards and guidelines and to perform evaluative studies, leaving technical designers to identify and build technical solutions within these constraints. Such a rôle model for the team may help to preserve the specification and ensure adequate tests of solutions. However willing and well intentioned, the technical designer is not in a good position to provide an objective assessment of the design solutions. Within large design teams it may be necessary to establish quality assurance checks as design proceeds and this may be one of the key rôles.

Within applications design a significant amount of the design work relates to working with users on technical specifications, job design, organisational change, etc. The rôle of the human factors specialists in this case is even more problematic. Ideally it should be the users who play the leading rôle in these procedures, designing their own future. They are unlikely to be able to do it effectively without professional help so that the human factors specialist should act as a facilitator, using the rôle model of the organisational development practitioner or 'change agent', e.g., Margerison (1978), identifying the procedures users might follow to undertake these tasks and supporting them as they do this work. Gower and Eason (1985) provide some examples of this kind of approach in planning implementation, furniture selection, workplace layout, etc.

The sensitivity of the rôle adopted by the human factors practitioner is important for another reason. Where there are users who need to feel commitment to the design solution or technical designers who feel it is their job to produce the technical solutions, there will be no welcome for a human factors specialist who attempts to occupy the same territory. The successful team has to be built with a multi-disciplinary base in which each specialist understands the rôle to be played and understands, and is sympathetic to, the rôles to be played by the others. This kind of understanding needs careful team building and any human factors specialist, as the source of expertise on group dynamics, should be capable of establishing their own rôle and of helping the team as a whole to develop constructive rôle models.

6.2 *Centralised human factors services*

If human factors specialists are in short supply or it is not deemed necessary to associate them with every design team, a conventional solution is to establish them as a central service. Most of the major suppliers have such central services; Hirsch (1981) and Shackel (1986) give accounts of the functions of such services in IBM. The rôles of central services are many. In some organisations they are research laboratories, e.g., developing new forms of interface. In others the major rôle may be to provide consultancy support for design teams. A common rôle is to provide human factors evaluation of products as the first versions are generated by design teams. One of the major movements at the moment is the creation of central usability testing laboratories where in an instrumented environment the behaviour of users with new products can be captured in detail and 'played back' to designers so that they can see directly how users interpret and misinterpret their design solutions.

Another major function is to act as an information dissemination centre. Boff (1987), and others, have coined the term 'gatekeeper' to suggest that centrally located specialists can filter available knowledge and make available that which is relevant to the non-specialists in the organisation. Returning to the debate in Section 4, the specialists inside an organisation may be able to make use of primary data sources and the bibliographic search systems which permit access to them, whereas the non-specialists may not find these useful. The specialists may then be able to process this data to provide standards and guidelines which could provide a consistent policy statement for the organisation. Many supplier organisations now have internal documents of this kind providing, for example, hardware and software guidance. The 'gatekeeper' may also provide *ad hoc*, specific advice to designers as it is required.

The central facility can then provide a very useful way of promoting human factors within an organisation. It tends to be a viable proposition when there is a large body of design work to be undertaken and, at the moment, it is the supplier organisations rather than user organisations which have created these facilities. Within user organisations the responsibilities for human factors issues tend to be taken by the users themselves or by centralised services that already exist, e.g., Personnel, Training, O & M, etc., who will be more concerned with the organisational ramifications of design solutions than with the technical systems themselves.

Central services can be very effective but human factors services are subject to the same organisational problems as other central services. They can, for example, become insulated from the rest of the organisation, developing their own work and resources with little reference to the needs of the design teams. They may be pushed in this direction if there is resistance or antipathy to human factors amongst design teams. An important function of any central facility is therefore to keep open the lines of communication to all parts of the organisation and to build an image of constructive support for design teams rather than irrelevance or threat.

6.3 *Training designers in human factors*

The need for some understanding of human factors issues is very pervasive, affecting many different design decisions. It is hardly likely therefore that a limited number of human factors specialists will be able to provide all the inputs that will be desirable. It is necessary for all designers to have some understanding of human factors, at least so that they know when to seek the help of a specialist.

It is useful to distinguish two dimensions of the knowledge that designers might require. Designers with different rôles may require different human factors knowledge. An interface designer may require knowledge about human-computer interaction that is, for example, not necessary to the systems analyst, who may need more help with user requirements analysis. The needs for training may extend beyond the design team. Users at all levels, for example, need training in how to participate in design; how, for example, to undertake job design studies and to evaluate technical options. Their representatives may also need training in how best to safeguard the interests of their members when a new system is being planned.

The other dimension is the level of knowledge required. For many purposes it may be sufficient to be aware of the human factors implications of the design work being undertaken in order to locate the relevant standard, set of guidelines or source of professional advice. This kind of knowledge will hopefully enable people to arrive at appropriate decisions without necessarily having a deep understanding of why they are appropriate. For the more limited number of designers who are regularly engaged in activities with a high human factors content, where there are many contingencies that have to be examined to establish an appropriate solution, a deeper understanding of the underlying principles and a working knowledge of the relevant analytic, design and evaluation techniques will be necessary.

There has been a rapid growth in training courses being offered for designers and users by human factors specialists. Many are at the general awareness level. There is a need for a detailed training requirements analysis to reveal the different kinds and depth of knowledge required in order to ensure that, when it does occur, training is targetted effectively.

6.4 *Professional contributions and types of design process*

Once again many of the issues which distinguish the different professional contributions required by the different design types have already been discussed and do not need repeating. Some further points may be noted. Given the relative shortage of human factors specialists it seems best to use them where they are most necessary. Three conditions seem to define this. First, there are circumstances where there is a heavy and difficult human factors content to the work and there is a low level of relevant expertise in the design team. This calls for direct involvement by a human factors specialist. It characterises some forms of innovative design where new interfaces are being created and, at the other extreme, some bespoke applications where major organisational upheavals may be necessary. Secondly, where there is widespread design effort making not very radical changes in human terms, the most appropriate professional contribution may be to fulfil the 'gatekeeper' rôle and, for example, to ensure there is a supply of relevant and accurate guidance documents at the disposal of everybody involved in design. Finally, the progress of human factors depends ultimately on its understanding and acceptance by everybody involved in design, so that perhaps the major contribution of the human factors specialist needs to be in training.

Ultimately the rôle the human factors specialist can play is determined by those designers and users already in control of the design processes. The imperative therefore is to seek rôles that can be effective in making human factor contributions acceptable to those who must make use of them.

7. Conclusions

The rationale for this review is that the 'media' by which the human factors 'message' is conveyed are very important. The analysis of the design processes shows that even the best contribution could be wasted if it is directed at the wrong people, is in the wrong form or serves only to threaten the job and work of existing designers.

The review makes clear that, whilst human factors might be perceived as an 'add-on' to existing design methods, the more seriously it is taken, the more necessary it becomes to question the fundamental design strategies being employed. Unless those seeking to make human factors contributions are able to cope with the problems of making fairly considerable changes in design practice, it is possible that many contributions will be rejected not because they are irrelevant but because they cannot be accommodated within existing practice.

The review has identified many different types of contribution. The conclusion has to be that all the different types are necessary but they need addressing to different types of design process and to different rôles within each design process. They also have to be established in a way that is usable and acceptable within each design environment.

The main dilemma in providing effective contributions appears to be the conflict between providing valid inputs and providing usable ones. To be valid the contribution has, in many instances, to reflect the specific contingencies of task, user, application and technology. To be usable to most designers, however, the contribution needs to be simple to understand and to execute. It will take considerable research to find ways of coping with this dilemma; maybe there are some human factors findings that can form the basis of simple yet valid contributions, maybe there can be procedures which are relatively straightforward to follow which will deal with the specific contingencies, or maybe we can identify those areas which need specialist treatment and we can train people to fill these rôles.

For the design community we hope this review will provide ideas of how to organise an appropriate human factors contribution in a specific design environment.

For the human factors community we hope that it shows that it is not sufficient to undertake research and generate new primary sources of relevant findings, but that it is necessary to put considerable effort into developing appropriate methods of delivering this knowledge where it is needed.

CHAPTER FIVE

HELPING THE I.T. DESIGNER TO USE HUMAN FACTORS

TOM STEWART

1. Introduction

The purpose of this paper is to review some of the practical issues involved in helping the Information Technology (IT) designer to use human factors. Unlike most of the other papers in this volume, this review largely ignores the established literature. The reason is not that there is little literature relevant to this topic, although that is largely the case; the reason is that the paper is an attempt to record some of the practical lessons I have learned in trying to earn a living as a human factors consultant.

One feature of life as a consultant of any kind is that time is very precious and is seldom available for retrospection. The opportunity to sit back and consider exactly what one does and what lessons may be drawn from it is a luxury indeed. Nonetheless, it is a luxury with some practical applications. Some of the lessons here may help others to use human factors in the IT design process.

However, before discussing what the different parties involved in IT design can do about human factors, I would like to consider why the IT designer ought to use human factors, where human factors fits into the design process and why it is not usually a high priority for designers. Finally, the paper ends with some thoughts on why it might always be difficult to use human factors in the IT design process.

2. Why the IT designer ought to use human factors

There are a number of reasons why the IT designer ought to use human factors as part of his or her design activity. Some of these are sufficiently well publicised to have entered the folklore of system design and have made it almost compulsory for designers to claim that they do indeed use human factors input. However, whereas Human Factors can now be regarded as a 'good thing' there is still considerable misunderstanding about what 'it' actually involves and indeed why it might be rather important and not simply be a frill or gloss which can be added just before a product is released to the unsuspecting customers. Let us therefore remind ourselves of the major justifications. These include the following.

2.1 *Poor interfaces cause systems to fail.*
There are some well documented cases where the user interface was such a critical component in an IT system that a weakness in it resulted in complete failure of the total system to achieve its design goals. There are almost certainly many more instances where the final system failure was never actually attributed to poor interface design or implementation but which was instead labelled as human error or poor training, etc. The following examples identify some of the human behaviour which can result from poor interfaces and illustrate how these have caused total systems failure.

(a) Human error
In 1974 the poor user interface to a road traffic signalling system resulted in police being unable to switch on the correct warning signs to alert drivers to a crash which was blocking both carriageways of the British M4 motorway. Due to heavy fog, drivers were unable to obtain sufficient warning of the accident and for some time continued to crash into the wreckage and the stationary emergency vehicles. The problem which faced the operators concerned correctly identifying the lights on both sides of the carriageway. The interface design had assumed that operators would only be interested in one direction of traffic at a time and made specifying equivalent lights on either side of the road difficult. Thus the emergency signalling system failed to signal the emergency and lives were lost as a result.

(b) Slow performance
In a mail order tele-sales system, the user interface was so cumbersome and imposed such an inflexible and unnatural structure on the customer transaction that some operators reverted to writing the customer's order on paper and entering it after they had completed their conversation with the customer. If the customer was kept hanging on after giving the order to allow for the stock availability to be checked then the system failed in its objective to improve the speed with which customers' orders could be received.

If, as happened more frequently, the customer rang off, then the system failed in its objective to provide customers with availability at the time of ordering and hence avoid the disappointment of non-delivery or the cost of accepting back rejected alternative goods.

(c) Low acceptability and industrial relations problems
After just two years of use, the key-to-disc data preparation equipment in a UK factory had to be completely replaced due to the total refusal of the staff, backed by their trade union, to operate the equipment. The normal life of the equipment would have been at least another three years but a succession of VDU ergonomics problems aggravated by an inappropriate management response rendered the system unacceptable to the staff.

Such examples are all too common, but in our experience are not often so badly mismanaged. Nonetheless, where staff have the industrial muscle, either due to trade union support or to the nature of their skills and jobs or the degree to which they have choice over their use of the system, systems fail because their users find them unacceptable.

There are probably more systems aimed at supporting managers which are disused, misused and abused because of inadequacies in their user interface than for any other group of users.

2.2 *Poor interfaces are expensive*
It is not necessary for the entire system to fail for the poor interface to cause significant problems. Even when the weakness in the interface is recognised and eventually remedied it is still an unnecessarily expensive venture. Apart from the costs which may be involved in identifying the poor interface as the source of the problem and the direct costs which may result from the interface problems, there are other costs which may be incurred.

(a) Repair and remedial work are expensive
Although there are different views on just how much more cost is involved, it is widely agreed that it is a much more complex, error prone and therefore expensive job to change systems or products once they have been implemented and are 'off the drawing board'.

(b) Lost credibility is expensive
Nothing is more damaging to the credibility of a product or system than for it to be introduced (often with excessive marketing zeal and hype) only to be withdrawn shortly afterwards for modification. This is particularly damaging when the area for modification is highly visible to the customer. Of course, this is one of the reasons for extensive in-house testing and the use of so-called alpha and beta test sites, but the loss of credibility still remains a problem even if the audience is smaller and better controlled.

(c) Extra hardware and software is expensive
Even just the replacement costs of any revised or modified hardware and software soon add up, especially when they are an unnecessary burden on budgets which are probably already stretched by contingencies and genuinely unforeseeable problems. Early involvement of human factors can prevent the user interface problems reaching major proportions and can avoid them becoming an expensive surprise.

2.3 *Users like and will pay for better interfaces*
Despite the initial scepticism of the computer establishment and the commercial uncertainty of some of the products, there is ample evidence that users like, and are prepared to pay for, better interfaces on products. Indeed, with the increasing convergence of technology and the impact of standards, products from traditionally rather different suppliers are becoming remarkably similar. It is often only in the user interface that there is any real differentiation between competing products. Certainly the interface provides an ideal vehicle for the designer to convey to the user the unique nature of his product and to demonstrate how much his product is superior to the competition.

This trend is encouraged by the growth in the number of discretionary users, i.e., users who can, and do, choose whether to use the system or product or not. The rise of the personal computer (PC) market illustrates this rather well. This market really took off when the price of a PC fell to a level where it was within the budgetary discretion of many managers. Thus they were able to buy PCs from the corner store without having to involve their own computer departments or make extensive financial justifications. Even where the proper approval procedures were followed, the fact that the users were paying directly out of their own budgets gave them a far larger say in the purchasing decision. Now, the price of the PC has fallen to the point where individuals are prepared to buy serious professional-quality PCs out of their own pockets. Here too we see evidence that improved usability is an important consideration for potential purchasers. This willingness to pay for user interface quality applies just as much to hardware (with users buying high quality monitors, etc.) as to software. The proliferation of software packages for PCs (often performing broadly the same functions such as word processing or spreadsheets) has as much to do with providing users with subtle interface choices as it has to do with functionality differences.

There are still many situations where the users themselves are not the purchasers of the IT products but here too there is an increased willingness to pay for improved interfaces to satisfy user demand and expectations, often in the interests of improved acceptability. A good example concerns the use of colour VDUs. We see many organisations invest in colour VDUs where the justification lies not in direct task performance (which may be at best unproven) but in the obviously greater acceptability of colour displays to users. The marginal cost of the hardware is easily outstripped by this improved acceptability. In any case, the relative costs of the hardware, compared to the software development costs and the staff costs, make the extra investment essentially trivial for many organisations.

Of course, there are costs which can be reduced directly if more attention is paid to the human factors aspects. These include training costs, documentation costs and other support costs. All of these may be reduced if the quality of the user interface is high.

2.4 *Availability and content of human factors information*

There is a rather weak argument sometimes used by human factors people that quite a lot is known that can help the designer and it seems a pity not to use it. Of course there is no immediately obvious reason why the interface designer should feel obliged to use the human factors material if he cannot see a use for it, and one would not wish to suggest that he should waste his time or indulge in undue altruism. However, since designers often claim (in mitigation for ignoring human factors evidence) that the material is unusable, there is merit in them trying to use the material and trying to improve it. After all, the more it is used the better it will get and indeed one might ask the question "how do you know it doesn't help if you haven't tried it yet?"

2.5 *IBM does it now*

The last reason which we address in this discussion is the rather stronger and commercially more compelling one that IBM does it now. Shackel recently described the internal 'revolution' which has occurred in IBM in the last few years when functionality was deposed as the ultimate god (Shackel, 1986). At least he states that IBM has made usability an equal god. This is not quite the same as saying the god of functionality is dead.

Certainly, if IBM do something, no matter what, then it is worth considering it very carefully because they clearly (a) seem to know something about computing, (b) seem to know something about marketing, (c) seem to be reasonably profitable, (d) tend to set the scene for everyone else, and (e) are regarded as *de facto* standard setters. Which tends to make me ask "do they know something you don't?"

3. Where Human Factors fits into the existing design process

One of the most important things which anyone who wishes to use human factors in the IT design process has to realise is that there is a pattern to the process. It follows a cyclical form which includes: 1. initiation phase, 2. planning and analysis phase, 3. design phase, 4. implementation phase, 5. operational phase.

At each phase in the design process, there are Human Factors inputs which are relevant to that phase. The report of a recent National Electronics Council Working Party (NEC, 1983) in the UK identified a number of key inputs and presented useful case studies illustrating the different contributions. Of course, there is no consistent universally agreed terminology for the design process, let alone for the human factors inputs. Nonetheless, the main types of contribution are relatively clear, see Figure 1. (For a discussion of some of these inputs see Stewart, 1985.)

- requirements analysis
- allocation of function
- interface development
- workstation design
- testing and user feedback
- quality control

Figure 1: The main Human Factors contributions to the design cycle.

Despite the proliferation of design and project management literature describing the ideal design process, the real life situation tends to be rather different. There are enormous differences between the grand design exercises where massive resources are thrown at a problem for a period of man years and the small scale *ad hoc* design activity which many individual system designers practise. One of the interesting developments in computer technology is the emergence of software tools which allow one person to design rather large and complex systems. These design processes have the advantage that one person sees the whole picture. Many of the discrepancies and anomalies which bedevil large projects quite simply disappear in a design team of one.

However, there is still a need for large design activities and a number of formal design techniques have emerged which aim to reduce the informality, improve the control and effectively eliminate dependency on the unique skill of a talented designer. Put that way it sounds very sensible. Put another way, it amounts to deskilling what is essentially a skilled job. Although the nature of creativity has been much researched and many authors claim to have developed methods and techniques which boost creativity, the element of chance still plays a major part. Unfortunately this is not always recognised, and we sometimes see relatively random decisions becoming perpetuated by myth and misunderstanding as the design continues.

I remember on one occasion tracing back a rather strange design decision on a computer terminal to the originator. When I had asked earlier why it was that way, the rest of the team assured me that it was for very good reasons (on a previous product) but that they could not actually remember just what that reason had been. However, when the originator was questioned, the reason turned out to be that the particular control knob "just happened to be handy" when he built the first breadboard prototype and everyone since then had assumed that it was the right control. It could have been, and one might argue that it had withstood the test of time. However, as I recall, it was unlikely to be the correct design. Certainly its choice had not reflected much in the way of analysis of user requirements, marketing requirements or anything else.

In such an environment, failure to use human factors properly is not a carefully slanted insult at human factors people, it is often simply a reflection that designers are busy and tend to try to get on with the job. When the human factors input appears to make life more difficult without any obvious advantage to the designer, then forgetting to use it is not unreasonable.

Another reason why human factors people may not be allowed to make an input is that they often function as advisers or consultants to the design process rather than being members of the design team. This certainly has its place and, for some issues, may be the most cost effective way of tackling the problem, but for others it perpetually relegates the human factors person to the role of outsider. Since much design is accidental and *ad hoc*, and design decisions often have to be made extremely quickly, the human factors person can easily get left behind and simply not be there when major decisions are taken. It may then be too late to change them and even quite difficult for the human factors person to discover exactly what has been agreed or changed. This can lead to a vicious circle of a changing design being mistracked by the human factors person who is unable to catch up.

When there are politically contentious design decisions and when the human factors person is opposed by some members of the design team, then it is all too easy for them to wait until the HF person is absent and then raise the damaging objections.

4. Why many designers do not use Human Factors at present

As we have already discussed, one reason why designers do not use human factors to help them make better design decisions is that they may not make the decisions actively or rationally. Many decisions are made by default.

However, there are a number of other reasons which are more rational and are therefore subject to argument, debate and persuasion.

4.1 *Error fix*

As far as the designer is concerned it seems cheaper to fix errors afterwards rather than go to all the trouble of getting it right first time. After all, much human factors is about predicting the future performance or reaction, and human factors people are often pessimistic. Even if they were not pessimistic, they are not infallible. There may appear to be some merit in waiting in case the human factors changes are unnecessary after all. Unfortunately, it can be very expensive trying to fix it later. Estimates vary of the exact ratio of post-implementation cost to pre-implementation cost, but ratios of 10:1 do not seem to be uncommon. All manner of other changes may be generated by the fix and the scope of remedial action will be greatly constrained by the design decisions which have by then been finalised. In addition there may be costs associated with lost credibility etc which add to the fix costs. So designers who take this approach are playing with fire.

4.2 *Specifiers lack understanding*

Until relatively recently, the purchasers of a computer system were extremely unlikely to be the ones who used it. For many IT systems and products this is still the case, and third parties buy, or at least specify, in an intermediary role between the designer and the end user. This means that human factors issues of importance to the end user may not be regarded as vital by the specifier and hence will not be regarded as vital by the designer. The advent of the personal computer has changed this to a considerable degree and many purchasers are now also users. This has led to increased opportunities for human factors, and it is no coincidence that the general standard of human factors in the design of hardware and software is much higher in PC products than it is for general computer terminals and equipment. However, there are still many cases where the specifiers do not have an appreciation of human factors and do not specify their requirements in such a way that designers take them seriously.

4.3 *Too much 'technopush' and too little business analysis*

It is interesting to note that all of our consulting clients are large organisations with substantial computer departments. They are not short of technical resources and although they may not have the specific skills in human factors that we offer, in many cases our role is to act as intermediaries between those who understand the technology and those who understand the business. The business people find themselves under pressure from suppliers and from their own technical people to exploit the apparent benefits of the technology. This is all very well, but the end result tends to be to find ways of using the technology for its own sake rather than ways of benefiting from the technology in a way that makes sense to the business. For example, we often see people who boast of rapid electronic communications between a selected group of managers or who produce near typeset quality documents regardless of purpose or content and feel pleased with the results. Yet often these benefits are superficial and may actually mask business damage being caused by systems. It may be anecdotal, but I have heard of a manager who made an important but flawed decision on the basis of a well-produced market report with convincing diagrams, graphs and charts. He later discovered that most of the figures were rough guesses which would have been more at home scrawled on the back of an envelope. In such an environment, the practical realities of making systems usable by ordinary staff are seldom heard. The wonderful 'gee whiz' world of high tech wins the day and the usability of the products is assumed because the mice and icons look pretty.

4.4 *Too difficult*

Some designers have been convinced that there is merit in human factors and can see how it might fit into their activities, but they get put off by the difficulty of applying it. They perceive, quite realistically in most cases, that it (a) needs extra skills especially in ergonomics, psychology, user interface design, etc.; (b) needs extra information — the user does not come with a specification manual and traditional designer training barely covers the area, although post-Alvey and post-Esprit this is beginning to change, albeit slowly; (c) adds to an already complex enough situation — human factors is by no means the only worthwhile thing the designer could take more seriously. Every day he is bombarded with leaflets for technical courses and conferences, demonstrations of new products and enhancements, modifications, exhortations to take other things more seriously, such as man management, time management, quality control, documentation, and project management. In an ideal world he would no doubt do them all, but life is short.

4.5 *Too much trouble*

Of course, many things that designers have to do are difficult, and that is not in itself a good reason for not using human factors. What underlies such reasons or excuses may be that the benefits are not obvious or may not be apparent until much later in the process so they are of little value to the designer.

Sometimes it is literally 'too much trouble'. The designer anticipates that involving human factors will make matters worse by raising expectations unacceptably high or by making an already complex design process even more complex. Especially where there is risk involved, the designer believes he has enough to worry about already. The most seductive of all these traps is "let's just get it running first and we'll clean it up later." In practice, it is far from minor cleaning up which may be required. Once early decisions have been made, it can be very difficult to un-make them and put them right.

4.6 *Too late*

One of the most common explanations for failing to involve human factors is that it is already too late to take it into account. It may be that the decision has already been made or simply that further delay would be totally unacceptable. It may appear better to proceed knowing that the system will be imperfect than to delay it further. This assumes that the changes are unlikely to be sufficiently significant to prevent the project from being a success and that the human factors is essentially a luxury which can be foregone. Of course, sometimes it really is too late by the time the issue is identified. In these cases it is important to document the problem properly so that the next time the same problem does not occur. It is also worth questioning just how late is too late. It can be that once the true significance of the issue is identified then justification can be made for a delay to the project. This means that the justification has to be more solid than if time were not of the essence. Certainly "too late" should not always be taken at face value.

4.7 *Competing priorities*

Designers and design teams usually have to compromise between competing requirements and priorities. For example, if it comes to making a choice between functionality and usability, it is hard to justify putting usability first (but see comments about IBM in Section 2.5 above). If the system does not work it does not matter how easy it would be to use. However, if the system provides at least some functionality then usability becomes important. Indeed, I believe it is inevitable that some functionality must be sacrificed in order to provide usability; just how much, depends on the user, the tasks, the users' experience with the system, and so on.

Other competing priorities include tight timescales and financial controls, and real (or imaginary) technical problems will naturally always take priority over human factors aspects in the work of the technical specialist. Finally, another type of competing priority is where the next job is coming from. Technical specialists do not gain technical credibility from helping users. I have witnessed a number of technicians who have lost out in terms of promotion because they have moved out of mainstream computing into user support, but who do not have the relevant qualifications for a career in the user area.

4.8 *Designers lack training*

One of the complaints which human factors people make about IT designers is that they lack the appropriate training to use or even to appreciate human factors. There may be some truth in this, although the question of territorial disputes between the different parties involved in design cannot be ruled out. Most participants feel that their own discipline is central and that others probably do not fully appreciate their contribution

4.9 *HF is often unusable*

By far the most justified of the reasons given by designers for failing to incorporate human factors in their design work is that human factors is often unusable in a practical design environment. Typically, designers complain that when they turn to the literature it is (a) incomprehensible, (b) pseudo-scientific and full of jargon, (c) written for other HF people, not potential users of the information, (d) difficult to apply to their own problems, and (e) difficult to find in the first place.

Such criticism may not always be justified. After all, many computer people have a love of jargon and obscurantism. But nonetheless, human factors people are guilty of treating designers in the way that designers treat users. In other words they do not take their specific requirements and task needs into account.

5. What the Human Factors specialist can do about it

In this environment, the onus is on the HF professionals to try to increase the use of human factors in the design process. There are a number of actions they can take to make matters better.

5.1 *Apply usability criteria to HF users*

The human factors professionals can try to understand the designer's tasks in the same way they expect the designers to try to appreciate the users' tasks. They should also try to understand the characteristics of the designers, and their preferences and individual differences in how they work. This then would provide them with the basis for matching the human factors input to the designer and his task.

5.2 *Try to understand the organisational constraints*

All too often, human factors specialists talk about 'what designers ought to do' without appreciating the organisational constraints within which they operate. One of the most damaging constraints to human factors is that of budget. It is therefore essential to cost-justify HF input in some way which makes sense to the designer and to the organisation. This should involve (a) assessing costs, (b) assessing benefits, financial and non-financial, (c) assessing costs of not doing it, (d) being realistic, and (e) trying to get the human factors input into the normal decision making process.

5.3 *Apply computer technology to the design process and develop appropriate tools*
Another approach involves applying computer technology to the problems of making human factors input usable to designers. Such tools have the advantage that they are in a medium with which the designer is already familiar and therefore start with some positive transfer and face validity.

A number of such tools and techniques are under development although few can be regarded as fully working tools. One of the most influential was Moran's Command Language Grammar (Moran, 1981) which was a representational framework of the conceptual user interface. A key feature of this is the notion of levels of interface (task, semantic, syntactic and finally interaction) and the representation of users tasks in terms of Goals and sub goals, the Operators for acting on the interface, the Methods used to achieve sub goals and Selection rules for choosing between two or more alternative methods (the GOMS model).

Another area of tool development concerns dialogue specification techniques which allow the user interface to be explicitly defined in interactive computer systems and handled by a User Interface Management System (UIMS). There are several promising specification and design tools based on transition networks including CONNECT (Alty, 1984), SYNICS (Edmonds, 1981) and RAPID/USE (Wasserman and Shewmake, 1984). These are primarily research vehicles at the moment. In the future, it is likely that fully developed practical tools will allow the designer to build a formally described specification which is executable at least as a prototype.

5.4 *Be prepared to spend some time transferring skills and awareness*
The human factors specialist must also appreciate the importance of spending time to transfer skills and awareness to the IT design community. This responsibility falls on us all, although not everyone will wish to take part in the full range of possibilities. These include (a) training courses, (b) seminars, (c) briefings, and (d) newsletters.

5.5 *Be more businesslike*
One of the barriers to effective communication between human factors specialists and designers is that there is a tendency for the HF specialist to believe that 'right' is on his side. This moral dimension, whilst commendable from some points of view, can lead to the human factors specialist 'preaching' his message and not communicating

effectively with the designers. In my view, the human factors specialist must become more business like and less like a social worker. In particular, he should:

(a) Understand commercial pressures and not make unrealistic demands on the designer, simply because it would improve the ergonomics of the product regardless of cost.

(b) Maintain professional standards in his contact with designers and users at all times, particularly in (i) presentations, (ii) reports, (iii) interviews, (iv) cost justifications, and (v) data analysis.

(c) Build trust and respect – one of the criticisms which is often levelled at human factors professionals is that they appear to devalue the contribution that other professionals can make. They are seen as unduly critical of the work of others and by constantly exhorting designers to take more account of human factors, show little respect for the skills which the designer already possesses. This is completely contrary to gaining trust and mutual respect which is essential, if they are to work together as a team.

(d) Avoid wasting time and take design seriously.

5.6 *In summary*

In other words, treat the designer as you would like him to treat the user.

6. What the IT designer can do about it

There are a number of things that the designer can do in order to make greater use of human factors or in order to avoid disuse becoming a significant problem. Thus the designer can adopt one or more of the following possibilities.

6.1 *Hope the problem, and those advocating HF, will go away*

This may be an attractive option to some designers but is hardly viable in the long term. The pressures for better human factors do not come just from human factors professionals; they come from the market place and are ignored at the designer's peril.

6.2 *Simply copy a good interface*

Copying a good interface is a more positive option and is also popular. There is ample evidence in the market of this approach and clearly there are circumstances in which it will work. After all, a clear example to follow is a powerful teaching device and a number of the significant interface innovations in recent years have been widely promulgated in this way with good effect. However, it is not always a good approach. There are a number of pitfalls for the unwary designer. For example, the interface:

(a) may not actually be good
Just because the interface has received widespread publicity or appears attractive to the casual observer, there is no guarantee that it will be the right interface for the user. Indeed, it is easy to misunderstand what it is that makes a good interface. By merely copying it the designer may miss the point. For example, many of the copies of the Xerox/Macintosh interface have focussed on the ability to illustrate objects with pretty icons. I believe that what made such interfaces attractive and usable had little to do with the graphics. It has more to do with the ability to alter contexts without the usual computer problems of having to terminate one activity before you can consider another. Many of the designers of these clones have missed that point and simply provide menus using icons which deliver little of the real benefit.

(b) won't give you a sales edge
In this harsh commercial world, simply copying a competitor will not give you a sales edge but will relegate you to a subordinate position. Increasingly IT products are becoming very similar in functionality through common components, standards etc. The user interface offers the most visible and perhaps the most attractive means of differentiating amongst products.

(c) may get you sued
In the worst case, copying an interface solution may result in litigation. There are already some court cases in session over the copyright of icons.

6.3 *Stick to designing systems for himself or his friends*
Some of the most successful systems have been the result of the designer creating a tool for himself or for his friends. This is not accidental. In such situations the designer has a deep understanding of the users of the system and of what they are trying to do with it. He also has good feedback from them so that he can revise and evolve the design over time to ensure that the match is optimum. However, it may not be an ideal solution in the long term. After all, (a) there may not be many of them, so the designer's target audience becomes rather limited, (b) he may not understand them as well as he thinks and this will only become clear once he creates systems for them, (c) they may prefer better systems and have different expectations, and (d) of course it gets pretty boring for the designer.

6.4 *Actively involve users in the design process*
There is much publicity about the virtues of involving users in the design process directly. This involvement may be as individuals seconded to design teams, as user led design teams or by using the user population as a reference group to test prototypes, evaluate designs, etc. Unfortunately, even though it is fashionable to talk about involving users and no self respecting design activity claims to do otherwise, taking such involvement seriously is another matter (see Chapters 12 and 13). In many cases the users are merely involved in a legal sign-off relationship. Once the specification is agreed it becomes fixed and the designer goes off to build whatever the users signed off regardless of whether that is the best way of dealing with the problem or not.

6.5 *Employ consultants in HF*
As a practising human factors consultant, I clearly have a vested interest in recommending that designers ought to employ human factors consultants; certainly this can be a cost-effective means of gaining human factors input. Nonetheless, I would stress that it is easy to misuse consultants, and employing the wrong consultants or giving them the wrong tasks can be expensive and counter-productive.

Consultants are particularly appropriate where there are some specialised skills required and these do not already exist within the organisation. This is usually the case with small organisations but even quite large ones may only require a particular specialisation occasionally; it may be better to bring in an outsider for a short time than to make a long term commitment to employing someone with the skills which may be seldom used and which may date rapidly.

It is important then to know what skills the consultant offers and how these can be used within your own organisation. Consultants may also be used to supplement existing human factors resources to meet intermittent demand which does not justify extending the human factors team permanently. This can be sensible use of external resources, but if such use develops into long term dependency on external resources then the organisation is not getting the maximum benefit from using the consultant. If the internal human factors activity or person is not involved then the skills and experiences of the consultant and the knowledge gained during their work will be lost to the organisation when the assignment comes to an end.

One of the strangest uses of an external consultant is to act as an authoritative platform for a message which may be already known to the organisation. Frequently the outsider is acting as a communication channel between parts of the organisation which ought to be capable of communicating but which clearly are not. Many times individuals have said to me "I am pleased you told them that, I've been saying it for ages but they never listened to me."

However, there are times when it is not the right answer to turn to outsiders. The requirements for continued presence and for extensive experience within the organisation mean that only an insider will do. Hence the need to employ in house ergonomists or human factors people.

6.6 *Employ ergonomists within the organisation*

Apart from their value in providing a focus for the use of external consultants, in house staff can provide day to day support in human factors. However, this is not without its own problems. The sheer volume of enquiries and demands may rapidly become too much for one person and so a small team may be required. This inevitably leads to problems of apparent empire building and resistance from other professional areas, especially those which see human factors as a threat or as competition.

There is also a conflict between employing relatively junior human factors specialists who will be cheap to employ and who will not threaten the career structures too much and getting the right level of authority, knowledge and experience. If the human factors staff are there to act as facilitators then they must be reasonably experienced and able to command authority and respect in the organisation. This neither comes cheaply nor does it fit easily within existing career structures.

The individual human factors specialist or the very small group dispersed throughout the organisation makes considerable sense in most cases. The economic and social climate are probably no longer correct for large decentralised human factors facilities to be set up. However, the lone human factors people may tend to wither and die if they are not nurtured. One form of nurturing is to create an informal support organisation which allows those with an interest in human factors to meet regularly and learn from each other. Often such groups have a formal or semiformal status within the organisation but by far their greatest strength comes from the informal network of communication and mutual support which develops. A popular name for such a group is a human factors forum. This can provide the right kind of support and organisational clout which a human factors department could never achieve or at least not achieve without some bloodshed.

6.7 *Acquire some knowledge and expertise himself*

The designer is always being exhorted by the human factors professional to learn more about human factors and to gain sufficient skills to know when to call in additional support if he cannot solve the problem himself. This at least would ensure that many of the major 'sillies' are avoided and certainly this in itself would greatly improve the situation experienced by users in many organisations.

There are many sources from which the relevant knowledge and skills can be drawn:

(a) Formal training
A growing number of short courses are available, in the range of a few days to a week or two. There are also a few part-time postgraduate courses which can lead to a professional qualification. However, there are no 'apprenticeship' or 'journeyman' schemes currently operating in human factors; this is a gap which needs to be filled.

(b) Going to conferences
It can be difficult to decide which ones to attend. Many conferences are aimed more at other human factors professionals than they are at users of human factors information. Certainly the average scientific conference in human factors will be of little value to the practising designer and will contain much irrelevant and perhaps contradictory material. This is not unique to human factors, it is just that the leading edge of human factors is not as well protected from the public as the leading edge of other more established sciences or disciplines.

(c) Reading books and journals
These can be a useful source of reference material but there is a considerable and growing volume of such material and it is often difficult to generalise from it. Much of the literature is also aimed at fellow professionals and scientists and is not easy to use in a practical setting.

(d) Buy and develop design tools
One particularly promising development is the creation of design tools which support the designer and bring human factors knowledge to him at the right point in the design process and in the right form for him to use it effectively.

Unfortunately, there are relatively few of these design tools available at the moment and those that do exist are still far from being the total solution. The danger is that by its very nature the design tool represents a simplified view of the problem and encourages simplified solutions. This can lead to the designer making totally unwarranted assumptions about the problem and not even being aware that he is making such assumptions. A small example of this is the use of statistical packages on personal computers which make it very easy for the user to apply all kinds of analyses and tests without understanding the assumptions about the data which are built into these tests. To a large extent, it was always possible for statistics users to misapply statistics, but at least the more complex and cumbersome procedures took considerable determination and some mathematical knowledge to perform. This tended to screen them from all but the most dedicated statisticians. Nowadays, anyone can perform multiple regressions, factor analyses and so on often on totally unsuitable data without being aware that the validity of what they are doing is at best suspect and at worst non-existent.

7. What users can do about it

Users have a number of options open to them if they wish to deal with the problem that IT design takes too little account of human factors. Some of these options are more appropriate if we are considering bespoke system design within a user organisation, some are more appropriate to the product design environment and some apply equally well to both. The users can:

(a) Put up with it
This is rather unsatisfactory solution although there is considerable evidence that many users do just this. The problem is that the penalties or costs associated with such a solution are seldom attributed to the poor design. All too often the blame for inadequate system performance or excessive error rates is directed at the users themselves and their 'lack of training' or some such excuse.

(b) Demand better systems
More and more users are demanding better systems and are in a sense 'voting with their feet' for systems which meet their requirements better. One method of achieving this is for the users to be responsible for purchasing their own systems. The personal computer market is one area where the users are often the same as the purchasers and there is ample evidence that they are making their demands for better products heard through their purchasing decisions. In bespoke systems development within user organisations, it can be more difficult for the users to make themselves heard. One technique which we find beneficial (in making the users' requirements drive the development process) is the use of business analysis techniques. These help to ensure that the design of the system reflects the business requirements and not just the technical computer design issues.

The implication of users demanding better systems is that they must be prepared to pay for them when making purchase and justification decisions. This is made more likely if the financial case for the system or product reflects the lifetime costs of the system and not just the once only purchase costs.

A more realistic view of the financial and non financial costs and benefits helps to ensure that rational decisions are made.

In bespoke systems development within user organisations, the user management play a vital part in achieving successful systems by concentrating on the design process itself. By managing the development project effectively and setting appropriate usability goals as part of the specification process they can achieve considerable results. However, if they do not make usability part of the buying decision then it will never be taken seriously by the designers.

8. What regulatory and standards bodies can do about it

One of the most influential impacts on the hardware interface was the German DIN standard for Visual Display Terminals (DIN 66234, 1981) which despite its faults has nonetheless been taken very seriously by suppliers who wished to enter or remain in the German market. Part 8 has recently been published for discussion and this deals with principles of dialogue design. This part has generated substantial controversy and may be significantly modified before it is finalised. Nonetheless, it is not the only standardisation effort currently under way and it may well stimulate those who criticise it to take part in the other standardisation activities.

As part of the UK's contribution to the international work, a six-part Draft British Standard was published in September 1987. The first four parts mirrored the ISO parts although differences in the administrative procedures of ISO and BSI meant that there were detailed differences between the two sets of documents. Parts 5 and 6 of the BS draft covered Workplace Design and The Working Environment for Office VDT work, which will be addressed by ISO in the future (British Standards Institution, 1987). During the comment period, the Ergonomics Training Centre organised a public conference in association with BSI and much valuable comment was generated. The full British Standard is due to be published in the Autumn of 1988 and will be substantially the same as the Drafts although greatly improved by the exposure to people outside the standards community.

The American National Standards Institute recently set up an HCI Standards committee and this has concentrated initially on identifying three areas where HCI standards might be developed. These are:

HCI Design Methodologies — user needs analysis; functional requirements; formal design specifications; iterative design.

HCI Interaction Principles — input devices and techniques; display techniques; output devices; dialog techniques; user guidance.

Evaluation and Testing

This work is only just beginning but by concentrating initially on getting the framework right , the group is setting the scene for making rapid progress in the straightforward areas and leaving the more complex ones till later.

One of the most important standardisation activities is that of the International Standards Organisation (ISO). In its main procedure manual *The Directives for the technical work of ISO*, ISO identifies four distinct sets of aims for standards any or all of which may be embraced by an ISO standard. These specific aims include:

- mutual understanding
- health, safety and the protection of the environment
- interface and interchangeability
- fitness for purpose.

Despite the improvements which have taken place in hardware and software design, it is clear that there is still much to be achieved in user interface standards in terms of mutual understanding, interchangeability and fitness for purpose.

8.1 *Problems with and improvements to current standards*

Apart from the problem that there are relatively few formal standards for VDTs, the main criticism to date is that those which do exist tend to be based on product design features such as height of characters on the screen. Such standards are very specific to cathode ray tube (CRT) technology and do not readily apply to other display technologies. they may therefore inhibit innovation and force designers to stick to old solutions. More importantly, the standards specify values for a range of different parameters quite independently and take little account of the large interactions which take place in real use, for example between display characteristics and the environment. The standards can also be criticised for being more precise than is reasonable in areas where research is still continuing.

To overcome some of the problems of current standards, the approach of Sub-committee 4 (SC4) of the Ergonomics Technical Committee (TC159) of the International Organisation for Standardisation (ISO) has been to place the emphasis on user performance standards. Thus, rather than specify a product feature such as character height which we believe will result in a legible display, we are developing procedures for testing directly such characteristics as legibility. The standard is then stated in terms of the user performance required from the equipment and not in terms of how that is achieved. The performance measure is a composite including speed and accuracy and the avoidance of discomfort.

Such user performance standards have a number of advantages; they are relevant to the real problems experienced by users, tolerant of developments in the technology, and flexible enough to cope with interactions between factors. However, they also suffer a number of disadvantages. They cannot be totally complete and scientifically valid in all cases. They represent reasonable compromises and obtaining the agreement of all the parties in standards setting take time.

The main focus of the work initially is on office tasks. This represents the area which is likely to affect most people in the short term. By mid 1988, we will have registered four parts of the proposed standard as draft international standards (DIS). These parts include: Part 1 – Introduction to the Standard; Part 2 – Task Requirements; Part 3 – Visual Requirement; Part 4 – Keyboard Requirements. Parts 1 and 2 contain much guidance material and general recommendations. Parts 3 and 4 in addition contain draft test methods for assessing legibility, discomfort and keyboard usability. These test methods will require considerable empirical testing and refinement before they reach the status of an international standard but they represent an important step in the right direction. The work of the sub-committee is truly international with the active participation of the following countries: Austria, Belgium, China, France, Germany, Italy, Netherlands, Norway, Poland, Sweden, United Kingdom, United States of America.

8.2 *Towards human computer interaction standards*

The initial focus of the work was purely on the hardware ergonomic issues as this was where the most obvious problems lay. Now that these are being tackled, attention is turning towards the software issues and the more general user interface considerations.

However, whereas most people agree that hardware standards are "a good idea", the same does not hold true for the human computer interaction standards. Indeed, there are often a number of objections raised.

(a) 'Not enough is known about good HCI to make a standard'

It is perfectly true that we do not know enough about what makes an interface good. But we do know a surprising amount which could aid the design process and improve interfaces. This objection usually stems from a misunderstanding about the nature and purpose of standards. It is entirely appropriate for standards to be guidelines and recommendations of good practice. Indeed, it is inevitable that human computer interaction standards will be just that. By the time we are sufficiently certain to be able to prescribe exactly, the technology will have moved on to leave us behind. One role of these standards will be to focus attention on good practice and principles, not to prescribe precise solutions.

(b) 'It is too early for standards'

Clearly there can be dangers in standards which are the results of rather hasty conclusions. When the technology is very fast moving it is all too easy for the relatively slow, conservative, standardisation process to be left behind. However, this is less likely to apply to the kind of user performance standards discussed above. In addition, one of the most important roles of standards for human computer interaction is to improve the consistency between different systems so allowing users to transfer skill between systems.

For example, not only is it likely that a key such as "delete" will be in different places on the keyboard but the function it performs can also differ from system to system. In some cases such differences may serve a valid purpose and should be retained. But in other situations the inconsistencies are inadvertent and could have been avoided had there been clear recommendations in a recognised standard.

(c) 'But a standard user interface would be very boring and unattractive'
No one is suggesting standard user interfaces. A good analogy is the telephone handset. There are certain characteristics it must possess if it is to connect to the telephone network. There are other aspects of design which can vary but which must conform to certain human characteristics if it is to work effectively with real people (e.g. microphone sensitivity, key button size, etc.). Within those constraints there are wide variations in functionality, aesthetics and concept which still allow product designers considerable scope for creativity.

(d) 'You will never manage to get agreement, look how long it is taking to get hardware standards'
On this point the critics could be right. But I remain an optimist that the common sense and self preservation will prevail. After all, the consumer electronics industry seems to have recognised that everyone benefits from common standards across manufacturers (whether they be formal or *de facto*) and that user confidence in technology actually increases sales and boosts the market.

Certainly, standards themselves are a relatively "blunt instrument" in the fight for better user interfaces but I believe they can make a worthwhile and useful contribution.

9. Why it is still difficult to apply Human Factors to IT design

One reason why, despite all the above, it is still difficult to apply HCI research to the IT design process is that we are too near the frontier of knowledge in HCI. There is no adequate filter which protects the potential user of HCI research from the uncertainties and extreme viewpoints and dubious claims which mark the leading edge of any field of endeavour.

In physics or chemistry or mathematics, there are layers of complex terminology which protect the user of these disciplines from the latest research and the wild men. Not so in HCI where the latest theory (and it may be doing it a compliment to call it a theory) may receive widespread publicity and hence achieve a degree of authority based on numerical support. Moreover, user interface issues are becoming increasingly important and are therefore likely to be favourite targets for any expansionist discipline or group. There are too many vested interests for them to be taken solely at face value and dealt with dispassionately. However, controversy and conflicting views can only confuse designers who cannot afford to become involved with research problems but simply want some clear advice on what to do.

Further, it is very difficult to pitch the degree of generality of the information and guidance at the right level. The information is often too general and potential users claim it is difficult to relate to their own problem or else it is too specific and users cannot find an example which is exactly like their own.

Then there are the problems of overuse and a naïve view of user and task. People like simple answers even if the question was rather difficult and complex. There is a tendency for good ideas in HCI to go through the phases of disbelief from the technology experts, gradual and reluctant acceptance, amazed acceptance and enthusiasm as users demonstrate strong views about the ideas, and finally over use where the basically good idea gets taken to ridiculous extremes. Such irrationality makes it difficult to implement the best scientific data available and achieve a logical optimised solution to meet the needs of the users.

10. Conclusion

The 'blame' if such is to be apportioned for the lack of human factors in the IT design process does not fall on a single set of shoulders. All parties can share the responsibility. However, all good management books emphasise that one person's problem is another's opportunity. The opportunity in this case is to get human factors into its rightful place in the design process. Human factors is not the centre of the design process but lies fairly close to it. To achieve this integration involves cooperation and commitment between the various parties involved. The end result of such integration is successful products which meet the needs of their users and bring glory and perhaps wealth to their creators. That does not seem a bad objective and one which is well worth working for.

[illegible]

[illegible]

[illegible]

10 Conclusion

[illegible]

CHAPTER SIX

INTERFACE DESIGN ISSUES FOR THE SYSTEM DESIGNER

WILLIAM NEWMAN

1. Introduction

The design of interactive computer-based systems forms the focus of much of the material in this book. One way to approach the subject is via the contributions that specialised disciplines such as Human Factors or Applied Psychology can make to the design process. A specialisation-centred approach has a number of advantages; in the particular case of designing for usability, such an approach helps to ensure that the designer has the fullest possible model of the human user as a basis for design.

An alternative approach is to view the subject from the system designer's standpoint. This approach typically looks first for structure in the system design process, and then for opportunities to introduce specialised knowledge (e.g., on human factors) to the process (cf. Chapters 4, 13, 7 and 5 by Eason and Harker, Damodaran, Gardner and Stewart). The process-centred approach is generally less thorough in dealing with user issues, which tend to be ignored if the process structure has no place for them. However it has the advantage that it results in methods that are more likely to be acceptable to system designers, because they bear a resemblance to the methods with which designers are familiar.

This paper takes a process-centred approach to the design of interactive systems, making some observations about the nature of the process and the opportunities to strengthen design methods. It is based on experience gained and documented by designers, experience that can shed light on the nature of the process that system designers follow. It is claimed here that this "actual" process differs in a number of respects from the "ideal" process advocated by a number of writers (Newman and Sproull, 1979; Foley and van Dam, 1982; Kloster and Tischer, 1985); it is also claimed that the "actual" process offers a number of opportunities to improve user interface design through proper attention to user issues.

2. User interface design: fundamental properties

Two fundamental properties of user interface design are (a) its overlap with the design of interactive systems, and (b) the shortage of models and representations to support the design process. This section is concerned with establishing these properties, on which the remainder of the paper draws.

2.1 *Overlap with interactive system design*

The user interface is that part of an interactive system directly concerned with end-user interaction. It supports the two-way flow of information between system and user, through its provision of:

(a) a *command language* in which the user can express actions to be performed on the stored information;
(b) *information display*, showing the state of the stored information.

Thus the user interface is not an interface *between* user and system: it is part of the interactive system itself. The software of the user interface is an integral part of the overall system, and relies on many of the same hardware components as does the non-interactive component: processor, memory, input-output bus, etc. The best illustrations of this relationship between the user interface and the interactive system are found in office applications such as word processing, graphics editors and spreadsheet programs where, if the user interface is taken away, very little of the system remains.

The literature on user interface design supports this view. Sufrin (1986), for example, states, "Designing an effective user interface to a complex system is difficult, since it cannot be done in isolation from the design of the information system itself." Authorities on user interface design, such as Foley and Shneiderman (1982) and Shneiderman (1987), advocate treating it in the context of system design. Individual papers on interface design reinforce this view (Smith *et al.*, 1982; Woodmansee, 1985). We do find evidence of other viewpoints, in particular the view that it should be feasible to design the interface independently of the supporting software (Pfaff, 1985); however, the fundamental issue here is modularity of software tools, rather than separation of design processes. Separation has been achieved in Fourth Generation Languages and similar "user programmed" systems, and is in general feasible where there is a high degree of interface standardisation.

2.2 *Models and representations*

All design activities rely on models and representations. Models provide the designer with abstract descriptions of the behaviour of the various systems involved in the design. With the aid of these models, the designer can make predictions about the performance of the implemented design and the changes that it will bring about. Representations offer the designer a means of specifying the design; they provide a framework within which to refine the design from a partial, abstract definition to a complete, precise specification. Models and representations complement each other in their support for the abstract and concrete levels of design work.

User interface design is not well supplied with models or representations. The lack of models arises because of the involvement with human users and the extreme difficulty of modelling human cognitive processes. Representations are in short supply, partly because they depend on models which are not available either, and partly because system designers have not devoted the effort necessary to develop them.

The lack of design models has been pointed out by many workers in applied psychology, notably Newell and Card (1985) in a recent paper. As regards representations, researchers such as Cook (1986) have pointed out that formal representations are still insufficient to meet designers' needs. Both design models and formal representations are active fields of research, but even the most optimistic would admit that years of effort will be needed to bring these into line with software engineers' methods.

3. Observations on the system design process

The process followed by most interactive system designers includes several standard sub-processes. In *requirements analysis* sets of constraints on the design are specified as a means of subsequently testing whether a satisfactory design solution has been achieved. In *conceptual-level design*, sometimes called functional design, the aim is to define the overall structure of the design solution as perceived by the end-user. In *detailed design* the command language and information display methods are fully specified. Finally, *prototyping and testing* determine properties of the design solution that cannot be derived on paper (e.g., user acceptability). When a satisfactory design has been produced and specified, implementation can be undertaken.

A number of observations can be made about the design process as described. This paper does not attempt a complete analysis, but concentrates on the following four observations which have major implications for interface designers:

1. User interface designs are never defined fully before implementation.
2. Experts recommend, "specify requirements first, design the user interface afterwards," but do the opposite.

3. User interfaces are mostly designed, not for a broad user population, but for a single user chosen to be archetypal.
4. Systems based heavily on Artificial Intelligence (AI) techniques cannot be represented except as prototypes.

The rest of this chapter is devoted to elaborating and justifying each of these four claims, and commenting on their implications.

3.1 *User interface designs are never fully specified*

User interfaces are never defined fully prior to implementation; on the rare occasions when thorough specifications are developed, this happens *after* implementation is complete, using the implemented system as the primary definition.

To find a basis for this claim, we need look only at the problems of specifying user interface performance. Consider the following cases:

- The user of a spreadsheet changes the contents of three adjacent cells by selecting the first, typing its new contents, stepping to the second, typing its contents, stepping to the third cell, etc. (Figure 1). How rapidly can this task be performed? If the system is in an "auto-recalculate" mode, what delay will ensue between stepping to the next cell and receiving a prompt or acknowledgement to continue?
- The user selects part of the text of a displayed document and changes the font size to 7.4 points (Figure 2). How will the characters be displayed? Will they be legible? Will the user be able to distinguish between similar characters, e.g., "l" (lower case 'L') and the numeral "1"?
- The user prepares a long document source file, containing references to other documents, and passes this as input to a document compiler to be formatted and printed. The compiler reaches part-way through the file and then stops, indicating that it has run out of storage space. How could the user have been warned of this beforehand? What should the user do to ensure that the document can be compiled successfully?

Answers to these questions are of prime importance to the user, but are extremely difficult for the designer to specify. The user in the first case needs to know how long recalculation will take, since it is better to switch off "auto-recalculate" if a lengthy pause will be introduced after each cell is changed. In the second case, if the user cannot read 7.4 point characters (as may happen with automatically generated screen characters) the text must be enlarged temporarily to support editing. In the third case, resource exhaustion during document compilation leaves the user unable to plan a strategy for success: should references to other documents be removed, or the

	Jan	Feb	Mar	Apr
	5.16	6.40	3.20	7.71
	8.74	8.19	7.52	12.03
	13.33	12.40	14.25	12.03
	20.28	20.38	20.99	12.03

	Jan	Feb	Mar	Apr
	5.39	6.40	3.20	7.71
	8.74	8.19	7.52	12.03
	13.33	12.40	14.25	12.03
	20.28	20.38	20.99	12.03

	Jan	Feb	Mar	Apr
	5.39	6.40	3.20	7.71
	8.97	8.19	7.52	12.03
	13.56	12.40	14.25	12.03
	20.51	20.38	20.99	12.03

	Jan	Feb	Mar	Apr
	5.39	5.18	3.20	7.71
	8.29	6.97	7.52	12.03
	12.20	11.18	14.25	12.03
	18.46	19.16	20.99	12.03

	Jan	Feb	Mar	Apr
	5.39	5.18	4.98	7.71
	8.29	7.97	9.30	12.03
	12.75	13.18	16.03	12.03
	20.13	22.15	22.77	12.03

Figure 1: Changing the contents of a succession of spreadsheet cells.

referenced documents shortened, or the main document split into two or more compilations? As we can see, the definition of the user interface needs to include definitions of how the system performs in such cases; the large number of different cases, and the difficulty of specifying performance in any of them, means that the system designer cannot address these aspects of the user interface.

These are not the only difficulties in specifying performance that lead to inadequate definition of user interfaces. As we have seen, available interface

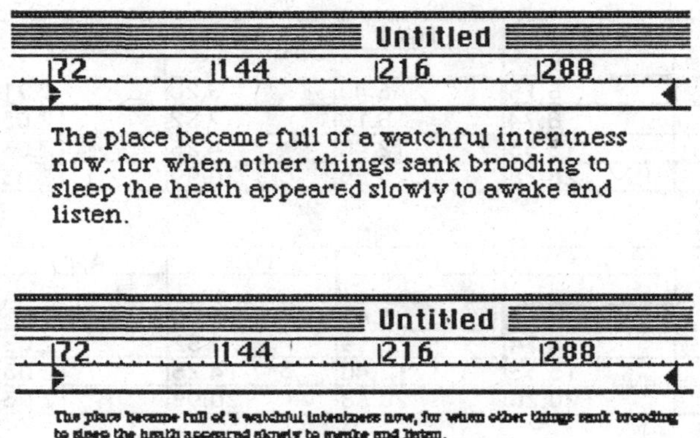

Figure 2: Changing text font size.

representations are weak. Few representations, if any, are in widespread use. Therefore when the designer wishes to document the interface, either to enable implementation or to publish the design, notations are not available for the job. In particular, there are no convenient notations for describing the appearance of screen objects. For example, how should we define the screen appearance of an arrow as the arrowhead is moved dynamically? Must the arrow always remain aligned with the shaft, or should it step through a number of preset orientations (Figure 3)? The only specification method offering a reasonably complete solution to information display is the use of a set of graphics functions such as GKS (Sproull, Sutherland and Ullman, 1985); this is a poor design notation that makes for difficult reading of a specification.

Figure 3: Arrows in which the arrowhead is kept parallel with the shaft (left) or steps through a number of preset orientations (right).

As the student of HCI literature well knows, this problem surfaces in virtually every published description of a user interface: in almost no cases is any attempt made to provide a full description. The definitive publications on Star (Smith *et al.*, 1982), Smalltalk (Goldberg, 1983), TEX (Knuth, 1979), etc., either omit most of the details, or bury the details in a lengthy system description. Examples of other published descriptions of user interfaces suffering from these problems are Vandor (1983) and Eisenstadt, Hasemer and Kriwaczek (1985).

The difficulty of providing even relatively complete specifications of user interfaces has several serious implications. For the designer, it hinders the traditional refinement process by which detail is added to an outline specification, until this specification is complete. For the implementer, it means that many of the design details must be defined as the system is implemented, with the danger that they may conflict with the designer's original intentions. For the student and the researcher, the lack of published interface descriptions is a serious impediment to progress.

3.2 *People design first, specify requirements afterwards*

It is publicly held that requirements analysis and specification should precede design. In practice, however, those who specify requirements do so in terms of a general solution to the design problem. Thus a design exists before requirements analysis begins.

Most textbooks and reference documents concur that requirements analysis should be the first step in system development (NCC, 1985; Jackson, 1983). There is a sound argument for following this sequence: requirements provide the criteria against which the designer can test design decisions. If no such criteria exist, how can design proceed?

Opposing this viewpoint is the evidence of design researchers such as Soloway (Adelson *et al.*, 1985; Soloway and Iyengar, 1986) and Swartout and Balzer (1982). Soloway has identified what he calls the *sketchy model* of the design, which the designer forms at the outset, before the design constraints are fully defined. Swartout and Balzer discuss several cases in which requirements undergo radical change as new directions are taken in the design. Thus there is conflict between recommended and actual practice.

One way to try to resolve this conflict is to gain a better understanding of requirements and of what they represent. The following points are helpful:

1. Requirements are constraints on the design: they state, for example, that a user interface must offer a certain range of functions, that it must be implementable on certain hardware, that it must respond within so many milliseconds, that it should react to user errors in certain ways.
2. The requirements analyst makes these stipulations on the assumption that they can be met. Nothing is gained, for example, by stating that a text editor based on a standard Telex terminal should offer multiple fonts and variable spacing: the hardware simply cannot support these requirements. Given a

bitmap screen and matrix printer, however, the constraint can realistically be satisfied.

3. The requirements analyst also confines his or her interest to issues that relate to meeting overall design objectives, such as competitiveness of the resulting product, or ability of the system to support a defined class of user performing a defined set of tasks. If a requirement appears unlikely to affect the overall outcome, it will probably be discarded.
4. The basis for specifying requirements is a set of models. These include models of the user, of the hardware-software system supporting the user interface, of the application process or task environment, and of the user interface itself. The requirements analyst tests each requirement against the relevant model to see if it is realistic.

In other words, when the designer says, "It is a requirement that...", he or she is saying, "I can model the effect of meeting or not meeting this requirement, and can show a correlation between these outcomes and achieving or missing the overall design objectives."

The reason, then, why design must precede the requirements analysis phase is to provide the models against which feasibility is tested. One of these is the model of the user interface itself: when stating, "There should be a function for performing x," the designer must feel reasonably sure that x can be accommodated in the interface structure. The "fuzzy model" of Adelson and Soloway is the model on which these decisions are taken.

There are several implications to be drawn from the relationship of requirements specification to design. The first concerns conventional system development: here requirements analysis is performed separately from design, by separate requirements specialists. They make assumptions about the design; the design team must understand these assumptions if they are to make sensible use of the requirements. There is a need for explicit definition of the models on which requirements analysis is based.

The second implication concerns designers who perform their own requirements analysis after adopting a particular "fuzzy model." All too often, this model is based on a narrow hardware or software solution; for examples, see Smith *et al.* (1982) and Sasso (1984). Overall design objectives, on the other hand, are more easily related to a model of the user interface or of the task environment. We should perhaps advise designers who are undertaking requirements analysis to start with a suitable initial model.

3.3 *User interfaces are mostly designed for a single user*

One property of the user interface design process that distinguishes it from conventional computer system design is its dependence on a *user model.* This term has a number of meanings, and it is important to state that we are concerned here with the *designer's model of the user*. User interface design cannot proceed without such a model — if no such model exists, then the activity cannot validly be called design, or else the resulting system does not include a user interface.

The designer relies on the user model in order to submit the design to hypothetical usage. The result is to show whether a particular function is useful, whether performance or response is adequate, whether the underlying conceptual model is comprehensible — in general, whether the system attains adequate usability. The degree to which this testing is possible depends on the strength of the user model. Generally speaking, user models are very weak: they cover only tiny portions of human behaviour and are highly fragmented. Two examples of useful models are Fitts' Law (Fitts, 1954), which predicts the user's speed of selecting screen targets, and the Keystroke Model (Card, Moran and Newell, 1980) which, using Fitts' Law, provides a means of estimating the performance of keystroke-based command languages.

Few of the decisions facing the interface designer can be resolved with the aid of isolated models such as Fitts' Law. Instead the designer needs a comprehensive user model that can provide the answer to questions such as, "Will the user understand the concept of a multi-level structured document?" or "Should menu items be displayed in a special typeface?" The psychological models available to designers in the literature cannot answer these questions.

In desperation, more than anything else, the designer turns to the nearest suitable human being to hand, whose behaviour can be predicted with reasonable thoroughness. The most accessible and predictable human is, of course, the designer himself or herself. The tendency for designers to use themselves as user models is at its most obvious when designers are heard saying, "What I need is a system that does the following..." Many experimental prototypes are the result of treating the designer as the user; see for example Boyle and Clarke (1985).

Rather than use themselves as user models, designers may turn to a specific person whom they know well enough to use in this rôle. One of the values of user studies is to acquaint designers with individuals who may one day become the users of their designs. For examples of designs performed on the basis of extensive user studies, see Officetalk (Newman and Mott, 1982) and Lisa (Morgan *et al.*, 1983).

User interface design cannot be considered satisfactory as long as designers rely on themselves or close acquaintances as user models. It produces systems full of idiosyncratic features, systems that prove unusable on reaching the real users.

Fortunately researchers are beginning to work on developing better user models (Whitefield, 1985) and tools for user modelling in the design process (Green and Young, personal communication). When these research efforts reach fruition, it may become possible to lessen designers' dependence on a single user model.

3.4 *AI-based systems can only be represented as prototypes*

The problems of user interface design are especially evident in the design of expert systems and other applications based on Artificial Intelligence techniques. The general outcome is to increase the designer's dependence on prototyping as a means of representing the design.

The problems facing the AI system designer may be summarised as follows:

1. *Modelling the application process*. It is difficult to predict changes in the application process caused by the introduction of expert systems. There are still too few documented examples of the use of these systems to support accurate modelling of their impact. The designer must therefore work partly in the dark in developing scenarios for the use of new system designs.
2. *Modelling the user*. There is no reason why user modelling should be any more difficult here than in other spheres of user interface design. However, the emphasis on building embedded models of the user can hinder the normal design process due to its concern to find properties of the user that can be embedded.
3. *A technology-based initial model*. Too often, expert systems are based initially on a concept of the technical solution, not on a well-understood set of user functions. Concern for user functionality and interface design often comes much later in the design process, when these are less easy to address.
4. *Deriving the user's conceptual model*. Here we are concerned with the user's model of the system — the "design model" of Norman and Draper (1986). It may prove difficult to develop a clear model for the user to adopt, because there are so many ways of representing expert knowledge. Some have advocated presenting the system as if it were a human expert, but it is unlikely that the user would adopt such a simplistic model.

Overall, the system designer works under a number of handicaps. Essential design models are either weakened or altogether lacking, and design representations do not support evaluation or subdivision of the design. It is not surprising, therefore, that AI-based system development relies so heavily on prototyping: a prototype can be evaluated without recourse to other representations, and offers a concrete model as a basis for further design iteration. Excessive reliance on prototyping has its risks, however: in particular, iterations take longer when each one involves prototyping.

We should hope that some of the problems with designing AI-based systems can be eradicated so that they can be designed using conventional methods.

4. Conclusion

This paper has taken a close look at some of the aspects of interactive system design from a designer's perspective. It has concluded that the design discipline still needs strengthening in a number of areas, especially in the development of stronger models and representations. Until this is done, we cannot expect radical improvements in the quality of design; progress can nevertheless be achieved if a realistic view is taken of the tools and methods currently available.

CHAPTER SEVEN

AN APPROACH TO FORMALISED PROCEDURES FOR USER-CENTRED SYSTEM DESIGN

ARTHUR GARDNER

1. Introduction

This paper stems from work recently completed at the HUSAT Research Centre to produce a new handbook on human factors in the design of computer based systems (Gardner and McKenzie, 1988). The handbook is now on public release.

During the course of preparing the new handbook it was necessary to study the existing sources of advice. What emerged was that different authors had focused their attention on different facets of the System Life Cycle: for example, it is rare to find an author who writes knowledgeably about both physical interfaces and organisational issues. It was found also that much of the existing advice is complementary rather than contradictory but that there has been little attempt to integrate the separate facets into a coherent methodology.

In addition, if one looks at existing sources of advice as components in an encompassing methodology then it is obvious that the advice available is not equally strong for all facets of the whole System Life Cycle. For these reasons, therefore, the new handbook is being written with a view to showing how the various design techniques and factual databases can be strengthened and integrated to form a more coherent and complete, formally structured, methodology for User-Centred Design.

This paper gives an outline description of a set of formally structured procedures for User-Centred Design and shows where selected, existing sources of advice are relevant within the User-Centred Design framework. The paper does not attempt to review all existing sources of advice. It is highly selective and mentions only recent sources which the author found particularly helpful and relatively easy to obtain. Mention of a source does not mean that the author necessarily endorses everything in it. Nor does it follow that a source which is not mentioned is rejected as being of no value.

2. The User-Centred Design framework

The formal procedures for User-Centred Design are intended to be used throughout all stages of the System Life Cycle. The System Life Cycle is conceived, see Figure 1 below, as having six sequential and iterative processes. The point to be made here is that the System Life Cycle does not stop when the System is installed. In-use Support, for example, is regarded as part of the cycle and, hence, needs to be included in User-Centred Design.

This paper concentrates on the second and third main stages or processes, i.e., User-Centred Design in "Requirements Specification" and in "Full Development and Build". Nevertheless, it should be borne in mind that the other areas are equally important.

Selected existing sources of advice which give an overview of human factors in the System Life Cycle are: Bailey (1982); Damodaran *et al.* (1980); Meisner (1982); and Salvendy (1987).

2.1 *Definitions*

It is as well to state some definitions at the outset since this paper uses certain terms in particular ways.

Users. The term "Users" means all the people who will use the System (for example: Operators, Supervisors, Managers and Maintainers). Users are components within the System.

System. The term "System" means more than just the machines (e.g., the computer hardware and software). It means all the components — human and machine — working together to achieve the purposes stated in the Top-level Specification.

User-Centred Design is user-centred in four ways:

(a) All Systems exist for human purposes. Advice is needed on how to identify Users' purposes and how to represent the information gathered so that it can be acted upon by Designers.

(b) The criteria on which Systems are to be judged are the requirements of those who must use it. Advice is needed on how to establish testable System goals from the point of view of the Users. (Usability criteria are examples.)

(c) The design team must have full User involvement in all aspects of systems development. Advice is needed on how to involve Users in design decision making.

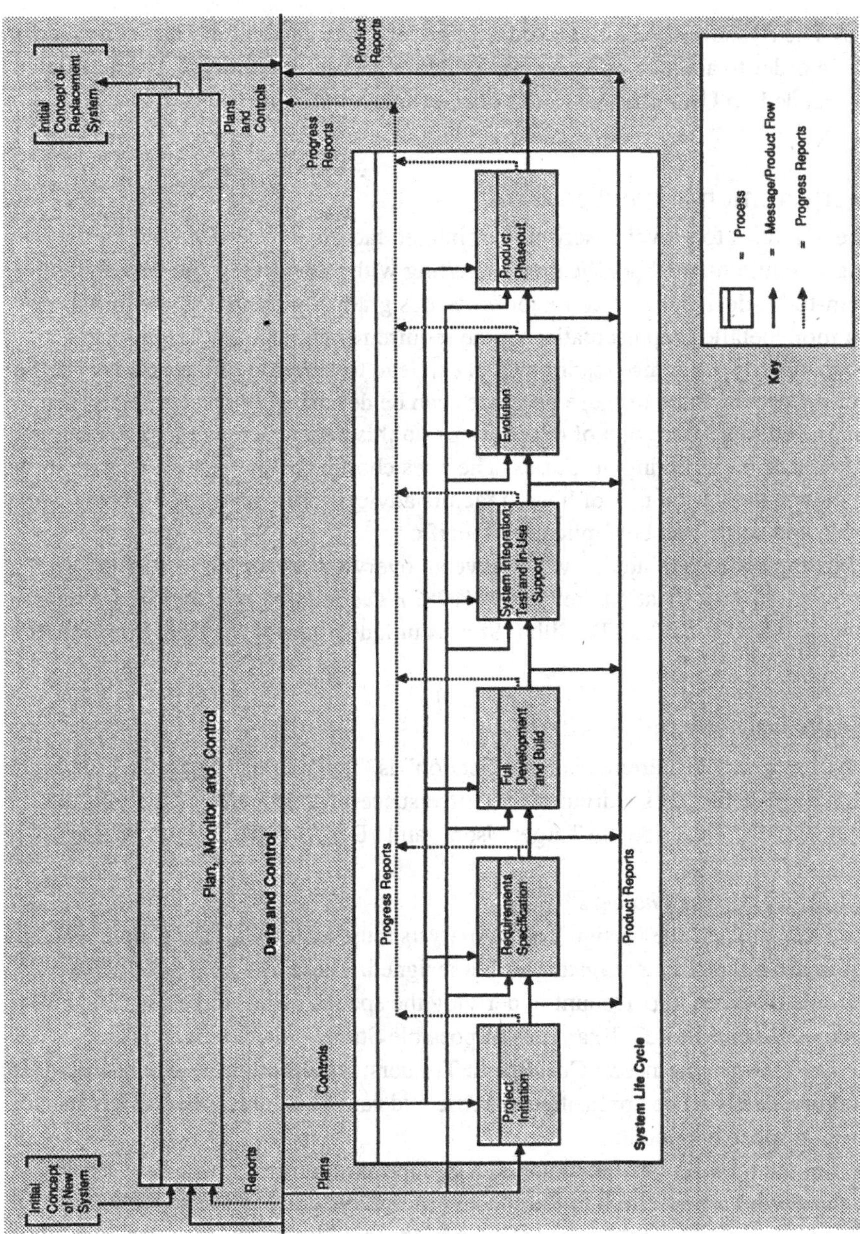

Figure 1: System Life Cycle.

(d) The System is to be designed explicitly to take account of User characteristics in order to achieve effective performance and acceptability to Users. Advice is needed on User characteristics of relevance to design.

3. Requirements specification

Figure 2 gives a top-level description of human factors in User-Centred Design during "Requirements Specification". Starting with a concept of the new System (the System-to-be-designed), three major processes gradually transform the initial concept into a more detailed representation of the requirements. Each of these processes involves quality assurance testing which can lead to iteration of the process itself or earlier processes. Each of these processes can be described in greater detail (i.e., decomposed to a finer grain of description). In this paper there is room to discuss only some of the enabling processes. The ones chosen (below) are illustrative in that they show a need for a mix of human factors advice, some of which will be general-purpose and some will be application specific.

Existing sources of advice which give an overview of human factors in Requirements Specification are: Bailey (1982); Damodaran *et al.* (1980); Wilson (1984); and Salvendy (1987). Gilb (1988) is uniquely useful for Goal Specification.

4. Stakeholder analysis

The first step in "Requirements Specification" is "Stakeholder Analysis", see Figure 3. This stage is further subdivided into three successive processes: "Identify the Stakeholders", "Describe the Target Users" and "Describe the System Scenarios".

4.1 *"Identify the Stakeholders"*

During this process the Design Team Analysts must identify all the people who have a legitimate interest in the System-to-be-designed. These are the people whose views need to be be taken into account in deriving the specifications to be used in "Full Development and Build". Examples of possible Stakeholders include Users; Analysts; Design Engineers; Customers; Trainers; and Recruiters. The resulting lists of Stakeholders will be application specific and cannot be prescribed in advance by a general-purpose handbook.

From the total set of Stakeholders, it is important to identify the "key people" (i.e., those who are essential to the success of the System and whose views must be taken into account). User-Centred Design holds that Users are always to be regarded as key-people. This does not mean that Users are regarded as always being right in all

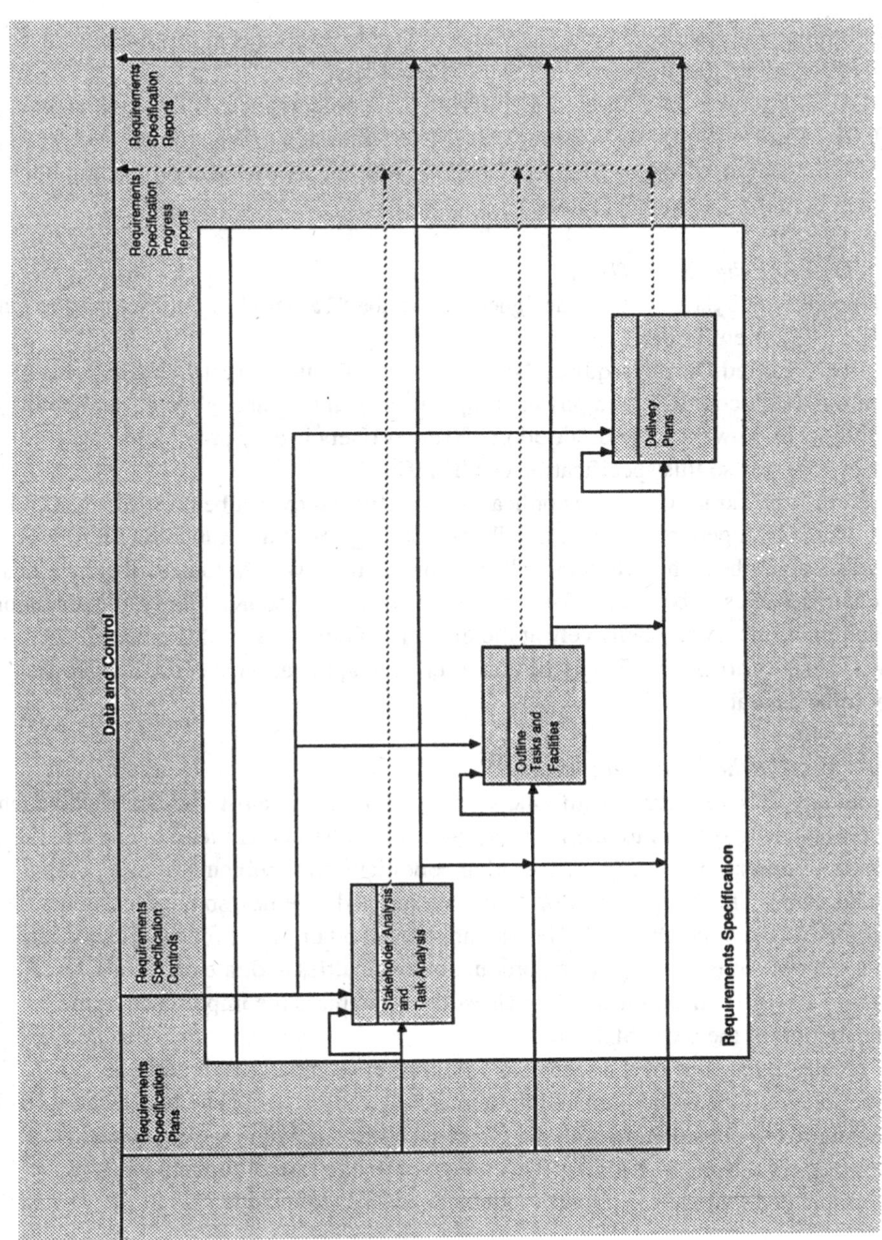

Figure 2: Human Factors in Requirements Specification.

their opinions. It does mean that the views of Users are always to be elicited and considered alongside the views of other Stakeholders.

Existing sources of advice on identifying Stakeholders include Damodaran *et al.* (1980), Mitroff (1980) and Wilson (1984). The discussion of Viewpoint Analysis in the CORE methodology by SDS Ltd (1985) is relevant as background reading but does not emphasise human factors.

4.2 *"Describe the Target Users"*

The people the System is to be designed for are the "Target Users". They may or may not be the Current Users.

User-Centred Design requires Analysts to describe the Target Users in terms of "quality" (e.g., cognitive and physical capabilities) and "quantity" (e.g., availability). At this stage, however, the description of Target Users is only provisional. As the design emerges so this specification can be refined.

Details of Target Users are application specific and cannot be prescribed entirely in advance by a general-purpose handbook, although Boff and Lincoln (1988) looks to be a step in the right direction. A handbook could be written to describe the kinds of characteristics to be looked for but there is no existing source known to the author which does this comprehensively at the moment. (Gardner and McKenzie, 1988, gives some information.) It may be that a series of application specific handbooks would be desirable.

4.3 *"Describe the System Scenarios"*

For all key Stakeholders, identify the scenarios for the System-to-be-designed which are particularly relevant to them. The scenarios from Users will tend to concern the System in operational use (e.g., operating conditions and problems from breakdowns). These types of information are lumped together, sometimes, under the heading of "mission analysis". The scenarios from other Stakeholders will concern other features of the System (e.g., production difficulties and rate of spend). User-Centred Design concentrates on the Users but recognises the importance of the contribution of the other Stakeholders.

Ideally, every one of the scenarios would be explored in detail with the Stakeholders. This is likely to be impracticable. Analysts will have to select a spread of scenarios in consultation with the Users such that the full range of intended operating conditions is explored. This involves an exercise of judgement. It is recommended that the selection should be done so as to include:

(a) All critical scenarios (i.e., situations which are central to the System's operational context or in which failure would have unacceptable consequences).

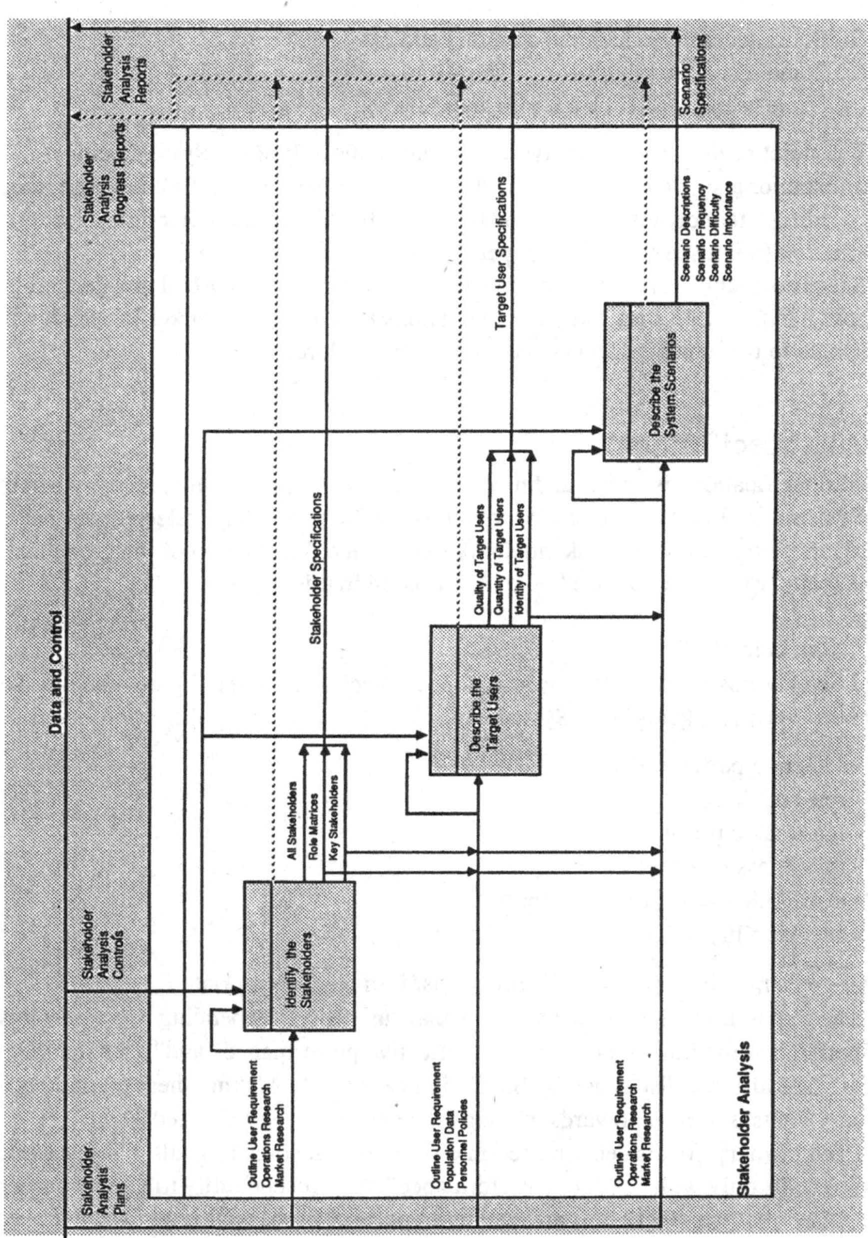

Figure 3: Human Factors in Stakeholder Analysis.

(b) Some scenarios which are common and easy.
(c) Some scenarios which are common and difficult.
(d) Some scenarios which are rare and difficult.

The point of the scenario analysis is to reduce the risk of the System being maximised for a single scenario to the detriment of others. It has the advantage, too, of providing a real context within which to elicit functional and other task relevant information (not discussed in this paper).

Scenario analysis is application specific and cannot be prescribed in a general-purpose handbook. In some projects, Operations Research and Market Research will contribute to the identification of scenarios to be explored.

5. Goal specification

"Goal Specification" is a vital and much neglected process. It is the process whereby the System "quality goals" (e.g., 'how well is it to be done?') are selected, defined and quantified. It follows "Stakeholder Analysis" and the eliciting of the functional goals (e.g., 'what is to be done?' — not discussed in this paper).

5.1 *"Goal Selection"*

Goal Selection is the first step towards a Goal Specification, see Figure 4 below. The so-called "primary goals" of a System are:

- effective performance
- reasonable cost
- reasonable profit
- timeliness
- availability in sufficient quantity
- acceptability to Users

Other goals may be added to this primary list if judged appropriate.

The important point, for this paper, is that "usability" (depending upon how it is defined) has something to do with both "effective performance" and "acceptability to Users" (see also the discussion by Shackel in Chapter 2). Making these explicit as primary goals is a move towards making Systems more User-Centred.

Each primary goal is decomposed into so-called "secondary goals". User-Centred Design deals only with "effective performance" and "acceptability to Users" but it is recognised that the other goals are equally important. Also, it is recognised that "effective performance" and "acceptability to Users" are interrelated since effective performance helps to make Systems more acceptable to Users and acceptability to

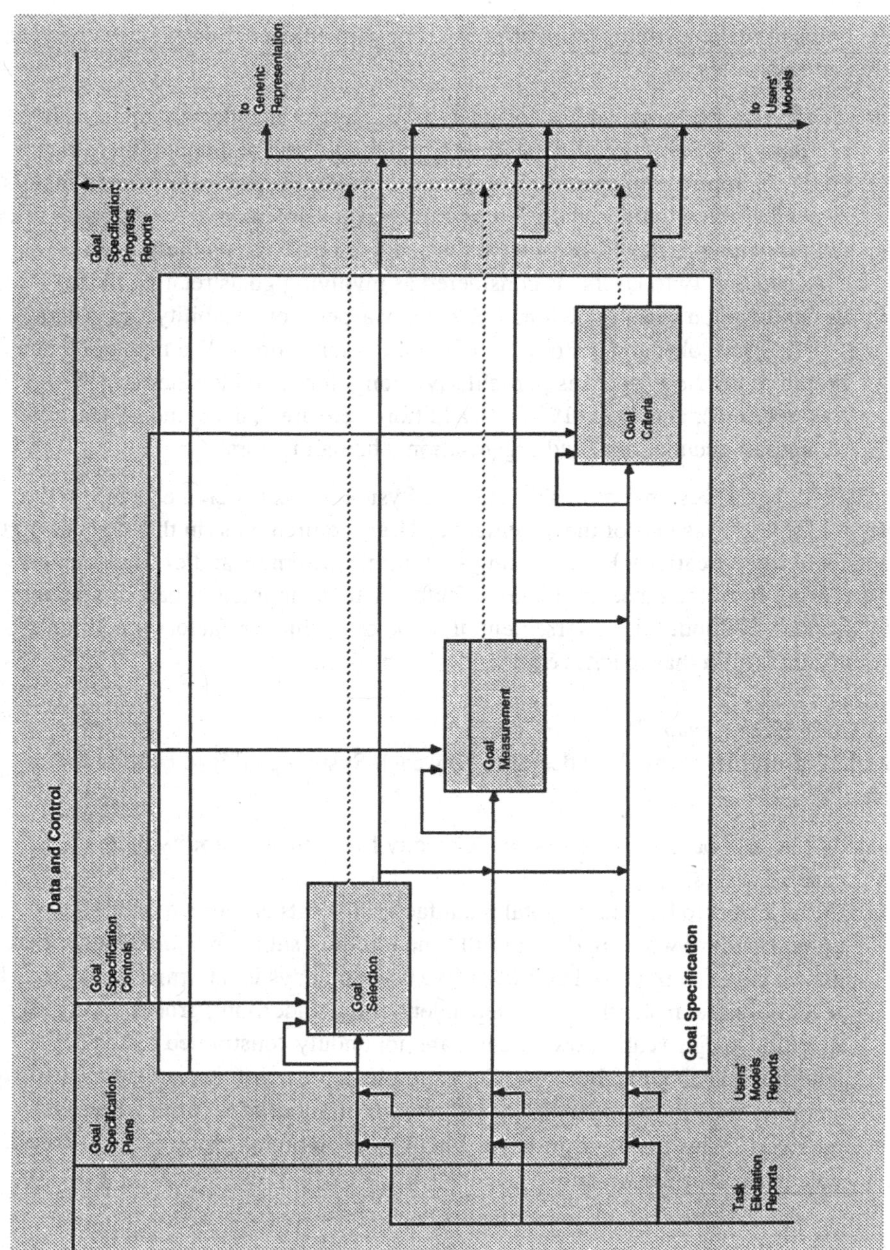

Figure 4: Human Factors in Goal Specification.

Users helps to make Systems more effective. For convenience, however, the two can be treated separately:

(a) "Effective Performance" is considered, usually, to include sub-goals such as: accuracy, availability, interoperability, reliability, and maintainability. Such goals are application specific and there seem to be no particular human factors issues involved in their inclusion or omission as System goals. This paper does not recommend, therefore, any existing source of advice on these goals.

(b) "Acceptability to Users" is considered as involving goals relating to the design of good tasks (which includes many aspects of "usability", cf. Shackel, 1984); good jobs; and good team and work organisations. The human factors literature on these issues is particularly strong, for example Cherns (1976); Eason (1983); and Trist (1981). In addition there are many standard texts on industrial, occupational and organisational human factors.

User-Centred Design requires that lists of System goals are created early in the System Life Cycle as part of the statement of User requirements (in this case, as part of the Goal Specification). By endorsing such lists, Customers and/or Management are declaring from the outset that human factors is to be an integral part of systems development. Without this endorsement, the role of the human factors practitioner is non-existent within that specific System design project.

5.2 *"Goal Measurement"*

"Goal Measurement" involves deciding how each System goal is to be tested. For each goal ask:

(a) What is to be measured? (errors; capacity for change; usability by the least capable Users; etc.)

(b) How is this to be tested? (total manufacturing costs amortized over 1000 units; standard working days in full time training; subjective judgement of an expert panel over a fixed period of five working days in a normal week; etc.) If at all possible, make the test independent of the underlying processes in order that the Design Team, downstream, are not unduly constrained by top-level assumptions about technology. For example, a process-independent measure of a communications system might be "average number of incorrect messages received". This does not prejudge whether the communication is paper-based, voice-based or whatever.

5.3 *"Goal Criteria"*

The setting of "Goal Criteria" involves deciding what is to be regarded as satisfactory for each goal. These are the criteria values to be used in choosing between competing designs and in quality control. For each goal it is important to ask:

(a) How good is the current System (if any) or its nearest equivalent? This information should be available as a result of In-use Audit of the current System. It establishes a base-line for future development. It ensures, also, that the Design Team really knows the characteristics of the present System.
(b) What is the best possible level of attainment? (The best that can be anticipated in the timescale given substantial resources.) This is obtained, usually, by the research departments making a technological forecast. Senior Managers and Customers cannot be expected to keep up with the details of technological progress. The value of this question is that it helps them to see the upper-limit of attainment and its cost.
(c) What is the minimum acceptable attainment? (The "worst case" that is still acceptable to Management or the Customer.) Often, this will be "at least as good as the current System".
(d) What is the planned outcome? (The 'to be aimed for' attainment.) This is the crucial decision. It is made in the light of the previous three questions. Typically, the planned outcome will fall between the "minimum acceptable" and the "best possible". It must be appreciated that the Design Team has no incentive to do better than this planned outcome. The planned outcome must be realistic.

The resulting document is a "Goal Specification". A useful format for recording this is shown in Figure 5. It is recognised that these numerical scores will be somewhat arbitrary and, at best, will give a crude summary of the judgements. The value of the exercise is that it forces everyone to be explicit about the goals so that misunderstandings and conflicts can be sorted out early rather than late in the development cycle.

"Goal Specification", as described here, is relatively neglected in Systems development but its potential impact on design is enormous (see also the discussion by Shackel in Chapter 2). Gilb (1988) is recommended reading.

6. Full Development and Build

Figure 6 below gives a top-level description of human factors in User-Centred Design during "Full Development and Build". This paper will illustrate some of the issues by describing the design of certain Users' Facilities (i.e., User-Computer Interfaces and User Workstations) which come within the stage "Detailed Tasks and Facilities".

Stakeholder: **Scenario:**

Time:

Date:

	Measurement Techniques		Criteria Values			
	What Measured?	How Tested?	Current System?	Best Possible?	Minimum Acceptable?	Planned Outcome?
Accuracy (priority 1.0)	Error Rate	Six Random Samples of output throughout the day, each of 30 minutes duration	20% Faulty	2% Faulty (see comment...)	15% Faulty	10% Faulty
Least Effort to Users (priority 1.0)	User Strain	Judgement of 3 experienced Supervisors about how much strain	100% (baseline)	150% (see comment...)	100% (ie at least as good as the current system)	120%

Figure 5: Example of Tabular Format for Goal Specification.

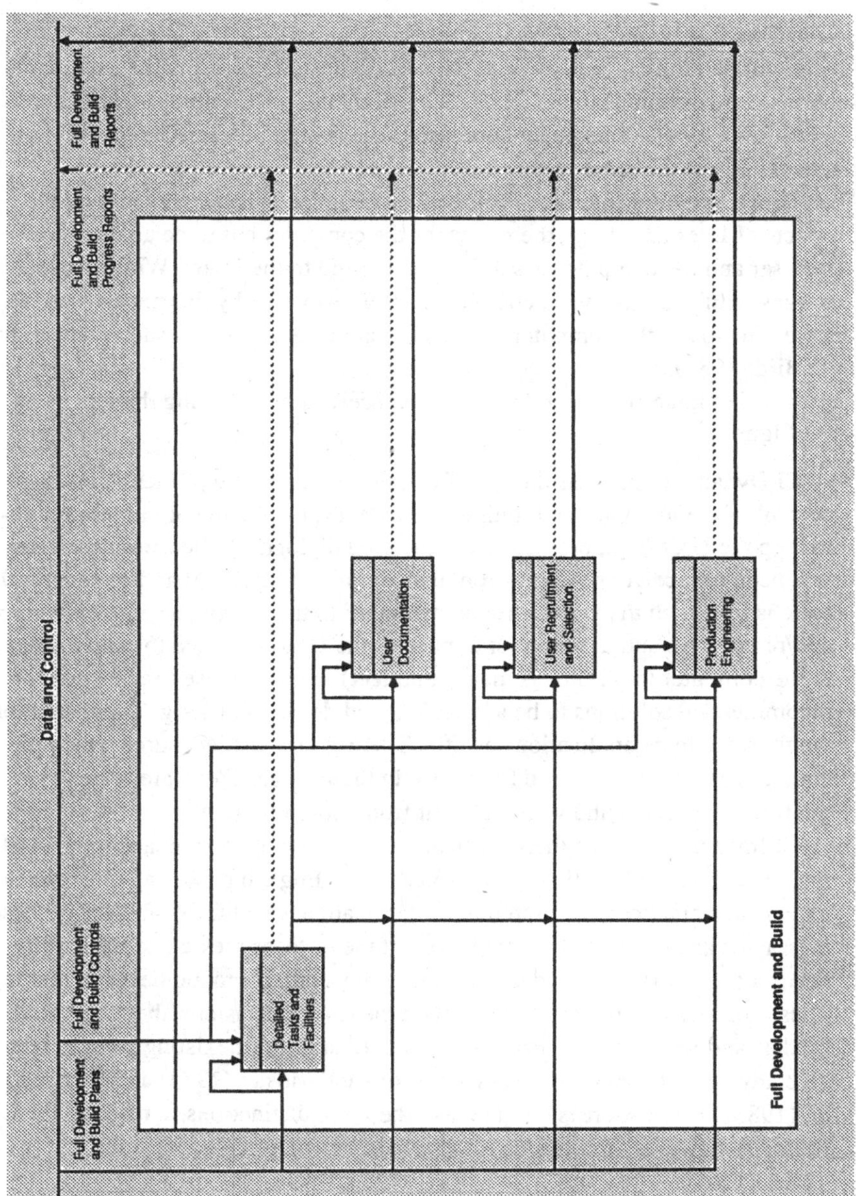

Figure 6: Human Factors in Full Development and Build.

6.1 *"User-Computer Interface Protocol"*

Designers will be familiar already with the need to design protocols (i.e., standard conventions) for communications (e.g., ISO/OSI model for Computer-Computer Interfaces – ISO, 1984). This paper approaches the design of User-Computer Interfaces (UCIs) in the same way.

The "User-Computer Interface Protocol" (see Figure 7) is concerned with the User aspects of Interfaces (e.g., the messages the computer has to be able to receive from the User and the computer has to be able to send to the User). Whilst protocols for messages within and between computers are not covered by this paper, interested readers are directed to the computer science literature for advice on such matters, for example Bird (1987).

The User-Computer Interface Protocol is conceived of as having three parts as shown in Figure 8.

(a) UCI Dynamics concerns the specification of: the routing of messages; the control of the initiation and timing of messages; the degree of guidance built-in to help the User (e.g., provision of structured dialogues); the senses the User will need to receive messages from the computer (e.g., sight and/or sound); the actions by which the User can send messages to the computer (e.g., movement and/or speech); and the limbs and muscles the User will need to send messages to the computer (e.g., fingers, hands and feet). Each of these needs a pool of recommended solutions to be available to aid decision making. These solutions would seem to be application specific. There is no existing source which the author is able to recommend for advice in these areas. These areas are relatively neglected and would benefit from more research.

(b) UCI Imagery concerns the specification of: the types of language to be used by the User in constructing the messages (e.g., English prose and/or graphics and/or mathematics); the grammar of these languages; the vocabulary of these messages; and the accent or emphasis or tone of these messages. Each of these needs a pool of recommended solutions to be available to aid decision making. These solutions would be contingent on the earlier decisions about cognitive models and would be application specific. Examples of existing sources which give advice at this grain of detail are Smith and Mosier (1984) and Parrish *et al.* (1983). These sources do not make the same distinctions as made in the UCI Protocol, however, and readers will have to evaluate such advice for themselves.

(c) UCI Devices have to be designed in the light of the decisions made about the interface dynamics and the interface imagery. Devices are defined in terms of "controls" (e.g., keyboard and/or mouse) and "displays" (e.g., screens and/or

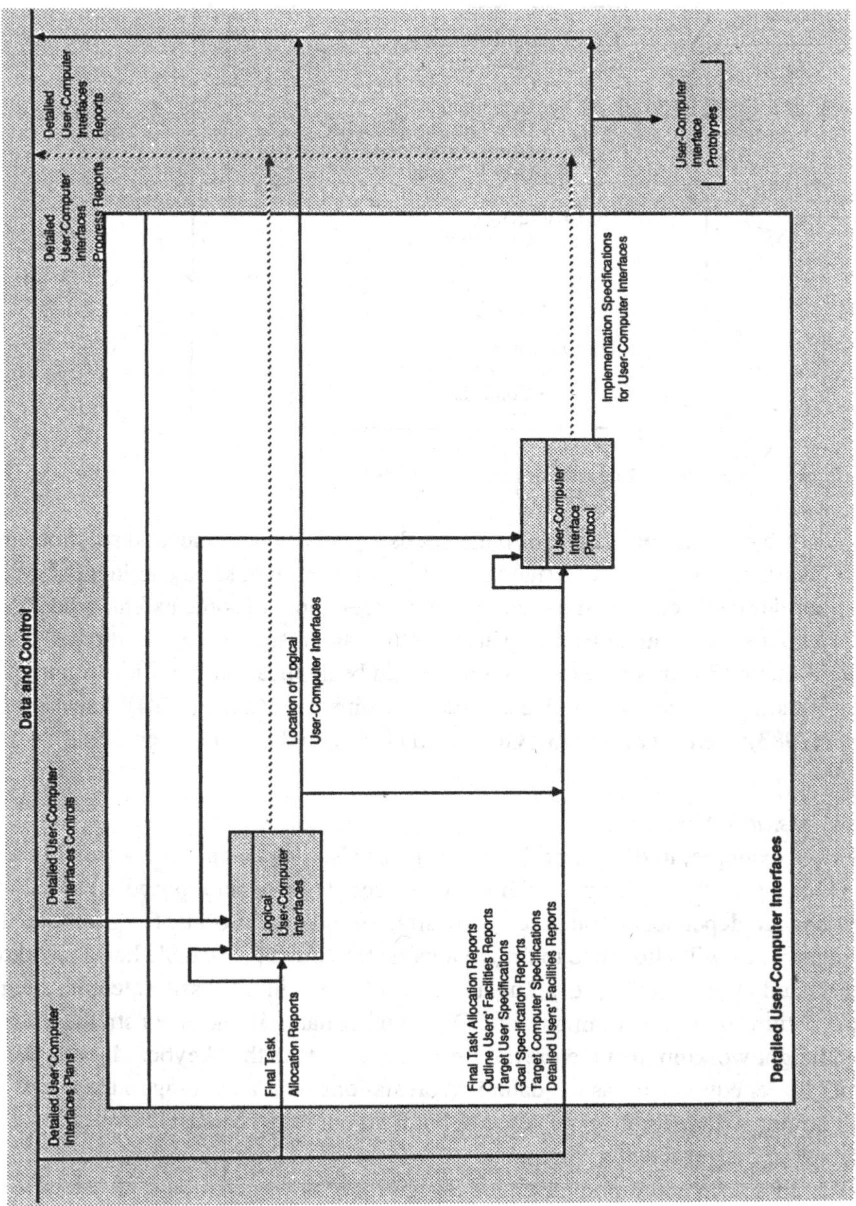

Figure 7: Human Factors in Detailed User-Computer Interfaces.

UCI Dynamics
- Routing
- Control
- User Guidance
- User Sensory Modality
- User Action Modality
- User Effector

UCI Imagery
- Language Type
- Grammar
- Vocabulary
- Accent

UCI Devices
- Displays
- Controls

Figure 8: Summary of main features in UCI Protocol.

voice synthesisers). Each of these needs a pool of recommended solutions to be available to aid decision making. These solutions would be contingent on the earlier decisions about dynamics and imagery and, to some extent, on decisions about controls and displays (since controls and displays may need to be designed in pairs). These solutions would be application specific. Examples of existing sources which give advice are Smith and Mosier (1984); Parrish *et al*, (1983); Benz *et al*. (1983); Grandjean (1987); and Shneiderman (1987).

6.2 *Workstation Design*

The final example, in this paper, is the design of User Workstations — see Figure 9.

Once again, the design procedures would seem to be general purpose but the solutions are dependent upon specific constraints and applications. For example, if the constraints will allow one to design a workstation with a variable height worktop for a seated User then the prevailing advice is to start with the "seat reference height" as the datum for all other dimensions. On the other hand, if one is constrained to a fixed height worktop then the prevailing advice is to take the "keyboard reference point" (or its equivalent) as the datum. Workstations built according to these two design rules will differ in some respects but both ought to be satisfactory and "usable" in their respective situations.

For advice on anthropometrics and design rules on workstation dimensions see Pheasant (1986). For advice on human perception and performance see Boff and Lincoln (1988) and Salvendy (1987).

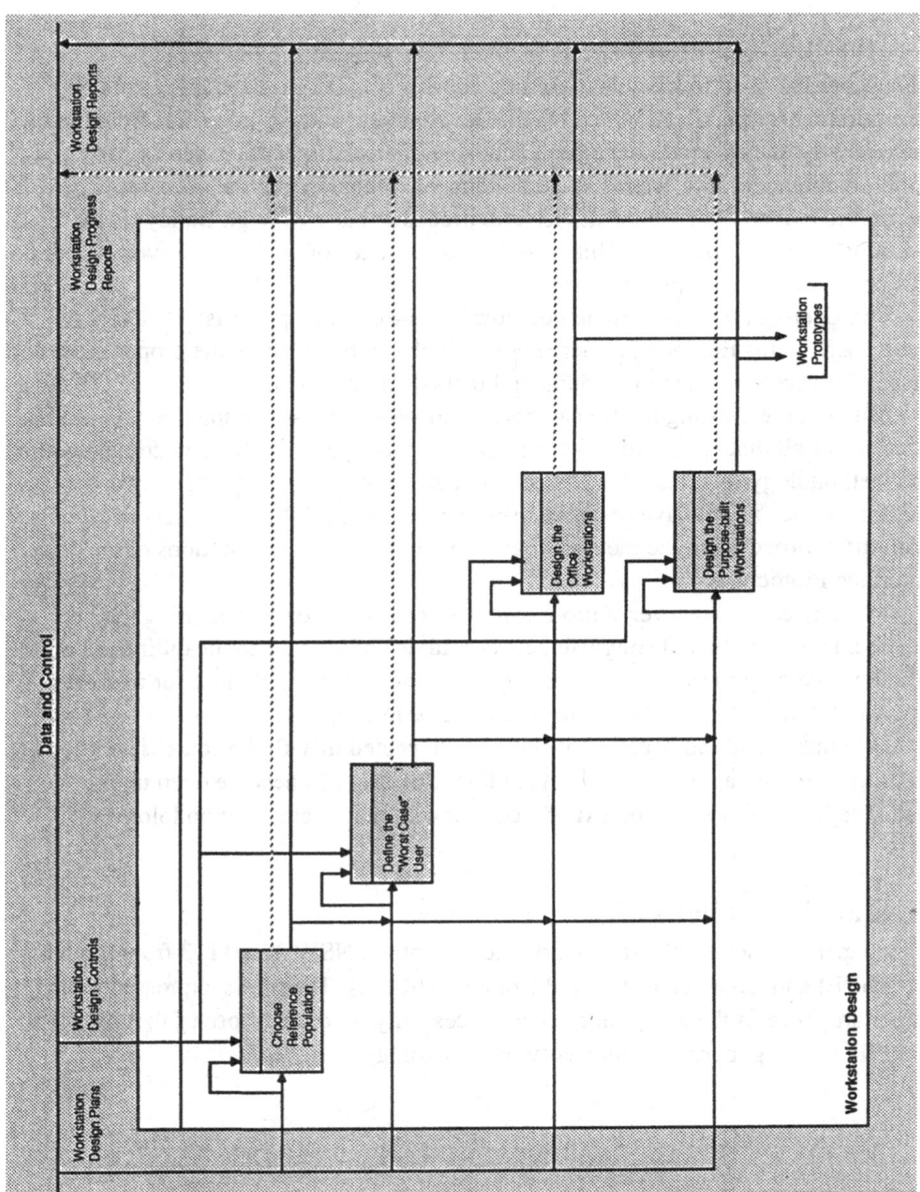

Figure 9: Human Factors in Workstation Design.

7. Concluding remarks

This paper has tried to show that existing sources of advice on human factors of "Requirements Specification" and "Full Development and Build" suffer from the fact that, usually, they seem to have been conceived in isolation rather than as parts of a coherent methodology. There are exceptions, of course, in that some sources do attempt to embed their factual advice into procedural advice (e.g., Bailey, 1982; Damodaran *et al.*, 1980; and Gilb, 1988). Most sources of advice, however, do not do this or do it only to a limited extent.

The User-Centred Design methodology outlined in this paper is an attempt to evolve a Systems Engineering framework which can better show the proper times and places for accessing both procedural and factual advice.

Much of the existing advice can be used to advantage within this framework. In some cases all that is needed is a cross-reference to place the advice in context within the methodology (e.g., use this advice at this stage of design). In other cases, the existing advice might have to be reworked or restructured slightly to accord better with the approaches in the methodology (e.g., to reflect the conventions of the "User Interface Protocol").

In many cases, however, a more extensive reworking or restructuring may be needed, for example to distinguish between advice of general applicability and advice of relevance only to specific applications or Target User Populations, or to create pools of advice which at the moment seem to be missing.

Lest this sound too negative, it should be repeated that all the sources mentioned in this paper are valuable and worth reading. But they can become even more valuable if set within the context of a common, human factors methodology.

Acknowledgements

This paper is based partly upon work under Contract NSW 32A/1113 from the UK MOD(PE) and Contract VM8 AAB from the UK DTI. The views expressed in this paper are those of the author and do not necessarily represent those of the MOD(PE), the DTI or Loughborough University of Technology.

PART 3

Special Topics in Depth

THE CONTRIBUTIONS OF APPLIED COGNITIVE PSYCHOLOGY TO THE STUDY OF HUMAN-COMPUTER INTERACTION

PHIL BARNARD

1. Introduction

1.1 *Human-computer interaction: the research context*

When a user is interacting with a computer system, two highly complex information processors are effectively conducting a dialogue. One of these, the user, will be engaged in some purposeful activity which is directed towards achieving a task objective in the home or workplace. The other, the computer system, is the tool that mediates the achievement of those objectives. Both parties to the dialogue are manipulating and acting upon information that represents concepts or entities in a particular task domain, for example, business accounts; the component reactions in a chemical plant; spaceships in a game; documents; or even computer programs themselves.

In order to achieve their particular objectives, individual users cannot typically rely on their knowledge of the task domain alone (cf. Morton *et al.*, 1979). They must also learn something about the way in which the tool behaves. They need such knowledge to interpret the state of information in the system; to assess how that state relates to their immediate goals; and to communicate to the system what action to take in order further to pursue those goals. These activities of interpretation, assessment and pursuing a course of action all occur in a specific context.

Obviously, that context is very much shaped by the particular style or form of human-computer interface that the system offers. As processors of information, any given generation of system is subject to the constraints of design practices within current hardware and software capabilities. Equally, the user shapes the context of a particular interaction. As processors of information, users are subject to different constraints — those of natural human cognition, their experience, their specific needs for using a computer tool and their broader motivations for doing so. The context is also determined by representations of the specific entities in the task domain that are being thought about by the user and manipulated by the system. In the course of a particular dialogue sequence these have a history. That history is likely to constrain both the user's interpretation of the system state and the system actions that can be carried out.

The study of human-computer interaction seeks to understand what it is about the factors within this total context that lead to productive and efficient use of computer tools. Once gained, that understanding should enable us to design new and better tools to support human endeavour and even to extend its horizons.

It has often been emphasised that this is essentially a multidisciplinary enterprise (e.g., Gaines, 1984; Norman and Draper, 1986; Carroll, 1987; Hammond, Christie and Marshall, 1987). In the process of development, software specialists, industrial designers and human factors engineers have all contributed to the evolution and enhancement of user interfaces. In the process of research many different disciplines have brought their concepts and methodologies to bear on the problems of usability. Computer science and its associated disciplines have led to enhancements in both hardware and software capabilities. The behavioural and cognitive sciences have also had very real influences. Some of these, such as psychology, ergonomics and sociology have assisted in the definition and analysis of the phenomena of actual tool use. Others such as linguistics and artificial intelligence have yielded important insights into the representation of knowledge and its manipulation.

In practical terms, cross-disciplinary understanding and cooperation are clearly of great importance for the productive advancement of both research and development projects. It is equally important for the effective transfer of new ideas from the research to the development communities. In more theoretical terms cross-disciplinary understanding is becoming essential. Although individual disciplines have their own objectives, methodologies and concepts, there is substantial cross-fertilisation. Both computers and users are representing and processing information and knowledge. Hence, concepts and techniques originating in one discipline are frequently of value in another.

For example, in order to analyse and explore the properties of the human information processor, psychologists may draw upon architectural concepts (e.g., transient and permanent storage) or functional concepts (e.g., executive processes) whose origins lie in computer science. Likewise, in order to analyse and explore how people represent and manipulate knowledge, psychologists may draw upon linguistics and artificial intelligence. Such intensive cross-fertilisation inevitably leads to a blurring of the boundaries between disciplines.

1.2 *Applied cognitive psychology*

Since its rapid evolution in the 1960s (e.g., see Neisser, 1967) cognitive psychology has sought to improve our scientific understanding of the fundamental properties of the human information processing mechanism. Its primary emphases have been upon developing and testing theories concerning the ways in which that mechanism constructs, manipulates and acts upon mental representations. Individual theories cover perception, language understanding and production, memory, problem solving, consciousness, intention and the control of action and many more. These areas of concern are all potentially relevant to the ways in which users will behave in the course of interacting with a computer.

Applying cognitive psychology directly to the problems of human-computer interaction is far from straightforward. Typically, individual theories are tested and evolve in the context of rather abstract laboratory tasks. These seek to isolate the influences upon behaviour of the component processes and mental representations which underlie cognition. Although substantial progress has been made towards defining and characterising important cognitive phenomena, there is little consensus concerning the theoretical concepts and principles that best explain them.

Typically, laboratory experiments focus upon repeated measurement of relatively "local" episodes of behaviour — as when subjects respond to discretely presented stimulus material. The basic phenomena obtained in these settings and the theories developed to account for them do not readily generalise beyond the confines of particular experimental paradigms. Also, it is often far from clear how the phenomena and theories relate to the settings of human-computer interaction where the component processes of cognition are coordinated to control extended and purposeful sequences of behaviour (e.g., see Barnard, 1987).

Applied cognitive psychology attempts to bridge the gap between the properties of cognition as studied in the more abstract laboratory tasks and those phenomena that are characteristic of cognition in the tasks of everyday life. There is considerable conceptual and methodological overlap between the core discipline of cognitive psychology and its applied counterpart. There are also differences. In the laboratory, hotly debated theoretical issues may focus upon predictions concerning relatively small differences in behaviour whose detection requires carefully controlled experimental conditions. The variables that give rise to those effects may be contributing relatively little to the overall ease or difficulty of carrying out the tasks of everyday life. As Landauer (1987) has remarked: "the point of applied research is to understand what matters in realistic contexts."

Knowing what is likely to matter in advance can be extremely difficult. There are many different ways in which an interface design may prove problematic. It might, for example, have an elegant and consistent command language. Users may nevertheless err when the command structures are incompatible with the organisation of information on the VDU (e.g., see Barnard *et al.*, 1981). Alternatively, a command language may prove problematic because it requires frequent use of shift key combinations on the keyboard (e.g., see Hammond *et al.*, 1980). Empirical evaluation may of course identify such problems. They nevertheless invite theoretical and practical analysis.

From a theoretical perspective this may require taking an integrated approach to the analysis of perception, cognition and action. This in turn may mean that our basic theoretical approaches need rethinking. Their scope may need to be substantially increased and this may require the development of concepts and techniques that enable us to generate approximate, but applicable, characterisations of cognition (e.g., see Card, Moran and Newell, 1983; Norman, 1986; Young and Barnard, 1987). From a more practical perspective, an integrated analysis of contributory factors may focus upon the various trade-offs that need to be taken into account in the actual process of system design (e.g., see Norman, 1983; 1986). Enhancing one attribute of an interface (e.g., displaying more helpful information) may have associated costs (it takes time to present and occupies VDU space). Viewed in this way there may be no clear resolution of a design problem, only trade-offs among alternative options.

Given the diversity of methods and theoretical concepts, as well as the broad range of practical issues associated with human-computer interaction, there are many different ways of pursuing research in applied cognitive psychology. The potential pay-offs are substantial. Sophisticated empirical methods, principled knowledge of the characteristics of user-system interactions and applicable models of user cognition could do much to enhance system designs and streamline their development. In moving towards these practical objectives, significant insights may also emerge concerning more fundamental theoretical issues, thereby also enhancing the core discipline of cognitive psychology itself.

1.3 *Key questions for this chapter*

The present chapter is set against the background of an interdisciplinary research context and the challenges of establishing systematic behavioural principles that encompass practical concerns. Its primary purpose will be to assess the contributions that can and are being made by applied cognitive psychology to the study of human-computer interaction. The blurring of boundaries between disciplines and between theoretical and practical issues means that the assessment will inevitably encompass a range of concepts and techniques. There is also a vast amount of research activity.

Hence, the assessment must be restricted to illustrations of the various types of contribution.

Many of the issues associated with design concepts and the application of behavioural methodologies within the development process are covered in Anderson and Olson (1985) and by other chapters in this book (e.g., Shneiderman; Shackel). Here the assessment will focus upon the use of interactive systems by those who are not specialists in a computer discipline. It will also concentrate upon two core questions: What progress is being made within applied cognitive psychology towards contributing a principled understanding of the phenomena or system use? What are the prospects for the systematic application of that principled understanding?

2. The visions

2.1 *Alternative objectives*

Cognitive psychologists actually turned their attention to the problems of human-computer interaction almost as soon as the technology became available to them. Over and above the immediate objectives of a particular study, most of the researchers had some broader vision concerning the potential of their concepts and methods.

Some concentrated upon the traditional goals of human factors. The measurement of performance with an appropriately sampled population of users could help choose among alternative interfaces with considerably better reliability than a designer's intuitions (e.g., see Ledgard *et al.*, 1980). Others were concerned with using behavioural evidence to formulate guidelines and principles which could be more generally applied early in the design process (e.g., see Black and Sebrechts, 1981). Systematic analysis also offered the prospect of potentially powerful alternatives to traditional emphases on empiricism and guidelines.

Such alternatives included the possibility of using formal methods to represent alternative interface designs in a way that would reveal their overall complexity or the presence of internal inconsistencies (e.g., Reisner, 1982). Others advocated using specifically psychological assumptions to model and predict key attributes of user behaviour — such as the time it would take users to learn a system or to perform specific tasks (e.g., Card *et al.*, 1983). For many of these approaches to apply, system and task specifications had to be predefined. For these, the visions remained essentially evaluative in nature. For others the vision included a more creative component. If cognitive concepts and methods were applied to furnish a deep understanding of the problems experienced by users, then that understanding could be used much more directly — to "invent" new types of interfaces that resolve the problems (e.g., see Landauer, 1985). A representative sample of these approaches will be examined in subsequent sections.

2.2 *An organising schema*

Before considering research achievements, it is helpful to have some kind of organising schema that can encompass key points of the different visions. In very general terms applied cognitive psychology can be viewed as bringing an empirical and conceptual "toolkit" to bear on the problems of human-computer interaction. Like any toolkit, its constituent elements fulfil different functions. One way of organising these elements into a broader research strategy is illustrated in Figure 1 (from Hammond and Barnard, 1984).

Some of the empirical methods focus upon observation and the acquisition of problem-defining data (cf. the "field" studies of Figure 1). They enable key phenomena of system use or user cognition to be charted. The problems associated with existing systems are, for example, frequently studied by obtaining session protocols of users attempting a realistic sample of tasks. Such information may be supplemented by measures of user perceived difficulties as assessed from their verbal comments or via assessment of their preferences. Such techniques are equally well suited to the exploration of the problems faced by designers as well as those faced by users. Alternatively, issues may initially be explored by studying users' basic conceptualisations within a task domain.

Explorational data of this type can fulfil both practical and research functions. They can, of course, be used to provide feedback to designers concerning usability. They can also provide a rich hunting ground for ideas and insight concerning the more basic causes of difficulties. Gradual accumulation of patterns of difficulties provide important signposts as to "what really matters" in human-computer interaction. This in turn helps to formulate hypotheses and to frame the requirements that our analytic and conceptual methods must meet (the "formal" tools of Figure 1).

Many of the more formal analytic methods can also have an exploratory character. Such is the case, for example, with many forms of task analysis. However, once such analyses are initially framed, or preliminary hypotheses formed on the basis of observational evidence, their ramifications can be tested in the laboratory using more classic experimental procedures and designs. Such tests may involve truly interactive systems or simulations of them. Alternatively, they may take key variables and study their consequences in tasks that are closely allied to those that might be accomplished with a computer system. If closely modelled upon a particular application, such studies can furnish a direct input to the design process. However, where variables are systematically manipulated they primarily serve to help define

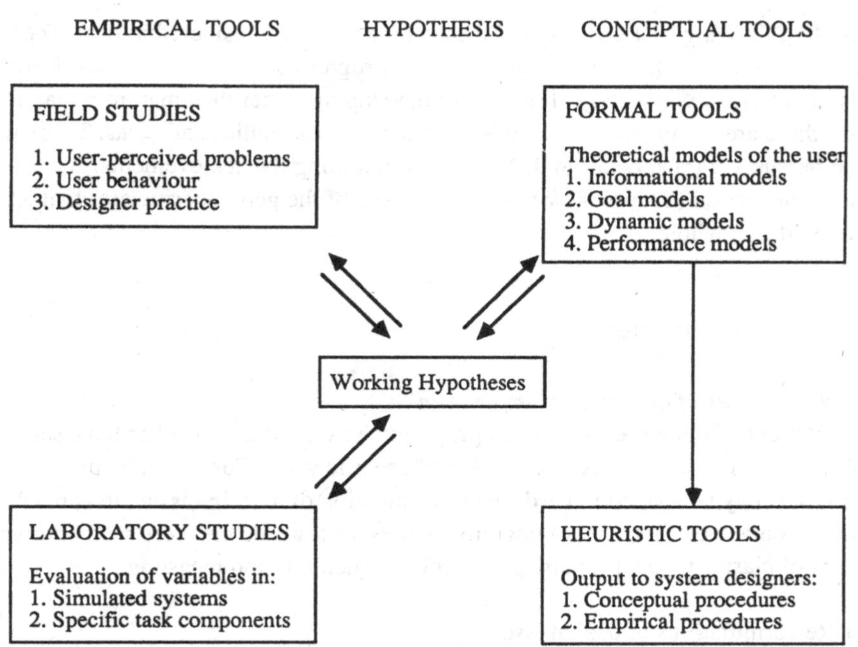

Figure 1. The toolkit organised into a research strategy (from Hammond and Barnard, 1984).

and delineate relationships between attributes of users, tasks and systems and attributes of performance. In short, such studies help us to understand the phenomena of system use.

Equally, those studies provide a basis for evaluating whether or not our more conceptual and analytic methods are accurately capturing and predicting what users are likely to do. Once such relationships are validated, the wider enterprise can really talk about heuristic engineering tools: conceptual and empirical procedures that can actually be used in system design and development. Naturally, the schema shown in Figure 1 does not accurately capture all the different research visions. The elements of the "toolkit" can be structured and used in a variety of ways. Research achievements can nevertheless be considered in terms of how our working hypotheses have been shaped (1) by exploratory studies; (2) by more conceptual analyses; (3) by experimental investigations of potential principles; and in terms of (4) the prospects for translating the products of such research into truly applicable tools.

In the following sections, each of these points will be considered in turn. The achievements will be presented in terms of the progress being made by the different kinds of activities. Since they all represent developing rather than mature research topics, there are many possible criticisms of the various studies and ideas. These will not be pursued in great detail in the context of outlining the achievements. A subsequent section (Section 4) will consider some of the general criticisms that apply to the field as a whole.

3. The achievements

3.1 *Achievements of exploratory empiricism*

In the context of longer term research programmes, exploratory studies have served to shape working hypotheses in a number of specific ways. For example, those hypotheses may be shaped towards the reformulation of a design issue, towards further scientific clarification of cognitive issues, or towards the more methodological concern of clarifying the properties of particular methods and measures.

3.1.1 Re-formulations of design issues

Work carried out by a group currently at Bell Communications Research (e.g., see Furnas *et al.*, 1982; 1983; Gomez and Lochbaum, 1984; Landauer, 1987) provides an excellent example of the reformulation of a design issue. One problem on which this group focused involved the way in which people name and categorise things: a problem of central importance to the design of information retrieval systems and command languages. The problem of naming and categorising was explored using a range of empirical methods such as name/descriptor generation, category assignment and sorting tasks. These techniques were applied across such diverse domains as text-editing, the contents of "yellow page" directories, cooking, and goods "wanted/for sale".

The common theme to emerge across studies, users and domains concerned the inherent variability in the way in which people name things. People can and do use a variety of different names or descriptions when referring to the same concept. The empirical data obtained in these studies added more than the simple identification of the problem. First, the variability could be quantified. The likelihood of any two people using the same name to refer spontaneously to the same concept ranged from a paltry 0.07 to a meagre 0.18. This reveals the likely extent of the problems for standard keyword retrieval systems which rely on the user generating one or only a few names that are the same as those chosen by the original designer of the system. Second, statistical simulations based upon the data were used to explore the probable success of alternative accessing schemes. Where target information could only be referred to by a single name, the probability of first try success was low (10–20%). However, the simulated probability of retrieval success could be dramatically improved (e.g., to 75-85%) by multiple "aliasing" — where the system accepts many, not necessarily unique, names for target information (Furnas *et al.*, 1983).

The same research group then went on to examine experimentally the issue of whether or not such enriched search vocabularies would actually enhance performance without an unacceptable cost in terms of the system retrieving many non-target items. Gomez and Lochbaum (1984) report one such study in which they systematically manipulated the richness of the search vocabulary with a database of 188 recipes drawn from cookbooks. As the size of the vocabulary was increased, so successful retrieval increased from some 12% to some 73%. Furthermore, the enriched vocabularies required fewer entries on average to reach the target than did the leaner vocabularies.

Another example of exploratory research with similar properties is provided by an IBM research group. Here the general problems of learning to use word processing systems were the focus of concern (e.g., see Mack, Lewis and Carroll, 1983; Carroll, 1984). In this case an initial study was conducted to identify the kinds of problems that "first time" users encountered. A small sample of users were asked to learn basic text entry and revision tasks by following a self-study training manual. While carrying out the tasks, users were asked to "think aloud" — to verbalise what they were trying to do and what they thought was going on. Records were preserved of both the explicit user-system exchanges and the users verbal commentary.

On the basis of these qualitative data, the investigators provide a rough taxonomy of the problems. Many of the difficulties could be attributed to a lack of very basic knowledge and the consequential difficulties of interpreting what the concepts and jargon mean. They report one user thinking that she might be "the printer". Similarly, users often did not appear to know what was relevant; they made *ad hoc* interpretations and inferences on the basis of very limited information; they generalised knowledge from their experience of typewriting; they assumed consistency of similar operations; they had trouble following directions and in gaining benefit from the help system and so on. Further examples of the individual categories need not be pursued here — they are well illustrated in Mack *et al.* (1983). Carroll (1984) concludes: "Learning in this situation appears to be very frustrating. System interfaces are inscrutable to the novice and the accompanying training materials provide little help in penetrating these mysteries."

The more general picture concerning user cognition during learning is evident from the taxonomic descriptions themselves. These make frequent reference to interpretation, assumptions, inference, and generalisation. Users were not slavishly following instructions, they were highly active participants in the learning process. Neither the training manual nor the interface provided appropriate support for active learners. In consequence, the researchers went on to explore ways of achieving more effective support.

In one series of studies, they examined alternatives to conventional documentation. The alternatives included "guided exploration cards" and "minimal manuals" (see Carroll, 1984). For example, the minimal manual drastically cut the amount of information presented; oriented the instructional material towards real tasks (rather than exercising facilities or functions); provided for more learner initiative (e.g., learners are left to explore deletions and insertions in a letter "on their own"); and provided greater error recovery information. Empirical verification of this approach showed that such manuals could be considerably more effective than their more conventional counterparts both in terms of acquiring basic skills and in terms of transfer to more advanced skills.

In a related series of studies, this same research group also examined a possibility for reducing initial learning difficulties. One way of protecting an active, exploratory user from making errors and getting into difficulties is to reduce the number of ways in which they can go wrong. This was achieved in a "training wheels" word processing system by initially disabling a whole range of functions required to carry out the more sophisticated tasks. In this system, the "first time" user only has access to very basic functionality. The more complex functions remained in the interface itself — as menu items in their appropriate contexts. However, if selected, the user was advised that that function was not available. Experimental studies were conducted in which basic tasks were learned on the training wheels system or on the complete commercial system. As with the minimal manual, the data suggested that the training wheels approach saved time and facilitated learning (again, see Carroll, 1984).

The achievements of this general approach are very real, whether applied to enriched keyword vocabularies, training manuals, or systems tailored for first time users. In each case, a mismatch between current design practice and users' natural predispositions has been identified and represented in terms of a general property of user cognition — variability in naming, or the active nature of human learning. In each case, the design problem is reformulated from the perspective of user cognition and the potential advantages of a possible solution are supported by empirical evidence. The "solutions" actually evaluated are not, of course, commercial products. They nevertheless stand in marked contrast to design "intuition" and constitute a clear demonstration of the potential benefits that could accrue were such solutions to be actively pursued in development projects.

3.1.2 Clarification of cognitive issues

Exploratory research has also helped to shape hypotheses primarily concerned with the further clarification of specific cognitive issues. For example, Hammond *et al.* (1980) studied users of an early relational database system which relied upon a highly notational command language. As with the Mack *et al.* (1983) study, the initial methodology involved obtaining session logs and "thinking aloud" protocols while users tried to solve a series of pre-set problems. Again, the investigators developed a taxonomy of errors and difficulties. Users frequently had problems with the form and content of the command language. One specific exchange was:

user types:	*t <- avg(age,people)
system responds:	age is an unset block

In this case, the command language required the arguments to be specified in a particular order — the block of data referred to had to be specified before the attribute over which the averaging was to be done. This kind of error could potentially have been due to users simply converting a natural language representation of the problem (I want the average age of the people) into a command string. However, such errors occur in the context of a set of command argument structures and in the context of other representations relevant to the particular instance of command entry (e.g., information on the VDU).

Having identified possible factors that could contribute to this class of error, Barnard *et al.* (1981) went on to explore experimentally their respective contributions to learning and performance in general. Several schemes for sequencing arguments were compared. In two schemes a pivotal argument always occurred in a constant position. In two other schemes the position of that pivotal argument varied. In these schemes the arguments were ordered in such a way as to be compatible or incompatible with users' natural language biases.

Three of these schemes led to roughly equivalent overall performance across initial learning. One scheme enhanced performance. That scheme involved placing the pivotal argument in a particular position (the first element) within the argument string. Positional consistency did not demonstrably enhance performance with the pivotal argument elsewhere in the string (i.e., the second element). Incompatibilities with natural language biases did not appear to retard learning and only contributed to argument reversal errors when the position of the pivotal argument varied from command to command.

Irrespective of the particular scheme for ordering arguments, performance was adversely affected when an information field presented argument identities on the VDU in an order that was incompatible with their ordering in command entry. A subsequent experimental study (Hammond, Barnard *et al.*, 1987) went on to show that the learning of argument structures was also influenced by the explicit prompting of command operations and by properties of the names used to refer to those operations.

The achievements and potential benefits of exploratory research of this kind are more indirect than those of the two preceding illustrations. These more factorial studies provide indications of the conditions under which particular variables can influence performance. They also provide some clues as to the relative magnitude of influences on user behaviour. However, the link to full blown designs with much greater functionality and richer tasks is often unclear. With larger command sets or different detailed constraints for argument ordering users may well behave differently.

What such studies achieve is twofold. First, knowing about the boundary conditions under which particular phenomena occur provides constraints for our working hypotheses concerning user cognition. As such constraints emerge over a series of studies they help us refine and reformulate our ideas as to what really contributes to error or ease of learning. Second, the nature of the phenomena enable us to pinpoint and illustrate how and why very general principles, such as maintaining consistency or natural language compatibility, may not necessarily be expected to provide the kinds of benefit often assumed by designers.

3.1.3 Methods and measures

The broader value of exploratory research clearly depends upon the properties of the methods used and upon the way in which qualitative and quantitative data are interpreted. The collection of "thinking aloud" protocols in conjunction with session logs, which played a part in two of the illustrations given above, is now a popular exploratory method. Its use, however, is not unproblematic. As a technique, it is highly laborious. In consequence, data are usually only collected for a relatively small number of tasks and users. This raises issues about the representativeness of such qualitative data. In addition, when users are reporting their thoughts verbally, they may not be performing the tasks in the same way as they would without concurrent verbalisation (e.g., Ericsson and Simon, 1980).

Such methodological concerns have led investigators to refine the techniques either to reduce the overall amount of effort involved (e.g., Hammond *et al.*, 1984), or to acquire other forms of verbal protocols. For example, O'Malley, Draper and Riley (1984) asked pairs of users openly to discuss problems during interactive sessions. This kind of technique provides enriched qualitative data concerning users' current concepts, rationales and explanations of system functioning. In contrast, Barnard, Wilson and MacLean (1986) discouraged verbalisation during actual interactive performance. What users could verbalise about the system was separately and quantitatively assessed using a different technique in which users described and explained pictures of system states to an experimenter.

In the Barnard *et al.* (1986) study, all users were queried on the same system states at two stages of experience. The contents of the protocols were quantified using techniques from the text memory literature in cognitive psychology. In this way the development of users' articulatable knowledge could be assessed and related to performance. As learning progressed the measures indicated that users' descriptions contained an increasing number of true statements about the system. Furthermore, this correlated with performance. Those users who performed well also verbalised a greater number of true statements about system operation. In marked contrast, the number of false statements about system operation did not decrease over the course of learning studied. Although apparently unrelated to overall improvements in performance, the pattern of false statements did appear related to the errors made during interactive performance. This led the authors to conjecture different relations between user knowledge and performance measures.

Other relationships among different "measures" have also been the subject of exploratory research. One major problem in relating design issues to research information is that alternative behavioural measures can tell different stories. This is often the case with measures of performance and measures of preference.

In one recent example, user preference and performance was explored in the context of different methods for entering data into a spreadsheet (MacLean, Barnard and Wilson, 1985). One method for entering data relied entirely upon the use of a mouse to point to each successive cell into which data had to be entered. An alternative method enabled the cursor to move automatically from cell to cell in a row or column. This method required a number of menu selections to determine the mode of cursor movement. This latter method required time and effort to set up but then saved on the number of mouse movements required during row or column entry. On this basis it would be efficient for entering large tables of data. However, for small tables the time cost of the additional menu selections should not be worthwhile.

MacLean *et al.* asked a sample of users to practise each method and then allowed them to make their own choice. This was done across tables of increasing size. To accrue maximum benefit from the alternative methods available, users should switch from the mouse method to the menu method when it becomes temporally efficient to do so. However, when the trade-off function was plotted, it was found that users tended to choose the menu method for the smaller sizes of table in spite of the fact that they were actually faster with the mouse method.

As with factorial studies aimed at clarifying cognitive issues, the potential benefits of exploratory studies of methods and measures are indirect. They are nevertheless of crucial importance: they help us to understand the nature of evidence and how it may relate to design issues. As with the uncovering of different relations among articulatable knowledge, overall performance and error (Barnard *et al.*, 1986), novel methodological techniques can provide a new perspective on an otherwise unclear problem. Likewise, understanding the relationship between performance and preference can help assess the validity of particular assumptions concerning, for example, user modelling. The MacLean *et al.* data queries the safeness of the assumption (Card *et al.*, 1983) that users will choose temporally efficient methods.

3.2 *The achievements of analytic approaches*

Empirical explorations of user performance help to define "what matters" in human-computer interactions; to delineate phenomena; and to strengthen methodologies. However, the systematisation of our empirical knowledge requires conceptual analyses of the properties of systems, tasks and users. Many "conceptual frameworks" are currently under development (e.g., see Olson, 1987). Here, a distinction will be made between those frameworks that focus on the knowledge requirement of tasks, and those that focus on the cognitive processes that occur during the execution of tasks. In a richly interdisciplinary context, broad distinctions obviously oversimplify the true state of affairs. Individual frameworks typically differ in their detailed objectives and in the precise way in which concepts are used. The distinction between knowledge- and process-based approaches nevertheless enables some of the major contrasts and similarities to be drawn out.

3.2.1 Knowledge based analyses

Since early systems more often than not made use of artificial command languages, several investigators made use of linguistic techniques to describe the ideal knowledge that a user would require to operate a system without error. Among the pioneers in this area were Reisner (1981; 1982), Moran (1981), and Payne and Green (1983).

The actual notations proposed by these investigators have very different properties. Reisner (1982), for example, proposed a kind of "psychological" BNF (Backus-Naur Form[1]). This distinguished overt actions that a user must perform ("input" actions) and mental operations ("cognitive" actions) associated with their execution. Key characteristics of user performance were assumed to be related to the number of terminal symbols in the "sentences" of the grammar and the overall number of grammatical rules required to describe dialogues.

Similar assumptions were made by Payne and Green (1983) in the development of their task action grammar (TAG). They argued that the kind of BNF form adopted by Reisner failed to capture high level regularities in command languages that users

---

[1] Backus-Naur Form is a notation for representing the syntax of a programming language.

were likely to abstract. They therefore proposed a two-level grammatical model which distinguished sets and rules. The sets represented entities with common properties in the relevant domain; while the rules determined how sets of elements could legally be combined into sequences. The authors argued that this was not only more realistic from a cognitive viewpoint but also that it was technically more economic. Systems could generally be described with fewer rules than would be required in a BNF grammar.

Moran's (1981) command language grammar (CLG) was developed to enable designers to separate different levels of system knowledge and their relationships. It distinguishes three components. The first is a conceptual component which represents task and semantic levels of description. A communications component distinguishes a syntactic level and an interaction level; while a physical component distinguishes low level considerations such as spatial layout and device requirements. The grammar specifies how symbols at one level of description are mapped onto lower level symbols. In this framework it is not assumed that users necessarily require all these levels to operate a system — they could rely on knowledge at an interaction level. However, without an elaborated conceptual component users would get into difficulties when something goes wrong.

Other notational techniques with similar characteristics have been developed to analyse the properties of tasks. Moran (1983) has himself proposed another form of analysis (ETIT — mapping from the External Task to the Internal Task) in which notations are used to represent an external task space (e.g., in terms of entities in documents such as paragraphs and words) and an internal task space (in system internal terms such as lines and character strings). The complexity of the mapping from one form of representation to the other is presumed to be related to ease of learning or of transfer from one system to another. In a different vein, Johnson and his colleagues (Johnson, Diaper and Long, 1984; Johnson, 1985) have utilised a form of action-object grammar to describe what people need to know about computer related tasks.

Perhaps the most influential form of task notation for human-computer interaction is the GOMS (Goals, Operators, Methods and Selection rules) approach proposed by Card *et al.* (1983). In this approach, high level goals, such as "edit manuscript", are decomposed into lower level goals, such as "delete word". Operators are elementary perceptual, motor or cognitive acts which change the task environment or a user's mental state. Methods are the procedures which must be followed to achieve individual goals. Selection rules are heuristics for resolving conflicts where more than one method is available. Explicit specification of these elements can be used to model how long it will take an expert to perform the tasks. As with the hierarchy of rules in CLG, GOMS models can be constructed at several levels of detail.

This general approach has recently been developed into production system simulations of the knowledge users need to acquire to support error free expert performance (e.g., Kieras and Polson, 1985; Polson, 1987). As with other approaches, properties of the set of production rules required to simulate a user's how-to-do-it knowledge are utilised to predict learning and transfer effects (e.g., see Polson, Muncher and Engelbeck, 1986). Ease of learning is viewed in terms of the "cognitive complexity" of the production rule representations that need to be "acquired"; while ease of transfer can be assessed in terms of the number of common elements shared by pre- and post-transfer knowledge.

Several of the formal approaches outlined above are given a much more detailed treatment in this book by Ziegler and Bullinger. They also consider their relative strengths and limitations. Their most obvious strength is that the notations make explicit otherwise informal constructs like the consistency or complexity of an interface design. Since specification forms a potential basis for assessing such designs, showing how this can be done is itself a considerable achievement.

As representations designed to predict key aspects of usability, their main limitation is their tendency to assume relatively simple relations between "knowledge" and user "behaviour". They also tend to focus upon rather idealised, error free, expert knowledge. Typically, the analyses make little reference to the kinds of mental activities that are involved in task execution — such as interpretation or problem solving. Likewise, very real constraints on human cognition, such as memory retrieval and the limited capacity of mental processing, tend to play only a minor part in the derivation of predictions. These aspects are the focus of attention for process based approaches.

3.2.2 Process based approaches

As a part of their general effort to provide a scientific basis for the study of human-computer interaction, Card *et al.* (1983), adopted a particular perspective on the constraints on human information processing. This they encapsulated in their "model human information processor". The model distinguished different processors and memory systems (see Figure 2). Each was assigned relevant quantitative parameters such as cycle times or capacities. These parameters were abstracted from the relevant psychological literature.

The model provided a general background against which their calculational methods could be developed. Indeed, these investigators gave a number of simple illustrations of the ways in which such parameter estimates could be used to work through fragmentary components of user behaviour. It is not difficult to see how a framework of this sort can be used to guide the construction of performance models concerning the temporal attributes of expert skills. However, it is difficult to relate it

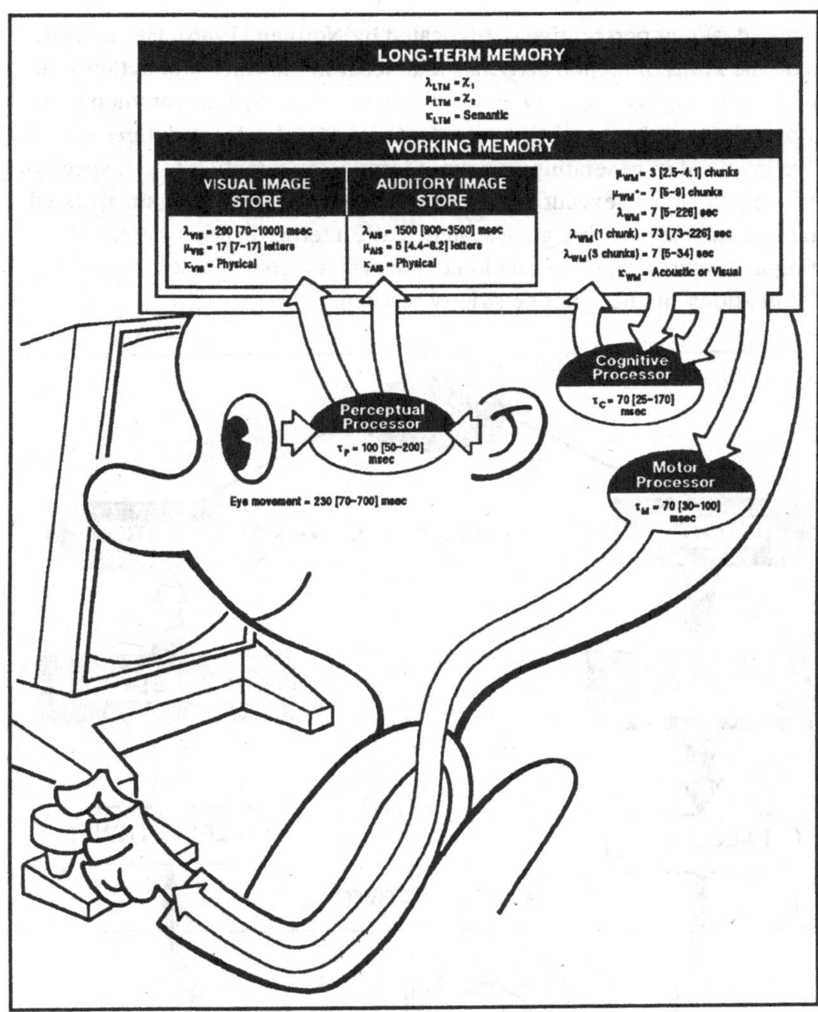

Figure 2: The model human information processor (from Card *et al.*, 1983).

directly to more qualitative aspects of cognition — such as how users manipulate their representations of knowledge. In fact, subsequent developments of the GOMS approach have tended to carry over only the more general assumptions concerning limited capacity working memory (e.g., Polson and Kieras, 1984) or the kinds of parameters required in memory access (e.g., John and Newell, 1987).

A rather different perspective is advocated by Norman (1986). His analysis focuses on the kinds of mental activities that occur in the control of action at an interface. Seven stages of activity are currently distinguished. In common with most other approaches, goals serve a pivotal rôle. Once a goal is formed, three further stages are involved in generating an action: forming an intention to act; specifying the action sequence; and executing it. The effect of that action is again assessed through three stages: perceiving the system state, interpreting that state; and evaluating that interpretation in relation to the original goal. These stages are viewed as approximations and need not be strictly seriated.

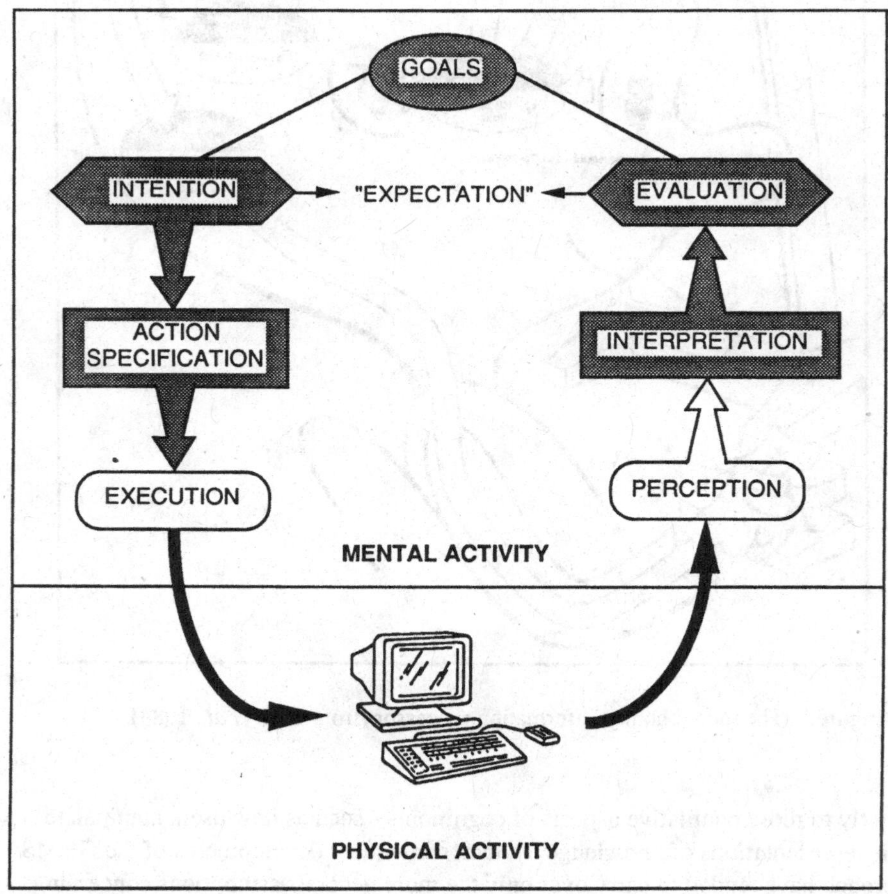

Figure 3: Seven stages of user activity (from Norman, 1986).

Norman's framework is not quantitatively predictive. Rather, it provides a basis for representing and understanding the cognitive consequences of particular designs. Menus, for example, can be thought of as devices that assist intention formation and action specification. Requirements for successive menu selections may nevertheless slow down execution in comparison to direct command entry. Likewise, it provides a clear conceptualisation of the potential benefits of direct manipulation interfaces. The use of iconic representations and pointing devices serve to reduce "the gulfs" between the system and the user. Users are directly acting upon representations of concepts in the task domain without requirements in action specification for command names or indirect menu selections. Similarly, where the consequences of an action are directly visible interpretation and evaluation are facilitated.

A framework that combines basic features of the two process based approaches outlined above has recently been proposed by Barnard (1987). This approach assumes a distributed architecture for human cognition with substantial capabilities for parallel processing of information (Figure 4). On this view different subsystems of cognition contain explicit processes that map from one kind of mental code to another (e.g., from a raw visual representation to an object based code). These processes embody the procedural knowledge required to execute the mapping. They also have access to declarative representations of information stored in "image records" (episodic memory structures) associated with each subsystem. On this view, there is no general purpose working memory. Cognition is viewed as being dynamically controlled via representations passed among subsystems.

The explicit decomposition of the memory and processing resources of cognition enabled Barnard to define a form of cognitive task analysis. It was assumed that key attributes of user behaviour could be inferred from a description of the way in which cognitive resources would function during task execution. The description incorporates components that refer both to knowledge and to information processing constraints:

User Behaviour <— Fn(Process Configuration and Procedural Knowledge and Record Contents and Dynamic Control)

In addition, different phases of cognitive activity, such as command entry or the interpretation of system states, are viewed as drawing upon different process configurations and memory resources. As with other approaches, this implies a family of models. In this case, members of the family describe the phases of activity that occur during task execution in a manner not dissimilar from Norman's overall view.

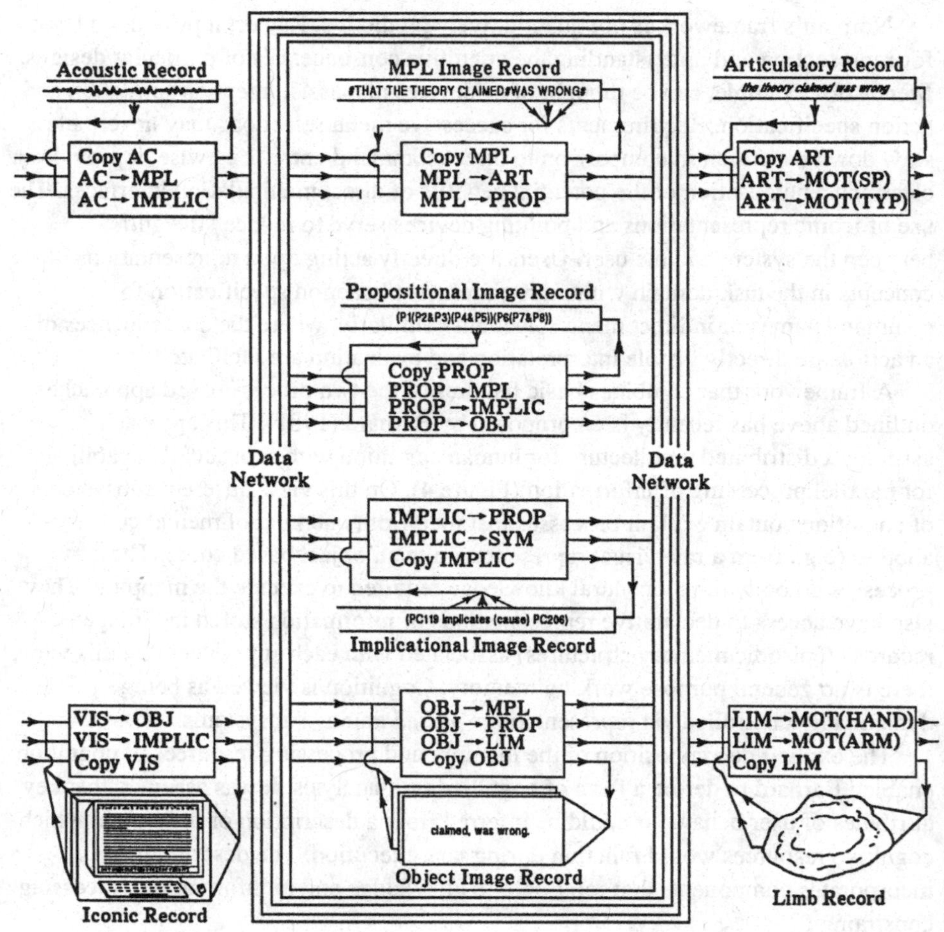

Figure 4. The interacting cognitive subsystems framework (from Barnard, 1987).

This approach is also intended to be predictive. Common patterns of mental activity are assumed to give rise to similar patterns of user behaviour. Such prediction requires principled relationships to be defined among the elements of the analysis and Barnard (1987) has proposed a number of such principles on the basis of experimental research on interactive dialogues. An illustrative example of the derivation of such principles will be given in the next section.

The process-based approaches illustrated here all attempt to capture, in an approximate manner, one or more aspects of what is going on in the user's head. In this respect, they complement the knowledge-based approaches described earlier. The key assumptions concerning user behaviour tend to be concentrated upon processes and their temporal or substantive properties. The assumptions concerning knowledge representation tend to be captured in a far more approximate way than is the case with grammars or production system representations. In effect, the individual analytic techniques are committed to different trade-offs in the depth and breadth of their coverage.

The advantages and disadvantages of the various different trade-offs is, of course, a matter for debate. However, user cognition is undoubtedly complex and it has often been pointed out that no single analytic technique will be sufficiently rich to capture all relevant features of user cognition (cf. Morton *et al.*, 1979). Against this background, the systematic development of a whole range of principled approaches can be regarded as a healthy state of affairs (cf. Norman and Draper, 1986). In contrast to the more classic style of theory typical of cognitive psychology, these approaches are making very real progress towards finding ways of specifying approximate models of systems, tasks and users.

3.3 *The achievements of experimental investigations of principles*

The experimental literature in human-computer interaction is now substantial. A significant proportion of this work has been directed at evaluating general issues associated with design alternatives. One example of an empirical "issue" is whether a few menus with many items are more effective than many menus each involving a few items (e.g., see Miller, 1981; Snowberry, Parkinson and Sisson, 1983). An earlier section (3.1) outlined other examples where experimental techniques were used to evaluate potential design alternatives (Gomez and Lochbaum, 1984; Carroll, 1984); as well as one example of experimental techniques being used to explore more cognitively oriented issues (Barnard *et al.*, 1981).

If our understanding of user behaviour is to advance in a systematic manner, then experimental research must go beyond the empirical facts to explicit statements of principles that can be generalised to new settings. For this to occur prototype principles and models need to be tested. Since the emphasis of the previous section was on the general properties of the different frameworks, experimental assessments of their predictions were not discussed. Indeed, as yet, the empirical ramifications of only some of those frameworks have been explored. The largest concentration of these concern various derivatives of the GOMS family of models (e.g., see Card *et al.*, 1983; Polson, 1987; John and Newell, 1987). There is also some data for the more grammatical formulations (e.g., see Payne and Green, 1983; Payne, 1984).

Where such assessments have been carried out, it is generally reported that the data fit the predictions of the model with reasonable accuracy. However, it is important to note that most of this type of empirical work is carried out by the originators of the model under test — and they get to choose the "testing ground". Where models have been evaluated by third parties, the fits can be less than impressive. Such was the case with an independent assessment (Allen and Scerbo, 1983) of the "keystroke level model" of Card *et al.* (1983).

As the various models evolve, it can be expected that many debates will focus upon concerns with the predictive accuracy and scope of the various modelling approaches. Rather than pursuing such detailed issues here, the present section will simply provide two illustrations in which experimental research is focused on an issue of principle. In the first illustration, classic principles from experimental psychology are applied to a setting in human-computer interaction. In the second illustration, evidence obtained in human-computer interaction is itself used to derive a principle.

3.3.1 An application of classic principles

In the opening sections of this chapter, it was pointed out that links between classic laboratory psychology and complex applied problems can be difficult to establish. Although they are relatively rare, there are clear cases where known principles of behaviour have been found to have utility in analysing problems in human-computer interaction. One such instance concerns principles that govern human choice and movement time. Indeed, such principles played a substantial rôle in the kinds of analyses advocated by Card *et al.* (1983). The present illustration concerns the application of principles to the depth/breadth issue in menu searches (Landauer and Nachbar, 1985).

In selecting items from a menu, users are making a choice among a specific number of alternatives. They must also carry out a movement to execute that choice. Hick's law governs the relationship between choice time and the number of alternatives; while Fitts' Law governs movement time as a function of target size and movement distance. Both of these laws have a logarithmic form:

Hick's law (choice reaction time) $T = c + k\log_2 b$

where b is the number of equally likely alternatives and c and k represent constants, and:

Fitts' Law (movement time) $T = c' + k'\log_2 d/w$

where d represents the distance, w the width of the target and c' and k' are again constants.

Landauer and Nachbar examined the applicability of these laws for menu choice where the user made a selection by pointing at a touch sensitive screen. This is an ingenious setting because the application of Fitts' law can be directly related to the number of menu options. The distance from the screen (d) is a constant under these circumstances and as the number of menu options available on the screen increases so the space available for each response sensitive area will reduce. Thus, both movement time and decision time could be expected to be a logarithmic function of the number of alternatives — or more conventionally, the branching factor in menu search.

Landauer and Nachbar report two experiments in which the depth and breadth menu searches were examined for a database of 4096 items. In the experiments, each menu contained 2, 4, 8 or 16 choices. In one case the targets were integer numbers; in the other they were alphabetically organised words. Pre-terminal choices were made by touching a sensitive band on the screen in which either an integer or alphabetic range was specified. In both cases the mean touch time per screen proved to be a linear function of the log of the number of alternatives in each panel. Their data are reproduced in Figure 5.

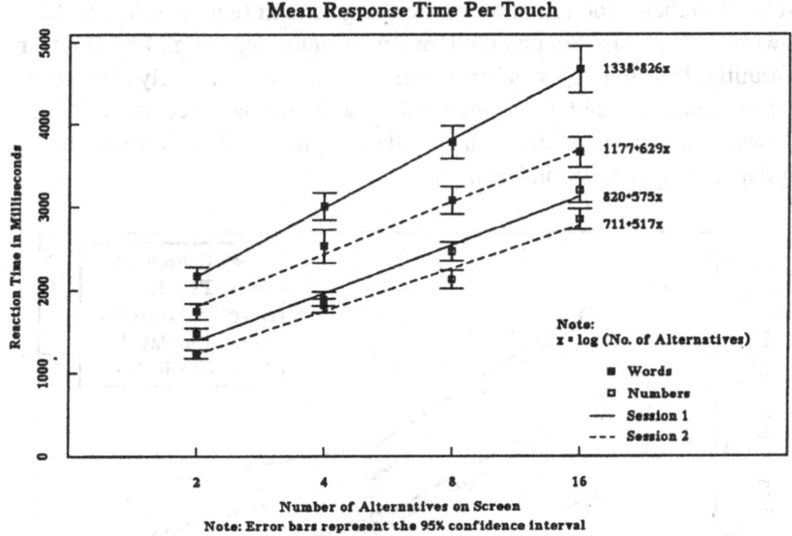

Figure 5. The logarithmic fit obtained by Landauer and Nachbar (1985).

Thus, in this setting, both laws applied. There must have been no substantial contribution from other processes, such as perceptual scanning, that was other than a constant or a log function of the number of alternatives. In terms of both mean and total search times the depth/breadth trade-off could be resolved in favour of breadth.

Of course, in this instance there could be no ambiguity in the assignment of a target digit or word to a particular range. With fuzzier categories of information (such as those characteristic of viewdata systems) other decisional processes may come into play. The generality of such results therefore requires further empirical examination.

3.3.2 From experimental evidence to principles

Demonstrations of the application of known principles seem unlikely to form a basis for resolving many of the issues in human-computer interaction. Novel approximate principles need to be sought. In developing an approach to cognitive task analysis (see section 3.2.2), Barnard (1987) attempted to define principled relationships between cognitive activity and overt performance on the basis of experimental evidence. Some of the principles were motivated on the basis of a particular experiment concerned with the learning of command namesets.

The experiment (Grudin and Barnard, 1984) examined the learning of five different namesets for text editing tasks. The namesets involved semantically specific names (e.g., delete); abbreviations of those names (dlt); known words whose meaning was unrelated to their function in the text editing context (e.g., parole); novel "pseudowords" (e.g., ragole); and random consonant strings (e.g., FNM). Over the course of initial learning, the specific names were learned relatively efficiently. The abbreviations and unrelated words incurred some performance costs; while the pseudowords and consonant strings incurred even greater costs. Representative learning data are reproduced in Figure 6.

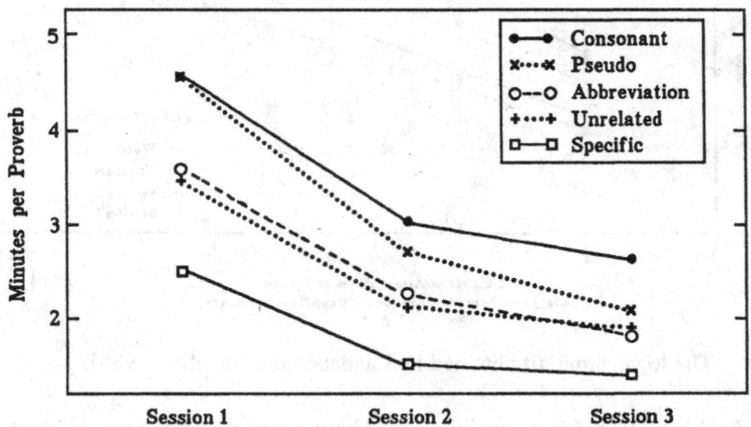

Figure 6. The mean editing times for learning the five command name sets (from Grudin and Barnard, 1984).

Barnard (1987) considered these data in relation to the demands placed upon the individual mental processes incorporated within his theoretical framework (see Figure 4). In order to issue a command name, separate processes must be recruited to map a semantic representation of the command operation onto its surface structure form (i.e., the name to be entered) and that surface structure form must be mapped onto motor actions for the control of keystroking. It was assumed that if individual processes do not embody appropriate procedural knowledge for effecting these mappings, then the dynamic control of action requires access to memory representations or inferential processing. These require additional information processing transactions among the subsystems of cognition. These extra transactions take time and increase the cognitive workload.

The Grudin and Barnard data suggested that the extra load could be approximated by assuming a principled relationship between the number of processes for which new procedural knowledge needed to be acquired and the complexity of dynamic control required within the human information processing mechanism. For the specific command names, it could reasonably be assumed that users would possess appropriate procedural knowledge both for the mapping from meaning to form and for the mapping from form to the required keystroke sequence.

With the abbreviations and unrelated words procedural knowledge would be absent for one processing component. In the case of abbreviations, procedural knowledge would be in place for mapping from meaning to the form of the full command word, but not for the precise sequence of characters to be keystroked. In contrast, with the unrelated words, the mapping from meaning to form would not be proceduralised. However, since the actual lexical items were known, the mapping from form to keystroke sequence would be proceduralised. With the pseudowords and consonant strings neither form of mental mapping would be known.

The resulting principles were specified in terms of general relationships between process configurations, procedural knowledge, record contents and the dynamic control of human processing activity (see section 3.2.2). Namely, if all elements in a configuration of processes required to support a phase of cognitive activity are fully proceduralised, then output can be controlled relatively automatically from the contents of a single image record. Where one process within a required configuration does not embody appropriate procedural knowledge then output cannot be controlled automatically and extra information processing transactions are required to control action. Where two (or more) processes are unproceduralised then many extra information processing transactions will be required.

These principles essentially account for the differences in initial performance depicted in Figure 6. However, performance with the pseudoword vocabulary improves faster than that for the consonant strings. In order to account for this pattern it is necessary to call upon another principle through which memory retrieval is enhanced by structural descriptions of possible lexical forms. The kinds of command names actually studied by Grudin and Barnard can be regarded as somewhat archaic when compared to more recent text editing systems. However, the important point is that the principles proposed are not restricted to that form of dialogue. They are stated in a very general form that can equally well be applied to the analysis of iconic interfaces or as yet undeveloped forms of dialogue style.

3.4 *Theory as a means to pragmatic tools*

In moving towards an applicable cognitive science, the various research projects described in this chapter have utilised very different tactics for calling upon principles and psychological theory. Some tactics have called for only the weakest form of synthesis. In problem-based solutions derived from exploratory research (section 3.1), such as the use of multiple aliasing or minimal manuals, theories were not systematically used. Rather, a psychological description of a usability issue is used to motivate a form of design. In these instances a general purpose application tool is not proposed. The gap between research and application is bridged by practical demonstration. This directly displays the plausibility of the idea to its target audience — system designers.

In other cases cognitive theory plays a direct rôle. In some instances, the application of the theory is best viewed in terms of a tool for thought rather than a tool for prediction. Such is the case with Norman's (1986) stages of mental activity. The kinds of subdivision proposed by Norman do not require a great deal of psychological expertise to understand. Accordingly, the distinctions themselves can have direct utility when supported by a few examples of how they relate to particular designs. They can help human factors practitioners, or even software designers, to conceptualise the nature of a design issue from the perspective of user cognition. Indeed, such conceptualisations are often felt to convey what is important about cognitive issues in a more relevant and digestible form than highly focused and technically presented models (e.g., see Whiteside and Wixon, 1987).

Much of the analytic emphasis in the study of human-computer interaction has been directed at stronger forms of synthesis. In strong synthesis, models based upon psychological principles are used to predict aspects of user behaviour in learning and performance. The intention here is generally to create tools that can be used to supplement empirical assessments. There are powerful arguments (e.g., see Reisner, 1987, Whiteside and Wixon, 1987) against any proposal to abandon empirical evaluations of designs and simply replace them with user modelling.

The encouraging feature of modelling activities in human-computer interaction research is the emphasis upon a rapid transition from theoretical discussion to the exploration of possible pragmatic tools. What research programmes have often strived to achieve is a practical demonstration of the utility of a tool and a methodology for its use. Representing a system dialogue in a formal grammar is, for example, a methodology in its own right. Although early examples tended to have an illustrative form, the potential utility of such techniques is now being demonstrated with significant coverage of the features of commercial products (e.g., see Green, Schiele and Payne, 1988).

The work of Card *et al.* (1983) also demonstrated a rapid transition from a theoretical representation (the model human information processor), to approximate engineering tools with very different methodological characteristics from grammars. In their case, the tools demonstrated were akin to mathematical methods employed in engineering disciplines. Task analysis and empirical estimates of relevant parameters could be used in mathematical modelling to predict key aspects of user performance, such as task execution times. These authors illustrate how such modelling could assist in design decisions concerning, for example, the range of different methods to incorporate into a system or the relative efficiency of different forms of input devices.

Although initially based upon the GOMS framework of Card *et al.* (1983), the work of Kieras and Polson has involved the demonstration of a different type of tool for use in an evaluative methodology (e.g., see Polson, 1987). In this case, a theory of cognitive complexity is explicitly realised in a working production system. This production system formalism is carried out with a real or envisaged system. Likewise, the way in which that system actually works is represented in a generalised transition network (GTN). The explicit representation of how-to-do-it and how-it-works knowledge enables both the user and the system to be simulated. Such simulations can then be applied iteratively both to explore properties of designs and to provide quantitative predictions concerning ease of learning and use.

The actual simulation of user knowledge means that some of the effort of a design team must be devoted to representing user knowledge. In order to do this, it is clear that someone on that team must have specialist how-to-do-it knowledge of cognitive complexity theory and how to implement it. Approaches that seek to avoid a requirement for specialist knowledge of cognitive theory are also under development. One possibility is to simulate theoretical constraints on human cognition, such as a programmable model of the user (Young and Green, 1986; Runciman and Hammond, 1986).

Operating within such a cognitively constrained architecture, designers would "program" user tasks that they have in mind for their envisaged system. If the designer finds it difficult to program the task, then by implication, users are also likely to find the task difficult. This kind of methodology involves designers using their own specialist skills to identify potential usability issues. By uncovering and exploring the nature of the problem for themselves, they should gain insight into how to create an alternative design that would avoid the problem.

A rather different kind of tool has been developed from Barnard's (1987) cognitive task analysis. In this analysis, a theoretical decomposition of cognitive resources (see Section 3.2.2 and Figure 4), is used as a language to describe mental processing. Principles governing cognitive activity were then inferred from empirical studies and represented in this resource based language (e.g., see Section 3.3.2). These were then supplemented by explicit rules for mapping from the principles to specific types of software application and to specific properties of user behaviour. These principles and mapping rules were then represented in the knowledge base of an expert system. A demonstrator system has been implemented for a restricted range of issues associated with command names, command sequences and menu sequencing (e.g., see Barnard, Wilson and MacLean, 1987).

This expert system builds approximate models of the way in which the human information processing mechanism will cope with the demands of a particular interface. On the basis of these models, the system draws principled inferences about both quantitative and qualitative aspects of user behaviour. Use of this tool does not require detailed specialist knowledge of the modelling process. The tool is aimed at human factors practitioners or designers with some knowledge of cognitive science. In addition, it does not require extensive formal specification of the interface. An analyst can approach the expert system with a specific design issue in mind. The system will elicit just that information it needs in order to build an appropriate "cognitive task model". Once that model is built, the system issues a textual report on the likely properties of user behaviour. If need be, the analyst can use the "what if" capability of the expert system to explore the consequences of modifying design features.

4. The realities of achievement

In the introduction to this chapter two key questions were posed. These concerned the extent to which applied cognitive psychology was contributing a principled understanding of the phenomena of system use and the prospects of that understanding being applied. There is a great deal of research activity, many empirical methods, a plethora of conceptual frameworks, a lot of evidence, and some prototype tools based upon theory. The ultimate value of research achievements in applied science must rest on the use of that science in design.

Obviously, much remains to be done by way of developing the various visions (Section 2) into a mature discipline that is routinely incorporated into system development. For such visions to be fully realised it is important to have a firm grasp of practical realities and to be in a position to respond in a positive way to more critical appraisals of the progress being made. From a purely scientific perspective, it is clear that there are many difficulties with our ideas, methodologies and evidence.

Exploratory methodologies have been used to great advantage and are being improved (Section 3.1). However, as Landauer (1987) has pointed out, the core discipline of experimental psychology has not been particularly productive in evolving the kinds of sophisticated exploratory paradigms that are really needed. It is also necessary to learn more about how to gain maximum benefit from those paradigms. In the case of exploratory studies using protocol methodologies, it is easy enough to collect the data. Then, much depends upon the skill and insight of a particular researcher in abstracting interesting or salient issues. Doing this successfully, particularly in relation to applicable theory, is often a matter of experience and judgement. Indeed, applied psychologists who are good at doing it may not be able to articulate how they do it.

Similarly, the different conceptual frameworks (Section 3.2) can all be regarded as capturing something important about cognition. However, they do make different trade-offs in modelling and in relation to the issues they address. The contrast between knowledge-based approaches (3.2.1) and process-based approaches (3.2.2) illustrated the kinds of trade-offs made. Most of the approaches remain partial and as yet have only been worked through for very restricted sets of circumstances. In this context, relatively little theoretical progress has been made towards dealing with all the different facets of interface use in an integrated way.

There are also problems with the kinds of assumptions made by the individual conceptual approaches. Predictions are usually based, not on a single simple assumption, but on a combination of assumptions. Under such circumstances a great deal has to be taken on trust. Sometimes constituent assumptions are open to debate. Most process-based approaches outlined earlier assume that human cognition is constrained by a central working memory of limited capacity. At least one makes a fundamentally different assumption. Barnard (1987) assumes that the restricted capability of the human cognitive mechanism to handle information in the short term is related to the coordination and control of distributed processes.

On other occasions, assumptions are implicit or only informally stated. This can make it difficult for people to agree on the content of a particular form of analysis. Such considerations can have profound consequences. To take just one example, the production system notation advocated by Polson (1987) enforces explicitness in the representation of user knowledge. However, the complete predictive mechanism assumes that productions are written in a particular "style". Variation in the style of writing individual production rules could in principle alter the outcome of the simulation (e.g., see Green *et al.*, 1988).

Uncovering and validating principles on the basis of experimental evidence (Section 3.3) can also be a difficult and lengthy process. The accuracy and generality of particular findings are a constant cause for concern. Furthermore, in some instances different pieces of evidence relating to a common topic can show markedly different patterns. Such has been the case with two of the topics considered earlier. Different experiments on the "naturalness" of command names for text editing have yielded superficially different results, sometimes coming down in favour of natural terminology (e.g., Ledgard *et al.*, 1980); sometimes in favour of computer-oriented terminology (Scapin, 1981); and sometimes showing that choice of terminology makes relatively little difference to performance (Landauer, Galotti and Hartwell, 1983).

Likewise, some studies of the breadth/depth issue in menu search have come out in favour of breadth (e.g., Landauer and Nachbar, 1985), while others have come down in favour of intermediate branching factors (Kiger, 1984; Miller, 1981). To the non-expert user of behavioural evidence these differences can be perplexing. However, it is frequently the case that factors other than the central topic of concern, such as the technique of assessment or the materials employed, are also varying from study to study. The real problem for the derivation of principles is to establish how all the relevant factors interact to determine the phenomena of system use. Such principles are unlikely to emerge from isolated or fragmentary pieces of evidence on any given topic.

In many respects applied research occupies the uncomfortable position of being squarely placed between the deep blue sea of science and the devil of practical application. There are equally powerful general criticisms from the perspective of those concerned with the practicalities of design and development. Many of the salient points have been recently discussed by Newell and Card (1985). They reinforce the general point that the theoretical contribution of applied science is too limited in scope. They also point out that there tends to be not enough knowledge to answer real design issues of current concern; and that when the researchers have obtained appropriate knowledge, its input is too late to be of real value. Thus, by the time scientific data for line editors is understood and accurately modelled, designers are building display editors; and by the time behaviour with these is understood, design attention is focused upon iconic interfaces, and so on.

There are also plenty of more detailed questions concerning the kinds of design tools that are under development (Section 3.4). One issue is the extent to which they are actually capturing the things that really matter in interface design. There is an argument, for example, that models of error free performance times for expert users are deficient in this respect. A substantial proportion of the variance in real performance times may be caused by a very small number of highly costly errors

(Landauer, 1987). Similarly, these models do not capture the real context in which users are likely to interact with a system. Whiteside and Wixon (1987) point out that modelling the complexity of the procedure for inserting a diskette is unlikely to predict very relevant problems in the context of system use. They report a user who physically inserted a diskette into a seam on the machine's plastic case rather than into the actual drive.

Another issue is the extent to which the kinds of tools being proposed actually mesh with the politics, schedules and practicalities of development teamwork (again, see Whiteside and Wixon, 1987). Theoretically motivated modelling may be all very well in principle, but it may call upon too many resources for too little gain in the context of a hard pressed development team. The kinds of theoretical models being developed are also primarily evaluative. With the possible exception of the idea of programmable user models (Young and Green, 1986), they do little to support creative design.

5. The future

Many of the critical points raised in the previous section can be answered sensibly. User cognition is complex. Although our scientific knowledge of the principles that govern these complexities is insufficient, enough is known to be of immediate conceptual and empirical value. The intuitions of system designers often display quite erroneous beliefs about user cognition (e.g., see Hammond *et al.*, 1983). In addition, the various criticisms and weaknesses are grounds, not for ignoring the progress that is being made towards an applied science of human-computer interaction, but for improving the discipline.

Thus, much can be done to address the problems of complexity, restricted scope, and the tendency for research to lag behind design (e.g., see Newell and Card, 1985). Issues associated with the complexity of cognition and the scope of our theories can be tackled by developing new forms of approximate cognitive modelling that have generalisable and cumulative properties. It may also be possible to speed up that process by making use of new methodologies for assessing the scope of models. For example, Young and Barnard (1987) have recently proposed a technique that involves a preliminary assessment of a model's scope by exploring how it copes with a range of scenarios describing different types of user-system interactions. This kind of assessment is itself approximate and could reduce our dependence upon lengthy experimental tests.

The particular issues raised by considering research achievements and their limitations also have implications for where future effort needs to be concentrated. In the present chapter the coverage has necessarily been selective. No reference has been made to popular concepts such as mental models (e.g., see Young, 1981; Halasz and Moran, 1983) or to the use of design "metaphors" (e.g., see Carroll and Thomas, 1982). On the basis of the issues that have served as illustrations here, three topics would seem to merit considerable future attention.

In order to deal with the many different things that can go wrong with an interface design, models are needed that integrate over the various perceptual, cognitive and motor resources of human cognition (e.g., see Barnard, 1987). In order to deal with the inherent variability of user behaviour, concepts are required to deal with the properties of individual differences and strategic variations in cognition (e.g., see Egan and Gomez, 1985). In order to develop our prospective design tools, it is necessary to improve our understanding of the ways in which designers make decisions and to find out what tools they really need (e.g., see Rosson, Maass and Kellogg, 1987).

6. Further reading

Many of the issues raised in this chapter are covered more extensively in the various chapters in J.M. Carroll (ed.) (1987) *Interfacing Thought: Cognitive Aspects of Human-Computer Interaction*. Cambridge, MA: MIT Press. Particular attention is drawn to the editor's introduction; to the chapter by Landauer; and that by Whiteside and Wixon. The rôle of cognitive psychology in system design is also the topic of a chapter by Hammond, Gardiner, Christie and Marshall in M. Gardiner and B. Christie (eds.) (1987) *Applying Cognitive Psychology to User-Interface Design*. Chichester: Wiley. Another critical appraisal of progress is provided by Newell and Card (1985) The prospects for psychological science in human-computer interaction. *Human-Computer Interaction*, **1**, 209-242.

CHAPTER NINE

FORMAL MODELS AND TECHNIQUES IN HUMAN-COMPUTER INTERACTION

JÜRGEN ZIEGLER AND HANS-JÖRG BULLINGER

1. Introduction

Models for the user interface are gaining increasing attention in the field of human-computer interaction (HCI) for analytic and constructive purposes. Different types of models can be identified in this context:

- Structural descriptions of the system architecture with respect to the different components of the user interface and the application.
- Formal descriptions of "dialogue processors", which are used for the specification or automatic generation of dialogue interfaces. These methods often form the basis for rapid prototyping tools.
- Task oriented models for analysing the structure and components of tasks.
- Cognitive models of the knowledge the user has to acquire in order to accomplish a set of tasks with a certain system. These models can be used for predicting usability characteristics like performance and learning times or consistency of an interface.

This paper presents a survey of relevant modelling techniques and formal methods with example applications and focuses particularly on cognitive modelling techniques. The research work related to this survey has been carried out in the context of the ESPRIT project HUFIT (Human Factors in Information Technology; Hoppe, Tauber and Ziegler, 1986). The strengths and weaknesses of the different methods are indicated. The survey allows us to identify promising applications of different methods and thus provides guidelines for human-computer interface specialists and designers of interactive systems.

Models and formal techniques can serve different purposes. Firstly they can contribute to a clearer understanding and separation of the different aspects of a user interface. This is an important aspect for the whole field of HCI because there are a fairly large number of studies in this domain which do not appear to have sufficiently clarified the specific aspects of the interface features under investigation or have compared interfaces with respect to characteristics belonging to quite different categories.

Secondly, models can support the design and implementation process of interfaces in a number of aspects. They can provide a useful framework for structuring the design process by grouping the necessary design decisions into classes which can then be elaborated at different stages. Formal methods are required and useful for the specification of interfaces. Such specifications can then be communicated among designers and implementors. Quite often, the need for a full specification of the interface can in itself help to avoid errors or inconsistencies in the interface design.

However, there is a strong trend in the design of interactive systems to avoid the time-consuming task of producing complete specifications before implementing a system. The technique of rapid prototyping relies on providing partial implementations at a very early stage of the design process which can then be tested and iteratively refined and improved. This technique is only feasible if suitable software tools are available which allow one to describe the system in terms of the interaction features of interest. In this field, formal methods are needed as a basis for user interface generation and management tools which can help to save a considerable amount of the implementation time and effort needed with traditional methods.

Finally, formal methods can be used for the description and analysis of the user's cognitive model of a system. This is a relatively new issue in HCI but appears to be of great importance because of its focus on the way a user perceives a system. Usability characteristics of an interface or certain interface components can be derived from such a model in predictive way, i.e., design alternatives can be evaluated before the system is built.

An important aspect of some formal methods is that they lead to models which are directly computable, i.e., the provision of a formal description can be fed to a compiler or interpreter and be executed on a computer. The resulting computer model can be a dialogue processor or a simulation of user behaviour.

The methods described in this paper are grouped according to their formal characteristics. The formalisms reviewed in this paper are:

- state-transition networks and finite automata,
- formal grammars, and
- production systems.

Besides these general formalisms, some more specific languages and tools for implementing user interfaces will be discussed. Figure 1 summarizes the different

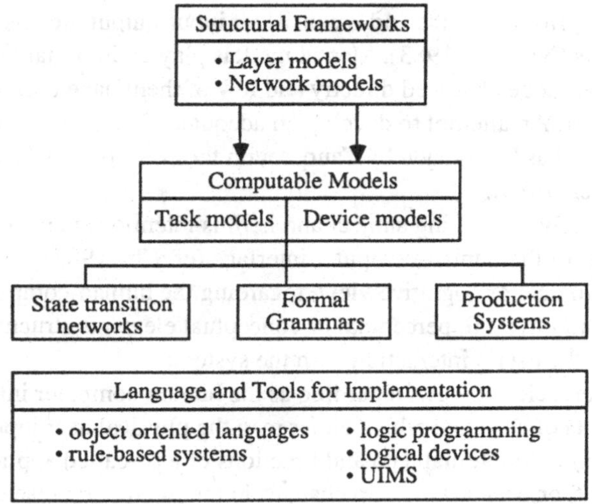

Figure 1: Structural overview of models and formalisms in HCI.

aspects of models and formal methods in HCI and provides a structure for the different categories of models and formalisms.

2. Models in human-computer interaction

In model theory (e.g., Stachowiak, 1973) a model is considered to be embedded in a ternary relationship R(M,S,O), with M standing for the model itself, S for the modelling or model-using subject and O for the object being modelled. When speaking about a model, this context should be clarified. Relevant aspects of models in HCI within this basic framework have already been worked out by Rohr and Tauber (Rohr and Tauber, 1984; Tauber, 1988).

Transferring the general conception of model theory to the field of HCI, we have to identify the relevant constellations of M, O and S with the specific purposes, interpretations and representations.

As subjects using or constructing models we have to consider users, designers, evaluators, implementors and systems. Systems are contained in this list, because they can be provided with explicit user models or task representations for purposes like adaptivity or active help facilities.

The so-called "mental models" refer to the user as the subject and a task or system as the object of the model. Mental models in this sense are internal and guide the activity of task completion using a certain device. They can be more or less elaborate, ranging from disperse and inconsistent input-output models to complete functional models (Norman, 1983). Mental models play an important role in HCI, although they cannot be observed directly and few of them have been presented in a formalised manner. An attempt to develop an adequate objective representation for this kind of model has been made by Tauber with the concept of a "user's virtual machine" (Tauber, 1985).

Depending on the modelling subject and her/his intentions there are basically two different "views" of the human-computer interface (cf. Chi, 1985):

- the psychological or cognitive view, regarding the human-computer interface as the set of all physical, perceptual or conceptual elements structuring and mediating the user's interaction with the system;
- the computer science view, regarding as the human-computer interface all the components of a system which either map the physical user input (usually keystrokes) onto internal data and functions of a so-called application component, or, *vice versa*, map changes in the internal representation of the application onto output operations perceivable by the user.

The first view is typical of the evaluator (often a psychologist), whereas the second is typical of the implementor, a computer scientist or an engineer. Designers may envisage each of the two aspects, according to the specific profile of their task. An integration of these two views in a common representation would be desirable but so far has not been achieved.

2.1 *Structural frameworks*

In the field of human-computer interaction, a number of models have been presented in the last few years which try to provide a structural decomposition of the user interface. The purpose of such models is to identify relevant distinguishable components of the complex phenomenon of human-computer interaction and to indicate the relationship between these different components.

This section addresses a number of such models which are only formal in so far as they provide a separation of abstract components and the structural relationship between the components. The degree of formalisation of such models is restricted to the structural properties without providing detailed formal descriptions of the contents of a component or for the information flow between components. For this reason, we will call such models structural frameworks.

Basically, two classes of structural frameworks can be identified. The first class comprises hierarchic, layered models of the user interface. The interface is seen as a communication process between user and system where information is exchanged on different levels of abstraction.

A second class of structural frameworks uses network models, e.g., to describe the different categories of knowledge which are used and required by two partners in order to achieve successful communication. At least one attempt has been made to allocate classes of communication knowledge in a network-like representation which includes user and system as main components (Kupka, Maass and Oberquelle, 1981).

The first attempt to apply models of communication theory to the field of human-computer interaction has been made by Foley and van Dam (1973). Their intention was to provide a structure for the interactive part of graphical applications. Foley and van Dam distinguish four levels of interaction: lexical, syntactic, semantic and conceptual.

The lexical level determines the surface appearance from the elementary input/output elements which are realised by different physical devices like screen, keyboard, mouse, etc. This level includes issues like naming of commands, function keys, visual representation of textual and graphical objects. Physical interaction only takes place at this level.

At the syntactic level, the validity of input/output sequences according to structural rules is defined. On the user's side, the input elements or tokens have to be combined according to these rules in order to issue a valid command to the system. The syntax determines when the system is ready to accept an input and when a system reaction or feedback can happen. On the output side, sequencing also includes spatial and temporal factors, like the 2D organisation of a display.

The semantic level describes the effects of user or system-initiated functions on the data objects represented in the system. From the user's point of view, the important aspect is which data objects are accessible and by which functions they can be manipulated.

There are usually numerous ways in which a task domain can be modelled by a computer representation of its objects and functions. A good example is the different geometry models used in the CAD area. The specific selection and design of such a model of the application forms the content of the top-most layer, the conceptual level.

On the basis of such a separation of the interface into different levels of abstraction, several models have been put forward, employing different objectives and criteria for the analysis of user interfaces.

The IFIP working group 6.5 has developed a model which consists of the following components: input/output interface, dialogue interface and tool interface (Figure 2). Both the user and the system are linked together with interfaces to the work organisation.

Besides providing a general structure for the user interface the model indicates several steps for standardising user interface components. If a standardisation of the

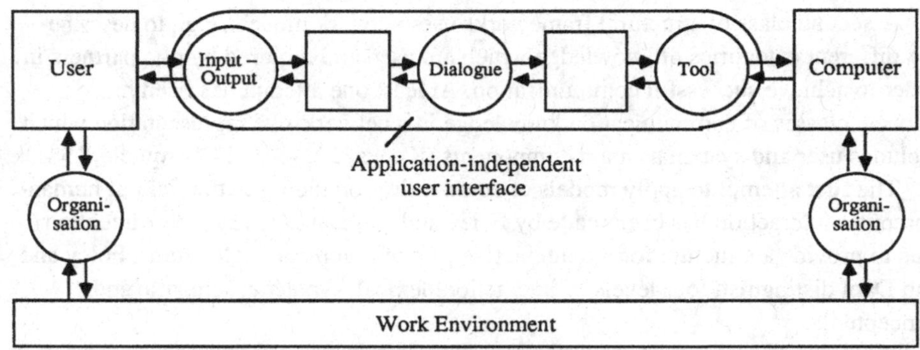

Figure 2: User interface model (IFIP Working Group 6.5).

three components (input/output, dialogue interface and tool interface) could be achieved, the user interface would be completely application independent. It must be noted, however, that such a general standardisation has not been accomplished yet.

Other models providing a layered view of the interface have been put forward by Gaines and Shaw (1984), Faehnrich and Ziegler (1984) and Nielsen (1986). The Command Language Grammar (CLG: Moran, 1981) is also based on the notion of hierarchic layers of the interface. This formalism will be described in a separate section. See also Barnard, Chapter 8.

3. State transition networks

Formal descriptions differ with respect to their capability to model explicitly the behaviour of the device or the interface. This distinction is especially important for analysing the properties of state transition techniques in comparison to formal grammars which are discussed in the next section. From the formal point of view, there is an equivalence between certain classes of state transition representations and context free grammatical formalizations. Yet, a pertinent difference is what is implicitly and what is explicitly modelled with a certain method. State transition networks explicitly model the behaviour of an interface, i.e., the model describes which reactions of the system (transition to another internal state and output) are caused by the user input.

State transition networks are one of the most frequently used methods for defining and describing user interfaces, especially in the field of user interface management systems (Green, 1985). The emphasis on state transition techniques clearly comes from the fact that they are formally well understood and relatively easy to apply. State transition networks are suitable for building computable models, i.e., models which can be interpreted and executed by the system.

State transition networks can be expressed in a graphical manner by state transition diagrams (cf. Green, 1985). In this representation, a user interface is seen as a collection of states. At any one time the user interface will be in exactly one state. The states are connected by arcs which are labelled by a user action or class of user actions. The interface will switch from one state to another according to the path indicated by the arc connecting the two states if the user performs the action by which the arc is labelled. Only those actions are valid user input which correspond to labels of arcs leaving the current state of the system. For processing the user's input program, actions can be connected to the different states or the arc which is currently being traversed.

The features described characterise the basic form of a state transition network. Users of this formalism have frequently found that even for moderately complex systems large transition diagrams may be needed which are difficult to construct, understand, manage and modify.

In order to overcome this problem, there have been three major extensions to this basic model. The first extension is to attach conditions to the arcs to further specify when the arc can be traversed. This can be used to describe whether a transition is dependent, e.g., on a specific value of a variable. Without this additional condition, it may be necessary to handle a number of additional states which do not differ in their syntactic properties.

The second extension introduces the possibility to treat states, labelled arcs (inputs) or conditions, recursively. This can be viewed as a subroutine capability; for instance, a single state can be a symbol for a subnetwork which is called and traversed if this specific state is entered. Recursive states and arc labels allow for a decomposition of complex diagrams into smaller subnetworks which are much easier to handle. Models incorporating this facility for states, conditions and labels have been called Generalised Transition Networks.

The third extension is the addition of memory to the states. This allows the states to remember the most recent path through them as well as default parameter values.

An important usability issue for state transition techniques can be seen in the way in which the interface designer can produce an interpretable representation of the state transition network. In a number of cases, the network is described by a sort of programming language in which states and transition attributes can be expressed in a verbal manner. However, more recently, graphical techniques for constructing and editing a network have also become available. The system can in this case directly interpret and execute the graphical representation produced with some appropriate network editor (cf. Wasserman, 1986). Graphical specification appears to be an important usability criterion for this graphically oriented technique.

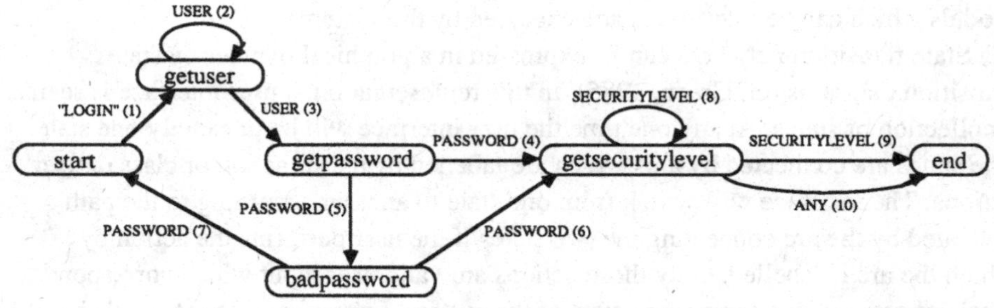

Figure 3: Example of a state transition network (Jacobs, 1983).

The following labels are attached to the arcs in Figure 3:

1. system response: 'enter name'
2. condition: not EXISTS_USER ($USER) (the prefixed $ indicates response: 'reenter username' the input of the user)
3. condition: EXISTS_USER ($USER) response: 'enter password'
4. condition: $PASSWORD = GETPASSWORD_USER ($USER) response: 'enter security level'
5. condition: $PASSWORD <> GETPASSWORD_USER ($USER) response: 'reenter password'
6. see (4)
7. condition: $PASSWORD <> GETPASSWORD_USER ($USER) response: 'start again'
8. condition: $SECURITYLEVEL > GET_ALLOWANCE ($USER) response: 'reenter security level'
9. condition: $SECURITYLEVEL < GET_ALLOWANCE ($USER) action: CREATE_SESSION ($USER, $PASSWORD, $SECURITYLEVEL)
10. response: 'unclassified security level' action: CREATE_SESSION ($USER, $PASSWORD, unclassified)

State transition networks are especially useful for implementation of dialogue management components. As they describe a model of the device — and not the cognitive representation of the task — their value for analysing usability characteristics is limited. Nevertheless, some authors have proposed that state transition networks can be used, e.g., for analysing modes of a system. Also, comparisons between the user's cognitive task representation and the dialogue structure might be a useful means for detecting task-device mismatches (Kieras and

Polson, 1985). An example of state transition networks is described by Jacobs (1983) for specifying a login procedure.

4. Formal grammars

4.1 *BNF: Reisner's Action Grammar*

A well established formalism for the description of context-free grammars is the BNF (Backus-Naur Form) notation. A BNF description defines the set of all syntactically correct sentences for a grammar by means of replacement rules. These rules (also called "productions") can be used for language synthesis as well as analysis ("parsing"). Each correct sentence can be derived from a starting symbol by subsequent application of some of the rules.

A BNF grammar consists of:

- a set of terminal symbols (the words of the language, here notated by words written in capital letters)
- a set of nonterminal symbols (constructs for explaining the structure of the language; e.g., verb phrase, statement,..., here notated by words in small letters)
- a starting symbol (e.g., 'S' for sentence)
- metasymbols defining the metalanguage by means of which an actual language is expressed (as, e.g., ::= for replacement of a symbol by an expression; + for a sequence of symbols on the right hand side of an expression, etc.)
- rules constructed from the elements above, e.g.,

  S ::= use_copy + use_delete I use_move.

In the field of human-computer interaction the use of formal grammars, especially in the form of BNF descriptions, was first introduced by Reisner (1981, 1983). She regards the sequence of actions performed by the user as a language. The physical actions are keystrokes, button presses, cursor motions, mouse actions, etc. These actions are regarded as the terminal symbols of the 'action grammar'.

Reisner's method refers to what Payne and Green (1986) call "a grammar in the head", as the object modelled. The purpose is to predict usability features of a system by means of a model described in terms of an action grammar. Three concepts derived from an action grammar are proposed to be used as predictors:

- the number of different terminal symbols
- the lengths of the terminal strings for particular tasks
- the number of rules necessary to describe the structure of some set of terminal strings.

The first expresses the total number of different action steps in the action language (number of 'words' of the language). The second reveals the number of single actions which the user has to perform sequentially for a given task. The third indicates the consistency in the steps required for a set of related subtasks. Also, inconsistencies of a system may be determined from "extra" rules which do not fit into the context of other rules for a certain task. It may be quite difficult, however, to determine such inconsistent rules in a particular case.

The following example taken from the model of ROBART1 (Reisner, 1981) demonstrates how consistency can be recognised in the formal description:

```
select_circle ::= select_circle_switch + PRESS_GO
select_line ::= select_line_switch + PRESS_GO
select_square ::= select_square_switch + PRESS_GO
select_text ::= NULL
```

All four rules concern the selection of some kind of objects in ROBART1. Whereas the first three rules have the same structure, the fourth is an exception, which indicates an inconsistency.

The nonterminal symbols in such a description can be regarded as describing tasks or subtasks of the user. An example taken from Reisner (1983) should illustrate the task aspect of the nonterminal symbols. It is a portion of an action grammar for a text editor and describes the deletion of one or more lines from a manuscript:

```
delete_line ::= use_Dn I use_backspace_key
use_Dn ::= identify_first_line + enter_Dn_command + PRESS (ENTER)
identify_first_line ::= get_first_line_on_screen + move_cursor_to the_first_line
......................
indicate_direction ::=
        PRESS (->) I PRESS (<-) I PRESS (CTRL-Y) I PRESS (CTRL-X)
```

Psychological experiments conducted by Reisner (1981) have demonstrated the usefulness of a formal grammar approach for representing user knowledge with respect to the actions to be performed. The direction of her predictions, as derived from the formal grammar, was confirmed by the experiments.

Reisner's method of the action language, however, has to be seen as the first step in modelling the knowledge the user has to acquire about a system. The missing of cognitive task concepts in this approach is a serious restriction in Reisner's method. Her choice of the nonterminal symbols is quite arbitrary, and no explicit assumptions are made about how users represent tasks.

4.2 *Task-action grammars*

Task-action grammars (TAG) try to overcome the above mentioned problems with BNF descriptions by providing a grammatical decomposition of mentally represented tasks into actions (Payne and Green, 1983; Green, Schiele and Payne, 1988; Tauber, 1988). The user's tasks are regarded as mental concepts. A concept, in turn, is defined by its features and possible feature values from well defined sets.

In the TAG method, the existence of so called "simple tasks" is assumed. These tasks do not require any problem solving or planning activity by the user. TAG directly describes the actions needed for the performance of a simple task by means of replacement rules.

A TAG description consists of three parts: the enumeration of the feature names and their possible values, the dictionary of simple tasks, and a set of replacement rules to map the tasks onto actions.

The following example (Figure 4) describes the main filing facilities of the Apple Macintosh. This is a direct manipulation interface with icons which can be selected and manipulated by means of the mouse.

TAG uses metarules which represent a class of single rules differing only in their feature values. TAG models the user knowledge which is required for solving a set of tasks with the system. The modelled knowledge is regarded as the competence needed to perform the task. TAGs are intended to be used by designers as well as by psychologists. For the designer, predictions similar to those used with Reisner's Action Grammar can be derived. Possible predictions regarding the performance and learning of tasks might be:

- performance time is dependent on the number of actions needed for a task;
- working memory load is dependent on the depth of the goal stack to be built up for mapping complex tasks onto simple ones;
- learning time is determined by the number of explicit rules per simple task;
- learning time is dependent on the number of semantic features and/or the degree of their familiarity to the user (influence of prior knowledge);
- errors can be dependent on the number of overlapping action sequences produced by the rules.

These possible predictions have, however, not yet been tested systematically. TAG has some advantages in comparison to BNF in checking consistency of a user interface by providing metarules which represent a class of individual rules in a very condensed form.

One of the problems when building a TAG model is to determine what features actually describe the mental representation of a task. Some work is under way to identify semantically primitive features for task descriptions (Tauber, 1988).

Features	**Values**
Unit	file-object, folder, copy-of-unit
Effect	deleted, copied, moved, renamed
Target	trash, folder, desk

List of simple tasks

delete object	::	Unit = any Effect = deleted
copy object	::	Unit = any Effect = copied Target = (folder, desk)
move object	::	Unit = any Effect = moved Target = (folder, desk)
rename object	::	Unit = any Effect = renamed Name = (new-name)

Task Rules

T (Unit = any, Effect = deleted) :=
    move (Unit = any, Target = trash)
T (Unit = any, Effect = moved, Target (folder, desk) :=
    move (Unit = any, Target = (folder, desk))
T (Unit = any, Effect = copied, Target (folder, desk) :=
    select (Unit = any) + menu ("duplicate") +
    move (Unit = copy-of-unit, Target = any)
T (Unit = any, Effect = renamed) :=
    select (Unit = any) + type ("new-name")

Subtask Rules

move (Unit = any, Target = any) :=
    select (Unit = any) + drag-to (Target = any)
select (Unit = any) := mouse (point) + click (button)

Primitives

type ("text"):	perform typing as stored by planning component
menu ("item"):	select menu entry
mouse (point):	point to appropriate unit object
drag-to (Target):	drag with mouse to target position and release button
click (button):	press mouse button

Figure 4: TAG description of Apple Macintosh filing tasks.

The TAG method might also be used for implementation purposes. A TAG description could be regarded as a knowledge base for providing help or more task-oriented explanations (Hoppe, 1987).

4.3 *CLG: the command language grammar*

The roots of the command language grammar (CLG: Moran, 1981) lie in artificial intelligence research, particularly in the field of notation systems for knowledge representation. CLG is essentially a metalanguage for the symbolic notation of human-computer interfaces. The basic formalism employed in CLG is the frame notation (Minsky, 1975; Winston, 1984). CLG cannot be directly regarded as a formal grammar in the sense of the previously discussed methods. In accordance with the frame notation, CLG reflects more the structural and functional aspects of a static knowledge representation than the procedural aspects of 'running' the knowledge.

Moran distinguishes two distinct conceptual models: the model the designer has and hopes the user will adapt to (this should be explicitly worked out by the designer) and the conceptual model the user actually has. For the psychologist, the central question regarding the CLG approach is what kind of conceptual framework can be assumed for the mental representation of an interactive system. For the interface designer, CLG can be used to specify interfaces and to derive usability ratings. However, there is as yet little concrete experience with respect to assessing system usability by means of CLG.

CLG proposes a structural representation of the system on different levels. Two components are described in CLG. These are the conceptual component and the communication component. The conceptual component contains the abstract concepts which define the system from the user's point of view; the communication component contains the command language and the dialogue. These components can be further subdivided:

Conceptual component:
- Task Level
- Semantic Level

Communication component:
- Syntactic Level
- Interaction Level

When constructing a CLG description, the first step is to analyse the tasks the user can perform with the system. Tasks are seen in the sense of the GOMS model, defined by a hierarchy of goals and subgoals. In this task hierarchy, each (sub)task is either a primitive task or composed of subtasks.

The task level description is refined in more detail at the lower levels of the CLG model. The semantic level defines the user's knowledge about the conceptual components of the system. It uses a representation of the objects as conceptual entities and of the conceptual operations on these entities which define the functionality of the system. Each task accomplishment is to be modelled in terms of the conceptual entities and conceptual operations. A CLG description for the semantic level may look as follows (the UNIX mail system is used as an example):

```
UNIX-MAIL = (A SYSTEM
    NAME = "Unix-Mail"
    ENTITIES = (SET: MAILBOX, MBOX, MESSAGE, HEADER, BODY, USER)
    OPERATIONS = (SET: SHOW, REMOVE, MOVE, DELETE))

MESSAGE = (AN ENTITY
    MEMBER = (A HEADER, A BODY))
    ......................

REMOVE = (A SYSTEM-OPERATION
    OBJECT = (A PARAMETER, VALUE = (A MESSAGE)))
(*the OBJECT is removed from the MAILBOX*)
```

At the syntactic level, command languages are described by the following syntactic elements: commands, arguments, contexts, and state variables. Each dialogue context is defined by state variables (like CURRENT-MESSAGE) and the commands which can be used in this context (for a detailed description see Moran, 1981). In this way, each conceptual operation is defined in terms of the commands which can be used to perform the operation.

The lowest level addressed by CLG is the interaction level. At this level, the sequence of physical actions the user has to perform for invoking a command is described. It is characterized by dialogue rules as well as by the association of the physical actions to each command. It must be noted that the value of the description technique for the interaction level seems to be questionable. Formal grammars like TAG, or state transition diagrams, are more efficient and transparent techniques for modelling this level.

The merits of CLG lie particularly in the explicit description of conceptual objects and operations. The description reveals the conceptual knowledge components relevant to the user for accomplishing the task. Hence, a CLG description can also be a basis for developing metacommunication facilities like help, tutorials, etc. (cf. Veer, Tauber, Waern and Muijlwyk, 1985).

5. Production systems and related methods

Production systems (PS) are a rule-based formalism for the representation of procedural knowledge. PS-rules consist of two components — a condition and an action in the form:

IF (condition) THEN (action).

What makes PS-rules much more flexible and powerful than IF-THEN statements in classical programming languages is the interaction of a rule-base (set of PS-rules) with a working memory (WM). The basic mechanism of this interaction is the recognize-act cycle (see Figure 5). In the first step of a recognize-act cycle the conditions of the rules are matched against the working memory entries and the potentially applicable rules (conflict set) are determined. This pattern matching process also yields the actual bindings for those rules containing variable parameters. Thus the conflict set contains rules in an instantiated form (i.e., rules with bindings). A conflict resolution mechanism decides which of the selected rules will "fire", i.e., the action part of the rule is evaluated. A simple, but in some cases effective solution is to write very specific rules, so that only one rule applies to any given context of WM.

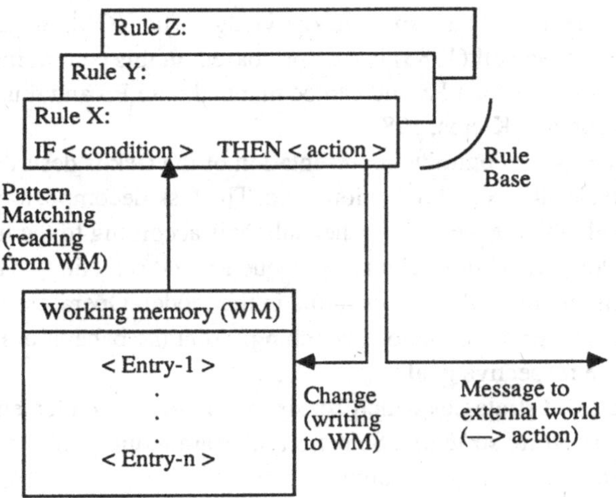

Figure 5: The basic mechanism of a PS interpreter.

The action part of PS-rules can produce different types of consequences. Internal actions change the contents of WM by adding or removing entries, whereas external actions send messages to an "external world", e.g., a simulation of a certain device. Internal actions are the only means for control and information flow between different rules. In other words, rules communicate only via WM. PS-rules can be regarded as independent, minimal elements of procedural knowledge.

The use of PS for modelling behaviour can be traced back to Newell and Simon's work on human problem solving (Simon, 1969; Newell and Simon, 1972; Newell,

1973). A combination of PS with semantic nets is used in Anderson's work on cognition (Anderson, 1983).

Problem solving is a goal-directed activity, which involves finding a sequence of operators leading from a given initial state to the goal. Tasks, as opposed to problems, do not require search in a problem space, but are associated with a fixed solution strategy. The distinction between tasks and problems can indeed only be made with respect to the knowledge of a certain person.

In the context of production systems and the notions of goal directed problem solving, we can identify two major approaches which can be used for cognitive task models in the field of human-computer interaction.

5.1 *The GOMS approach to task modelling*

How can procedural task knowledge be represented? The notion of goals, subgoals, methods and operators, originally developed in the context of problem solving, can readily be used to represent task-specific knowledge. The GOMS approach developed by Card, Moran and Newell (1983) is a theory based on this central idea. It uses higher-level descriptions than PS and can be mapped onto PS and thus be made computable (Polson and Kieras, 1985).

In GOMS, the user's cognitive representation of the task is described by a tree of Goals, Operators, Methods and Selection rules. The task decomposition starts with one top-level goal which generates further subgoals according to the hierarchical structure with additional control elements (sequence and selection). These regulate the actual sequencing of goals and operators in the model. Operators are elementary perceptual, cognitive or motor actions which represent the behaviour required for accomplishing the respective goal.

Methods are fixed strategies which consist of subgoals and elementary operators with a predefined control structure. Selection rules are required if alternative goals or methods can be chosen at a certain point.

Figure 6 shows a GOMS description of the Macintosh filing system tasks which have already been used as an example in the section on task-action grammar.

GOMS models can be used to analyse different aspects of user behaviour for a given task. Performance times can be derived from the number of steps (goals and operators) required to accomplish a task. Method selection can be predicted from selection rules. Also, sequences of user operations can be determined from a simulation based on a GOMS description.

One can make an important distinction between different GOMS models with respect to the grain size of analysis in them. The granularity of a GOMS analysis is determined by the elementary operators used in the model. Depending on the degree of detail which is expressed by the elementary operators, four levels of refinement

```
Top Level Goals
< 1 > : do filing task
        {repeat until no more unit tasks}
        < 2 > :  get next unit task
        < 2 > :  perform unit task
Task Level
< 1 > : perform unit task
        {select}
        < 2 > :  delete file
        < 2 > :  copy file
        < 2 > :  move file
        < 2 > :  rename file
DELETE-FILE-METHOD
< 1 > :  delete file
        < 2 > :  move file to waste paper basket
                 {use MOVE-FILE method}
MOVE-FILE-METHOD
< 1 > :  move file
        < 2 > :  select file
                 {use SELECT-FILE method}
        < 2 > :  position cursor to target position
                 {use POSITION-CURSOR operator}
        < 2 > :  verify target position selected
             {if target displayed as icon}
                 < 3 > verify target highlighted
             {if target is open folder}
                 < 3 > verify cursor in folder window
        < 2 > :  release mouse button
        < 2 > :  verify move
SELECT-FILE-METHOD
< 1 > :  select file
        < 2 > :  lookup position of icon {LOOKUP Op.}
        < 2 > :  position cursor {POSITION-CURSOR}
        < 2 > :  press mouse button
        < 2 > :  verify file selected
COPY-FILE-METHOD
< 1 > :  copy file
        < 2 > :  select file
                 {use SELECT-FILE method}
        < 2 > :  select function duplicate
                 {use SELECT-FUNCTION method}
        < 2 > :  move copy to target position
                 {use MOVE-FILE method}
SELECT-FUNCTION-METHOD
< 1 > :  select function
        < 2 > :  lookup position of menu title
                 {use LOOKUP operator}
        < 2 > :  position cursor to menu title
                 {use POSITION-CURSOR operator}
        < 2 > :  press mouse button
                 {MOUSE BUTTON operator}
        < 2 > :  lookup position of function name
                 {use LOOKUP operator}
        < 2 > :  position cursor to function name
                 {use POSITION-CURSOR operator}
        < 2 > :  release mouse button
```

Figure 6: GOMS description of Macintosh filing tasks.

can be distinguished. At the unit task level, the elementary operator is perform-unit-task. Performance time is estimated by the number of unit-tasks the task involves. On the functional level, specification and execution of a function (with parameters included) form elementary units. Input of each function and specification of arguments are separate operations on the argument level, whereas single keystrokes are operators on the most detailed level of task description (keystroke level).

GOMS models have been successfully applied and tested in the field of text editing where the sequential processing of single edits can be well expressed in the hierarchic representation of GOMS.

5.2 *Cognitive complexity theory*

Based on the GOMS model, Polson and Kieras (1985) have developed a theory of "cognitive complexity". The theory is used to analyse and predict learning and performance of routine skills which occur for instance in the use of text editors. In the framework of cognitive complexity theory (CCT) a GOMS analysis is transformed into a set of production rules and the production system is used as a simulation model of user's behaviour. Figure 7 shows a GOMS description and the corresponding production rules (the example is part of a model of text and graphics editing tasks on the Xerox Star system, cf. Ziegler, Vossen and Hoppe, 1986).

GOMS	Production Rules
MOVE Method GOAL <1>: Execute Move . GOAL <2>: Select Object {use SEL OBJ method} . GOAL <2>: Press MOVE Key {use keystroke operator} . GOAL <2>: Select Targetposition {use TARGETPOS method} . GOAL <2>: Verify Move	(ExecuteMove (IF (GOAL EXECUTE MOVE ?OBJ) (NOT (?OBJ SELECTED))) (THEN (ADD (GOAL SELECT ?OBJ)) (CALL OBJ . SEL))) (MoveKey (IF (GOAL EXECUTE MOVE ?OBJ) (?OBJ SELECTED) (NOT (MOVEKEY PRESSED))) (THEN (SEND "Press MOVE") (ADD (MOVEKEY PRESSED)) (ADD (GOAL SET GOALPOS)) (CALL TARGETPOS))) (VerifyMove (IF (GOAL EXECUTE MOVE ?OBJ) (GOALPOS SET) (NOT (TARGETPOS TESTED))) (THEN (SEND "Look Doc. – Verify Move") (ADD (TARGETPOS TESTED)) (DELETE (TARGETPOS SET)))) (FinishMove (IF (GOAL EXECUTE MOVE ?OBJ) (GOALPOS TESTED)) (THEN (DELETE (GOAL EXECUTE MOVE ?OBJ)) (DELETE (TARGETPOS TESTED)) (DELETE (TRANSFERKEY PRESSED)) (ADD (MOVE EXECUTED))))

Figure 7: Comparison of a GOMS description and corresponding production rules.

Predictions of observable parameters are derived in the following way: execution time for a given task is estimated by the total number of recognize-act cycles in the simulation. The time to learn a new method is considered to be a linear function of the number of new productions which have to be acquired. Thus transfer of skill between two different tasks is determined by the number of shared productions relative to the total number of productions needed for the new task. This is a modern version of the classical "common elements" theory of transfer (Thorndike and Woodworth, 1901).

In this way, quantitative predictions can be derived from a CCT model. Empirical tests of the predictions have shown good results for different text editors (Polson and Kieras, 1985), filing systems (Polson, Muncher and Engelbeck, 1986) and an integrated text and graphics editing system using direct manipulation (Ziegler, Hoppe and Faehnrich, 1986; Ziegler, Vossen and Hoppe,1986).

There are some inherent limitations to cognitive complexity theory due to the fact that the model does not deal with problem solving, choice of alternatives or errors and regards perceptual actions as undifferentiated "black box" task units. The different semantic properties of objects are only reflected implicitly in the operative task structure.

Both GOMS and the Polson and Kieras theory deal with fixed strategies of task completion. Features of the system are only considered if they are used for correct completion of the given tasks. Not the whole interaction space offered by the system, but only a special path through this space, is modelled. There is an underlying assumption that interaction is driven by the user's procedural representation of the task, but this view might not always be adequate. For example, using a menu system the user might find a correct path through the interaction space without any specific procedural knowledge, only guided by the menu choices offered by the system. On the other hand, learning difficulties resulting from semantically unknown menu items could not be explained by a cognitive complexity model.

For simulation purposes Kieras and Polson introduced a representation of the system using generalised transition networks (Kieras and Polson, 1984). This component serves as a device model and evaluates the external actions produced by the PS. This can be seen as a correctness test for the PS. Although the system model is referred to as a representation of the user's "how it works" knowledge, it does not directly influence the theoretical predictions.

6. Languages and tools for implementing user interfaces

Today, a large number of different tools and techniques are available which can facilitate the implementation of user interfaces.These techniques can only be briefly addressed here.

Besides tools which are directly intended for user interface design there are very high level languages, like object-oriented and logic programming languages which can provide the degree of abstraction necessary to make interface implementation easier than with conventional programming languages.

Object-oriented languages (e.g., LOOPS: Bobrow and Stefik, 1983) are based on objects and classes. Objects can have slots with associated values or methods to calculate those values (corresponding to procedures). Classes provide a structural description of a whole set of objects or instances of this class. Classes are structured in a class-subclass relation with inheritance facilities. The communication between objects is based on the mechanism of message-passing.

Object-oriented languages can especially facilitate the construction of highly interactive, e.g., graphical surface objects which "carry" their interaction methods with them. The user can be seen as just another source of messages sent to an object. The use of universal methods which are understood by all objects can support uniform and consistent interaction structures.

Logic programming (PROLOG) can support the implementation of the logical structure of a dialogue. It is relatively easy to implement a grammatical dialogue description in PROLOG. However, the input/output capabilities, e.g., graphics output, of PROLOG are not very far developed at present. Like productions systems, logic programming may help to include knowledge bases and inference mechanisms into the user interface, providing, e.g., better query, explanation and help facilities for the user.

6.1 *Special representation languages for UIMS*

User Interface Management Systems (UIMS) are gaining increasing importance in the HCI field. Edmonds (1982) proposed the following architecture as a logical model of a user interface management system (Figure 8).

Figure 8: Architecture of a UIMS (Edmonds, 1982).

The presentation component has to provide a processing unit or "manager" for the external representation of the user interface. This presentation manager is responsible for the generation of the screen contents and reads input from the input devices. We will focus here on the dialogue control component which defines the syntax of the dialogue between user and the application programs. It also handles the flow of control in the dialogue. Firstly, it mediates between the user and the application program; secondly, it decides on the next action to be initiated by the system.

The application component holds a representation of the application programs, which are implemented internally. It knows about the input and output parameters of the applications as well as of their effects.

6.2 *Dialogue representation*

This section deals with representations used for the generation of dialogue control components. This has been the main issue of research on UIMS. Basically, these methods for the description of the dialogue component are applied:

- state transition diagrams
- formal grammars.
- event-response systems.

The use of state transition networks and their graphical representation has already been briefly described in Section 3 of this paper (Jacobs, 1983).

A similar method is used in the SYNICS user interface management system (Edmonds, 1981; Guest, 1982). Like the method for the execution of a dialogue proposed by Jacobs, this system is a general compiler for formal descriptions of dialogue components. Input strings are analyzed by the SYNtax rules and then the rules of the semantICS produce the translated output. In SYNICS, both recursive transition networks (RTN) and extended BNF descriptions are used. Additionally, a dialogue design system is realised. The main program is the so called "dialogue processor" which takes the dialogue description and generates the dialogue manager. The dialogue language is defined by a description of system states as nodes of a net. Transitions from one state to another depend on the responses from the computer program which controls the dialogue.

An example for a grammar-based UIMS is the the XS-2 system, developed at ETH Zürich and BBC Baden (cf. Sugaya *et al.*, 1984). It provides both types of functionality, a dialogue generator and run-time support. XS-2 is based on a uniform representation of commands by means of trees. The underlying tree structure is derived from an extended attribute grammar. The system includes a presentation component, which follows the sites-modes-trails concept proposed by Nievergelt and Weydert (1979). Figure 9 shows an example of a XS-2 screen.

The XS-2 system is an example of a uniform, self modifying standard user interface. Its deficits lie in the restrictions imposed by the fixed presentation structure and the high level of abstraction required for working with the command tree. Alternative ways of presenting the command structure to the end user are missing (e.g., different forms of menus). Event-response systems (cf. Hill, 1986) bear some similarity to production systems, but are different in two important aspects: there is a limited, predefined set of events (like mouse-clicks, button-presses, etc.) which can be handled by the system (as opposed to arbitrary working memory entries in any production system). Secondly, events are tied to interface objects (e.g., a mouse-click which occurs on a certain menu entry). Each event can produce an action which changes the state of the dialogue or state of some application. Event-response systems are becoming the most frequently used technique for UIMSs, especially for window-based systems and interactive graphical interfaces. Green (1986) states that the event model has the greatest description power. Its main advantage is that multi-threaded, parallel dialogues (as they typically occur in window systems) can readily be expressed in this model.

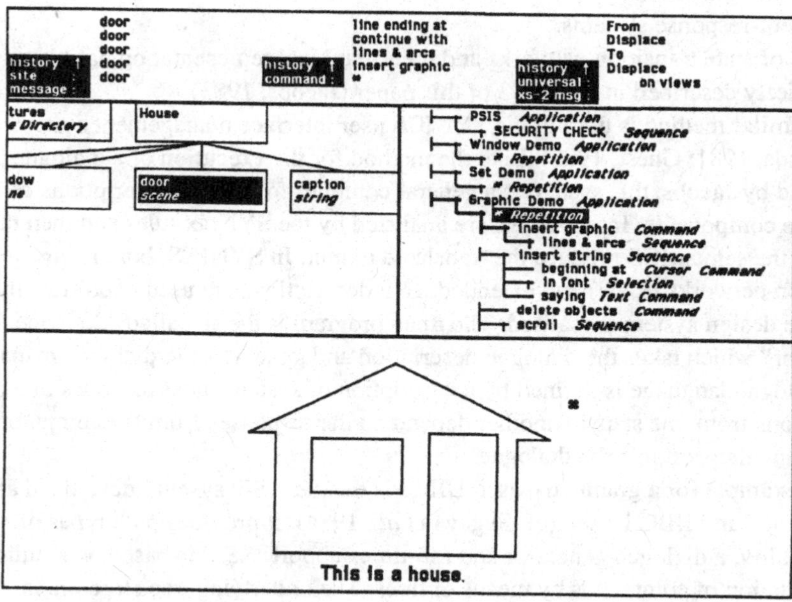

Figure 9: Example of a XS-2 screen (from Sugaya *et al.*,1984).

7. Conclusions

This paper has shown that the use of formal models and techniques can bring considerable advantages both for analysing and constructing user interfaces. However, there is evidence that there is not a single formalism which is suited to all problems in the large field of HCI. The most important question a user of formal techniques should ask is whether the specific problem of human-computer interaction addressed is explicitly modelled by a particular formalism. Other methods may describe the object of interest equally well from a logical point of view, but only implicitly model the target issue.

Very useful developments can be seen concerning user interface management systems. In this area, formal techniques are required by the very nature of the problem. One can expect that the different components and tools necessary will be integrated in user interface development environments in the near future.

In the field of analysing the user's cognitive representation of an interactive system, very promising progress has been made. Predictions obtained from formal models could be confirmed in a number of studies. However, it should be noted that only small interaction tasks have been studied so far in highly controlled experiments. Modelling a user's cognitive representation of a complete system seems to be out of reach at present for theoretical and practical reasons. In order to complement these formal studies, one will certainly need experimental work with realistic tasks and a higher ecological validity in the field of HCI.

To summarise, the last figure gives an overview of the formal techniques discussed and the respective purposes they have been used for.

Method	Description		Usability Predictions	Specification (System)	Generation (System)
	System	User's Model			
CLG	X	X	?	X	
GOMS		X	X		
PS		X	X		
BNF	X	X	?	X	X
AG	X	?	?	X	X
TAG		X	X		
ATN/GTN	X			X	X

X : Method applied for this purpose
? : Potential use in this field, application not known

CLG : Command Language Grammar (Moran)
GOMS : (Card, Moran and Newell)
PS : Production Systems
BNF : Reisner's action grammar
AG : Attributed Grammar
TAG : Task Action Grammar (Green and Payne)
ATN/GTN : Transition networks

Figure 10: Overview of formal methods and their application.

Acknowledgements

This paper draws upon a survey performed in the ESPRIT project HUFIT (Human Factors in Information Technology) to which H.U. Hoppe (now GMD, Darmstadt) and M. Tauber (University of Paderborn) have extensively contributed.

CHAPTER TEN

DESIGNING EXPERT SYSTEMS FOR USABILITY

BRIAN GAINES

1. Introduction

The initial success of expert system developments (Michie, 1979; Gevarter, 1983; Reitman, 1984) and the development of a number of reasonably domain-independent software support systems for the encoding and application of knowledge (Hayes-Roth, Waterman and Lenat, 1983; Waterman, 1986) has opened up the possibility of widespread usage of knowledge-based information systems. Most major new applications of information technology bring with them novel problems of user interfaces, operational procedures, training and the conceptualisation of the rôles and activities of the people and computer systems involved. Expert systems are no exception. They involve significant problems of informatics usability because:

- expert systems may be used in sensitive decision-support applications where errors are highly significant;
- expert systems are usually partially specific to the local application and require customisation;
- expert systems are usually not static and require updating according to changing circumstances and experience in use;
- expert systems usually require users to answer queries couched in specialist terms with no assurance that these terms are understood as intended;
- expert systems attempt to provide explanation facilities enabling users to understand the reasoning involved in the conclusions reached;
- expert systems often use uncertain inferences and facts which cannot be validated precisely, making it difficult to check their operations and conclusions;
- expert systems often require access to multiple forms, levels and types of inter-related data and processes, involving a complex inter-linked, multi-window interface.

In particular, the design, development and implementation of expert systems involve significant informatics usability problems in that:

- expert systems development requires knowledge acquisition from people, involving both knowledge engineers and application domain experts in specialist interactions with computing systems.

In addition, expert systems are relevant to informatics usability not only as a source of new problems but as a significant new opportunity in that:

- expert systems may be used to provide support and advice to a user of any complex information system and hence to improve the human-computer interface.

This paper considers expert systems technology as generating new modes of interaction between people and computing systems, and analyses a number of issues that arise:

- How does the nature of expert systems lead to the need for major differences in approach to systems and usability design?
- What special problems of usability arise in explanation facilities?
- What special problems of usability arise in knowledge acquisition and transfer?
- How appropriate are existing dialog design styles and guidelines?
- What additional human-computer interaction theories and guidelines are appropriate to interaction with expert systems?
- How can expert systems technology be used to improve human-computer interaction?

2. The nature of expert systems

In applying concepts of usability to expert systems it is important to distinguish those features which differentiate them from classical data processing. It is clear that expert systems use some new computational techniques, but it is perhaps less apparent that the system design approach involved is itself fundamentally changed. However, major paradigm shifts are involved (Gaines and Shaw, 1985). The classical approach in decision and control system design is the instrumentation, data collection, modelling and optimisation sequence shown in the top section of Figure 1. This approach to system design underlies the methodology of the physical sciences and technologies based on them. It has the merit that it has been extremely successful in engineering much of the technological infrastructure of our current society including our manufacturing industries.

However, this approach is successful only to the extent that the systems under consideration are amenable to instrumentation and modelling. Its greatest successes have been where this amenability can be achieved normatively, that is in cases where

Classical System Design	a) thoroughly instrument the system to be controlled or about which decisions are to be made b) use the instrumentation to gather data about the system behaviour under a variety of circumstances c) from this data build a model of the system that accounts for this behaviour d) from this model derive algorithms for decision or control that are optimal in terms of prescribed performance e) implement the algorithms as a decision or control system
Problem 1	The models available are inadequate to capture the system
Old Approach	Procrustean Design. Change the world to fit the model — normative technology
Paradigm Shift	Model Realism. Use system methodologies and information technology that enable the natural world to be modelled without distortion and destruction
Problem 2	Optimal control is over-sensitive to system uncertainties
Old Approach	Sub-optimality. Use a sub-optimal controller that is robust
Paradigm Shift	Model Uncertainty. Model the uncertainty as part of the system
Problem 3	Data is unavailable or inadequate for modelling
Old Approach	Managing. Do not automate — leave to human control
Paradigm Shift	Expert Systems. Model the person as a decision-maker or controller
Problem 4	Neither a human nor an automatic system alone is adequate
Old Approach	Ad Hoc System Design. Use a mixture of automatic and human decision/control
Paradigm Shift	Accountable Integration. Integrate automatic and human activity — make the automation accountable — "why?"

Figure 1: Paradigm shifts in system design.

the system to be controlled is itself a human artifact. For example, linear system theory has become a major tool in systems engineering not because most natural systems are linear — they are not. The implication is in the opposite direction: that linear systems are mathematically tractable and that we design artificial systems to be linear so that we may model them readily.

The application of "a linear model with quadratic performance criterion" to natural systems is often attempted but, in general, it does not work. We have done so not because the tool was appropriate, but because it was the only one we had. However, the use of a hammer to insert screws, although partially effective, tends to distort, destroy, and generally defeat the purpose of using a screw. Similarly, the use of an inappropriate system theory to model a system may give useful, but limited, results when we have no other, but it distorts reality, destroys information and generally defeats the purpose of modelling that system.

Much of our current technology succeeds to the extent that it is normative. In agriculture we reduce the complexity of a natural ecology to a comprehensible simplicity by the use of pesticides, herbicides and chemical fertilisers. We reduce the system to one which is amenable to our modelling techniques. That simpler is not necessarily better and that re-engineering nature to impose uniformity destroys variety which is itself valuable have only been realised in recent years.

This shift in the paradigm of system design, from procrustean design to model realism, results in the first perspective shown as a response to Problem 1 in the lower section of Figure 1. Three other changes in perspective stem from this first one.

The second perspective is that which led to new techniques for dealing with uncertainty and approximate reasoning (Gupta, Kandel, Bandler and Kiszka, 1985). Optimal control theory was regarded as the peak achievement of system theory in the 1950s and 1960s. However, it proved limited in application because it demanded precision in system modelling that was impossible in practice. It was too sensitive to the nuances of system structure expressed through over-precise system definition.

The third perspective is that which is primarily associated with the stereotype of expert systems. Hayes-Roth (1984) has noted that many problems that have been felt to require human management are now amenable to expert systems. Modelling the way the expert performs the task rather than modelling the task itself is the primary characteristic of an expert system.

The fourth perspective is an important one for expert systems. They are knowledge-based systems because they make provision for explaining the decisions reached. The "why?" question has important implications for both the practical and theoretical significance of expert systems and the logics on which they are based. Expert systems represent new maturity in information technology by providing an audit trail of the data and inferences on which their recommendations are based.

Each of these paradigm shifts has implications for the usability of expert systems:

• the approach underlying *model realism* also leads to systems that conform more closely to user's conceptual models and vocabularies;

- modelling *uncertainty* mimics human reasoning more closely but also makes the explanation and comprehension of the inference processes used more difficult;
- the *expert systems* paradigm of modelling the person, not the problem, enables advice-giving support systems to be generated for a wide variety of situations including those directly affecting usability;
- the *accountability* of expert systems through the "why?" and "how?" explanation capabilities greatly increases usability by allowing users to explore the operation of the system in comprehensive terms — however, the effective presentation of such explanations generates new usability problems in its own right.

3. The architecture of expert systems

In considering the usability of expert systems, it is important to realise that they are complex integrated systems involving a variety of tools and associated user environments, and that they also involve different categories of operator. Figure 2 shows the basic architecture of an expert system.

Knowledge base: the central ring shows the knowledge base of facts and inference rules that is the heart of an expert system. This extends the facilities of a conventional database by enabling the storage not only of facts but also of rules that further enable facts to be derived. These rules may both be explicitly expressed (production rules) and implicit in the conceptual structure in which the facts are expressed (objects, frames).

Expert system shell: the middle ring shows the expert system shell that provides computational facilities for applying the knowledge base to user decision support:

— the *application system* at the bottom tests the user's hypotheses or seeks to satisfy his goals by deriving the consequences of facts about a particular situation reported by the user, using the general facts and inference rules supplied by the expert and edited by the knowledge engineer;

— the *explanation system* to the lower left answers queries about the way in which facts have been derived in terms of what information and inference rules have been used;

— the *acquisition system* to the upper left provides tools for interviewing the expert to obtain his vocabulary, and general facts and inference procedures in terms of it;

— the *display system* at the top provides tools for presenting the knowledge base in an understandable form, and the relations between facts and inference procedures it contains;

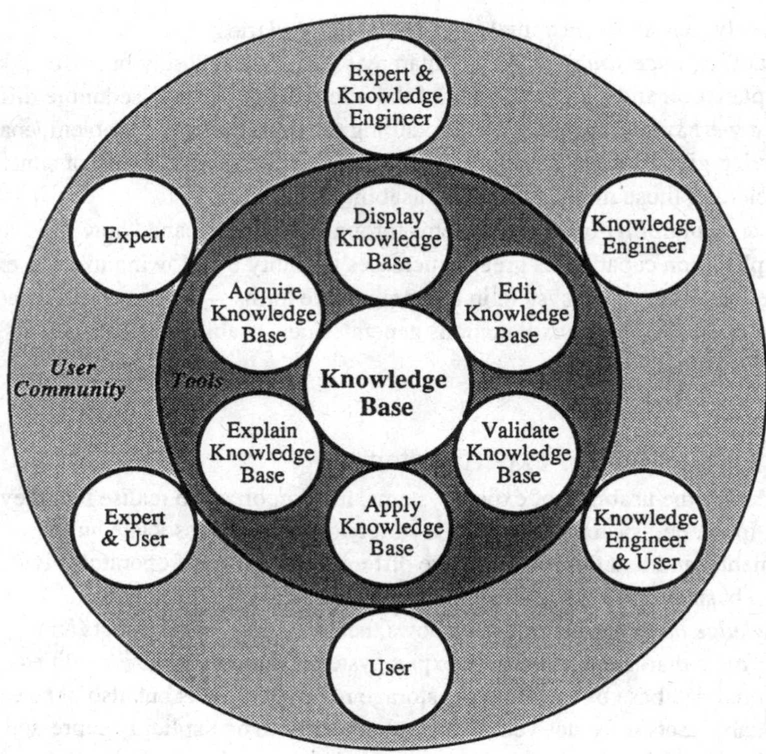

Figure 2: The architecture of an expert system.

— the *edit system* to the upper right provides tools for editing the knowledge base while maintaining its integrity in terms of the vocabulary, variables and operations used;

— the *validation system* to the lower right provides tools for checking the knowledge base against specific case histories with known consequences.

Operators: the outer ring shows the three classes of operator of expert systems:

— *users* come to the system for advice on specific problems in a particular domain, supplying it with specific facts and their hypotheses about consequences or goals;

— *experts* come to the system to transfer their knowledge about the problem domain, supplying it with generally applicable facts and inference procedures;

— *knowledge engineers* act as intermediaries between the expert and the system, helping him to encode his knowledge and validate the operation of the resultant expert system.

In terms of usability considerations, it is important to note that these operator rôles may be combined within a single individual, such as the 'expert and knowledge engineer', making it dangerous to assume that three self-contained user environments can cater for the different levels of skill and conceptual frameworks involved. It is better to think in terms of a single integrated environment that allows different levels of access through mutually consistent operating procedures. Most current expert systems do not provide such an integrated environment, and complete modules are missing or inadequately implemented, but Figure 2 provides a framework within which all existing systems can be embedded. Most current expert system shells:

- offer a limited knowledge base represented in terms of production rules and frames;
- have weak application capabilities limited to deriving consequences and testing assertions;
- give simple explanations in terms of the facts and rules used;
- have no integrated acquisition capabilities;
- have limited capabilities to display the knowledge base, sometimes in graphical form;
- have a user interface to the knowledge base editor which requires understanding of internal data structures;
- have limited validation capabilities and no integrated database of case histories.

However, rapid improvements are taking place in the knowledge representation, inferencing, explanation, display and editing capabilities of expert systems (Hayes-Roth, 1985; Michalski and Winston, 1986; Pearl, 1986; Swartout, 1986; Rappaport, 1987). Most current knowledge acquisition is done by manual knowledge elicitation which places too much load on the knowledge engineer and inadequately involves the expert. However, automatic tools for rapid prototyping are becoming increasingly important (Shaw and Gaines, 1987; Gaines, 1986c; Boose and Bradshaw, 1987) and are described in a later section.

4. Usability and explanation

The significance of the explanation facilities of expert systems has already been emphasised. Explanation makes the system accountable for its recommendations. From a usability perspective it allows the user to explore the inference processes leading to the system's output, what data has been used, what inferences have been made from it, and what rules have been used in generating those inferences. Explanation was a natural feature of the production-rule backtracking approach to early expert systems. The chain of inferences from data to conclusions could easily be backtraced to provide a natural sequence of explanation. (In a later example, in

Section 7, the interaction dialog with TEIRESIAS in Figure 10 shows this backtracing used very effectively to aid debugging.)

As expert systems become more complex, however, it is unlikely that simple backtraces will be regarded as providing adequate explanations. They are, in any event, inadequate if uncertain reasoning and accumulation of evidence are involved in the inference chain — many partial inferences may contribute to the final conclusions and some ranking of their significance is required. The move towards 'deeper' reasoning in expert systems, involving multiple levels of inference, also raises the possibility of multiple levels of explanation. The fundamental problems of the nature of explanation in scientific reasoning are well-known in the philosophical literature (Salmon, 1984), and one should not expect easy solutions to the general requirement.

These considerations have led to a number of studies of explanation in knowledge-based systems from both psychological and technical points of view. Kidd (1985) has studied the forms of explanation requested by those asking for advice from a 'phone-in' radio program. Hughes (1986) has developed Lehnert's (1977) taxonomy of forms of question to apply to the forms of explanation in expert systems. Pollack (1984) has reported a system designed to infer a user's goals in order to give appropriate answers to badly posed questions. Swartout's (1986) XPLAIN system demonstrates how appropriate multi-level organisation of domain knowledge may be used to generate explanations that show characteristics of dialog with human experts.

The availability of explanation in expert systems is not just a minor advance but rather a major paradigm shift towards accountable integration as shown in Figure 1. Usability considerations in explanation are as yet poorly understood, however, and major advances in both the psychology and technology of explanation may be expected over the next decade.

5. Usability and knowledge engineering

As might be expected the new technology of expert systems has also generated new problems of usability, particularly in regard to the specialist problems of its new classes of users, the knowledge engineers and experts. Feigenbaum (1980) defined *knowledge engineering* as the reduction of a large body of knowledge to a precise set of facts and rules, and it has already become a major bottleneck impeding the application of expert systems in new domains. We need to understand more about the nature of expertise in itself (Hawkins, 1983) and to be able to apply this knowledge to the elicitation of expertise in specific domains.

The problems of knowledge engineering have been stated clearly:

"Knowledge acquisition is a bottleneck in the construction of expert systems. The knowledge engineer's job is to act as a go-between to help an expert build a system. Since the knowledge engineer has far less knowledge of the domain than the expert, however, communication problems impede the process of transferring expertise into a program. The vocabulary initially used by the expert to talk about the domain with a novice is often inadequate for problem-solving; thus the knowledge engineer and expert must work together to extend and refine it. One of the most difficult aspects of the knowledge engineer's task is helping the expert to structure the domain knowledge, to identify and formalise the domain concepts." (Hayes-Roth, Waterman and Lenat, 1983)

This bottleneck is the major impediment to the application of expert systems, and to the realisation of their full industrial potential. The automation of knowledge acquisition and transfer has become a major research and technological goal.

The human factors problems of expertise elicitation from a skilled person are well-known in the literature of psychology (Nisbett and Wilson, 1977; Broadbent, Fitzgerald and Broadbent, 1986). Hawkins (1983) has analysed the nature of expertise and emphasises its severe limitations and dependence on critical assumptions which are often implicit. Dixon (1981) has surveyed studies showing that much human activity is not accessible to awareness. Collins (1985) has studied knowledge transfer processes among scientists and suggests that some knowledge may not be accessible through the expert, not only because he cannot express it, but also because he may not be aware of its significance to his activity. Bainbridge (1979, 1986) has reviewed the difficulties of verbal debriefing and notes that there is no necessary correlation between verbal reports and mental behaviour, and that many psychologists feel strongly that verbal data are useless. Clinical psychologists see the problem as one of cognitive defences that impede internal communication, and have developed techniques of verbal interaction to identify underlying cognitive processes (Freud, 1914; Kelly, 1955; Rogers, 1967). These can be used to by-pass cognitive defences, including those resulting from automation of skilled behaviour, and Welbank (1983) has surveyed the psychological problems of doing this. Kidd and Cooper (1985) have given a practical case history of the human interface problems of transferring knowledge to an existing expert system shell.

The main problems identified in accessing an expert's knowledge are as follows (Gaines, 1987a).

- Expertise may be fortuitous. Results obtained may be dependent on features of the situation which the expert is not controlling.
- Expertise may not be available to awareness. An expert may not be able to transmit the expertise by critiquing the performance of others because he is not able to evaluate it.

- Expertise may not be expressible in language. An expert may not be able to transmit the expertise explicitly because he is unable to express it.
- Expertise may not be understandable when expressed in language. An apprentice may not be able to understand the language in which the expertise is expressed.
- Expertise may not be applicable even when expressed in language. An apprentice may not be able to convert verbal comprehension of the basis of a skill into skilled performance.
- Expertise expressed may be irrelevant. Much of what is learnt, particularly under random reinforcement schedules, is superstitious behaviour that neither contributes nor detracts from performance.
- Expertise expressed may be incomplete. There will usually be implicit situational dependencies that make explicit expertise inadequate for performance.
- Expertise expressed may be incorrect. Experts may make explicit statements which do not correspond to their actual behaviour and lead to incorrect performance.

In the development of knowledge engineering methodologies and rapid prototyping techniques for expert systems the emphasis has been on interviewing experts, and hence on linguistic transmission of expertise. A rich variety of alternative methods for expertise transfer exists in human society.

- Expertise may be transmitted by managing the learning environment. A trainer may be able to establish effective conditions for an apprentice to acquire expertise without necessarily understanding the skill or himself being expert in it.
- Expertise may be transmitted by evaluation. A trainer may be able to induce expertise by indicating correct or incorrect behaviour without necessarily understanding the skill in detail or himself being expert in its performance.
- Expertise may be transmitted by example. An expert may be able to transmit a skill by showing his own performance without necessarily understanding the basis of his expertise.

There are many sources of expertise that do not involve others.

- Expertise may be acquired by trial and error learning. This is the basic inductive knowledge acquisition process that is always in operation although heavily overlaid by the social transfer processes already discussed.
- Expertise may be acquired by analogical reasoning. The transfer of models and skills from one situation to another is an important source of knowledge.
- Expertise may be acquired by the application of general laws and principles to new situations. The use of physical laws and systemic principles to generate specific expertise is the basis of scientific and engineering expertise.

These many aspects of the problems of knowledge acquisition and transfer are further confounded by the combinatorial possibilities resulting from the recursive nature of knowledge processes. We can acquire knowledge about knowledge acquisition. We can mimic the behaviour of an expert coach managing a learning environment. We can give evaluative feedback on analogical reasoning or the application of principles and laws. We can express the principles behind the effective management of learning in specific domains. The knowledge processes of human society are rich and complex, and, in practice, many of these possibilities will be instantiated as parallel, inter-related activities in any knowledge acquisition and transfer situation.

In an industrial context the application of techniques derived from clinical psychology to problems of hard systems engineering is not an obvious or probable step to take, and the early approach to knowledge engineering was to 'manage' it by inventing the profession of knowledge engineer as defined in the quotation above. It has been possible that knowledge engineering might develop as a profession on a par with systems analysis and programming, and that an initial shortage of skilled knowledge engineers would cause problems to be overcome eventually as the profession developed. However, this scenario now appears less and less likely. There is certainly a shortage of knowledge engineers and problems in developing applications, but doubts have been cast on the notion that human labour is the appropriate solution to the knowledge engineering problem.

- The decline in costs of both hardware and software support for expert systems has brought the technology into a mass-market situation far more rapidly than originally envisioned.
- This has led to a growth in demand for expert systems that is proceeding far more rapidly than the growth in supply of trained and experienced knowledge engineers.
- The declining costs of expert system technology are also making the expense of human labour in tailoring the technology for particular applications appear to be the dominating constraint and an excessive cost.
- A move towards a labour-intensive activity such as knowledge engineering is contrary to all trends in industry.
- In particular it is contrary to the trend towards automatic programming techniques in the computing industry.
- The rôle of the knowledge engineer as an intermediary between the expert and the technology is being questioned not only on cost grounds but also in relation to its effectiveness — knowledge may be lost through the intermediary and the expert's lack of knowledge of the technology may be less of a detriment than the knowledge engineer's lack of domain knowledge.

These considerations of the previous section have heightened interest in the possibility of providing knowledge support systems to automate knowledge engineering as a process of direct interaction between domain experts and the computer (Shaw and Gaines, 1987). A brief review of such developments is given in the next section.

6. Automating knowledge acquisition in expert systems

Figure 3 shows the classical system paradigm (as shown in the top section of Figure 1) extended to include the derivation of design information from the human operator. The obvious approach is interview analysis, and this has been used in many studies. However, often the operator is unable to give a verbal description of his skill, or suggests an incorrect basis for it, and computer modelling of his input-output behaviour gives better results. Textual analysis of the operator's handbook is another significant source of information about his intended behaviour.

These techniques are in fact just part of a hierarchy of knowledge transfer methodologies which defines the areas of application of the knowledge engineering techniques already in use (Gaines, 1987a). Figure 4 shows this hierarchy in relation to the basic architecture of an expert system.

• *Knowledge base*: at the centre, as before, facts and inference rules.

• *Expert system shell*: in the lower oval, the operational system for applying the knowledge base to knowledge support:

— the inference system derives the consequences of facts about a particular situation;

— the planning system determines how to use the inference system to satisfy the specified objectives;

— the explanation system answers questions about the basis of the inferences made.

• *Knowledge acquisition system*: in the upper oval, the knowledge transfer processes that may be used to establish the knowledge base:

— the knowledge generation system implements knowledge acquisition by the raw induction of models from experience without cultural support as exemplified by ATOM (Gaines, 1977) and AM (Davis and Lenat, 1982);

— the expertise modelling system implements knowledge acquisition by mimicking an expert's behaviour as exemplified by INDUCE (Michalski and Chilausky, 1980);

— the performance reinforcement system implements knowledge acquisition from performance feedback as exemplified by the PERCEPTRON (Rosenblatt, 1958) and STELLA (Gaines and Andreae, 1966);

— the knowledge elicitation system implements knowledge acquisition by interviewing experts as exemplified by ETS (Boose, 1985), KITTEN (Gaines and Shaw, 1986b), MORE (Kahn, Nowlan and McDermott, 1985) and SALT (Marcus,

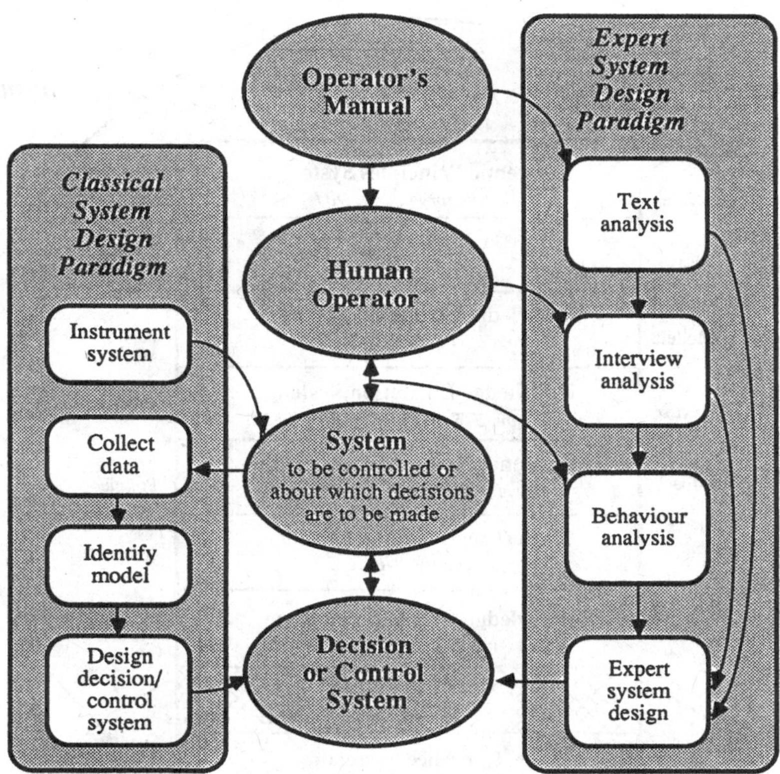

Figure 3: Expert system design paradigm.

McDermott and Wang, 1985);
— the knowledge structuring system implements knowledge acquisition by analogy as exemplified by TEIRESIAS (Davis and Lenat, 1982) and CYC (Lenat, Prakash and Shepherd, 1986);
— the basic laws system implements knowledge acquisition by building physical models as exemplified by simulation languages such as SIMULA (Nygaard and Dahl, 1981);
— the systemic principles system implements knowledge acquisition by derivation from abstract principles as exemplified by the category-theoretic language OBJ (Goguen and Meseguer, 1983).

The knowledge base and shell have been incorporated with the acquisition methodologies in Figure 4 to show the natural relationships between all three. Shell structure and knowledge acquisition research and development have so far been

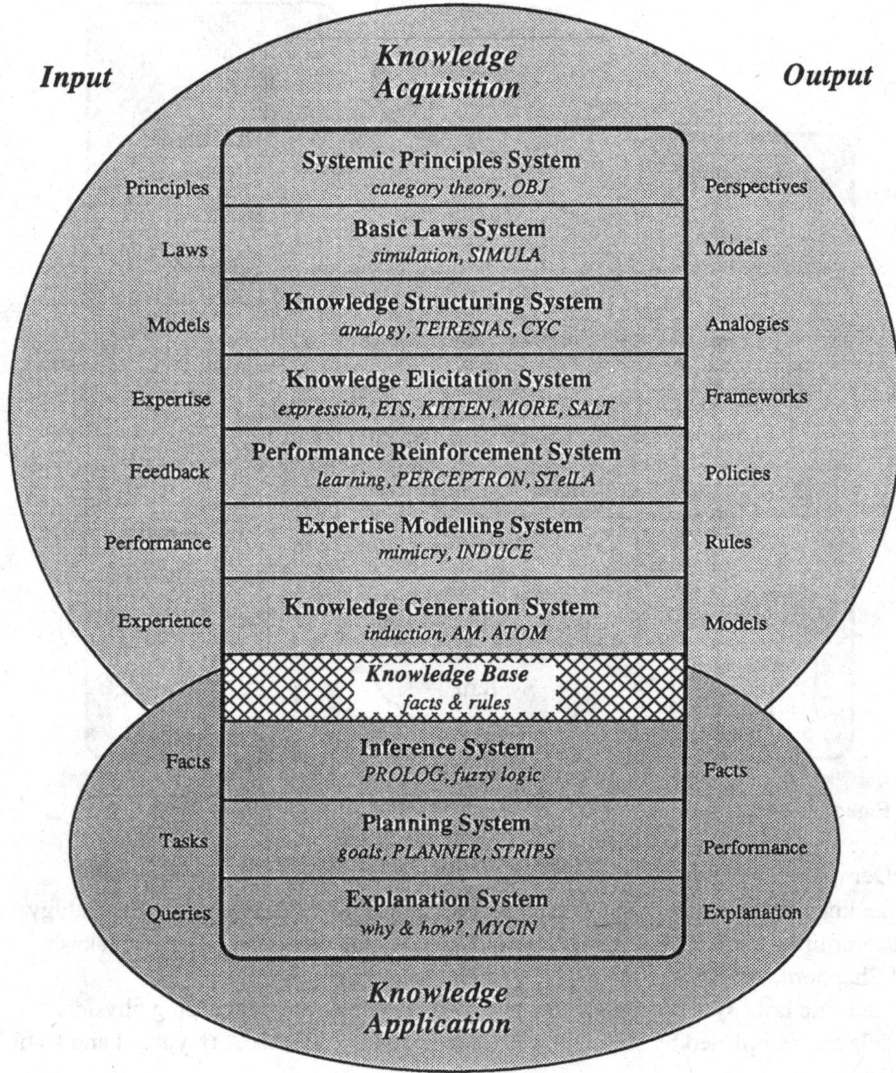

Figure 4: The hierarchy of knowledge acquisition methodologies.

treated as separate enterprises. Integrating the two is essential to future knowledge-based system applications so that the combined system provides maximal and coherent support to the expert and knowledge engineer.

The general requirements for a knowledge acquisition system to automate knowledge acquisition for expert systems are:

- the knowledge acquisition system tools should be domain independent;
- the tools should be directly applicable by experts without intermediaries;
- the tools should be able to access a diversity of knowledge sources including text, interviews with experts, and observations of expert behaviour;
- the knowledge acquisition system should be able to encompass a diversity of perspectives including partial or contradictory input from different experts;
- the system should be able to encompass a diversity of forms of knowledge and relationships between knowledge;
- the system should be able to present knowledge from a diversity of sources with clarity as to its derivation, consequences and structural relations;
- users of the knowledge acquisition system should be able to apply the knowledge in a variety of familiar domains and freely experiment with its implications;
- the system should make provision for validation studies;
- as much of the operation of the system as possible should be founded on well-developed and explicit theories of knowledge acquisition, elicitation and representation;
- as the overall knowledge acquisition develops it should converge to an integrated system.

All of these requirements are subject to caveats — some domain dependence may be appropriate for efficiency in specific knowledge acquisition systems — some human intervention may be helpful or necessary when an expert is using the system — and so on. However, the broad design goals stated capture the key issues in the knowledge acquisition system design community.

The PLANET system for repertory grid elicitation and analysis (Shaw and Gaines, 1986) is a basic knowledge acquisition system satisfying the first two requirements for domain independence and direct use. Its foundations in personal construct psychology, which itself has strong systemic and cognitive science foundations, are attractive in terms of the requirement for theoretical grounding. Boose (1985) in evaluating ETS has noted the limitations of basic repertory grid techniques in terms of requirement for a diversity of knowledge — that the methodology is better suited for analysis than for synthesis problems, for example, debugging, diagnosis, interpretation and classification rather than design and planning, and that it is difficult to apply to deep casual knowledge or strategic knowledge — and is attempting to overcome these using grid hierarchies in NeoETS (Bradshaw and Boose, 1986) and AQUINAS (Boose and Bradshaw, 1987). The TEIRESIAS extension to MYCIN is an early form of knowledge acquisition system providing debugging support for an expert system using basic analogical reasoning (Davis and Lenat, 1982).

Figure 5 shows the structure of KITTEN, an integrated knowledge acquisition system (Gaines and Shaw, 1986b; Shaw and Gaines, 1987). It consists of a knowledge base, various analytical tools for building and transforming the knowledge base, and a number of conversational tools for interacting with the knowledge base. Its operation is best understood by following sequences of activity that lead to the generation of a rule base and its loading into an expert system shell.

- A typical sequence is text input followed by text analysis through TEXAN which clusters associated words leading to a schema from which the expert can select related elements and initial constructs with which to commence grid elicitation.
- The resultant grids are analysed by ENTAIL which induces the underlying knowledge structure as production rules that can be loaded directly into an expert system shell (Gaines and Shaw, 1986c).
- An alternative route is to monitor the expert's behaviour through a verbal protocol giving information used and decisions resulting and analysing this through ATOM which induces structure from behaviour and again generates production rules (Gaines, 1976).
- These two routes can be combined. KITTEN attempts to make each stage as explicit as possible, and, in particular, to make the rule base accessible as natural textual statements rather than technical production rules.

Figure 6 shows a graphic dialog in KITTEN in which a manager is encoding the dimensions of his thinking in relation to his expertise in personnel assessment. He has entered the distinction *need supervision — don't need supervision* as a way of distinguishing among a triad of three subordinates randomly presented to him, and is now placing his other subordinates along this dimension by clicking on their names and dragging them to the rating scale. This natural visual approach to the expression of knowledge is very easy to use, and it is interesting to relate it back to Smith's original rationale for graphic interfaces in his development of *Pygmalion* — that it was natural to human creative thinking (Smith, 1977).

KITTEN analyses the data as it is entered and attempts to use it to continuously extend the range of dimensions of the expert's thinking in the relevant problem domain, feeding back queries based on the knowledge already entered. Figure 7 shows another graphic dialog relating to the match between two dimensions and suggesting that another subordinate be entered who might reduce this match. A similar approach is taken to matches between the subordinates themselves, prompting the elicitation of a new distinction. Such feedback tends to change the expert's focus of attention, triggering off thought processes relating to dimensions of his thinking that might otherwise be missed. It is interesting to compare the KITTEN dialog of Figure 7 with the TEIRESIAS dialog shown in the next section in Figure 11. Note how in both cases the reasoning within the system is used to focus attention on very specific

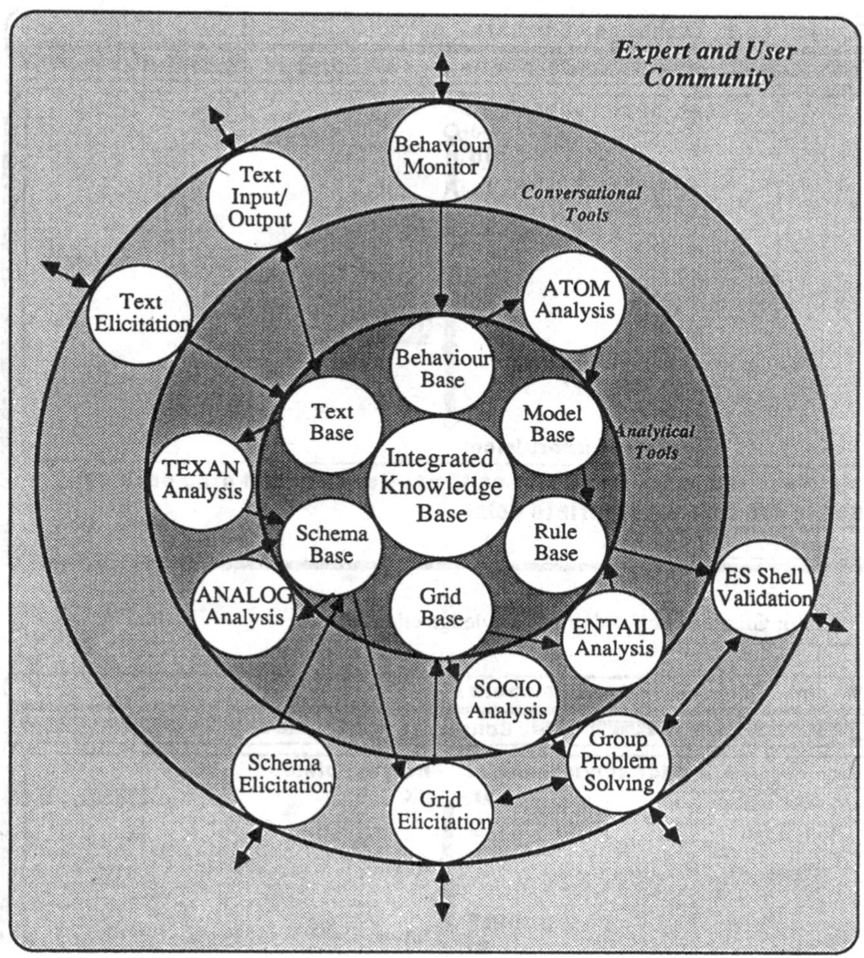

Figure 5: KITTEN – Knowledge Initiation and Transfer Tools for Experts and Novices.

issues and guide the expert in expressing just that knowledge that would improve the performance of the system. This directed guidance, while still leaving the expression of knowledge very open-ended, is the key to effective automation of knowledge engineering.

The group problem-solving component of KITTEN is particularly important because it goes beyond the stereotype of an 'expert' and 'users', and allows the system to be used to support an interactive community in their acquisition and

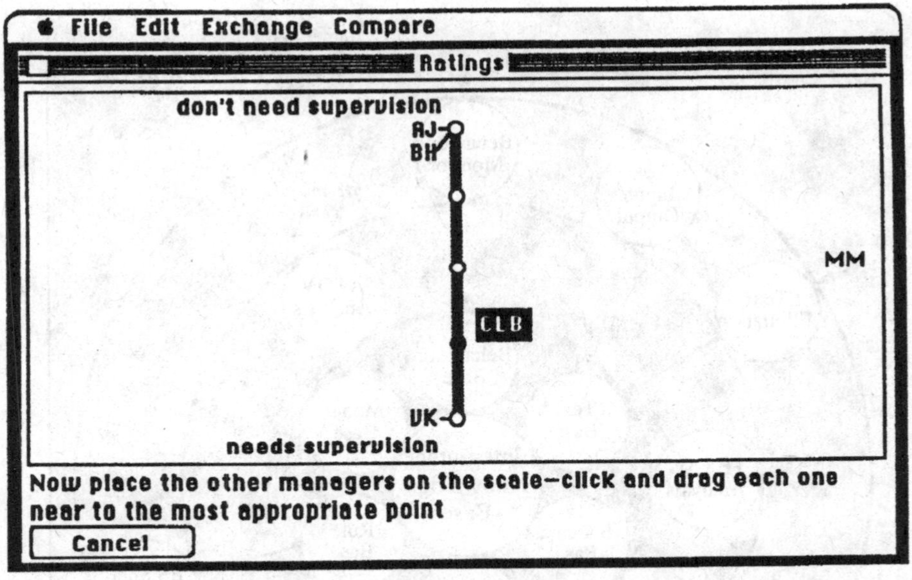

Figure 6: Graphic click and drag knowledge elicitation.

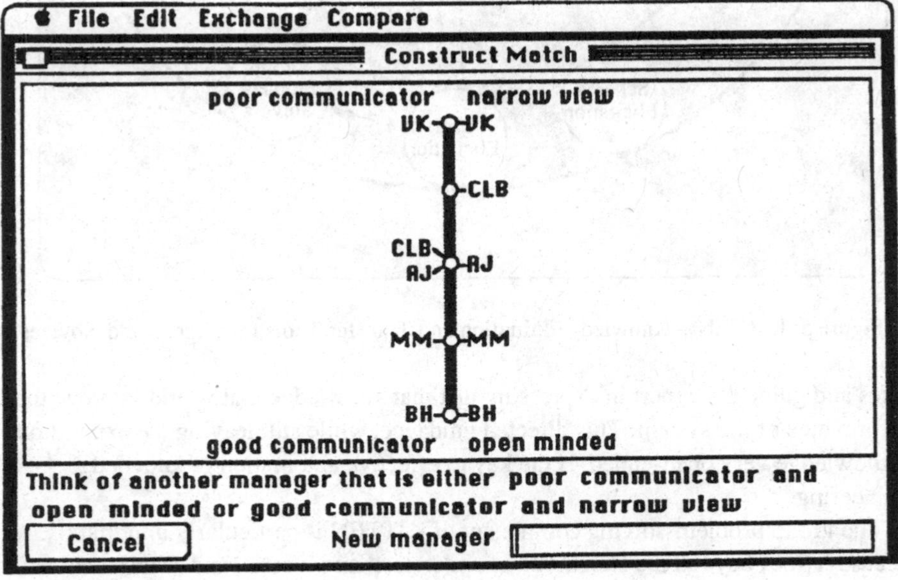

Figure 7: Feedback of matches to re-direct attention during elicitation.

transfer of knowledge and mutual understanding. The SOCIO analysis allows members of a community to explore their agreement and understanding with other members, and to make overt the knowledge network involved.

Various forms of data analysis and graphic presentation are available in KITTEN and in related systems such as ETS (Boose, 1986) and AQUINAS (Boose and Bradshaw, 1987), including the automatic generation of conceptual hierarchies and production rules with which to prime expert system shells. However, much of their success in aiding the rapid prototyping of expert systems comes from the very basic operations involved — that of eliciting the experts' own distinctions and personal vocabularies with no injection of concepts and terminologies from those outside the knowledge domain. Expert systems developed with these tools are natural to use because they operate within the same conceptual framework, using the same terminology, as normally expected by experts in the domain.

7. Dialog styles in expert systems

In the evolution of interactive systems three main styles of dialog may be distinguished (Gaines and Shaw, 1986a) as shown in Figure 8.

— *Graphic Dialog*: in which the human manipulation of objects within the world to communicate information and commands is simulated to access the activities and data structures within the computer.

— *Formal Dialog*: in which the activities and data structures within the computer are presented externally in a direct representation with the minimum syntactic sugar necessary to aid human cognition.

— *Natural Language Dialog*: in which the human use of language to communicate information and commands is simulated within the narrow context of the activities and data structures within the computer.

All three styles are found in expert systems with the variations being primarily based on the underlying technology rather than consideration of user needs.

As shown in Figure 8, the trend in the fifth generation is towards the integration of all three styles and recent expert systems reflect this. For example, GURU (Holsapple and Whinston, 1987) is a decision support shell incorporating an expert system shell that makes available a combination of formal dialog through prompt-response, menus or form-filling, coupled with natural language interaction. This makes it possible to access the same knowledge base through a variety of interactive styles that may be made to correspond to existing user experiences and preferences. Since it is designed to operate on personal computers without graphic facilities, it does not offer graphic dialog through icons and a mouse, although it would not be intrinsically difficult to incorporate this in its architecture.

<table>
<tr><th>Generation</th><th>Graphic Dialog
Representing world</th><th>Formal Dialog
Representing computer</th><th>Natural Language Dialog
Representing person</th></tr>
<tr><td>2
1956-63</td><td>Expensive
Flight simulators & process simulators for limited military and industrial use</td><td>Simplistic
Job control languages giving operators access to machine features</td><td>Output Only
Natural language output from stored script in early computer-aided instruction</td></tr>
<tr><td>3
1964-71</td><td>Practical
Mimic diagrams
Light pens
Touch screens</td><td>Standard
Simple prompt-response
Menus
Form-filling</td><td>Primitive
Keyword recognition
Incorporation of words from input in output</td></tr>
<tr><td>4
1972-79</td><td>Creating Reality
Windows
Icons
Desktop simulation</td><td>Sophisticated
Dialog-engineered prompt-response
Interactive form-filling
Intelligent form-filling</td><td>Practical
Understanding fixed domain
Understanding DBMS domain
Meta-level understanding</td></tr>
<tr><td rowspan="6">5
1980-87</td><td>Low-Cost</td><td>Integrative</td><td>Sophisticated</td></tr>
<tr><td>PC flight simulators</td><td colspan="2">Integration through INTELLECT & GURU</td></tr>
<tr><td colspan="2">Integration through Macintosh</td><td></td></tr>
<tr><td colspan="2">Integration through Symphony & Framework</td><td></td></tr>
<tr><td colspan="3">LISP machine applications</td></tr>
<tr><td colspan="3">Fifth generation objectives</td></tr>
</table>

Figure 8: The development of styles of dialog through generations of computers.

The best known early expert system, MYCIN (Shortliffe, 1976) was developed prior to both the Lisp machine and personal computer technologies and used a simple prompt-response dialog. It aids a clinician to make decisions about the diagnosis and treatment of microbial infections using rules of the form shown in Figure 9(i). The illustrative dialog shows MYCIN first gathering data about the patient and then using this to make inferences about the probable infections present. The first support system for knowledge engineering was also developed as part of the MYCIN project since it was found that it was difficult to trace the rules causing errors in the deductions of MYCIN if the clinician felt that something had gone wrong. TEIRESIAS (Davis and Lenat, 1982) was added as an auxiliary expert system with expertise *about* MYCIN, and the facility to explain MYCIN's decisions, and help the clinician amend the rules when they lead to incorrect conclusions. It uses a similar rule-based approach to

RULE 50
If 1) the infection is primary-bacteremia, and
2) the site of the culture is one of the sterile sites, and
3) the suspected portal of entry of the organism is the gastro-intestinal tract,
Then there is suggestive evidence (.7) that the identity of the organism is bacteroides.

(i) Rule from MYCIN medical diagnosis system.

METARULE003:
If 1) there are rules which do not mention the current goal in their premise
2) there are rules which mention the current goal in their premise
Then it is definite that the former should be done before the latter.

(ii) A TEIRESIAS metarule.

Figure 9: Examples of expert system inference rules.

reasoning as does MYCIN but the rules are now *metarules* about the forms of rules and the use of rules as shown in Figure 9(ii).

The effect of the metarules on the dialog is that the clinician and MYCIN-TEIRESIAS can discuss the rules and inferences made as well as the patient, organisms and infection. Figure 10 shows a debugging sequence in which the inference made by MYCIN is noted to be incorrect and TEIRESIAS aids the clinician in correcting it. In this dialog the clinician noticed an identity was missing in those deduced by MYCIN. He chose to allow TEIRESIAS to guide the debugging, and it used the metarule of starting with the identity which appeared incorrectly. The program then reconstructed the deductive process, asking the clinician to confirm its actions at each stage, or comment on anything incorrect. It confirmed the facts about the particular case in hand and checked that the rules were correct. Before very long the issue has become sharply focused for the clinician and the system.

Many significant expert system developments in recent years have taken place on Lisp machines which provide a powerful graphic dialog environment derived from the Xerox Star design (Smith *et al.*, 1983). This has proved particularly significant in the implementation of the knowledge base display module in Figure 2 where a network representation of the conceptual hierarchies being used is very effective. This approach has been taken down-market also with expert system shells such as

---

INFECTION-1 is PRIMARY-BACTEREMIA
<Item 1> E.COLI [ORGANISM-1]
<Item 2> PSEUDOMONAS-AERUGINOSA [ORGANISM-1]
Are all these identities correct? **N**
Are there any identities missing? **Y**
Which one(s)? **KLEBSIELLA-PNEUMONIAE PROTEUS-NON-MIRABILIS**
Are there any identities that shouldn't have appeared? **Y**
Which one(s)? **PSEUDOMONAS-AERUGINOSA**
Do you want to
    1] track down the problem yourself,or
    2] allow me to guide the debugging, or
    3] ignore it for now and fix it another time?
Type 1, 2 or 3 **2**
We'll start with the PSEUDOMONAS-AERUGINOSA first. The following rules were used
    in deducing that the identity of ORGANISM-1 is pseudomonas-aeruginosa
RULE184
Since [1.1] the category of ORGANISM-1 is not known
    [1.2] the gram strain of ORGANISM-1 is gramneg
    [1.3] the morphology of ORGANISM-1 is rod
    [1.4] the aerobicity of ORGANISM-1 is facultative
There is weakly suggestive evidence (.3) that the identity of ORGANISM-1 is
    pseudomonas-aeruginosa
Is this rule correct? **Y**
Should its premise have failed for this case? **Y**
Which clause of the premise should have been false? [give #] **1**
No conclusions were reached concerning the category of ORGANISM-1. Should it
    have been possible to conclude a category? **Y**
Which one? **ENTEROBACTERIACEAE**
There were no rules successfully invoked in the attempt to deduce that the category
    of ORGANISM-1 is enterobacteriaceae.
The following (potentially applicable) rules were NOT executed because the starred
    [**] clause failed
RULE116
If   1) the identity of ORGANISM-1 is not known
  ** 2) the gram strain of ORGANISM-1 is not known
    3) the morphology of ORGANISM-1 is not known
    4) the site of CULTURE-1 is csf
    5) the infection is meningitis
    6) the age (in years) of Albert Hall is less than or equal to .17
then there is weakly suggestive evidence (.33) that the category of ORGANISM-1 is
    enterobacteriaceae
RULE050
If   1) the morphology of ORGANISM-1 is rod
    2) the gram strain of ORGANISM-1 is gramneg
    3) the aerobicity of ORGANISM-1 is facultative
  ** 4) the infection with ORGANISM-1 was acquired while the patient was
    hospitalised
then there is suggestive evidence (.7) that the category of ORGABISM-1 is
    enterobacteriaceae
Are all these rules correct? **Y**
Should any of them have been successfully invoked? **N**
Is there a rule missing? **Y**
Ok, then I need a rule that would allow me to deduce that the category of ORGANISM-1 is
    enterobacteriaceae.
Would you like to give me such a rule now? **Y**

Figure 10: A knowledge engineering dialog with TEIRESIAS.

Nexpert (Rappaport, 1986) which operate in the Apple Macintosh environment. Figure 11 shows some of the uses of windows in Nexpert.

- *Transcript* window keeps a log of the complete interaction, data entered, hypotheses entered, inferences made, conclusions reached, and so on.
- *Categories* window shows the conceptual structure of the rules and data.
- *Rules* window shows the rules in the knowledge base.
- *Hypotheses* window shows the hypotheses entered.
- *Data* window shows the data entered or inferred.
- *Hypothesis* window shows the current hypothesis under consideration.
- *Conclusions* window shows the conclusions reached during inferencing.
- *Prompt* window (a one-line strip at the bottom of the screen, just visible in Figure 11) shows what action would take place if the mouse were to be clicked at the current cursor position.

The prompt window is an important contribution to the usability of a complex window, icon and mouse environment where the user often finds it difficult to determine which of the many actions available will achieve his objective. As he moves the cursor around the screen using the mouse the text in the prompt window changes

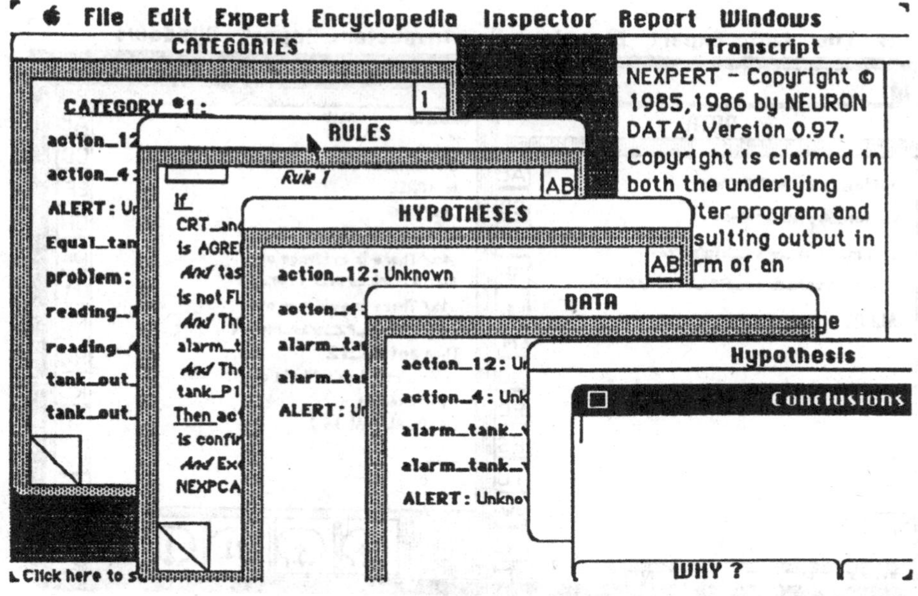

Figure 11: A modern multi-window, menu and icon environment in Nexpert.

continuously to show what action would be initiated if he clicked the mouse in that position.

Figure 12 shows a further window, the *rule editor*, which illustrates some of the care taken about human factors in Nexpert's design:

- the use of the four "head" icons at the bottom to indicate how to add a rule, modify a rule, make a copy of a rule, and delete a rule, respectively;
- the use of the "writing" icon at the bottom right to indicate how the rules may be written to disk;
- the use of the "page turning" icon at the lower left of the window to indicate how the next rule may be accessed;
- the use of the "alphabetic index" icons on the right to indicate how the rules may be accessed by the first letter of their conclusion.

Note also how the rule itself is automatically formatted for clarity in presentation. The prompt window is particularly helpful for initial users who are not familiar with the icons since moving the cursor to an icon brings up an explanation of the action involved as a prompt.

The graphic dialog capabilities used in Nexpert are important not only in their

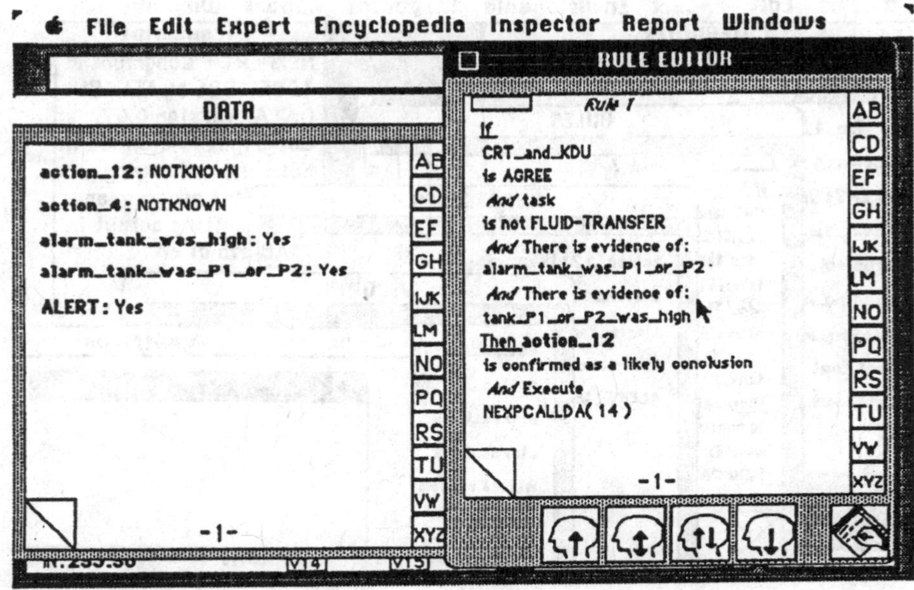

Figure 12: The rule editor dialog environment in Nexpert.

standard window, menu and icon forms, but also in their capability to allow mimic diagrams to be used in highly customised user interfaces. Figure 13 shows a mimic diagram monitoring the status of a chemical plant through data received from instruments communicating through a Macintosh serial port. The operator can see the status of the plant through the numeric indicators and also actuate the plant by clicking on the valve symbols causing them to open and close.

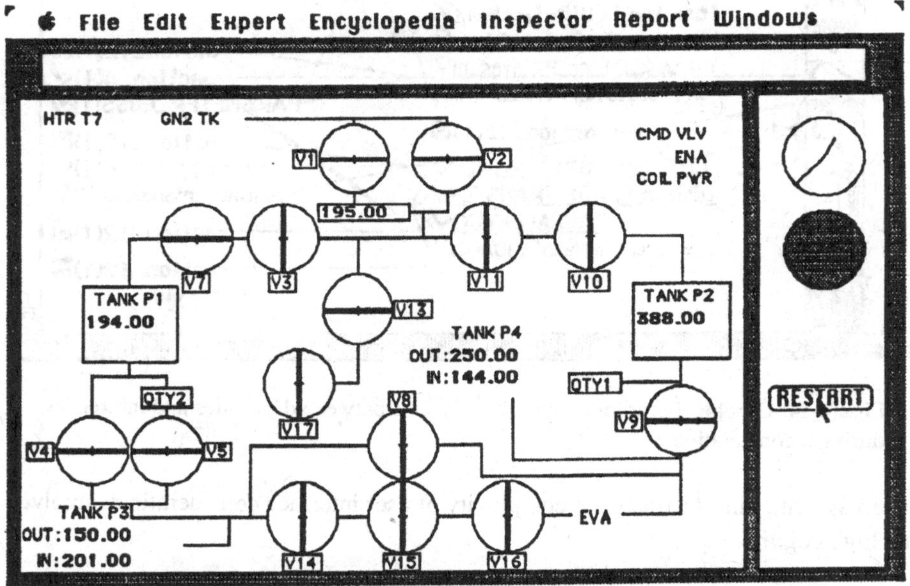

Figure 13: Dialog through a mimic diagram of gauges and semaphores in Nexpert.

Nexpert also uses the graphic capabilities to show the data and inferences in graphic form as shown in Figure 14. The knowledge engineer can navigate the knowledge base during an interaction and determine which rules have been invoked, and which rules are capable of being invoked, based on the data entered through the instruments and by the operator.

An important capability of Nexpert is that it allows a user to enter a hypothesis which it takes as a goal to be derived from inference rules and facts in the knowledge base. However, if it disproves the hypothesis, it takes the data gathered from the user during its attempt to derive the hypothesis and draws whatever conclusions it can from them. The result is that it often comes up with a hypothesis that the user regards as the "nearest" true one to that which he suggested. This is a powerful feature in an

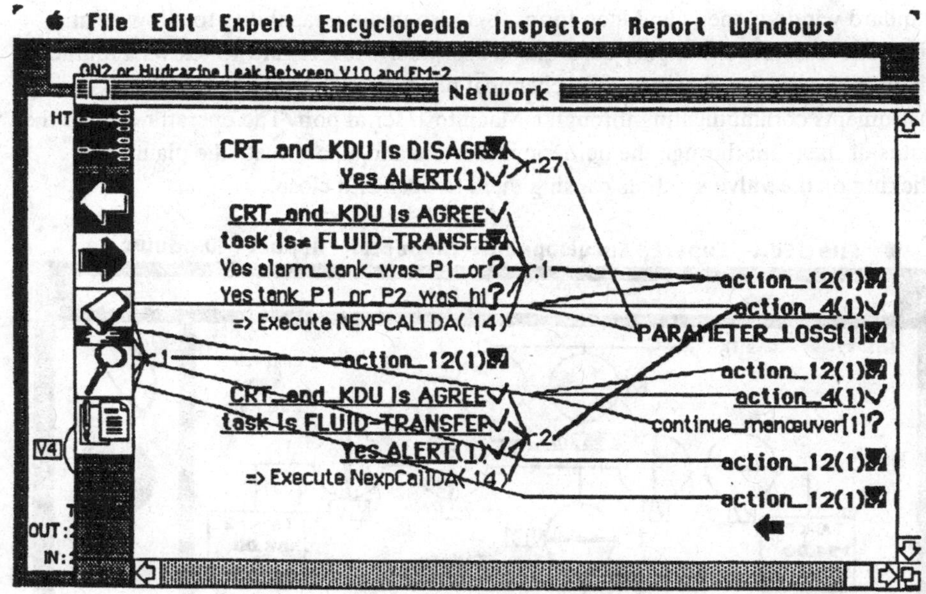

Figure 14: Graphical presentation of the relations between data, rules and inferences during a consultation.

expert system, but illustrates the complexity of user interface considerations involved at a high cognitive level.

8. Standard dialog guidelines applied to expert systems

As experience in the design and use of interactive systems has grown, guidelines have been developed for the design of effective human-computer dialog, commencing with Hansen (1971) and culminating in the very detailed review of Williges and Williges (1984). Shneiderman (1980) has collected many of these rules together, and Maguire (1982) has analysed some of them systematically, noting contradictions and proposing their resolution. It is interesting to apply such guidelines to expert systems, both to use them to design the user interface and also to see how well the guidelines apply in the context of new technology. The following sub-sections recapitulate the 30 guidelines given by Gaines and Shaw (1984) and discuss their application to expert systems.

8.1 *Principles of responsibility*

8.1.1 We are all responsible for computer behaviour

Remember when you treat computer-people interaction as if it were people-people interaction that the computer is behaving as it was programmed to. We, as specifiers, programmers and users, are all responsible for the behaviour of computer systems.

This guideline emphasises a particularly sensitive issue relating to expert systems — who is responsible for their advice and the adverse effects of actions resulting from errors in the system? It is surprising that accounting, medical and military use of conventional data-processing has not already led to major issues of legal responsibility for computer malfunction. Expert systems introduce a very direct link between the human professional and the information processing of a computer system and, since professionals can be held liable for the adverse consequences of their advice, it is reasonable to ask whether that liability perseveres when their advice-giving procedures are transferred to the computer.

8.1.2 Computers provide a new medium for communication

Remember when you try to understand the rôle of computers that they provide a new medium for communication that will be used in part to mimic those already existing. However, they will also change our society and modes of thinking in ways that we are not able to predict.

Books have long been used to encode expertise. However, the interaction with a book is one-way. The medium does not make provision for us to ask questions if we do not understand the book. Expert systems may be seen as the initial development of two-way, interactive books. The forms of knowledge that can be encoded and the richness of interaction possible are still very limited compared with those with the human author. However, as expert systems develop they will provide a radically new medium for human communication.

8.1.3 Computer programs encode expertise

A computer program encodes the expertise of a person to make it accessible to others. The effectiveness of dialog depends on encoding expertise in communication.

Expertise in communication can be encoded in an expert system and, hence, one major application is to provide better interfaces to existing programs.

8.1.4 Programs create the reality experienced by the users of computers

Remember that the computer is a tool for simulation and that what is simulated becomes reality for the user. The power of the computer should be used to create worlds that are simple for the user and natural to the task.

Most expert systems currently operate through keyboard input and textual output. However, the combination of expert systems and simulation techniques to provide knowledgeable environments is extremely powerful and will be an increasing basis for significant applications.

8.1.5 The rôle expected of the system should be maintained

Tricks of dialog should not be used to give a false impression of the capabilities of the computer system. A rôle should be accurately projected that can be maintained throughout the interaction.

The rôle integrity of expert systems is particularly important if they are to be used in error-sensitive applications. Computer advice still bears the stamp of unreasonable authority. Uncertain advice should be clearly presented as dubious. If there is more than one option, alternative advice should be made available.

8.2 *Principles of past experience*

8.2.1 Users already have expectations about computers

Take into account the possibility that the user's expectations of the computer will affect his interpretation of any dialog with it. The dialog should be designed to minimise confusion arising from these prior expectations.

The dialog conventions of early expert systems have already become well-established so that "how" and "why" questions are expected and well-understood.

8.2.2 Choose through experience

Conversational systems should be experienced before they are talked about. Prospective users should experience interaction with a related system before specifying their requirements for their own system.

The emphasis in expert system design has been in getting the experts to act as specifier rather than the users, presumably on the assumption that users will accept the authority of experts in relation to the computer system as well as in relation to their expertise.

8.2.3 Use the vocabulary of expert and user

Listen carefully to conversations between experts and users, and design the dialog using their normal vocabulary.

The vocabulary in expert systems is very important. The expert specifies his conceptual framework and inference rules, and it is assumed that the user can communicate and understand facts within that framework.

8.2.4 Users readily think of computer systems in the same way as they think of people

One expectation of computers is that they will behave similarly to people in their conversation and modes of operation. If we do not wish this to occur then we have to be careful that the program presents the computer as a piece of equipment and not as the simulation of a person.

It is natural to adopt an animistic approach to expert systems because they are expected to mimic the advice-generating processes of a human expert. The danger that the user will take the system outside its range of competence yet still assume it to be expert is still highly significant.

8.3 *Some principles of understanding*

8.3.1 Make the system easy to understand

Users will model the computer system and form new expectations based on their interaction with it. The system should be designed to induce accurate models and correct expectations.

The system needs to project to the user the scope and limitations of its knowledge base and inference processes.

8.3.2 The system should be consistent in operation

The commands should always do the same thing throughout. The information presentation should always mean the same thing throughout.

Consistency needs to apply not only to the user interface but also to the access to the knowledge base and inference system through that interface.

8.3.3 The system should be uniform in operation

The facilities which users have learned to use in one part of the package should be available to them in other parts if they might reasonably expect this.

Uniformity needs to apply to the forms of knowledge representation as well as to the user interface to those forms. Some expert systems still drop into Lisp-like data structures for certain editing operations.

8.3.4 The state of the system should be clear to the user

Computer systems can be complex and their internal state is not easy to see. Important information about the state of the system should be shown to the user in such a way that it is easily assimilated.

The state of an expert system is very complicated. The user needs to be able to review the facts he has entered, the facts already in the knowledge base, those inferred, and the inference rules in the knowledge base.

8.3.5 The user should be shown the choices available

At any point in a formal dialog sequence the user will have a limited range of options available. There should be a facility to enable the user to find out his choices.

Queries to the user in expert systems are often open-ended yet the values tested in the rules are often highly restricted. The user should be able to determine significant replies which will actually cause different rules to be used.

8.4 *Some principles of adaptation*

8.4.1 The system should adapt to the user under user control

Provision should be made for various levels of user knowledge but no attempt should be made to estimate this automatically. The user should be given control over the level of help provided by the system.

Users of expert system shells vary widely in their computer literacy. Knowledge engineers, experts, frequent users and casual users, all have different support requirements that should be available under user control.

8.4.2 The system should minimise the user's workload by anticipating responses

The most likely user response should be made the default option that can be selected by a single user action.

Procedures which reduce the complexity of user decision making in expert systems are very important to the acceptance of the technology.

8.4.3 The system should cooperate with the user in validating responses

Information should be checked as it is entered and queried if it appears unlikely to be correct. The consequences of significant actions should be made clear to the user and confirmation requested before they are carried out.

Response validation can be more thorough in a well-designed expert system because the programming environment provides for the expression of complex validation procedures. Thus checking information entered should be part of the expertise embedded in the system.

8.4.4 It should be easy to escape from a dialog cleanly

At any point in a formal dialog sequence the user may wish to abort the dialog and escape any consequences of his preceding responses. There should be a

facility to enable the user to escape at will leaving the state of the system well defined.

Care is needed with the abort facility to determine which information that has been entered should be deleted. The deletion of inferences made from it is not a trivial problem, particularly if the system operates on a resource allocation rather than exhaustive inference basis.

8.5 *Some principles of style*

8.5.1 The style of dialog varies with the computer technology used

Some aspects of computer dialog style will be dependent on the type of person-computer interface available. Be aware of the capabilities and limitations of different interfaces.

Every form of dialog style is being used in expert systems: prompt-response; form-filling; menus and function keys; windows and mouse; and natural language. Many mixtures of these also occur and a good shell provides all styles so that it can mimic existing interactive procedures for particular user groups.

8.5.2 Be aware of the repertoire of techniques for person-computer dialog

The range of styles and techniques for dialog is continually increasing as is the experience in their use. Approach new situations with an open mind as to what techniques would be appropriate and maintain awareness of new approaches as they develop.

The availability of an expert system shell allows the dialog itself to be generated through knowledge-based procedures and hence introduces new programming styles and techniques.

8.5.3 Natural language may be used in a variety of different ways

In considering the use of natural language dialog with computer systems note that it can be used for output independently of input.

Most shells provide natural language output in prompts and explanations. This should be parametrised so that values of variables can be used within it, otherwise the external dialog may get out of step with the internal operation of the system as it is developed or modified. Writing the system for ease of modification is a significant software engineering skill in its own right.

8.5.4 Fluent language may not imply fluent understanding

Take into account when evaluating any system that apparently good conversational dialog may be generated through rules that are based on little understanding of what is being said. There can be widely differing degrees of understanding underlying the same dialog.

Most shells do not provide a deep natural language analysis capability. Where they mimic this through some elementary keyword recognition procedures it is important that the user becomes aware of its limitations. Translating the internal representation of a natural language request back into natural language and showing it to the user is a good way to accustom the user to what is actually happening.

8.6 *Some principles of presentation*

8.6.1 Programs require presentation

Programs in the new medium for communication provided by computers require the same attention to techniques of presentation as have those in past media.

It is important to encourage experts to interact with, edit and validate the knowledge base of the expert system that encodes their expertise. Mediation by the knowledge engineer is an impediment to system development and should only be used for initial hand-holding to accustom the expert to the system. It is important that the system market itself to both expert and user — certainly that it places no impediments in the way of their use.

8.6.2 Know the market

The designer of a new computer program should have in mind a clear market defined by customer needs and requirements.

The top-down approach is very important to expert system design. The technology is attractive and many applications are being considered which will not prove cost-effective. The ultimate "why?" question to any expert system has to be "why should you exist?", and it should be asked at a very early stage of development.

8.6.3 Users should be informed

At every stage in the chain from marketing through selling, training and routine use of a computer program, users of that program need to be kept informed of relevant information about it.

The problems of keeping users well-informed are exacerbated in expert systems by the complexity of the systems, their local customisation, and the need for continual local and global updating. Knowledge is complex and dynamic, and the systems reflect this.

8.6.4 Programs should be self-sufficient

Computer programs developed for a particular application should be extended to present themselves to potential customers and to tutor their users.

Good expert system shells have the capability to present knowledge-based tutorials and provide knowledge-based help facilities. Indeed, these may be the main applications of the shell in a system that gives improved access to conventional data-processing.

8.7 *Some principles of development*

8.7.1 Design never ceases

Systems evolve as users gain experience and develop their requirements. The interactive facilities of the computer should be used for development also to aid the enhancement of a system in the light of experience.

Expert systems are subject to local customisation and updating, and hence the developmental tools should be fully integrated with the application environment.

8.7.2 Dialog should be logged and analysed

The computer should be used to maintain selective records of dialog and programs provided to analyse these in terms of, for example, errors broken down by user and dialog sequence.

Dialog logs are valuable with expert systems as audit trails of the advice generating process, not only to capture awkwardness in dialog but also errors in the user's understanding and the system's knowledge processing.

8.7.3 Design for a changing and uncertain future

User requirements will change, possibly unpredictably. Systems should be designed to allow for enhancements and to leave the possibility of open-ended extension.

The knowledge base in current expert systems tends to be very shallow, reflecting the surface structure of the expert's skill rather than the deeper principles behind it. Hence, the system needs to change as new knowledge is acquired.

8.7.4 Make the best use of today's technology today and tomorrow's tomorrow

Do not wait for the pace of change in computer technology to slow down. It will not. Do not assume that what is an appropriate use of today's technology will be appropriate for that of tomorrow. It may not.

Expert system technology is changing very rapidly. Shells are offering a wider variety and more powerful forms of representation and inference. User interfaces are improving. Simulation, graphics, communications and links to other programs are becoming widely available. However, we are in the early stages of a new and immature technology and the pace of progress will increase not slacken. System designers have to make use of what is available without becoming locked in to obsolete conceptual frameworks.

9. Specific dialog guidelines for expert systems

Section 2 suggests that new informatic technologies will require new approaches to design for usability; and the analyses of explanation in Section 4, of knowledge engineering in Sections 5 and 6, and of expert system dialog styles in Section 7, have provided examples of new usability considerations in expert systems. However, Section 8 has shown that existing guidelines continue to apply. The overall situation may be captured in two *meta-principles*.

9.1 *Some meta-principles for expert systems usability*

9.1.1 Previous guidelines continue to apply

> *Guidelines developed for effective dialog with previous generations of interactive systems continue to apply to knowledge-based systems.*

Principles of responsibility, past experience, understanding, adaptation, style, presentation and development continue to be important for new generations of knowledge-based systems. Violations of these guidelines will result in problems for the user which cannot be overcome by the use of "intelligent" processing. Conformity with these guidelines will at least give the user a secure foundation on which to build experience of the new technologies. The interpretation of the guidelines should be widened to take into account particular features of knowledge-based systems.

9.1.2 Additional guidelines are required

> *Guidelines developed for effective dialog with previous generations of interactive systems do not encompass some critical features of knowledge-based systems and require specific extensions.*

The critical areas where knowledge-based systems have made significant advances that affect usability are primarily in the explanation facilities and in knowledge acquisition. There are some side-effects of expert systems being part of the trend towards complex integrated systems, possibly involving multiple tasks and multiple users, that also need to be taken into account.

9.2 *Principles of explanation*

9.2.1 Make provision for multiple levels of explanation

Recognise the plurality of possible explanations for the conclusions reached by a knowledge-based system, and match the level of explanation to the user's requirements.

It is likely that the requirements for adequate explanation are more severe than those for valid advice, and hence this usability requirement may be a very important dynamic in the development of expert system shells.

9.2.2 Allow for ill-posed questions

User requests for explanation may well be ill-posed and provision should be made for inferring the question to be answered rather than deriving it directly from the request.

Explanation facilities may be seen as an extension of past 'help' facilities. When users requires help it is likely that they are not in a position to be clear and correct in specifying their request.

9.3 *Principles of knowledge acquisition*

9.3.1 Integrate knowledge acquisition with knowledge application

Make no unnecessary distinctions between the processes of applying a knowledge-based system and those of developing it.

The distinctions between expert, knowledge engineer and user are ones of rôles rather than people. Many users will play more than one rôle and will be confused by unnecessary changes in the modes of operation and data presentation.

9.4 *Principles of integration*

9.4.1 Generate dialog from knowledge structures

Generate all dialog directly from the same knowledge structures used for inference and do not have separate structures for questioning and explanation.

The complexity, customisation and rapidity of change of knowledge-based systems makes it very difficult to keep the main system and its support systems in step unless there are automatic links between them. Documentation, dialog and explanation should be generated from the knowledge structures rather than as separate entities. This requirement may be more severe than that for valid inference and hence should be a major design consideration for expert system shells.

9.5 *Principles of rationality*

9.5.1 Match the behaviour of the system to the cognitive expectations of the user
Structure dialog, inference and explanation to appear as the reasonable behaviour of an expert advisor.

The generation of requests for data through backtracking is known to appear reasonable to users. Nexpert's technique of using data elicited to test a false hypothesis to generate the 'nearest' true hypothesis also appears very reasonable to users. We need greater understanding of these criteria of rationality in order to optimise the usability of knowledge-based systems.

Many more dialog rules at greater levels of detail could be generated for informatics usability of expert systems. However, the following section suggests that it may be more productive to use knowledge-based systems to express the knowledge structure underlying effective human-computer interaction, and derive specific guidelines from general considerations.

10. The impact of expert systems on usability

The move to knowledge-based systems is not just creating new problems of usability, but also offering new solutions to old problems, including direct application to the user interface itself and indirect application to our conceptualisation of its design. The direct application of expert system techniques to improve the human-computer interface is an attractive possibility, for example, in replacing simplistic *help* facilities with a more flexible expert advisor. Such possibilities have been studied in the literature under the heading of *intelligent user interfaces*, and Rissland (1984) gives a number of knowledge requirements for intelligent interfaces:

- knowledge of the user — for example, preferred style or level of expertise;
- knowledge of the user's tasks — for example, context or ultimate use of results;
- knowledge of the tools available and being used — for example, protocols for invocation and use of resources needed;
- knowledge of the domain of the user's task — for example, epistemological knowledge or measures of importance;
- knowledge of interaction modalities — for example, how to communicate graphically or by speech;
- knowledge of how to interact — for example, when to intervene or look over the user's shoulder;
- evaluation knowledge — for example, how to judge effectiveness or act on gripes.

There are few examples of practical applications of intelligent user interfaces as yet. Totterdell and Cooper (1986) have reported a study of an adaptive front-end to an electronic mail system. Chalfen (1986) has developed an expert shell for easing user access to integrated heterogeneous software. This is particularly important in enabling third generation simulation software already existing to be brought into a fourth generation interactive environment through the use of fifth generation knowledge-based techniques. Kitto and Boose (1987) have described an intelligent user interface to a knowledge acquisition system which guides the expert through the complexities of the acquisition process. This is significant in demonstrating that the new problems created by knowledge-based systems may also be alleviated using knowledge-based techniques.

The growing complexity of guidelines for informatics usability suggests that the use of knowledge-based systems for the design and evaluation of human-computer interaction may be attractive. Wilson, Barnard and MacLean (1986) have described an expert system development that makes user interface guidelines available as a decision support system for system design. Gaines (1987b) reports a systemic analysis of the knowledge structures underlying a human factors evaluation methodology for complex multi-modal, multi-user, multi-task systems developed by Edwards and Mason (1987).

Figure 15 is a synopsis of the Edwards and Mason evaluation methodology. They analyse an intelligent dialog system in terms of the eight aspects shown at the top of Figure 15, and then evaluate it in terms of the four dimensions shown at the bottom of the figure: *elegance*, capturing the notion of efficient design; *understandability*, capturing the notion of comprehensible design; *functionality*, capturing the notion of potential capability; and *suitability*, capturing the notion of usable capability. The knowledge structure of the basic distinctions underlying this evaluation methodology arise from the basic distinctions of structure and behaviour, and the evaluative dimensions arise from the basic distinctions of actuality and agency.

The development of knowledge structures underlying human-computer interaction will enable the empirical rules for effective dialog design to be subsumed into deeper principles applying at each level of the hierarchy of analysis of intelligent interactive systems. These structures are also the knowledge engineering foundations for knowledge-based advisory systems on complex human-computer system design and evaluation. Thus, as usual, progress in informatics is recursive with the next generation of knowledge-based systems providing both a range of new problems and also a range of techniques to cope with them.

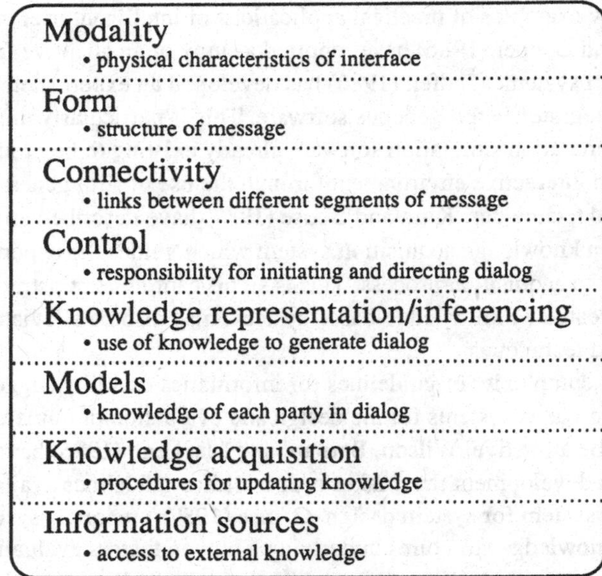

Aspects of Dialog

Observer / *System*	Structure	Behaviour
Logical	Elegance *Efficient design*	Functionality *Potential capability*
Psychological	Understandability *Comprehensible design*	Suitability *Usable capability*

Dimensions within Aspects

Figure 15: Aspects and dimensions of an evaluation schema for human factors in intelligent dialog systems.

11. Conclusions — steps toward knowledge science

The domain of knowledge-based systems creates many new problems and opportunities for research, studies, guidelines and theories relating to informatics usability. This paper has surveyed many aspects of expert systems usability including

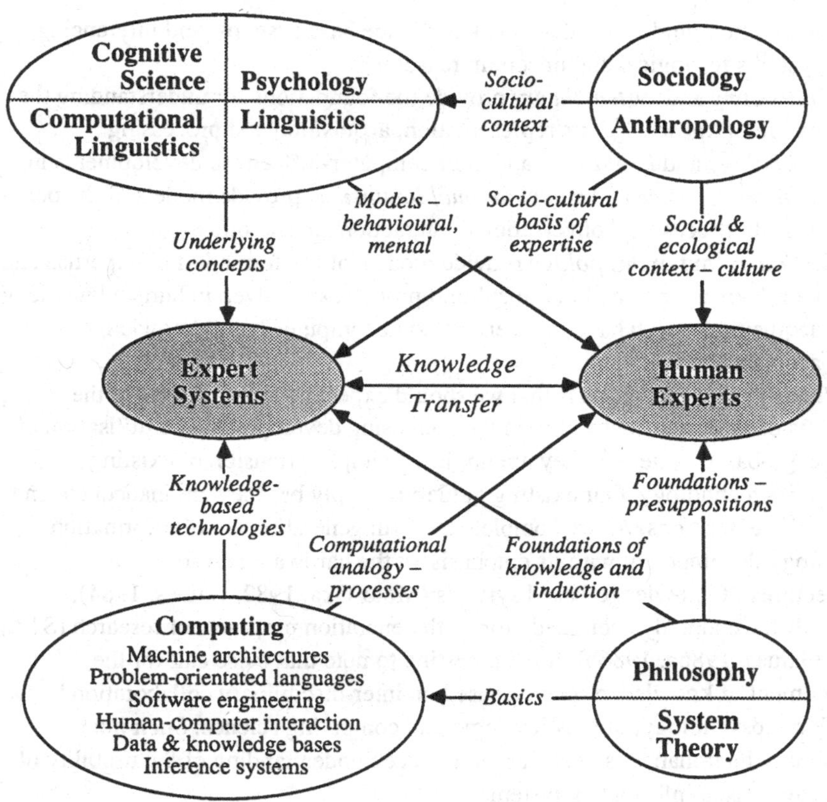

Figure 16: Relationships between the many different disciplines contributing to the usability of expert systems.

the relevance of existing human-computer interface guidelines and the new problems that arise from these systems. In conclusion it is interesting to note the very wide range of disciplines necessary to support the scientific development of usability considerations for expert systems. Figure 16 shows the wide range of relationships and contributions necessary:

- The fundamental problem is that of *knowledge transfer* between computer-based expert systems and human experts of various kinds, including users and knowledge engineers as well as domain experts.
- *Computing science* provides the required technologies with special-purpose machines, languages, software engineering techniques, human-computer

interaction guidelines, data and knowledge base systems, and inferencing systems for logical and uncertain reasoning.

- *Philosophy* and *system theory* provide the foundations for understanding the nature of knowledge, its representation, acquisition and processing.
- *Psychology* and *linguistics*, and their computer-influenced developments in *cognitive science* and *computational linguistics*, provide models of the person, thought processes, conversational interaction, and so on.
- *Sociology* and *anthropology* provide models of the formation of expertise and its rôle in society, and of the cultural processes involved in human knowledge acquisition which have to be emulated in computer-based knowledge acquisition.

What Figure 16 suggests is that we should expect no easy answers to the problems of informatics usability in the increasing development and utilisation of knowledge-based systems. They are not just a simple extension of existing informatics technology. Our existing guidelines apply but they are inadequate and need major extensions. As we complete the fifth generation era of information technology development with its emphasis on the hardware and software architectures of knowledge-based systems (Moto-Oka, 1982; Gaines, 1984), proposals have already been made for sixth generation programs of research (STA, 1985; Gaines, 1986a, 1986b). It is interesting to note that these call for the development of knowledge science based on inter-disciplinary collaboration between neurology, psychology, linguistics, logic and computing science. Such inter-disciplinary interchange is necessary to the deep understanding of the usability of knowledge-based informatics systems.

Acknowledgements

Financial assistance for this work has been made available by the National Sciences and Engineering Research Council of Canada. I am grateful to my colleagues John Boose, Jeff Bradshaw, Alain Rappaport and Mildred Shaw for many discussions and access to material used in this paper.

Part 4

Organisational Aspects and Design in Large Systems

CHAPTER ELEVEN

ORGANISATIONAL ISSUES AND TASK ANALYSIS

SIEGFRIED GREIF

1. Introduction

The allocation of tasks between humans and technology within many organisations seems to depend more on the qualities of increasingly sophisticated informatics systems than on the qualities of the human user. Rarely does an organisation achieve an appropriate balance between the two. Whatever the balance there will be implications for organisational structure, particularly in such aspects as the division of labour within it, the structure and arrangement of tasks and the structure and arrangement of communication networks.

Unfortunately the reciprocal and interactive effects which exist between organisational design and informatics design are often overlooked. Research clearly shows that in the future the organisation must go beyond a strategy of simply implementing the newest or best hardware and software system in the organisation and "muddling through" the resulting problems of organisational changes. Informatics design, organisational tasks and training have to be integrated from the beginning if high standards of efficiency and humanisation of working life are to be met.

Several authors, for example, advocate as an efficient and innovative model, high technology production systems organised around small, decentralised or independent units. Other authors suggest that there will be an increase in centralisation and control supported by more potent reward and feedback systems which are made possible by the new technologies. Either situation is possible; much depends on the decisions that are made about when, why and how new technology is to be used. It also, of course, depends on whether the reward and feedback system is used to control completely the task performance of organisational members or whether it is established as a means of self controlled management and learning.

Other major dimensions which must be considered in the design of informatics systems are the division of labour, the competences of the members of the organisation and the extent to which the organisation is segmented. Some authors consider the informatics system, which has multi-task potential and which can be used by heterogeneous users, may well bring an end to the traditional industrial forms of the division of labour, i.e., specialisation, etc. Other authors predict an even more radical segmentation of the labour force between the unskilled and the highly qualified computer experts. Complex psychological models have been developed, like Hacker's (1985) action theoretical concept of "complete activities" which directly aim at guiding future informatics design. Another approach involves the concept of "task and competence oriented software design". Other models like Ulich's (1978) concept of "differential job design" allow for different individual needs, problem solving strategies and competences of people doing the same job.

The construction of adequate methods for the assessment and evaluation of changes is by no means a problem which is only important for scientific progress. In the long term the organisation needs reliable and valid data on organisational changes and their effects in order to make valid and appropriate decisions. It is conceivable that instead of global scales of organisational dimensions and behaviour, "task analysis" will be the preferred basic methodological perspective, giving precise observation data on keystroke times and errors in human-computer dialogues. There are many problems in analysing complex jobs and organisational interactions in this way. An illustration of the technique used at the University of Osnabrück is given which attempts to overcome traditional, mechanistic approaches by the incorporation into task analysis of psychological and cognitive modelling, etc.

In this paper a number of illustrated models of organisational change are discussed. These clearly demonstrate the need for an integration of informatics design and organisational development. A number of basic dimensions of organisational structure are also examined. Informatics design may be seen as conflicting with, or acting in support of, characteristics of these dimensions.

2. Technological determinism

It is the position of technological determinism that organisational structures and processes are dependent on the technology applied (Woodward, 1958, 1965). Reviews of empirical studies show (cf. Staehle, 1985, p. 502 ff), that simple models assuming direct causal effects of technology have to be abandoned or to be replaced by complex interdependency models which allow for additional moderating influences like the predictability and complexity of environmental conditions (e.g., the stability of the market). Despite this, there seems to be a revival of simple models of technological determinism regarding the assumed consequences of informatics design on organisations. If we apply a different informatics design philosophy to maximize the criteria of usability like, for example, "flexibility" (cf. Shackel, 1985; Ulich *et al.*, 1986) then the interdependencies are changed completely. The informatics design is determined by variations in tasks and by the individual preferences of the user. This can enlarge the degrees of freedom beyond the possibilities of older technologies.

The determination of organisational structures and human behaviour processes therefore depends on the informatic design philosophy, which is applied by the organisation. Following Ulich *et al.* (1986, p. 38 ff), technology may be called an "option", because "it can be put to use in very diverse ways for various purposes... Whether or not the possibility of using technology to benefit men and women is realized, however, remains largely a political question".

Such political decisions on technologies have complex and uncertain consequences for the members of the organisation and for organisational efficiency. They raise new political conflicts on the priorities between organisational design or informatics design and the design principles which should or should not be put into practice. A wrong decision may be very dangerous for the survival of organisations. This explains perhaps the failure to reconcile different and opposing views and the tendency to adopt any design solution which has worked and has been used — perhaps even with doubtful success — by a leading organisation.

3. Coping strategies

The implementation of new or updated computer-based production and information technologies into an organisation can be both a challenge and a threat for individuals and groups within it. In the early days of implementation there is often a quick polarisation of opinions pro and contra computer-based technologies and a fractionisation of organisational members. This may even occur between groups supporting the new technologies. Systematic strategies of planned organisational changes to cope with resistance to change — which of course may be rational — are seldom applied (Hirschheim *et al.*, 1985; Pava, 1983). It is possible to divide the observable strategies of implementation into the following three broad categories:

(i) Buy and apply the best technological system (human needs and competences are secondary) and 'muddle through' the organisational problems.

This simple implementation strategy seems to be the one most often used. (For overviews of implementation studies see Bjørn-Andersen, 1985; Dzida *et al.*, 1984; Gottschall *et al.*, 1985; Otway and Peltu, 1983; Pomfrett *et al.*, 1985; Ulich *et al.*, 1986). 'Muddling through' may be an adequate rational choice in a complex and unpredictable situation. But organisations which do not have any coherent idea at the outset which facilities they might require from a new word processing system (the majority of the 92 companies questioned by Pomfrett *et al.*, 1985) and which do not plan an adequate redesign of organisational tasks and training facilities, are risking organisational confusion, conflict and unnecessary costs.

(ii) Active or passive resistance for as long as possible (informatics design is secondary) and 'muddling through' the resulting technology problems.

If the resistance to new computer technology is very high in the organisation, the decision may be not to buy any new system. This decision may be rational, where computer technology still is less efficient than traditional technologies or where it is too expensive (when all secondary costs like training have been included) for profitable use in the organisation. Even more interesting are the cases of real resistance in organisations, which then decide against buying new or updated computer technologies, especially where there is an obvious potential to increase profits or other benefits. In one situation farmers resisted computer technologies even when they have been shown to be efficient for the mass keeping of cattle, have been recommended by official consulting organisations and will be funded by government.

When systems are implemented in these circumstances the resulting problems are mainly ones which relate to lower levels of efficiency which may in turn lead to other consequences (e.g., loss of profits and future investments, market position). There may be other disadvantages too. In many industries, computer controlled production processes or robotics have reduced unhealthy working conditions and have helped to achieve high productivity gains for the organisation. But they have also contributed to high rates of unemployment on the general labour market. Unemployment itself is a plausible cause of negative attitudes, computer anxiety and passive or active resistance.

(iii) Planned integrative change of organisational tasks, informatics design and training.

It is possible to find cases where the implementation of new computer technologies in an organisation have been systematically planned. These are characterised by the analysis and redesign of organisational tasks, planning and experimentation. There are case studies of the planned implementation of computer-aided offices (cf. the ASTEX project of BMW, Munich, or three Swiss projects of Ulich *et al.*, 1986). But in all these projects, the integration of organisational tasks, informatics design and training together has not gone very far. It is noticeable that the informatics design concepts have not been altered much in direct relation to, or after, any analysis of tasks or possible training procedures.

A well balanced integrative strategy remains nebulous in the absence of theoretical models and methods to assess the criteria which have to guide the integrative solution.

4. Dimensions of organisational change

There are four basic dimensions, which are essential considerations for effective informatics design: (1) size, (2) centralisation versus decentralisation (3) reward and feedback system and (4) the division of labour or specialisation. (For other dimensions of organisations see Kubicek and Welter, 1985.)

4.1 *Size*

The number of organisational members has often been used as an elementary structural dimension. Simple theoretical models assume size to be an important independent variable in its own right which directly relates to other dimensions — like specialisation and coordination (cf. Kieser and Kubicek, 1976). For example, greater effort is needed to solve communication and information problems when larger numbers of people are involved. This results in a clear structure of subsystems with different tasks or activity fields. As a consequence it is necessary to develop coordination processes if the organisation is to function as an efficient and coherent system.

Since these demands are often very difficult to meet and since size is normally negatively correlated with satisfaction and innovativeness, small organisations ("small is beautiful") are often theoretically preferred. Ulich *et al.* (1986) explicitly takes this position and argues that new computer technologies allow for the future growth of small but innovative and highly productive organisations. It is interesting to note that a survey of 5051 firms in West Germany, by the journal *Impulse*, showed that 55% of the workforce worked in organisations with less than 500 members. The mean number of employees was 11.

Supporting the foundation of new small firms in fields of future growth through tax reductions by the government and professional counselling seems to be a successful strategy for partly reducing unemployment. In consequence Ulich has begun to carry out more projects investigating small and middle sized industries in Switzerland. A project on multi-task office software and training has also been carried out in Osnabrück, directed towards regional small and middle sized firms (Greif, 1989).

4.2 *Degree of centralisation*

Power and influence, information flow and the degree of control concerning organisational tasks (definition of goals, operations or operational criteria which the members have to reach) can be distributed differently in the organisation. Theoretically the highest degree of centralisation is reached if the leader (or a homogeneous leading group) influences and controls the tasks of the organisational members completely. (In large organisations this "ideal" is reached by perfect control of tasks through a hierarchy of managers. Therefore a hierarchical organisation is often taken as the typical model of a centralised organisation). The decentralised organisation can be defined by a situation where all members can decide completely which tasks (including goals, operations and operational criteria) they want to do. (They may also, of course, voluntarily discuss and co-ordinate their work.)

Both extremes are only theoretical models. Modern organisation theories, at least the psychological models (cf. Greif *et al.*, 1989) advocate decentralised, democratic organisations rather than autocratic and centralised ones. The hypothesised reasons are concerned with better job satisfaction, achievement motivation, higher competence development, better health, long term efficiency and a flexible adaptation to market changes. Informatics design may support both centralisation and decentralisation. For example, if all organisational members have been trained to interact permanently, or at regular intervals, with a centralised computer network and to communicate with other members only via a computer network, it would be theoretically possible to design a precise top-down software design — a downward flow of commands and an upward flow of information. This would apply to the whole organisation of all tasks, the flow of information and the control of the operations and communications of all organisational members. Let us hope that such an Orwellian vision of future organisation remains fiction!

There may well be projects which integrate informatics design with the training of organisational members in respect of this basic dimension of centralisation/ decentralisation. But the explicit and systematic design procedures still have to be developed. It would not, however, be satisfactory for the designer to simply discuss different models with experts or, say, the head of the organisation. An empirical analysis of organisational structures and tasks is a fundamental step in arriving at an appropriate design solution.

4.3 *Reward and feedback system*

A centralised organisation needs information on task performance if it wants to control the whole organisation. Reward and feedback are therefore tools of management to exercise control over organisational members. Organisational members deviating negatively from the established and observed standards of task performance have to risk short or long term negative feedback and punishments.

Members reaching the standards or deviating positively get positive feedback and are rewarded. This simple model is not without problems. It may be sufficient here to mention some of them:

(i) The validity of the basic assumption of the centralised control model is that it is possible to influence the behaviour of organisational members through a personnel appraisal system. This has still to be proven. Empirical surveys show, that "there is no particular reason for enthusiasm about the predictive powers of the appraisal systems currently used" (Drenth, 1984). An alternative in a decentralised model might consist of individual self-feedback. Here the individual member defines and controls his/her appraisal and task performance.

(ii) It is often difficult to select and agree on criteria for personnel appraisal for all members which are subjectively fair. Criteria which are unfair in the opinion of organisational members are those which stimulate active or passive resistance (cf. Katz and Kahn, 1978; Greif, 1983). Drenth (1984) recommends participation of all members to develop an appraisal system which is not only a "tool of management" but allows for a transition from appraisal to participative task redesign and career counselling.

(iii) Similarly there are difficulties in constructing criteria which have sufficient discriminating power to describe relevant differences between organisational members. The tendency to avoid conflicts, leniency and subjective preferences may reduce or change the information value of subjective rating systems. Narrowly defined objective criteria may stimulate the members to reduce their performance to an optimisation of observable outcomes. Spontaneous activities which are necessary for the efficient functioning of organisations, e.g., Katz and Kahn (1978), are reduced.

It is technologically possible to program a personnel appraisal system which completely protocols and appraises the total interaction process of the operator. However, the most likely outcomes of such projects will be a growing fear of Orwell's negative utopia ("big brother is watching you"), the development of mistrust about computers and informatics designers and the stimulation of active and passive forms of resistance. Having said that, a 'self-reflexive system' could be designed which helps the user to analyse and change his operations and procedures, giving him all the available performance data he wants to know and all the information on relevant training facilities. Modern theories of achievement motivation (cf. Heckhausen, 1980) suggest that tasks which are easy to perform and where the difficulty is always the same and cannot be adapted to individual preferences will reduce achievement motivation. Therefore it could be more appropriate to design tasks which allow for individual choice of the preferred level of difficulty.

4.4 *Division of labour, specialisation and member competences*

Two hundred years ago Adam Smith (1786) demonstrated the resulting efficiency from a division of labour into small and simple subtasks, using the example of needle production. The division of labour on this basis has become a universal model of task design for industrial societies. The labour market has been differentiated accordingly into different segments of high and low competence levels and branches (cf. Sengenberger, 1978). The whole economical system of Adam Smith is based on a sufficient percentage of low competence jobs and workers at the bottom of the pyramid, with low salaries but with a high flexibility of the working force.

Many observers assume that the implementation of microelectronics will cause a "Second Industrial Revolution" and fundamental changes of the division of labour. Most authors are predicting a more extreme segmentation between the low and the high competent or the extremely specialised employees created by the introduction of new computer technologies (cf. Dzida *et al.*, 1984). Some like Kern and Schumann (1984) view the end of the division of labour, at least in the long run, while only very few like Silberman (1966) predict only small impact on work and education. In the meantime, technological determinism is simplifying the complex relation between informatics design and division of labour. Bjørn-Andersen (1985), however, says that "microelectronics is an abstract technology which has very few deterministic features in itself." Ulich *et al.* (1986) also see new technologies as an "option" for different design solutions especially for job enlargement.

Bjørn-Andersen (1985) has developed and evaluated training programs for participation in the organisational redesign of tasks. His "firm belief" is that only training programmes, combined with elements of organisational development strategies, will provide future changes which result in a move towards less division of labour. Ulich and his coworkers (Ulich *et al.*, 1986, p. 4), using as a basis psychological action theory, are analysing and designing computer-aided office work in Switzerland. Their aim is to create "work systems and organisational structures better adapted to human needs and qualifications". They recommend complex software systems which allow for flexible adaptation, complex tasks and more training of the personnel.

5. Assessment and evaluation of organisational structures

Informatics design will have an impact on the future development of organisational research and assessment methods. The assessment of attitudes and global scales on organisational behaviour (like job satisfaction, organisational climate, leadership questionnaires, job demands) may be useful as global screening instruments. The "precision instruments" and important "tools" for task and informatics design will be methods of task analysis. These can provide concrete data on human-computer dialogues, possibly using keystroke times and error data on the human operator or process times and error of the computer system. See also Chapanis, Chapter 16 in this volume.

In their broad review of approaches and measurement methods of structural dimensions of organisations Kubicek and Welter (1985) describe 280 methods constructed for the assessment of dimensions. Nearly all empirical studies are aimed at assessing organisational dimensions either by (a) analysing documents (of official task descriptions, rules and procedures), or (b) by asking experts or samples of organisational members to describe the attributes of the organisation. But looking at the different results of different correlational studies (cf. Staehle, 1985) the validity and practical utility of the resulting descriptions have still to be proven.

It is important to define the concept of "organisational structure" and the basic model of relationship more precisely. From the view of systems theory the "structure" of an organisation is defined as the set of all binary "if–then" relations between all analysed sets of attributes or operations of the elements of the system (or organisation) (cf. Greif, 1978 for a precise predicate logic definition). The basic elements of an organisation may be simply divided into humans and tasks. These broad classes can of course be subdivided, depending on the type of organisation and the goal of the analysis.

If we use conditional probabilities to describe the strength of the relationships, we may summarise all relations between the observed attributes of all elements of the organisation by a "structure matrix".

In order to describe the practically relevant structural relationships of our organisational elements with input criteria (like quality of raw materials, technology and qualification of organisational members) and output criteria (like profit, efficiency and well-being of the members), we should include all relevant input and output elements and their important attributes in our matrix.

The major problem is in finding adequate methods which help us to assess valid and relevant attributes and operations of the related humans and tasks of the organisation precisely. If we are able to assess such attributes and operations, we are able to apply time series observations to estimate precisely the strength of the relations between attributes of the inputs or human and task elements of the organisation and the output criteria selected. In other words we have all necessary data to derive empirically observable organisational structures (since the structure is simply defined by the set of binary relations between the human and task elements). Methods of task analysis may be constructed to solve the major problem of finding valid, relevant and practical attributes to describe precisely the concrete interaction processes between humans and between humans and non-human objects. Therefore we will concentrate on the methods task analysis, even if we are trying to assess dimensions of organisational structure.

The practical value of such a methodologically stricter model of an empirically founded structure matrix, which is based on attributes assessed by precise task analysis and a model of relationship based on time series observation, should theoretically be very high, if and only if there is a high systemic relationship or a high empirical predictability between the selected attributes of the inputs and of the organisation, as independent variables, and some important output criteria (like profit, efficiency and wellbeing). Time series observations are time consuming and such an approach requires the development of precise theoretical models and new statistical tests for the analysis of individual interaction processes (cf. Holling, 1987, for elementary models and methods).

6. Task analysis and informatics design

The concept of a 'task' plays a central role in different scientific disciplines, beginning with traditional management sciences, sociology and different branches of psychology. Between different disciplines there is a remarkable similarity of the elements used to define the task concept. Even where the concepts "rôle" or "problem" are preferred to "task" there are identical or similar defining elements. Even so, different aspects remain, depending on the special approach and its central objectives, which should not be overlooked and which might contribute to a broader and interdisciplinary understanding of the task concept.

Frese (1975) prefers to define a "task" by its transformational characteristics, in particular:

(a) the given starting state
(b) to any final state or goal
(c) through any mean or set of operations
(d) with existing or missing criteria, which have to be followed, and which execute the operations.

This general definition refers to certain basic defining elements which seem to be applicable to the task concept for different scientific disciplines and approaches, ranging from management sciences and decision theory, problem solving theory, work and organisational psychology, sociological and psychological rôle theory and developmental psychology.

Card, Moran and Newell (1983) apply a method of task analysis which attempts to construct general hierarchical models of the goal directed (keystroke) operations of the expert user. Their "fundamental principle" of task analysis is the "rationality" of the person. "A person acts so as to attain his goals through rational action, given the structure of the task and his inputs of information, and bounded by limitations on his knowledge and processing ability" (Card *et al.*, 1983, p. 86). The central goal (or efficiency criterion) which has to be attained is a high speed of errorless performance.

Card *et al.* (1983) also describe the basic principles of task analysis as a tool for informatics design which follows the traditional model of time and motion studies. The designer has to observe and protocol time and error data of elementary operations of expert users and then analyse the protocols trying to find the "best way" solution (least time and errors). He may creatively use these data to construct an alternative hardware and software design, which reduces times of finger movements or unnecessarily complicated chains of commands over error prone procedures, etc. Afterwards the new design solution has to be evaluated again by task analysis and the results compared with the initial design. Here task analysis is merely used as an evaluation method, helping the designer to get concrete empirical models and criteria which lead to optimised solutions. The construction and evaluation of models is a simple method. If used by creative engineers it has nevertheless been successful in many fields of application.

But the value of the model depends on the validity of the basic models and the criteria used to test the design solutions. As such the basic models of Card *et al.* (1983) are inadequate (cf. Barnard, Chapter 8; for experimental results, see Greif and Gediga, 1987) and it is insufficient to analyse 'one best way' keystroke models and non-conflicting short term goals like minimal keystroke and error times. Therefore we have, at Osnabrück, tried to develop a method of task analysis, which may be applied if the user follows different or conflicting goals (e.g., speed and accuracy, or efficiency and well-being, or short and long term goals which are not homogeneous) and if different users prefer to operate in very different ways (some planning many steps in advance, others using "trial and error" and some "systematic exploration"). To analyse the "psychologic" of human action, "objective" data have to be supplied by information on the subjective mental models of the task, the computer system and the subjective organisation of the observable operations. The keystroke times will give insufficient or even misleading data, if their psychological meaning cannot be understood.

6.1 *Subjective or objective task analysis?*

In the field of work and organisational sciences 'objectivity' is a highly valued criterion. Psychological instruments, especially questionnaires are often criticised as being merely "subjective". "Objectivity" has a special meaning, not to be mistaken with the concept of "objectivity" in classical psychological test construction. According to classical test theory "objectivity" refers to the independence of the test results of different users or observers. Scientific methods have to lead to reproducible results, independent of the person using the method (scientists or other persons). There is no question that the results of a task analysis have to be "objective" or independent of the observer in this basic sense. To avoid misunderstanding we will prefer to call this criterion "observer reliability" following the literature on observation methods.

Gablenz-Kolakovic *et al.* (1981) discuss different meanings of "objectivity" which mirror the criterion as it is used in the field of work and organisational sciences. They distinguish between "subjective" and "objective instruments" of task analysis. "Instruments" of task analysis are called "subjective" if the results of the analysis (e.g., the worker's core values on "job complexity" and other dimensions of the instrument) are dependent on the attributes of the working individual (the "subject"). "Objective instruments" try to assess attributes, which are valid for different individuals (e.g., job demands for all trained workers on the same job). But both types of instruments have to consider the individual "redefinition" of the task.

Even if such a construct of "objectivity" is highly esteemed in the field and "subjective instruments" (and the individual worker as a reliable source of information) are sometimes mistrusted by managers, psychology has to be careful analysing individual performance of workers before attributes and demands can be generalised. For instance when describing the 'complexity' of the "Tower of Hanoi" we might study a population with two completely different action paths. The resulting distribution of 'complexity' would be bimodal. An assumed 'mean complexity' may be a value describing none of the existing modal values of the sub-samples. Experimental psychologists would claim that we have to prove the validity of our constructs or show that assumed attributes are generalisable across individuals. Thus scientifically "objective" and "subjective" instruments are not independent. We need both types for task analysis.

6.2 *The "cyclic unit" as basic element*

Miller, Galanter and Pribram (1960) have developed a descriptive cybernetic model of human action where the "TOTE unit" is the basic element. Planning and goal directed behaviour is analysed as a complex cybernetic network of "TOTE units". Volpert (1982) in generalising this concept prefers the term "cyclic unit". "Cyclic units" are, according to Volpert (1982, free translation), defined by a "goal" and "transformations" in the same way as we have used them according to the definition of "task". The "transformations" may be observable patterns of movements or steps of mental information processing, lower level micro-units or higher level planning processes.

The term "goal" might be interpreted misleadingly as if the individual is always consciously setting goals by himself regardless of the environmental demands and of the concrete stimulus situation. In general the influence of the environmental demands, the concrete stimulus situation and the dependent selective attention processes on the development of the redefined micro-goals which the individual is trying to reach at a micro level of cyclic units should be stressed. (Typists or laboratory subjects normally do not report any goal setting or decision process in routine writing words or using the cursor keys with a keyboard — of course there may be interesting exceptions). Therefore for our purposes we prefer to use the term "final state" (F) instead of "goal" if we are describing the expected end state of micro level cyclic units.

Following a similar definition of Card *et al.* (1983) it is preferable to use the term "operations" (O) instead of the more abstract term "transformations". "Operations" may be defined as elementary, observable and delimitable steps of actions, related to task elements or partial goals and are discriminable by actors or observers. (The concept of "concrete action" of v. Cranach *et al.* (1980) has a similar meaning.) Computer commands or discriminable perceptual or problem solving acts may be used as examples of "operations".

The following Figure 1 describes the procedural structure of a cyclic unit with four operations. Complex or simple "hierarchic" or "heterarchic action structures" may be described in interrelated networks of cyclic units. A heterarchy might even be a set of loosely connected groups of cyclic units.

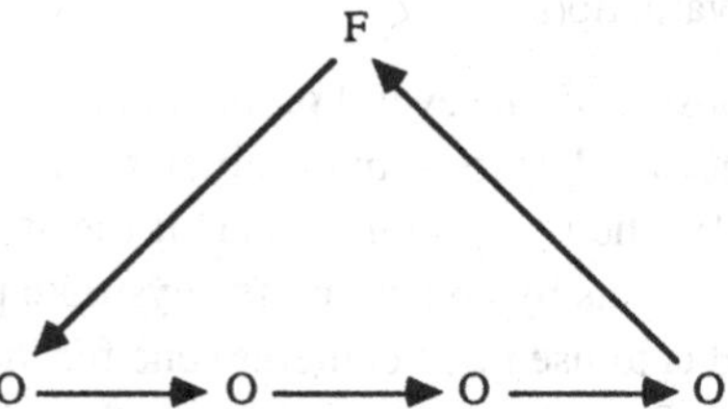

Figure 1: The "cyclic unit" (F = final state; O = operations).

6.3 *"Heterarchic task analysis"*

Heterarchic task analysis is a retrospective method of task analysis which will help to assess the individual micro-style of a person with a task and in a given time after the task has been done. The task performance on the job has to be observed only through keystroke times and protocols, registered automatically by special computer programs or possibly by unobtrusive measures. In the retrospective interview situation, the subject is asked to remember the typical working situation. This gives us much more background information to understand precisely their particular operations and problems.

The basic units of this description of the interaction process with the computer are subjective "cyclic units" (subjective grouping of operations into tasks and subtasks). The "cyclic units" may be combined into a comprehensive hypothetical network model describing the individual self-regulating process at the given time and task. The method is called "heterarchic task analysis" to accentuate the possibility of multiple and heterogeneous or conflicting tasks and subtasks (hierarchical structures are special cases of the heterarchy).

The method has been developed from the early problem solving research of Duncker (1935) who used problem solving protocols together with introspective reports or 'thinking aloud'. Cranach *et al.* (1980) have also applied a similar approach to analyse "concrete" goal oriented micro-interactions between people. The "objective" keystroke data and time values which Card *et al.* (1983) prefer in their method of task analysis are also contained in this method, but they are not the major source of information used to interpret the results. The major steps in our method are as follows:

0 Preparation.
1 Sequence of operations, cognitions and emotions.
2 Subjective tasks and subtasks.
3 Goals, methods and choice points.
4 Description and evaluation.

Before beginning the observation, several preparatory activities have to be done (step 0). For example, a decision has to be made about the time sample and working sequence to be observed (0). The first major step (1) is the assessment of the sequence of all micro-movements by an automatic keystroke protocol and by video tape. The preferred method is to use three cameras (one for the face, one for the keyboard and one for the screen). Special recorders cut the takes together with time values on one single video screen. The video film and keystroke protocol are then used to confront the user subject with his/her task performance and explore his/her cognitive processes, reasoning and attention processes, and emotional reactions. After this in the next step (2) the subjective "tasks" (or working steps) and "subtasks" (or task elements) are explored, which gives an image of the hypothetical subjective organisation of operations or mental representation of the network of "cyclic units" of the acting person. In the next step the user is interviewed about goals, inner conflicts and conflicts with environmental demands or stress, general methods of operation, choice points and the selection rules which are applied to choose between alternative methods. In the last step (4) depending on the objectives of the study the interview protocol is used to describe and evaluate the operations, subjective tasks and other attributes of the protocol. Each step is described in detail by Monecke (1987). Greif, Monecke and Tolksdorf (1986) and Monecke (1987) demonstrate that the first results of retrospective validations in a laboratory experiment with three tasks and 80 subjects are encouraging. Gediga *et al.* (1989) show its combination with other methods of job analysis in a larger field study. In the following we will concentrate on the instrument as a tool for task and informatics design (cf. Hamborg, 1989).

It is recommended that an automatically generated TASK ANALYSIS PROTOCOL sheet (see Figure 2) is used with all key strokes and time values. For the interviewer it should give enough space for written comments on each operation.

At every step of the first video confrontation the following aspects have to be recorded and explored (in the "time", "operations" and "remarks" columns, Figure 2):

(i) Operations/times assessed automatically by a logfile program (what has been done?)
(ii) Thoughts, plans or decisions (which ones?)
(iii) Attention (to what aspects or stimulus and environmental attributes?)
(iv) Sensations and feelings (neutral/ positive/ negative; which ones: overload/ anxiety/ aggressiveness/ conflict/ activation/ monotony/ fatigue/ self-satisfaction?)

The "cyclic unit" is used as a model for the division of the sequence of operations into the subjective groups or cognitive representations of tasks and subtasks. According to the theoretical approach we assume that not only can the observable micromovements of different individuals show psychological relevant inter- and intra-individual differences (in reaction to the stimulus or task conditions) but they can also show the cognitive organisation of the inner regulatory structures and processes. Experience with this type of exploration has shown that it seems to be possible for most people (sometimes there are difficulties) to define the subjective "cyclic units" when confronted with a video tape of their performance shortly afterwards, provided clear instructions and good examples are used. But it must be admitted that this is a critical point of this method because an assumption must be made that such observations and reports are valid and reliable. But as long as we seem to have no better information and instruments to derive the "cyclic units" of action, we have to use the verbal reports of the subjects.

The interviewer marks the divisions of the subjective cyclic units by ">" (see the column "substeps" in Figure 2) and is asked to find 'names' for the steps described. Thus the whole protocol is shown stepwise. After this the subject and the interviewer, both being familiar with the whole sequence, use the step or (sub-) task names for

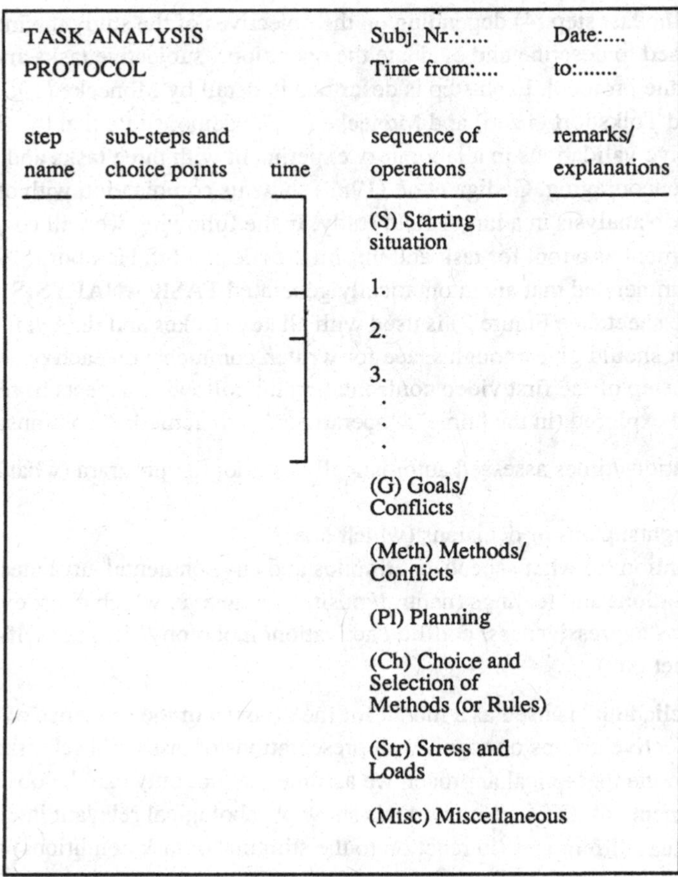

TASK ANALYSIS PROTOCOL

Subj. Nr.:...... Date:....

Time from:.... to:.......

step name	sub-steps and choice points	time	sequence of operations	remarks/ explanations
			(S) Starting situation	
			1.	
			2.	
			3.	
			.	
			.	
			.	
			(G) Goals/ Conflicts	
			(Meth) Methods/ Conflicts	
			(Pl) Planning	
			(Ch) Choice and Selection of Methods (or Rules)	
			(Str) Stress and Loads	
			(Misc) Miscellaneous	

Figure 2: The task analysis protocol sheet.

exploring possible subdivisions and aggregations into possible macro-units.

The "choice-points" and the possible alternatives have to be marked symbolically (by "< >"). If the alternative paths and subjective probabilities of the alternatives have been explored in the interview then the alternative paths leading to other 'pyramids' in the 'multiplex network' may be drawn by arrows.

6.4 *Evaluation and redesign*

The task analysis protocol allows one to construct meaningful indices descriptions of the subjective tasks and cyclic units of an individual person. In this 'subjective' or ideographic approach the attributes of the task are not independent of the micro-style of the acting individual. Depending on the special goal of the research or applied project, different evaluations are possible:

(i) Efficiency measures (time for single operations and overall time needed to reach the goal, number and type of mistakes, etc.)
(ii) Complexity of subjective tasks (number of operations, number of tasks, subtasks or hierarchical levels, etc.)
(iii) Variability/stability of subjective tasks (number of varying/stable tasks and structures of subtasks in a defined time period).
(iv) Degrees of freedom (number of subjective choice points in the "problem space").
(v) Integration of subjective tasks (number of relations between subtasks and between tasks).

These results may be used either for the description of the task structure of individuals or a comparison of different subjects (or the same individual at different times) on the same tasks (or task conditions) or different tasks (and the same subjects). Looking at inter-individual (or intra-individual) differences we might compare a single efficiency index with one or several 'optimal solutions' (for example the cyclic units with the shortest times, and minimum number of mistakes) and compare the complexity, variability, degrees of freedom and integration.

The method of "heterarchic task analysis" is an exploratory technique, which can be used to evaluate observable task operations (with or without computer technology) and their psychological background. An evaluation tool of task and informatics redesign may be evaluated by the quantity and quality of concrete modification ideas which are stimulated by applying the instrument. Experience so far shows that in the first place the application of our method stimulates the observed person to reflect critically about the organisation and problems of his/her work on exactly the concrete level which is useful for redesign. Our experience is that even users who do not know much about the computer system are able to formulate suggestions for the redesign of the task and the hardware and software which should be evaluated. Users reflect and plan changes to their operations after this intensive self-confrontation and will talk frankly about their lack of knowledge and their training needs. Even if the subjects do not mention knowledge problems, the task analysis protocols may be used to compare it with other, obviously better, organisational arrangements of operations (in terms of efficiency and well being) and this enables the discussion of the resulting problems with the user. Therefore the method is a tool which allows for the assessment and evaluation of three important aspects of organisational tasks, informatics design and training together, which have to be changed in an integrated way.

If the tool is applied by the designer or an analyst who is well informed about the possible design alternatives, the major advantage of using the method is that it helps to get a concrete and intuitive model of the way the user is working and his problems with the system. We therefore apply our method for individualised models for 'task oriented informatics design'. The units preferred by the individual and its subjective task organisation are used to develop a first draft of a 'top-down design' of an individual hierarchical menu structure and individual labels of the commands. The resulting individual menu solutions can be tested experimentally in regard to efficiency or learnability.

Task analysis, then, is the basis of the software evaluation and development work being carried out at Osnabrück. The first findings show that the practical handling of typical tasks by most standard office software systems is too complicated and troublesome. Informatics design is not supporting the observable, individual differences in subjective tasks and organisations.

In May, 1987, we started a project at Osnabrück on multifunctional office software and training especially for small and medium sized companies (cf. Greif, 1990). Our approach integrates field research on practical problems, systematic methods of task analysis and an empirical evaluation of modern software systems and training methods. The first prototype of our program, called "individual System (iS)" constructed by Günther Gediga, is easily adaptable to tasks, competences and individual task organisation or preferences. The program has a special architecture which allows the use of different versions of the program package for different "levels of complexity".

Level 1 is a safe and easy to learn or remember 'direct manipulation' and 'menu selection system' (see Shneiderman, Chapter 14 in this book). Here the thinking level is concrete and operational. This level is preferred by beginners and infrequent users of the system. Professional users often prefer 'command systems', or individually adapted combinations of different interaction styles (see Shneiderman in this book), since they are often faster and more powerful in a mathematical sense. In our system this is the fifth, 'professional', level. But competences for abstract thinking are necessary to understand and apply command syntax efficiently. Task oriented software has therefore to be integrated with an adequate training concept to reach this level of competence. For this we developed and experimentally tested a concept of exploratory learning by errors (cf. Greif, 1990).

7. Conclusions

'Muddling through' strategies are not an adequate answer to dealing with the complex and practical problems arising from the implementation of production and information technologies. The more efficient alternative, which may reduce the risks of organisational failure, is to adopt a strategy of planned organisational change which integrates the analysis and redesign of organisational tasks, task oriented informatics design, training and the development of competences.

The practical value of informatics design based on task analysis and which is adapted to individual competences and demands can be easily demonstrated in organisations or departments where tasks, competences and individual preferences are extremely different. Standard software, which is very difficult to adapt to such differences, confronts the organisation with a decision conflict: either to implement complex standard software packages which embrace all necessary functions of all important tasks and operations or to apply simple standard systems for the majority of tasks with special programs for special tasks and professional users. The advantage of the first alternative is that all necessary tasks can be done by a single integrated system. But the organisation has to invest permanently in the training of all members to master a software system which is too complicated for the routine jobs of many — sometimes most — users and embraces procedures which are embedded in a complex and difficult to remember environment. The second alternative puts the burden of complicated and inefficient procedures on the professional users, who have to apply software combinations or different systems to do their job.

This is not only a problem of professional programmers in organisations but also of other professional software users, e.g., secretaries and assistants. Our experiences show that managers with complex jobs, who seldom use computer systems, are likely not to want to be overloaded by complex software and therefore prefer simple, 'low level' systems without any unnecessary or risky functions. It would not be appropriate for these same managers to implement the identical systems their assistants and secretaries possess.

Studies at Osnabrück show that standard software systems or combinations of different programs are inadequately designed for most tasks, even if they allow for some adaptation. We therefore need integrated software systems, which allow for a better balance between practical demands of the job, software and the design and development of competences and people's needs in organisations. Psychological research has shown that 'imbalances' as well as simplified work are dissatisfying and can affect peoples' mental health and performance. Therefore we should seek to build variety, action completeness and substantial levels of autonomy into peoples' jobs (cf. Hacker, 1985; Ulich *et al.*, 1986; Wall and Clegg, 1981).

'Muddling through' strategies may be rational today, since informatics design is not yet adequately adapted to typical differences of tasks and peoples' needs in modern organisations. But these strategies may have complex long term costs because of alternative design "options" (Ulich *et al.*, 1986) which might be more beneficial, efficient and humane may be overlooked. For an adequate future balance between organisational tasks, informatics design and the needs of people, methods of task analysis should not only be applied for the description of practical problems, for planning and redesign of jobs and software and hardware but will also provide the last word in evaluating the long term outcomes.

Acknowledgements

The "Multifunctional Office Software" project is funded by the German Minister of Research and Technology (Programme "Humanisation of Working Life"). I also gratefully acknowledge the editorial help of Simon Richardson on an earlier version of this paper.

CHAPTER TWELVE

PARTICIPATION IN SYSTEMS DESIGN — WHAT CAN IT OFFER?

ENID MUMFORD

1. Introduction

Participation is a facilitating process which involves users in systems design with the objective of improving the design process and making computer-based systems more acceptable and relevant. This paper will examine the concept of 'design', the nature of systems design, and a methodology — ETHICS[1] — which deals with organisational factors in design. It will also discuss the contribution that participation can make to 'good' systems design; provide examples of the use of participation and suggest how it can be introduced and structured both now and in the future.

2. What is design?

2.1 *Various definitions*

Design is something that everyone does, whether it is designing a garden, a kitchen, a house or a complex computer system. It is hard to define although the Oxford dictionary makes a brave attempt and sees it as 'a plan or scheme conceived in the mind of something to be done' or 'the preliminary conception of an idea that is to be carried into effect by action.' These definitions tell us that design is something to do with a kind of thinking that leads to subsequent activity. Professional designers have more specific definitions and some of these are quoted by Freeman (1983) in a paper on Fundamentals of Design. Engineering design is defined by Asimow (1962) as:

"a purposeful activity directed toward the goal of fulfilling human needs,

---

[1] ETHICS — Effective Technical and Human Implementation of Computer-based Systems.

particularly those which can be met by the technological factors of our culture."

A committee appointed by the UK Council for Scientific and Industrial Research in 1963 — the Fielden Committee — defines mechanical engineering design as:

"the use of scientific principles, technical information and imagination in the definition of a mechanical structure, machine or system, to perform pre-specified functions with the maximum economy and efficiency. The designer's responsibility covers the whole process from conception to the issue of detailed instructions for production and his interest continues throughout the designed life of the product in service." (Fielden, 1963)

Lucas (1974), a computer specialist with a great interest in organisational issues, has another broad definition. In his view:

"Creative design techniques are focussed on solutions to organisation behaviour problems in systems design."

Design then is about change — needs are met and problems are solved through the design process with the result that something new replaces what existed previously. It is therefore a process which leads to an output.

Design as a process has always been recognised in the computer world and there has been a proliferation of methods directed at assisting the different tasks that make up this process. Most of these methods have been directed at facilitating all or part of the system 'life cycle' concept which describes systems design as moving through a number of stages — feasibility study, requirement collection and analysis, design, implementation, validation and operation (Ceri, 1986).

The system life cycle concept defines systems design as a set of sequential steps taking place over time. The technical specialists who use the concept also frequently interpret it as applying to a set of technically oriented activities directed at the analysis and collection of data which will enable a computer to produce a required output. Given that computers in industry and commerce are only useful so long as they make a contribution to the performance of a business, it is surprising that the life cycle concept pays little attention to business needs and problems and fails totally to address issues of organisational design which may be key factors in enabling the technical system to work successfully.

Attempts to broaden the definition of systems design are now taking place. The concepts of socio-technical design, developed by the Tavistock Institute of Human Relations in London in the 1950s, are now attracting the attention of systems designers. The Tavistock group recognised that technical and organisation systems had to fit together and be mutually supportive if the larger work system was to operate successfully and they developed excellent theories and methods to assist organisational design. They did not venture to question the design of the technical system, however, and their efforts were often directed at ameliorating poor technical systems through compensatory good organisational design (Trist, 1981).

Managers would argue that neither the technical nor the socio-technical approaches to design really address issues of business needs and business effectiveness and this is another critical factor that should be incorporated in the definition of systems design.

If the business, organisational and technical aspects of systems design are recognised as important then the following is a possible definition of the systems design process when used in industry and commerce:

> Systems design is the process of creating and introducing new systems which incorporate technical and organisational components to improve business efficiency and effectiveness and the quality of working life of the employees who use or are affected by them.

By efficiency is meant removing and reducing problems so that costs are also reduced and the business works in a dynamic, flexible and streamlined manner. By effectiveness is meant carrying out critical business activities at a higher, and more successful, level than before and introducing new activities which contribute to the better achievement of the business mission.

2.2 *The system design cycle*

If the definition given above is accepted then system life cycle activities might look like the following:

1. A recognition of business needs and problems and a decision to consider organisational change incorporating a computer-based system.
2. A clear specification of the business mission of the firm as a whole and of the department or departments which will be using or affected by a new computer system.
3. An analysis of business efficiency needs — problems which are increasing costs and reducing the ability to achieve the business mission.
4. An analysis of effectiveness needs — critical tasks and functions which will 'add value' to the work of a department if existing ones are improved and new ones introduced.
5. An analysis of job satisfaction and quality of work needs. Aspects of work and the work situation which are lowering morale and causing frustration.
6. An analysis of future change needs. Likely or planned change to which any new system must adapt.

This is a requirements analysis, but it is a *business* and not a technical requirements analysis.

This business requirements analysis leads to the specification of *system objectives*. This step translates the needs which have been identified into a series of precise objectives which the new system must be designed to meet. It requires the:

7. Specification of efficiency, effectiveness, job satisfaction and future change objectives.

The next step is:

8. Systems design.

This will have two components — technical and organisational. Both must contribute to the achievement of the objectives which have been set in stage 6. Technical design requires the acquisition or development of software and hardware that will enable a computer system to provide the information or data that the business efficiency and effectiveness objectives require. Organisational design is the creation of a viable work structure that will facilitate the achievement of the business mission, contribute to the efficiency and effectiveness objectives that have been set for the new 'business' system, provide job satisfaction and accept easily the new technical system. As organisational design is directly related to the achievement of the business mission, ideally it should precede technical design. The technical system should be designed to fit with it and not *vice versa*.

This analysis of business and human needs and problems at the systems requirement stage, and combination of technical and organisational factors at the design stage is the basis of the author's ETHICS design methodology which will be briefly described later in this chapter. A more detailed description can be found in Mumford (1983a, 1986). Few other methodologies encompass this degree of breadth. Most methodologies which address the automation of the office ignore behavioural criteria and are based on a model of the office viewed as a set of task-related activities (Hirschheim, 1985). Because behavioural criteria are often not seen as important at the design stage, although it is increasingly recognised that they are critical at the implementation stage, there are still few serious attempts to involve users in the design of the systems which they will subsequently use.

3. Participation in design

3.1 *Why is user participation still so rare?*

Participation in systems design is still relatively uncommon despite the fact that many writers now stress its importance (see, for example, McCosh, 1984). There appear to be a number of reasons for this lack of use. One very practical reason is that people do not know how to organise participation. Some would like to but shy away because it seems difficult, complex and uncertain. Occasionally technical designers are willing to try and involve users but find that the users are reluctant to be involved. This can be due to bad relations in a firm and a lack of trust and confidence between management and lower level employees; it can sometimes be due to deferential relationships with people wanting to be told rather than involved. The author has occasionally encountered this reaction with groups of secretaries.

A second reason is that participation does not yet form part of the culture of many organisations. Usually this is because management is not accustomed to consulting and may feel that this threatens their 'right to manage'.

Third, technical specialists may not be favourably disposed towards participation. They may regard the design task as theirs, and as a means for demonstrating their knowledge and skill; they may fear that the intervention of users will show that non-specialist groups can also acquire and use some of these skills. Their training may also militate against participation. They may have learnt that systems analysts collect information through interviewing individual members of the future user department and believe that this is an effective method for identifying system requirements.

However, it seems that we are now experiencing a cultural shift. Many UK companies are asking for assistance in changing their cultures to make them more open and flexible and to diffuse skills and decisions more widely. Many US firms are practising very open and participative management and finding that it produces results that both assist the company's profitability and raise employee morale.

Fourth, in the past systems design could often succeed without participation. It usually affected most the lower levels of staff in the office and on the shop floor. These groups might not get systems that they liked and found useful, they might not be motivated to use them effectively, but at least the systems did work and sometimes produced good results. Management had no means of knowing that things could have been better.

Today, it can be argued that participation is not just involving those at the lower end of the work hierarchy in the systems design process. It is also crucial to ensure that those higher up are actively involved in designing the decision support and expert systems that they will use. There is already considerable evidence that these kinds of management system cannot be successfully designed without the involvement of the future users.

3.2 *What is participation and what can it contribute?*

Participation in systems design is 'the involvement of the end users, and others who will be affected by the system, in its design'. Experience with participation suggests that it has many advantages. These are reviewed below.

3.2.1 Participation as a statement of company philosophy

Many companies today are trying to alter the traditional bureaucratic and authoritarian style of management. They are anxious to introduce a more employee centred style, with open communication, the opportunity for debate and question at every level, and a high emphasis on personal responsibility and development. Participative systems design is yet another means for demonstrating this open management philosophy. Surprisingly, it is one that is often neglected. Firms that pay great attention to communication and consultation in their day-to-day management practice may not be able to persuade their systems analysts to use a similar approach when new systems are being designed.

3.2.2 Participation as a contribution to knowledge

A design task shared between future users and technical specialists should assist good design. The users are expert in the operation of their department and aware of all its faults and problems. They have probably been trying to draw management's attention to these for years. They can be helped to change their focus of attention from what is happening to what should be happening if problems are to be removed and improvements made. Users therefore have a great deal of important knowledge to contribute to the design of a new system.

They are better able to contribute this knowledge if they are able to share ideas in a group situation. The department can then be looked at as a whole and the contributions of different rôles and functions identified and examined. This would seem to be an improvement on the traditional systems analysis approach of the individual interview. With this, the analyst, who probably knows little in depth about the department, has the task of assembling a mass of parts into a meaningful whole.

Individuals also provide a particular, and often idiosyncratic, perspective whereas groups are able to put their knowledge of the parts together and see a meaningful whole. The ability to do this has become increasingly important as we move into the era of the expert system. Experts often disagree with each other and if a single expert is relied on the result can be an expert system that no one except the person who contributed to its design will want to use. The author's experience when working with firms developing expert systems has been that those using a participative approach for knowledge elicitation get better systems than those that rely on a single expert.

3.2.3 Participation as a learning experience

As well as assisting the contribution of knowledge, participation can also provide an important learning experience. When the design task is shared both users and systems analysts learn from each other. The systems analysts get a level of knowledge about the user department and its needs that would be very difficult for them to achieve through individual interviews. They can discover not only how the department does work, but also how it could work and perhaps should work. This means that an existing unsatisfactory method of operation is not simply polished up by the introduction of some new hardware and software — a practice that often results in greater inefficiency and higher costs. Attempts are now made to improve the ability of the department to achieve its business mission by introducing organisational and technical enhancements that together create major improvement.

Similarly, the future users of the system learn a great deal from the technical specialists. If hardware and software options are examined as part of the design process then the users will have an opportunity of evaluating these and relating what is on offer to the department's needs. If prototyping is used, or a pilot system developed, there can be opportunity for trying out different kinds of hardware and software before a final decision is made.

Both users and systems analysts leave a participative experience with greater knowledge and understanding than they had before, and with sympathy for each others' point of view. This will be of considerable benefit when they come to design their next system.

3.2.4 Participation as a means for giving a sense of ownership

Many books and papers on systems design stress the need to make users feel that they 'own' the system — that it is theirs to operate and manage. They then recommend the systems analyst to transfer the system to the user at some, usually advanced, point in the systems design process. Often this transfer process is formalised and the user manager is asked to 'sign' for the system, indicating that it is what he or she wants and that major responsibility for its successful operation now lies with the user.

It can be argued that feelings of ownership are difficult to develop when one group is handing over to another something that is the creation of the first group. Participation enables this problem to be avoided. Users can now really claim ownership of a system that they have developed to meet their own needs; that they fully understand because they have helped it grow and mature; that they feel is their 'baby' and therefore want to succeed; and that they are determined to use in an effective way.

3.2.5 Participation assists effective use of a new system

Participation means that not only do users want to use the new system effectively, but also they have the knowledge to do so. Because they have lived with the development of the system over many months they will have an excellent understanding of what it has to offer, and of its advantages and limitations. They will also understand where the business needs of their department require most assistance from it. Too often, sophisticated equipment is bought by companies and then used at a level way below its potential because users do not have the knowledge and motivation to operate it at a higher level.

3.2.6 Participation as a means for developing good human relations

It is difficult, if not impossible, to introduce new systems easily in a situation where there is conflict between management and employees. Either the new system will be used reluctantly and seen as yet another imposition by an uncaring management, or, if the firm is unionised, it will become a victim of protracted industrial relations feuding. It may eventually have to be abandoned or else bought in at a price.

But even in firms with good management/employee relations major change can cause stress and conflict and damage these relationships. Participation, by providing an opportunity for collaboration between technical specialists and users, and consultation and discussion between managers and those lower down, can act as a vehicle for improving and cementing relations. Everyone is involved, as a team, in overcoming the inevitable problems associated with change and in jointly striving towards the accepted goal of a viable and working system. Change then becomes an exciting integrator and not an unwelcome disrupter.

3.2.7 Participation as a provider of change skills

Today, experienced systems analysts are in short supply and have to spread their talents thinly around a company if new systems are to be introduced. Situations in which they have to spend long periods with a user identifying and correcting defects in a badly designed system can seriously delay computer developments in other departments.

Participation means that users become increasingly expert in managing their own change. They come to understand how to analyse their own needs, how to design new systems, and how to introduce these successfully. This means that technical specialists are called upon only for advice and are not required to control the total design process. Handing over the management of change to the users has many advantages. It helps the users to introduce the kind of system that they want and need, and to associate an organisational structure with the technology that provides efficiency, effectiveness and job satisfaction. Too often technical specialists who exclude users from the design task end up misinterpreting their needs and provide a system that is not liked or understood. With the management of change becoming a continual ongoing activity in most firms, user involvement can help ensure that it is carried out with interest and enthusiasm and a minimum of human problems.

Participation then can provide something for everyone. It enables the future users of a system to participate in its design — in this way ensuring that their business and human needs are effectively met and that they become skilled in the management of their own change. It helps ensure that management gets systems that are good for the firm. Such systems assist productivity, provide job satisfaction, help the achievement of the business mission and do not turn out to be expensive white elephants. Also, the trade unions are able to establish that their members are not being exploited when new technology is being introduced, although it must be recognised that trade unions are not always enthusiastic about participation. They can mistrust management's intentions in permitting it to take place and may regard it as a way of 'conning' the workers to accept change that is really against their interests. They may also object to the fact that their members are protecting their own interests and are not permitting the unions to look after these for them.

Participation does not mean that the normal management-union bargaining processes are eliminated. Negotiation will take place over job evaluation and rates of pay in even the most participatively designed systems, and there is always a rôle for the trade union. Participation in which the unions play an active part means that management-union bargaining issues will be based on real and understood issues and not become associated with incorrect fears and assumptions about the consequences of change.

Participation, as we have seen, also helps the technologists by releasing them from parts of the design task and enabling them to spread their skills and knowledge more broadly around the firm. It also helps them to understand organisational design factors which they might otherwise neglect.

Customers and clients of the firm should also gain when their needs are met more effectively and quickly by a well organised department, with knowledgeable staff, who use technology to increase their efficiency.

3.2.8 For whom is participation relevant?

Participation is often seen as a process that helps groups at the bottom of a company to influence their own future work situations, and it has a very important rôle to play in this respect. But it is also useful for other groups, and may be essential as decision support and expert systems increasingly affect managerial and specialist groups.

It can be argued that it is extremely difficult for a group of computer specialists located in a Management Services department to understand top management's complex information needs. Management, no matter how senior, must spend time examining its own needs and objectives and discuss these with the technical specialists before a successful system can be built.

The author recently watched an expensive information system for senior management fail in a British company as the computer technologists desperately strove to understand the information needs of a top management group which would not spend time examining these themselves. Inevitably, the technologists produced a system that did not fit what senior management wanted, did not work well technically, and was rejected after a great deal of money had been spent on its development.

Experience with the design of expert systems suggests that both experts and future users need to be involved in the design processes. Knowledge that is elicited solely from a single expert is likely to be idiosyncratic and not accepted as valid by other experts. A group of experts looking critically at how they work will produce a better result. Similarly, if an expert system is being developed for a group different from those with the original knowledge, then design must take account of the way the system will be used. The inclusion of users in the design task will ensure that this happens (Wilkerson, 1985).

A major computer manufacturer found that it could not design an expert system to help salesmen produce accurate quotations and orders for customers without the involvement of both engineers and salesmen in the design task. The engineers had the knowledge, the salesmen would use the system.

3.3 *Structure and method for participation*

Participation, like most things, has to be managed if it is to work successfully. Part of this management is ensuring that a situation exists in which participation can successfully develop and creating a group structure which will enable discussions to take place and decisions to be made.

The first step in successful participation is to ensure that people want it and are willing to work with a democratic approach. Top management must be made aware of what is involved and promise their support, interest and assistance. Similarly the trade unions must not be opposed to participation and must believe that it is a genuine attempt to share decision taking and not a trick to make employees accept change that is not really in their interest.

Most important, the future users of any new system that is being considered must understand what participation involves, be prepared to devote time to the design of a new system and, ideally, be enthusiastic about participating in the design process. Participation will be difficult to manage successfully if any of these groups are uninterested, suspicious or hostile.

Second, a 'facilitator' must be identified. Someone who will assume the rôle of guide and helper and assist those participating to move purposefully along the road leading to a successful system. The facilitator should have good social skills, understand group processes and be experienced in working with groups, be familiar with the design methodology that is being used and have a good knowledge of the principles of organisational and job design. If a skilled outside consultant is not available then a member of the personnel or systems department can successfully fill this rôle. The person chosen as facilitator should not have a vested interest in the new system and so should not be a member of the user department or a system analyst involved in the project. His or her rôle will be to provide advice and guidance to the participants in the design process; help resolve any conflicts that arise and maintain the user group's interest and enthusiasm during the period that design is taking place. It is usually best if the facilitator does not assume the Chairmanship of the group responsible for the design task. This should be given to the member of the group likely to be most competent in this rôle.

Third, once the facilitator is recruited, the participative group structure needs to be created. There are many ways of doing this and the most appropriate for a particular situation needs to be carefully thought through. Three decisions have to be taken at this stage:

1. What is the best kind of participation structure to adopt?
2. How shall group members be selected?
3. Who needs to be a member of any groups that are formed?

The structure favoured by the author of this paper is to create a steering committee and one or more design groups. The steering committee should consist of representatives of top management who have an interest in the system. These will include the senior managers of the user area, the head of management services, a senior personnel manager and, where appropriate, a senior trade union official. The rôle of the steering committee is to set the framework and guidelines for the project, to provide information on company policies and objectives and to provide support, guidance and help throughout the period that the project takes place.

Each user area needs its own design group. If the proposed system will affect one department only then a single design group will suffice, although groups with an indirect interest in the system will need to be involved to some extent in design decisions. If more than one department will be a direct user of the system, then it is advisable to have a separate design group for each — although the groups will have to meet together at regular intervals to ensure that none of their decisions are in conflict.

Design groups should be small, with not more than eight to ten members; they should be fully representative of the user department and contain members of each of the principal interest groups — staff from different functions and grades and from different age groups. They should contain the technical specialist, or specialists, allocated to the project by management services or the computer department, and they may or may not contain the line manager of the department. In the author's opinion, it is better not to have the line manager in the group on a permanent basis as he or she may play too dominant a rôle in the design process. The line manager's view on issues is clearly important and must be known to the design group, but it can be effectively ascertained by inviting him or her to a part of each meeting or to some of the meetings. It is essential for the line manager to have comprehensive and up-to-date knowledge of what the group is doing, and he or she must be constantly informed of what is taking place through regular discussions with the design group chairman and facilitator and through written minutes of the design group meetings.

There are no rules on how to select or elect the members of the design group and it is best to choose an approach that fits with opinion in the user group. Sometimes a formal election is preferred; in other situations volunteers are accepted. Sometimes management wants to choose the design group, believing that if this is left to the users unsuitable people may become members. Although this attitude is understandable management selection does not work well in practice. It can leave the impression that a group of management stooges has been created, who are more likely to represent the views of management than those of their colleagues.

Once the design group or groups has been created a decision has to be taken on how they can best keep in touch with the colleagues they represent, and to what extent they want to involve these colleagues in the decision processes. Many groups believe that regular reporting of what is taking place with requests for suggestions and feedback is sufficient. Others want important decisions to be taken by the department as a whole, with a department meeting being held whenever these are necessary.

The sixth step is to make sure that the design group understands its rôle and responsibilities. These will have been defined by the steering committee. Clearly, all design groups are formed to contribute to the design of a new system but the boundary around their responsibilities can be set in different places. Some steering committees may give the design group an open book — with a brief to examine the advantages of computerising a part of the department and only if this is seen as worth while to go ahead with the design task. Other steering committees will take a firm decision that a particular project is to go ahead but give to the design group the responsibility for choosing hardware, software and the organisational structure that will surround the new system. Others again may want a particular technical solution but allow the design group to create an appropriate organisational structure to fit with it.

There may be other decisions that the steering committee will wish to reserve for itself because they affect company policy. All of these constraints must be made clear to the design group by the steering committee at the start of the project. A written statement of the objectives of the project and the design group's terms of reference is very important.

It has to be recognised that there are difficulties here. The steering group will prepare its terms of reference and guidelines when it has little knowledge of the realities of the design task. It is not unusual for design groups to go back to the steering committee at an early stage in the project and ask them to rewrite the terms of reference as they are proving too broad or too narrow.

The design group also has to decide how it is going to keep in regular communication with its constituents. Each member of the design group should regularly report back to the group he or she represents, discuss what is taking place and ask for ideas and comments. Minutes should be written after each meeting and circulated to constituents and other interested individuals and groups with requests for comment. Companies which have sophisticated electronic mail systems can send information and receive comments through the telecommunications network. This works well when constituents are scattered over a large area.

4. The design task — using ETHICS

A methodology is only a means to an end — that end being the effective realisation of a set of objectives. With computer-based systems the end depends on the values of those concerned but is likely to be: the creation of a well designed, efficient, easy to operate new system, that can be introduced without difficulty and provides users with a set of tools that enable them to work more effectively and obtain greater job satisfaction from their work.

With computer applications, methods should assist both technical and organisational design and contribute to systems which fit easily into the work culture and environment. At present there are few methods of this kind apart from Checkland's soft systems methodology (Checkland, 1981) and the author's ETHICS methodology (Mumford, 1983a). A facilitator working with a design group would use ETHICS in the following way.

Before starting the design task, the members of the design and steering groups would take part in a two day training course in which ETHICS would be explained and they would carry out an exercise based on a simplified form of ETHICS. A video film made by the author, which demonstrates how groups in other firms have used ETHICS, would also be shown.

The objectives of this course would be twofold. First, to give the design and steering groups some picture of the design task ahead and the activities which they would have to undertake to achieve it. Second, to provide an appreciation of what is meant by organisational design — the creation of rôles, relationships and task structures to enable a department to achieve its business mission.

Many people working in industry seem either not to have a clear perception of the work organisation which surrounds them, or else they believe that it is closely controlled by technology. An important message provided by the course is: technology and work can be designed in many different ways. There are always choices.

Once the course is over the first meeting of the design group has to be arranged and a decision taken on how frequently to meet in the future. A half day weekly or fortnightly meeting is often seen as the best approach. Members need a period between meetings to collect information and the 'learning to design' process takes time and cannot easily be compressed. Deadlines are a good idea and a stimulus to the group to progress the task, although these may have to be revised if they prove unrealistic.

At their first meeting design group members will be apprehensive and uncertain of their ability to design a new system. The first task of the facilitator is to provide reassurance and generate some confidence. ETHICS does this by having as its first step an analysis of the present method of work in the user department. This is a subject on which each member of the group is an expert. They know exactly how they do their own job and the problems which they experience in carrying it out.

4.1 *Describing what happens now*

ETHICS STEP 1. Analysis of the present work situation.

Each member of the group describes their own job and this description is written on flip charts, which are hung around the walls of the meeting room. An extensive use is made of flip charts and other visual aids throughout the design process.

The description of the current situation is not only to provide confidence. It also enables the group to understand how the department as a whole is working now, before they start analysing needs in detail and thinking about redesign. It may take one or two meetings to complete.

4.2 *Making clear the business mission*

ETHICS STEP 2. Identify the mission of the firm and of the user department.

This is a critical step. The objective of any new system should not be to add polish to an existing, perhaps badly organised, work situation. If this is done a new computer system may cause productivity and efficiency to become worse rather than better. It is to reorganise and introduce new technology so as to achieve more effectively the business mission of the department — the reason why it exists at all. Therefore *the subsequent steps of the design task will all be directed at the more effective achievement of the business mission.*

In most industrial and commercial situations it is not difficult to define the business mission, although the facilitator needs to make sure that everyone agrees with the definition before proceeding to the next step in ETHICS. In other situations

— educational establishments and some government departments, the mission is less easy to identify and may change over time. Considerable discussion may be required before agreement is reached on a definition.

Once the business mission is clarified and agreed the design group starts on its diagnosis of problems and needs. This is to establish those factors in the present situation that are preventing or slowing down the achievement of the business mission. Steps 3, 4, 5 and 6 in ETHICS all form part of this diagnosis.

4.3 *Diagnosing needs and problems*

ETHICS STEP 3. Identify those problems in the present organisation of work that are reducing efficiency and hence the achievement of the business mission.

Efficiency is defined as keeping things working smoothly, without errors and at low cost. Efficiency problems are behaviour and procedures that slow work down, cause errors, unnecessary work duplication and other kinds of poor work performance.

A technique called variance analysis, developed and used by the international group that operationalised the socio-technical approach, is used at this stage (Mumford, 1983a). A variance is defined as: a tendency for a system, or part of it, to deviate from some desired, or expected, norm or standard.

The design group therefore examines their own jobs and the work of the department as a whole to identify those parts where problems tend to occur. These are listed on flip charts. The design group looks for two kinds of variances:

1. *Key variances*. These are deep seated problems which may be impossible to remove altogether but which can be more effectively controlled. They are frequently associated with the need to deal with other groups such as suppliers and customers, or individuals and groups in other departments.
2. *Operational variances* are problems which arise in the user department through poor work procedures, poor organisation and shortage of information. Many of these can be removed altogether when the work system is redesigned.

The design group will ask and answer such questions as: what is the nature of the problem, what is its cause, where does it originate, where does it appear, how is it corrected now, who corrects it, what information is required to correct it? At a later stage in the design process they will ask: how can this problem be removed altogether through work reorganisation and new technology?

The design group now moves on to:

ETHICS STEP 4. An analysis of job satisfaction needs.

All change can be used as an opportunity for considering and improving job satisfaction and this is an important objective of the ETHICS approach. But for job satisfaction to be improved the factors causing frustration and low morale have to be carefully identified. In situations where there are more than a small number of employees in a user department this is done with a self completion questionnaire plus small group discussions of the results.

For job satisfaction to be improved it has to be defined and measured. In ETHICS it is defined as: the fit between what individuals or groups are seeking from work (job expectations) and the reality of what they are receiving (job experience).

The definition of job satisfaction as a 'fit' means that good and bad fits can be measured. The variables measured in this way by ETHICS are:

Knowledge needs — the use and development of skills and knowledge
Psychological needs — based on the Herzberg motivators (responsibility, recognition, status, sense of achievement, advancement)
Efficiency and effectiveness needs — the provision of required resources (training, information, supervisory assistance, acceptable controls)
Job design needs — work interest, use of skill, variety, discretion, autonomy, use of judgement and opportunity to take decisions.

The mix of these characteristics that employees prefer will differ from individual to individual and from group to group. The analytical breakdown is usually done by occupation, grade, age and sex.

The ETHICS method has its own questionnaire for eliciting this information but design groups often wish to add questions (Mumford, 1983a). The management of the questionnaire and the analysis of the results should be carried out by the design group facilitator who will give the design group a detailed picture of the good and bad fit aspects of work in the user department. Each member of the design group will then meet with his or her constituents, discuss the questionnaire results with them, check that they give an accurate picture of job satisfaction needs and problems and ask for suggestions on how the situation could be improved.

Both the variance analysis and the job satisfaction analysis provide an opportunity for involving all users in the systems design process.

ETHICS STEP 5. Identify effectiveness needs.

Effectiveness is defined as: doing things that may already be done well, even better, and doing new things — so that the business mission is more easily achieved.

The design group are now asked to examine the 'critical' activities of their department — those aspects of work that most directly contribute to the achievement of the business mission. Factors which are inhibiting effectiveness are listed on the flip chart and discussed.

ETHICS STEP 6. Consider the future.

Most systems today have a limited life span and have to be flexible enough to accommodate frequent changes in the internal and external environment of the firm. It is useful for the design group to identify both those changes that they know will occur in the near future and those that may occur. They can then ensure that organisational and technical restructuring is flexible enough to receive and assimilate these changes.

This is the end of the diagnostic phase of ETHICS. During this period the facilitator will have to help the design group members in various ways: for example, to keep them interested and motivated when inevitable frustrations occur; to help resolve conflicts that may arise between members representing different interest groups; and to assist them in communicating ideas, options and decisions to their constituents and to the steering committee. Most important, the facilitator will have to ensure that management allows the design group members time to attend meetings, and help from the steering committee may be needed to ensure that higher priority is given to these meetings than to urgent day-to-day tasks.

4.4 *Setting objectives*

ETHICS STEP 7. Consider what should be changed.

This step requires the design group to identify (1) those negative efficiency and job satisfaction factors that are having the greatest influence in preventing the easy achievement of the business mission, and reducing the quality of working life in the department; also (2) those effectiveness factors that could be strengthened and made to have a more direct influence on the achievement of the business mission. This process, together with an assessment of 'likely' and 'possible' future changes, takes the group into:

ETHICS STEP 8. Set objectives for the new system.

This step produces a set of clear, well defined objectives, which can be tested for attainment once the new system is in and working. This means that 'measures', or other forms of systematic evaluation, should be attached to each objective wherever this is possible and appropriate.

Objectives will be listed under the headings of efficiency, effectiveness, job satisfaction and future change. They will be prioritised into 'key' objectives and 'desirable' objectives.

Because a design group represents a number of different departmental interests objective setting is not necessarily an easy process and is likely to involve negotiation. There will be some objectives that everyone agrees are necessary and important, and these can be placed at the top of the 'key' objectives category. Other objectives will be seen as very important by some representatives but as less important by others, and agreement must be reached on the priority to be given to them.

Occasionally the objectives specified by the representative of one departmental group will be seen as threatening to the interests of another. Again, this problem must be discussed and an attempt made to reconcile the different interests before moving into the design stage of ETHICS. The advantage of the ETHICS approach is that differences of this kind can be brought out into the open and discussed rationally before a decision is made.

Steps 7 and 8 form the objective setting phase of ETHICS. Step 8 is the most important step as it provides the basis for the design of the new system and a set of clear targets that can be checked once the system is operational to ensure that they have been achieved.

4.5 *Designing the new system*

ETHICS STEP 9. Redesigning the organisational structure.

A source of failure with many new technical systems is that they are introduced into a department that is inefficient and badly organised. The result may be that efficiency is reduced even further. In order to ensure that this does not happen and also to take advantage of the opportunities for improvement provided by a major change, the design group now takes a decision on how the department can be reorganised to achieve the efficiency, job satisfaction, effectiveness and future change objectives that have been set. Reorganisation needs to be based on a careful consideration of the department's business mission, on the 'key' tasks that must be carried out if this mission is to be achieved, and on the rôles and relationships that are required for the accomplishment of these key tasks.

Ideally, a number of organisational options should be identified and set out in detail on the flip charts. The principles of socio-technical design will be useful in assisting the creation of these options. The organisational option most likely to assist the achievement of the system objectives should be noted.

ETHICS STEP 10. Choose the technical solution.

The technical solution may be an entirely new technical system to be designed by the in-house computer specialists, it may be a package solution, or it may already exist in other departments and the intention is to extend it to the department of the design group. In Step 10 the design group is very dependent on the advice of the technical systems analysts who are members of the group. Ideally, they should be able to present a number of technical options so that the design group can match these against the system objectives, the preferred work organisation and the business mission and decide which provides the best fit.

After discussions with the steering committee and with all staff in the user department a decision must be taken on which organisational and technical solution to introduce.

ETHICS STEP 11. Prototyping.

The reorganisation of the department should take place and have settled down before any new technology is introduced. This time space provides an opportunity for creating a prototype of the new technical system and noting any problems associated with it. It also enables staff to become familiar with using the technology, and for comprehensive training to take place, before it becomes an integral part of the department.

ETHICS STEP 12. Job design.

The assimilation of new technology requires some job design to take place. Decisions will have to be taken on who is to use the hardware and software, and how. New tasks will be created and old ones removed and care must be taken that this change leads to an enhancement and not a degradation of work. The principles of good job design need to be applied to all jobs so that job interest, challenge, responsibility, discretion and autonomy are increased, if this is what staff desire. The pre-change job satisfaction survey and discussions will now be an important source of information for the design group.

4.6 *Implementation*

ETHICS STEP 13. Getting the system in and working.

This is a critical step and requires a paper on its own. It is important to maintain user involvement throughout this period and to remember that bad implementation has made many potentially good systems unacceptable.

4.7 *Evaluation*

ETHICS STEP 14. Checking results.

Once the system is in, working and has settled down the design group should make a careful evaluation to find out how well the system objectives are being met and the business mission achieved. A number of the diagnostic tools can now be used again. A second analysis of variances will show the extent to which old 'key' variances are being better controlled and old operational variances have been eliminated without new ones being introduced. A second job satisfaction survey and discussions will show the extent to which bad fits on the job satisfaction needs list (knowledge, psychological, efficiency and effectiveness, and job design needs) have been reduced, again without new ones being introduced.

The systems design task may now be seen to be over. It must be remembered, however, that today design is a continuous activity. New systems soon become obsolescent as circumstances change and new internal and external pressures affect the work of the user department. There is an ongoing rôle for the design group in monitoring these pressures and establishing when the system's organisational or technical components need redesigning.

They have a second important rôle in spreading the knowledge of how to carry out participative design throughout the rest of the company. Video films can also be useful here and it is a good idea for the facilitator to arrange for some of the proceedings of the design group to be recorded on video-tape, if they have no objection to this.

It may be expected that the facilitator will now be able to move on to help another user group participate in the design of their organisational and technical systems. For the facilitator the most difficult stage is likely to be the first — when the diagnosis of needs and problems is being carried out. Difficulties will arise in dealing with a design group uncertain of what is expected of them and of their own abilities, and who get frustrated with having to examine the present before designing for the future. But once the third stage of designing the system is reached, morale is likely to be high and the group will enjoy the creativity of rethinking their own organisation of work and choosing a new technical system. They are also likely to be good at doing this once they are made familiar with the concepts of organisational and job design.

5. Case studies in participation using ETHICS

The author has now been associated with a considerable number of participative projects, most recently in the design of expert systems. Three are described briefly below.

The author's first experience of user participation was fourteen years ago when the systems analysts in Turner's Asbestos Cement (TAC) were anxious to change the firm's sales office from a batch to a terminal based system for customer records and accounts. They approached the author for help saying that they were anxious to associate good organisational and job design with the new technical system and would she advise them. A job satisfaction survey was carried out in the office and the results discussed with all the clerks, bringing them together in small groups. At these meetings a large number of organisational problems emerged and the author suggested to the clerks that they should think about how these might be solved.

The author then forgot about this suggestion and fed back the results of the survey to the members of the technical computer group, who designed what they thought was an excellent socio-technical system. They then called a meeting of all the clerks, described their proposed system to them and sat back and waited for the applause. To their astonishment, there was silence. Then one of the senior clerks said very politely, "Thank you for your presentation, your ideas are quite good, but while you have been designing a new work structure for our office we have been doing the same thing, and this is how we should like to be organised". He then produced an excellent blueprint for a work structure that solved most of the office's efficiency and job satisfaction problems.

The TAC computer group recognised the excellence of the clerks' suggestions and it was the clerks organisational solution that was implemented. It was a great success. The author personally learnt a very important lesson that she has tried to apply ever since. This is: *people at any level in a company, if given the opportunity and some help, can successfully play a major rôle in designing their own work systems* (Mumford, 1981).

The second example is a group of sixty clerks in Rolls Royce UK who handled invoices coming in from the firm's material and service suppliers. The department was poorly organised, morale was very low and it had an aging labour force as young people did not want to work there. The Rolls Royce systems manager, who wished to introduce an on-line office information system into the department, said that whenever he walked through he thought all the clerks were dead.

This seemed an excellent situation for a participative approach. A design group of eight people was created, each member representing a particular group of clerks in terms of age, grade and function. Two systems analysts from the computer centre were asked to join the group, and a senior clerk became the chairman. A steering committee was also formed to set the guidelines for the project and ensure top management commitment. This included the senior user manager, the manager of computer services, the firm's medical officer and the chairman of the trade union branch.

The design group worked together for a period of about six months analysing their own needs, setting precise efficiency and quality of working life objectives for the new system and examining the organisational and technical alternatives that could contribute to the achievement of these objectives. The author acted as facilitator to the design group and at regular intervals throughout the design process we tried to involve all members of the department in the analysis and discussions.

The result was a new organisation of work based on self-managing groups which the clerks liked, because they had created it themselves, and which had a very positive impact on morale. The clerks became multi-skilled and were then offered promotion by other Rolls Royce departments. This movement unfroze the situation and young people began competing for jobs there. An inefficient, demoralised clerical group was transformed into a group that was successful and motivated (Mumford, 1983b).

The third example was a group of bank officers in a London based international bank which was introducing the latest real-time technology into its dealing room. The dealing room was supported by a foreign exchange department that handled all the administration for the buying and selling of currency on the money markets.

Here the initiative for a participative approach came from the Bank's systems analysts, who recognised that 'dealing' was a highly specialised area and accepted that they must have user assistance in designing the new system.

Once again a representative design group was created to identify problems and needs, both business and job satisfaction. After consultation with their colleagues, the design group members decided to associate a new organisation of work with the proposed computer system. This was based on currencies. Each work group in the foreign exchange department now had responsibility for all the activities associated with buying and selling a particular currency — the dollar, the pound, the franc, etc. This more challenging work structure replaced a factory-type paper flow line which had largely consisted of small, routine jobs, many involving only the checking of a colleague's work (Mumford, 1981).

6. Conclusions

Today, participation is taking different forms. The author's most recent project has been working with a computer manufacturer who has used participative design for two different kinds of projects — assisting staff in a number of departments to do their own strategic planning and creating design groups of experts and sales staff to develop and test a major expert system for improving the sales function.

All of the projects described in Section 5 were successful in that good, acceptable systems were a result of the design processes — although the route to success was not always an easy one.

6.1 *When can the participatory methods of ETHICS be used, and by whom?*

Because ETHICS is a general problem solving approach it can be used in most situations although it may require modification. It can be used exactly as described in this paper or it can be regarded as a bag of tools, with some parts used, but not others.

It is useful both when a firm's own systems analysts are designing a technical system or when a package solution is being selected. In the latter case the diagnostic and objective setting process provides a set of criteria against which different packages can be measured.

Situations where modification will be required are for very large systems and for systems where there is as yet not enough experience to identify good organisational solutions. Examples of the first are systems in banking where the same technical system may be introduced into many branches, or systems which are crossing national or international boundaries and going into many different units of a particular company. Here it must be recognised that many different organisational forms can be hung onto the same technical system. Therefore a good strategy is to create local design groups, each of which comes up with its own organisational solution. Common organisational solutions do not usually work well as they fail to cater for differences in culture, environment, attitudes and work practices.

Very large systems will require complex participation structures, with steering, planning and design groups being established at different organisational levels. Companies with electronic mail systems will find that these greatly assist communication, consultation and feedback at every level.

The participation of all staff in design is probably only possible at the grass roots, where the design of a department or relatively small unit is taking place. Nevertheless participation does produce positive attitudes and acceptable systems, and efforts should be made to encourage this to the fullest extent wherever possible.

Another problem in today's use of ETHICS is that organisational solutions may be difficult to determine because the impact of a new form of information technology is not known. Ideally, organisational solutions should be created to achieve the business mission, not to fit technology, but it is clear that new developments such as networks will have a dramatic effect on work structures. One way of tackling this problem is organisational prototyping. Different organisational structures can be tested out in pilot situations until the one which best assists the business and fits with the new technology is identified.

ETHICS can also be used in the development of standard mass market packages but here it will be used in a very general way. Members of the design group will not be the future users of the system but representatives of these drawn from different industries and occupational groups.

ETHICS was developed to assist the future users of a system to participate in its design. But it can also be of use to a number of other groups. Consultants and sales executives may find it helpful in diagnosing client needs and problems before recommending changes that should be made, or products that should be bought. It has also been used for assisting with problems other than the introduction of new technology. For example, a major American computer manufacturer has used it as a means for helping staff improve their productivity.

6.2 *Where is ETHICS going next?*

Hopefully ETHICS will continue to be developed. It needs constant improvement and adjustment to meet new organisational and technical challenges. It also needs incorporating with some of the good technical approaches to systems design. The author hopes very much that someone will be interested in doing this.

CHAPTER THIRTEEN

TOWARDS A HUMAN FACTORS STRATEGY FOR INFORMATION TECHNOLOGY SYSTEMS

LEELA DAMODARAN

1. Introduction

For more than two decades it has been recognised that Information Technology has human and organisational consequences — not all of them positive. However, awareness of problems does not necessarily result in constructive efforts either to reduce negative consequences or to promote the benefits for the IT user.

Early on-line systems were designed with little knowledge of or concern for the end user. User issues were typically considered only when problems in training, implementation and normal use were encountered. Often the ergonomists, behavioural scientists or other specialists in the Human Sciences (henceforth referred to collectively as Human Factors (HF) specialists or practitioners in this paper) were called in as consultants to investigate "resistance to change", complaints of visual and postural fatigue, low productivity, high labour turnover and absenteeism, etc. Since the technical systems had already been designed, the best that these HF specialists could do was to modify environmental conditions, or suggest adjustments to job design and work organisation to compensate for the constraints imposed by the technology. This practice of "palliative ergonomics" to remedy design faults has been a prevailing demand placed on HF specialists for many years. Such work is characterised by involvement of the HF specialists either very late in the design cycle or well after development has been completed and operational difficulties are arising. At this stage the technology is not usually amenable to fundamental change. Even suggestions of relatively minor changes so late on can bring shudders from the design team at the "heavy programming" required to make changes required by the users.

Widespread disappointment at the failure of IT to deliver the expected rewards has spawned a multiplicity of projects, methodologies and techniques to improve user participation, develop "user friendly" interfaces, etc. Surveys of users' attitudes, investigations into job satisfaction, countless man-years of negotiations to agree rest pauses for screen-based work, ergonomic design and evaluation of interfaces, and usability laboratories proliferate endlessly. From this surge of activity some useful knowledge and guidance has undoubtedly emerged but its influence and value appears to fall far short of its volume. Too often the advice and recommendations provided by HF practitioners and specialists are either rejected, inappropriately implemented, or only partially implemented. Reasons given for low utilisation of HF advice often relate to cost, to the lateness of the guidance relative to the stage of the design cycle, to incompatibility with other organisational or business constraints, or to lack of understanding on the part of the client.

Sixteen years of research and consultancy experience in the HUSAT Research Centre suggest that for Human Factors expertise to be successfully applied requires recognition that it must take account of the socio-technical framework which incorporates IT. Socio-technical theory, rooted in early studies of coal-mining (Trist *et al.*, 1963) established that human and organisational issues cannot be considered in isolation from the technology. The interdependencies between the social and technical systems are fundamental to the structure and function of any work organisation and are powerful determinants of job design.

Most HF projects concerned with such things as designing interfaces, evaluating training, investigating user reactions, address just one element of a total socio-technical system. Failure to take account of the interdependencies between the element under study and other elements of the total system render many recommendations for action nugatory. To implement recommendations derived in such a highly focussed way would often result in unacceptable knock-on effects in areas not considered in the project. This reality leads to many reports and recommendations being dismissed as impractical or inappropriate — although from an academic standpoint the studies may well have been methodologically sound and have produced statistically valid results.

Experience of numerous projects, the literature on planned change and socio-technical systems theory have led the author and co-workers in HUSAT and the Tavistock Institute of Human Relations to suggest that the application of Human Factors expertise can only be meaningful and effective within a socio-technical framework.

Fragmented, piecemeal HF projects concerned, for example, with specific interface characteristics in isolation have in general failed to enhance IT from the viewpoint of the user organisations. Such experience has fostered a growing belief that only a more holistic approach to the exploitation of IT will benefit IT users. This belief has in turn led to the concept of a Human Factors Strategy for IT systems being suggested. This paper describes the emergence of the concept and an attempt to develop such a strategy. The paper describes work conducted by the HUSAT Research Centre, a member of the Tavistock Institute of Human Relations and many members of the client organisation. The programme is still underway and is two to three years from completion.

In Section 2 the Case Study is described, covering a period from 1982 to 1986, which charts the development of the strategy from its earliest conception to its formal implementation. The nature of the consultancy experience, the achievements and some of the unresolved issues are also described. The work was commissioned by the DHSS and represents a major pioneering venture in Human Factors. The DHSS is the first large UK non-military Government Department to have recognised the benefits which could accrue from serious application of Human Factors in the IT context. The programme presents an entirely new and exciting challenge on an unprecedented scale to the practice of Human Factors in the 1980s. The DHSS deserves much credit for commissioning and supporting a programme of such national significance.

In Section 3, prescriptive advice is offered to assist in the design of future Human Factors strategies relating both to the technical content of the strategy and the mechanisms to be deployed within it.

2. The case study

2.1 *Social Security operations in the UK*

The Department of Health and Social Security employs 93,000 people, of whom approximately 74,000 are located in Regional and Local Offices around the country, engaged in the administration of a range of social security benefits. Figure 1 gives some idea of the current scale of this operation. Over £40 billion a year is being awarded in benefits, by means of more than 1,000 million separate transactions.

The DHSS is a large bureaucratic organisation with a strict hierarchical structure and well-established staff grading and promotion policies. Staff are recruited typically at several levels of the organisation ranging from school-leaver entry to graduate entry. Career progression occurs by movement through varied positions in the organisation and represents a strong orientation to develop generalist rather than specialist skills. As a consequence of frequent transfers of staff and minimal hand-over from one job occupant to his successor, lack of continuity in development projects is a characteristic feature of the Department.

2.2 *Computerisation of Social Security operations*

The Department has had considerable experience and success with very large-scale

Social Security Today

- 25 million claims a year
- 24 million beneficiaries at any one time
- 1 billion payments a year
- £42 billion benefit expenditure a year
- 106,000 staff in DHSS and DE
- £1.7 billion administration costs

(1 billion = 1,000 million)

Figure 1: Scale of Social Security operations

batch processes since the 1960s. Success with more up-to-date computing processes has been more elusive. The demise of the CAMELOT project in 1979 led to formulation of a working paper in 1980 (DHSS, 1980) which outlined plans for computerisation of the administration of benefits. A second paper which took account of the initial consultations and early actions was published in 1982 (DHSS, 1982). Three major objectives were identified, as follows:

- Better Service to the Public
- Greater Administrative Efficiency
- More Rewarding Jobs for Staff

In order to meet the objectives listed the Operational Strategy was conceived:

"This is a plan for a network to connect the 500 or so Social Security local offices and the 1000 or so Unemployment Benefit Offices to the mainframe computers which will hold the claimant records. It is anticipated that there will be over 35,000 terminals on-line to this network by 1992.

One of the principal driving forces behind the strategy is the desire to unite the multiplicity of hitherto completely separate benefits in what is known as the 'Whole Person' concept, so that claimants will no longer have to deal with a confusing diversity of agencies. The ultimate aim is to establish a single logical database for all benefits." (Spackman, 1987)

The main benefit systems concerned are:

1. The contributions system (with over 52 million records) which keeps a complete record of National Insurance contributions throughout a person's working life.

2. The National Insurance recording system.
3. The Benefits, specifically
   — Retirement Pensions,
   — Unemployment Benefit,
   — Child Benefit,
   — Supplementary Benefit (soon to become Income Support),
   — Family Credits,
   — Various Incapacity Benefits,
4. Departmental Central Index to link these systems together.

Each of these is a very large system in its own right!

> "Modernising existing systems while preserving the current level of service, building the major new systems, like the Local Office Project (LOP) to deliver income support, and eventually unifying these into one integrated service, can only be accomplished step by careful step. This gave rise to the first and possibly most important architectural decision — all benefit systems from now on to be built to a completely uniform technical architecture. There was no other means by which this number of very large projects, each with a different priority and each in a different stage of development, could be separately managed in a way that allowed eventual convergence" (Spackman, 1987)

The green paper published in 1980 described the technical systems which would comprise the Operational Strategy. However it was clear that it was not just the technical system which would change. The whole human and organisational systems in DHSS, including claimant contact, would change with the introduction of information technology. Thus an immensely large and complex socio-technical system was to be changed.

2.3 *Initial Human Factors consultancy contract*

In recognition of some of the Human Factors issues to be addressed, two Human Factors consultants were commissioned in 1982 to undertake a small (6 man months) initial project in DHSS. The terms of reference of the project defined by the DHSS were as follows:

(i) advise on the design of the system interface being developed for the Local Office Project (LOP) and the standards to be employed — in particular, the form the system dialogue should take; the job design implications of this for local office clerks; and the Human Factors which should be taken into account in introducing the system;

(ii) take account of the wider considerations of future requirements of the DHSS

Operational Strategy as a whole in framing this advice;

(iii) report on progress to a joint steering committee of the Strategy Team and LOP Team

(iv) provide a report jointly to LOP and the Strategy Team on completion of the study and contribute, as required, to the LOP Full Study Report.

The initial study was intended to focus upon dialogue design issues. However, the presence of Human Factors consultants in the client organisation for the first time meant that they provided a legitimate focus for DHSS staff to raise wide-ranging human and organisational concerns. As a consequence the consultants were asked to address a host of significant issues, including education in Human Factors, user involvement processes, and the design features of a benefit assessment system based upon microcomputers.

2.4 *Formulation of a Human Factors Strategy*

The multiplicity of requests for Human Factors consultancy led to the consultants recommending to the steering committee that issues arising should not continue to be addressed in an *ad hoc* and fragmented fashion. Instead it was proposed that a coherent and systematic Human Factors Strategy should be formulated, in order to take account of the human implications of Information Technology. The steering committee accepted this recommendation (so changing the terms of reference for the initial study). Thus, dialogue design received only a small part of the consultancy effort originally intended; but nevertheless 'first pass' guidelines to be refined in the local office context were subsequently produced. The major output from the initial contract was a Human Factors Strategy. The key elements of this strategy are shown in Figure 2.

The Human Factors (HF) Strategy was outlined in a short discussion paper entitled "Social Security Human Factors Strategy" and was promulgated to approximately one hundred managers primarily of Principal grade and above. A two-year programme was then commissioned.

2.5 *Staffing*

Work on the two year contract began in February 1983 and continued under the direction of the author. The programme was staffed by a core team of three HUSAT consultants. Other HUSAT directors and a senior consultant in HUSAT provided advice and support on an *ad hoc* basis as required by the work programme. Additional members of HUSAT and the Department of Human Sciences at Loughborough University were also involved in the work when their specialist knowledge was required. The resources of the whole Research Centre were utilised on the project

- User-Centred Focus
- Analysis of User Needs
- Liaison between Users and Designers
- Design and Development Support
- Implementation Support
- Post-Implementation Reviews/Audits
- Feedback to Designers/Manufacturers/Management/TUs, etc.
- User Involvement in Every Stage
- Organisational Learning
- Multi-Skilled Design Team

Figure 2: Key elements of a Human Factors Strategy.

through use of brainstorming techniques and workshops. This was especially important when new techniques and approaches had to be developed to meet client needs. Thus, while the contract supported the equivalent of seven full-time consultants, in practice a team averaging 14 members was available to resource the project. The complex and varied nature of many of the assignments required a multi-disciplinary approach and led to secondment of a member of the Tavistock Institute of Human Relations to enlarge the resource pool supporting the programme of work further.

2.6 *Nature of the work*

The terms of reference of the two-year programme were as follows:

"Following on their initial studies, the Contractor's personnel are to advise and assist DHSS on Systems Interface Design. In particular they are:

a) To advise on the system interface design aspects and Human Factors associated with projects within the Operational Strategy: in particular hardware requirements for terminals, the form the system dialogue should take, the job design implications for local office clerks and the approach which should be taken to introducing technology.

b) To assist in developing design standards in these areas to apply to all projects within the strategy.

c) To provide written material in the form of papers/reports and undertake oral presentation of findings/recommendations as required.

d) To assist in training DHSS design and training staff working in these areas."

2.6.1 Diversity of Work

To provide Human Factors consultancy in the DHSS context involves a multiplicity of activities at different levels of the hierarchy and in a variety of client locations in the UK. Considerable parallel activity occurs as the norm and can involve contact with Senior User Management, Project Managers, members of Headquarters guidance teams, ADP (Automated Data Processing) analysts and designers, trades union representatives, user representatives, local office managers and staff. The diversity of activity required in the work programme is illustrated by the following list of meetings, working practices and procedures which take place:

- Sub-contract negotiation
- Contract management meetings
- Internal HUSAT team meetings
- Design team liaison meetings
- Local office Project Steering Committee meetings
- Technical meetings with client
- 'Brainstorming' sessions
- Running training workshops on HF topics (e.g., data collection techniques, dialogue design)
- Running seminars (e.g., Managing Change; Introduction to Ergonomics)
- 'Trouble-shooting'
- Project Manager meetings
- User Manager meetings
- Interview/questionnaire surveys
- Environmental surveys
- Walk-throughs
- Review of documents to comment on HF aspects
- Review of 'State of the Art' in HF specific issues
- Presentations of products from the sub-projects
- Reviews of HF literature

2.6.2 Starting the work programme

The first task was to progress the dialogue design guidelines originally commissioned in the initial contract. In order to tailor general guidance compiled from the literature into guidance relevant to the leading strategy project, the Local Office Project (LOP), the HF consultants sought to develop some understanding of the local office environment. Accordingly, a familiarisation study in one local office ensued in March 1983 and involved the following activities:

- An interview survey of a sample of staff
- Discussions with the manager and assistant managers

• An observation study of the caller area

Work proceeded on dialogue design for LOP and, at the same time, a short course on 'Introductory Ergonomics' was constructed and presented by the HF consultants in response to a request from the newly appointed Regional New Technology Officers.

Momentum on the project was then lost for a period of several months as a result of movement of a key member of the DHSS. From the beginning of the initial contract the HF consultants had reported to an appointed officer who had initiated the procurement of HF consultancy and therefore had some understanding of the subject area of Human Factors. This appointed officer had been chairman of the steering group for the initial contract which had seen the birth of the Human Factors Strategy. He was promoted to a quite unrelated post in early 1983. His successor thus "inherited" management responsibilities for a contract in disciplines entirely unfamiliar to him. The purpose and value of the contract to the DHSS were unclear to him, as were the means of assessing and controlling the work. A constructive relationship between the Human Factors consultants and the new appointed officer took some considerable time to develop.

Recommendations for LOP Dialogue Design were presented to DHSS in June 1983 on the basis of the earlier Local Office familiarisation work. However, the idea of producing guidelines on the basis of the work done in Local Offices was later rejected by the DHSS in favour of generalised standards. Throughout 1983, work on such standards documents continued and a range of other work arose, still largely on an unplanned *ad hoc* basis. For example, work was done in response to a request to explore the advantages and disadvantages of claimants' viewing screens.

One of the specified tasks required of the HF consultants during this 2-year period was to conduct an evaluation of the 'Local Office Microcomputer Project'. Microcomputers were introduced into local offices as an interim measure prior to LOP system implementation. In Autumn 1983, the report of the microcomputer evaluation was produced and it identified some significant difficulties. For example there was a mis-match between the format of the source document (claim form) and that of the screen dialogue. This evaluation also highlighted other issues that were relevant to the LOP system: the need for support and some options for job design and work organisation.

2.6.3 Appointment of Operational Strategy Director

In October 1983 a director for the Operational Strategy was appointed. Recognition by the director of the crucial significance of Human Factors in IT gave powerful impetus to the work programme.

In 1984, work continued on the evaluation of dialogue and screen designs but the major project involving the HF consultants was another of the tasks specified in the contract: "A socio-technical analysis of work done at present in local offices, including comments and advice on the document being produced on equipment and environment".

A detailed study was made of the work in one large inner-city local office. The methods included structured and unstructured interviews, observation of individuals and working groups, some self reporting questionnaires and the "tracing" of some items of mail received, some phone calls received and some personal enquiries at the reception desk. As well as a descriptive report it led to a number of technical papers to be used by the LOP design team.

Consultancy was also carried out on a user acceptability audit of the Family Income Supplement minicomputer system.

The work commissioned during this two-year period frequently came about in response to concerns arising in the client organisation and requiring attention — often at short notice. The concept of a planned HF Strategy had been eroded by pressing project demands. The concept of a strategy only really continued in the minds of the HF consultants since those in the client organisation who had shared ownership of the concept and plan, and who had supported it, had moved elsewhere. The steering group of the initial project had ceased to operate and was not replaced until a Human Factors Steering Committee was established in mid-1985 by which time a further contract for HF Consultancy had been placed.

2.6.4 Continuation of the HF work programme

Through 1985 and 1986 a range of important work was undertaken to inform LOP design and implementation decisions. The data collected for the socio-technical analysis was validated and reported. To build upon the local office data collected in the socio-technical study a survey of local office organisation was commissioned. This was based upon a carefully designed questionnaire which was sent to a sample of 50 local offices distributed throughout the UK. The questionnaire provided information about present local office organisations and the viability of other stated organisational options. These data were collected to inform strategies for implementing the IT systems as well as to ensure adequate flexibility of the IT design.

Several education and training activities in HF were also conducted during this time. These activities generated a number of products including seminars on the Management of Change, material for a distance learning Core Concepts training package for ADP staff, a one-day workshop in dialogue design, and a two-day workshop on user analysis and task allocation. HF contributions were also made to formulating a strategy for User Education and Training.

In addition to the local office studies and the educational activities cited above work was frequently done on an *ad hoc* basis in response to specific short term requests from the client, e.g., an evaluation of database software, a report on user acceptability criteria, comments on the Human Factors considerations in data conversion and take up, comments on client produced system architecture papers, etc.

2.6.5 Contractual structure from 1985

The largely reactive work programme during 1983/84 was stressful for the HF consultants and difficult for the client organisation to monitor, control and evaluate. As a result of the difficulties experienced in managing the Human Factors consultancy during this two-year period a new contractual structure was formulated for the subsequent work which began in mid-1985. Under this modified contractual arrangement a core contract was set up which essentially provided the infrastructure for specific technical subprojects.

The core contract made provision for the following activities:

- Advice/Assistance to identify consultancy requirements
- Attendance at Project Managers Meetings
- Meetings with Departmental and Regional Trade Unions
- Attendance at User Managers Meetings
- Attendance at HF Steering Committee Meetings
- Meetings with Operational Strategy Directorate's Senior Management
- *Ad hoc* Presentations/Papers/Reports
- Preparation for Meetings
- Briefings for HF Consultants
- Project Planning and Resource Management
- Administration

The appointed officer in the DHSS had responsibility for commissioning work, requesting proposals, agreeing the terms of reference, objectives and work plan with the consultants. As well as the general activities described above, the core contract made provision for subprojects which were contracted individually. Subprojects undertaken in 1985/86 included the following:

- Local Office Project: Prototyping
- Local Office Studies: Office of the Future
- Local Office Project: Implementation and Training
- Strategy Training Unit: Dialogue Design Course
- HF Input to system design methodology
- Applications Architecture: HF Standards — Advice and Guidance
- Retirement Pensions: Prototyping
- *Ad hoc* advice and guidance on HF to Regional Directorate

- Strategy Training Unit: Core Concepts Training
- Advice and guidance of HF and Ergonomics in Prototyping

These arrangements offered a great improvement in the management of the consultancy. Benefits of the changed structure were short lived, however, since financial cut-backs on consultancy spending occurred throughout the DHSS before the new arrangements had really settled down. A decreased budget for HF consultancy led to a policy decision on the part of the client to concentrate the consultancy effort into giving centralised guidance which would therefore benefit all the operational strategy projects. Thus direct HF consultancy support to IT projects was withdrawn in favour of supporting the drafting of guidance to be provided for example on how to apply human factors principles throughout the design and development life-cycle.

2.6.6 Integrating HF into the Design Methodology

Thus, work also began in 1985 to incorporate Human Factors within the design methodology which was being developed for all systems development. This subproject assignment is proving to be particularly influential in promoting application of HF principles and techniques. The HF consultants were assigned to develop material for incorporating into the methodology to ensure that relevant HF elements are included and appropriately represented. This was to encompass the:

- Identification of worksteps within the methodology which need to take into account HF considerations
- Documentation of the relevant reference material.

The material developed had to meet the following requirements:

1. To be suitable for use by staff not trained in HF
2. To be usable with little initial training and a minimum of direct consultancy support.

It was intended that the HF activities incorporated in the methodology were to be carried out by representatives of the user population and the guidance has been drafted accordingly.

The subproject work concerned with methodology continued throughout 1986 and was expected to be completed at the end of that year. A methodology team had been established earlier in the DHSS led by a civil servant. This Methodology Team included a senior ADP consultant from a small consultancy house and a junior consultant from a large management consultancy firm which is employed widely in the Department. These consultants were charged with integrating features of SSADM (Structured System Analysis and Design Methodology) and PROMPT (Project Resource Organisations Management and Planning Technique) to provide a standard approach to be used on all IT projects underway in the Department.

The Human Factors expertise was to be provided by the HF consultants for the other consultants to integrate into the Methodology. The new integrated methodology was entitled Departmental Integrated Application Development Methodology (DIADEM).

The documentation for DIADEM is structured hierarchically in three tiers. The infrastructure required to support the methodology is described in a 'Management Binder'. The specific activities required at each stage in the system development lifecycle are described in a 'Technical Binder'. Detailed descriptions of the techniques and procedures required to carry out the activities in the Technical Binder are provided in a 'Techniques Reference Binder'. The methodology is further supported by a range of Application Architecture Standards documents including standards addressing hardware and software aspects of human interface design. Training in some of the required techniques is provided by the consultants; direct consultancy support from the Methodology Team is also available to projects.

Use of the brainstorming technique identified the following as key HF inputs to IT Design:

1. User Analysis/Socio-Technical Systems Analysis
2. User Involvement in Decision Making
3. User Acceptability Criteria
4. Methods of User Involvement
5. Job Design and Work Organisation
6. Task Allocation/Jobstream Charts
7. Human Computer Interface Design
8. Prototyping
9. Workplace and Workstation Design
10. User Support
11. Management of Change
12. Institutionalising Human Factors

Material in these twelve key HF areas has now been incorporated into the Management Binder, Technical Binder and Techniques Reference Binder as appropriate.

The main focus of the work undertaken in this subproject was on the early stages of the life-cycle since they are crucial from the user's viewpoint. In the Initiation Stage (which is the first stage of DIADEM) exploratory investigations are conducted to provide the data for defining the requirements of the system. Conventional system analysis techniques do not take a user-centred approach and therefore fail to provide critical user data. To remedy this deficiency user analysis techniques have now been integrated into the methodology. User data collected at this stage also form the basis for subsequent evaluation purposes. Crucial decisions relating to the allocation of function between people and technology are also made during these early stages. These decisions have profound impact upon job design and work organisations. To improve the quality of the decision-making, task allocation techniques and job design considerations are now integrated into the methodology. Although the bulk of the HF activity is required in the early stages of DIADEM, some important additions have also been made to later stages. For example Acceptance Testing and Quality Assurance procedures have been expanded to include HF evaluation criteria. The post-implementation audit now also includes such criteria.

2.7 *The consultancy experience*

2.7.1 Mission

The HF programme began with excitement and enthusiasm to take on the challenge for Human Factors to contribute to the effective use of IT. The scale of the undertaking and the problems were of such magnitude that inevitably the work proved difficult, demanding, frustrating and often unrewarding and demoralising for the consultants — especially the younger members of the HF team. The sustaining motivation throughout has been the sense of mission to develop ways of incorporating Human Factors into a major civilian IT application for the first time in history. In the face of day-to-day pressures it was often not easy to maintain the vision of the long-term aim of the HF Strategy, and some of the younger members chose to leave the project.

There are clearly many problems in any new venture — especially on the scale of the Operational Strategy. Some of the more intractable ones which have yet to be resolved concern client attitudes towards HF and particularly the lack of tools and techniques available in many areas.

2.7.2 Ambivalence towards Human Factors

There is widespread recognition in the DHSS that human and organisational issues are important. However, these issues are seen as requiring "common sense" rather than specialist skills and experience to deal with them effectively. This perception of HF skills contrasts with the widespread acceptance that consultants were needed in other areas where skills are in short supply in the DHSS, e.g., in project management, in computing and in telecommunications. The net result of this view of the subject area is that adequate commitment of resources to HF is resisted at policy level while enormous demands for HF work are experienced "on the ground".

2.7.3 Competition between consultants

The existence of other consultants within the organisation, whose specialities apparently do not evoke such feelings of ambivalence in the client, leads to complex relationships in the field. HF consultants not only have to do the normal educating and convincing of members of the client organisation; they are frequently challenged, including on committees or in public meetings, by members of the competing consultancies. Sometimes these are wanting to increase their own HF repertoire, and it is difficult to know when to assist in this.

2.7.4 Undifferentiated view of Human Factors

It has frequently been the experience of the HF Consultants in this programme that they are expected to be equally competent in all areas of psychology and ergonomics. Thus HF specialists in interface design could be asked and indeed have been asked to give guidance on, for example, job design and work organisation. Client displeasure is considerable when HF consultants approached for advice outside their area of specialism suggest seeking advice from other consultants in the relevant subproject area. This unwillingness for the HF consultants to provide guidance in areas outside their specialism tends to be interpreted as lack of competence and confidence on the part of the consultant. It is not seen as reflecting a professional concern for validity and a sound basis for recommendations — rather it is regarded as 'sitting on the fence' in many instances.

2.7.5 Client expectations about HF

The diffuse and uncodified nature of the HF knowledge base has proved to be a considerable burden throughout the work programme described here. The academic literature includes many areas relevant to IT but the information is not organised into a body of knowledge concerned with the psychology of the IT user. There are some areas where considerable knowledge and experience exists which has yet to be codified and yet other areas where there are gaps in existing knowledge. This 'state of the art' in HF is generally neither credible nor acceptable to the client organisation. In addition there are areas which will never be codified.

The lack of 'off the shelf' guidance, techniques and tools in many HF areas tends to be seen not as a limitation of the current state of HF or as a realistic indication that some joint work must be done, but as a shortcoming of the individual consultant. Generally the client seeks rapid application of HF expertise to the task in hand and is unprepared for an investigative or development process before a valid HF input can be made.

2.7.6 Demands on the consultants

Considerable effort and resources beyond what was contracted by the client have been expended to cope with the mismatch between client expectations and reality. The HF consultants have had to engage in a range of activities in parallel. It has been essential to the progress of the work to provide the client with explanations of the 'state of the art' and in general to provide education in basic HF principles at all levels in in the DHSS. At the same time a research process to cull available knowledge has been required as well as 'brainstorming sessions' to utilise the collective knowledge and experience of HUSAT personnel. Development of quite new techniques, for example to handle task allocation in system design, has also been required. Thus it has been a characteristic of the work since 1982 that education in HF has to be provided continuously while also conducting a research and development process, providing support to the IT project underway and managing client relationships. Each of these important functions is in itself demanding and time-consuming. To accomplish them all in parallel is challenging in the extreme and places a heavy toll on human resources.

2.7.7 Experiences of success

When one is immersed in such a wide-ranging and complex assignment, one is more likely to be aware of the problems than of the successes. Nevertheless there are substantial achievements as well as positive experiences and these are described below.

2.8 *Achievements*

Developing and implementing a HF strategy in a large bureaucracy which is in the throes of computerising local office administration for the first time is a difficult and often frustrating undertaking. Progress has been slow but significant. As a result of the HF work programme there are some tangible products of particular importance, three of which are outlined below. In addition other more diffuse but positive changes are occurring in the approach to IT in the DHSS which are discussed in Section 2.8.4 below.

The first of the specific 'products' mentioned includes the training in Human Factors for all new computer staff. The second is the introduction of Human Factors into a structured design methodology. The third is the development of a considerable body of knowledge relating to Local Office operation. These three achievements are outlined below. As the work continues it can be expected to produce other significant outputs, enhancing the DHSS's Human Factors Strategy.

2.8.1 Human Factors training

All new staff at the level of Higher Executive Officer (HEO) and above who are working with computers are now given instruction in the basic principles of Human Factors. Training occurs at the earliest stages of their general computer training, giving the staff an introduction to the concepts of Human Factors at the same time as they are learning about the new technology. Such an approach offers several advantages, not the least of which is the emphasis it gives to considering the end users. It should significantly improve the design of new systems and ensure that the users are considered throughout the design process.

For the more experienced ADP staff a one-day workshop on dialogue design has been constructed which provides a combination of theory and practice to designers and programmers.

2.8.2 Human Factors in a structured design methodology

As a result of incorporating HF into DIADEM the methodology now specifically addresses the need for user involvement. It allows (and requires) users to play an important and legitimate rôle in the design process. This rôle includes involvement in the specification, acceptance testing and the quality assurance of any IT project.

Integrating HF into the methodology has succeeded in giving user issues at least a share of the attention they merit. It is now not just legitimate but essential to address human and organisational issues.

One particularly important achievement here has been to overcome or to reduce the limitations of conventional systems analysis by introducing the concept and techniques of user analysis. As a consequence user concerns and characteristics are now investigated from the earliest stage (Initiation) of the 'development life-cycle' and more adequately reflected in the "User Requirement" document. This should result in the specification and design of an IT system matching user needs more closely than is usually the case. Further, there is now a requirement in the methodology to allocate tasks between the computer and human beings in a considered way with due regard for job design implications. This process demands exploration of long term human and organisational impact and an identification of viable options for evaluation. In addition User Acceptance Testing has been expanded to ensure that issues of crucial relevance to the users, such as ease of use, are included in the test procedures.

2.8.3 Database on local office operation

A unique body of information concerning local office operations has been constructed from the detailed study of one local office and survey data from 50 local offices. It provides an invaluable resource for application to the following areas:

i) IT project design decisions
ii) Management of Change strategies
iii) Management training
iv) Job design
v) Model Office Exercises (i.e., Simulation)
vi) Developing evaluation criteria for local office effectiveness.

The studies of local offices have generated a vast amount of rich socio-technical data which is now available to inform the processes such as those listed above. The data will be particularly helpful to the user organisation as it begins to prepare for the implementation of the proposed IT systems.

2.8.4 Diffuse achievements

In addition to the specific tangible 'products' described above there are more diffuse but nonetheless important achievements occurring across projects. These include the first signs of a transition towards a socio-technical systems design process for IT, development of a strategic approach to managing change and, perhaps most significantly of all, moves to involve users in the design and development process.

(a) *Transition towards socio-technical system design*

The introduction of information technology to facilitate delivery of benefit to claimants will automate certain processes (e.g., calculation of benefit) and facilitate others (e.g., case paper location) by assisting local office staff in their work. The point has been made that it is not just the technical system which will change but the whole way in which local office work is organised and contact with claimants is managed.

Computer systems design methods have not embraced socio-technical theory or practice in the past. For example conventional systems analysis procedures begin by examining the technical procedures and the flow of information. These data are then represented in a variety of formalised structures such as flow-charts or data-flow diagrams. These processes exclude — sometimes explicitly — all human activity associated with performance of the technical tasks. This separation of technical procedure from human practice is misguided and damaging in its effects on IT design. The artificial division of 'social' from technical is a root cause of the poor match frequently observed between the real needs of the computer user and the actual characteristics of the computer service provided.

(b) *Progress towards a strategic approach to the Management of Change*

A considerable body of knowledge relating to planned change exists (Bennis, Benne and Chin, 1969). This knowledge is not generally taught to computer specialists and only rarely to managers. It is quite customary to hear senior as well as middle ranking junior people in large bureaucracies explaining problems experienced in any new venture as manifestations of 'resistance to change'. Indeed, the phenomenon often provides an acceptable reason for failure of the project.

In reality resistance to IT generally stems from negative user experiences. For example, initial enthusiasm for new systems is often reduced or destroyed by system flaws such as lack of 'user-friendliness', lack of relevance of facilities and inappropriate system response times. Serious 'resistance to change' is often associated with reduced job satisfaction and 'de-skilling'. All of these problems can be successfully addressed by ensuring users have influence over the design process and ownership of the resultant system. The literature on planned change provides extensive guidance on how to achieve change successfully.

In order to overcome the all too familiar problems sketched above, steps towards developing a strategic approach to the management of change are being taken in the social security computerisation programme. Earlier parts of this paper have described the attempts to reflect operational requirements of the user in the design and development process. For example in the structured design method being developed the user acceptance testing now includes user acceptability criteria as well as technical performance criteria. Thus, task match, ease of use, user support, job design and work organisation criteria are recognised as legitimate requirements of an IT application.

(c) *Promoting user involvement*

A key essential in effective management of change is involvement of those to be affected by change in the planning of that change. In a vast bureaucratic organisation with a multiplicity of future users spread over a considerable geographical area it is far from easy to involve the users in the development and design of the system. The difficulties are compounded when implementation is still several years away from the present day.

The challenge is being taken up in the social security computerisation in two ways. First, an ambitious user education and awareness programme is being mounted to inform and to stimulate interest in the planned projects throughout the system development cycle. Second, user involvement is being promoted by assigning individuals from the user organisation to work on design issues in user teams. Thus selected user representatives with experience in the organisation are tackling system development tasks such as the conduct of simulation exercises, planning implementation strategies, etc. The most serious obstacles to be overcome here are:

i) the 'hostage phenomenon',

ii) the short term focus of the user organisation, and

iii) the dearth of methods and techniques for helping the user to contribute meaningfully to design.

These problems which emerged during the HF work programme are discussed in the next section.

2.9 *Some unresolved problems*

2.9.1 The need to institutionalise Human Factors

Experience throughout this assignment and elsewhere points to the conclusion that to be effective and influential HF must be 'institutionalised', i.e., built into the whole policies, practices and infrastructure of an organisation (Klein, 1986). Where projects have run into difficulties it has often been because the demands of the project run counter to accepted practice or because of lack of understanding of the role of HF in IT design and implementation. Thus it is crucial that application of HF should cease to be dependent upon a few enthusiasts in an organisation but should be a normal part of management thinking, part of the repertoire of skills of ADP staff, integrated into design methodology (including the QA process) and reflected in standards, guidelines, procurement, recruitment and staff appraisal. In Section 3 of this paper the actions necessary to progress towards institutionalisation are presented.

2.9.2 The hostage phenomenon

Involving such large numbers of users in the IT development is clearly a formidable problem. It has already been indicated that involvement through education is underway. In addition user involvement in design is being sought through setting up user teams to work alongside the technical design teams. This is an important and helpful development but gives rise to the problem characterised as the 'hostage phenomenon' (Hedberg, 1975). This problem arises when a user representative is plunged into the unfamiliar world of ADP specialists. The language, concepts and focus are technology centred and often foreign to the user representative. Uprooted from his/her home ground there is a powerful drive to make sense of the new environment and to feel more comfortable in it. To achieve this requires the user representatives to learn the ADP jargon and take on the ethos of the technical specialists. As a result the user 'representative' very quickly develops characteristics which are not usually those of the user population, i.e., the 'representative' quickly ceases to be representative of the users once he has been assigned to an IT project for some time. He/she is also a hostage of the project in the sense that he/she becomes a kind of scapegoat who can be 'blamed' if the eventual project fails to meet the needs of the wider population since he/she was party to its development.

The hostage phenomenon is exacerbated when user representatives are assigned on a full time basis to projects and are physically separated from the rest of the user population. This is the situation in the DHSS. A consultative programme is required to reduce the hostage phenomenon by ensuring the user representative communicates with the wider user population. Support from senior management in the user organisation is also required when conflicts arise with the technical teams.

2.9.3 The paucity of psychological techniques

The absence of developed tools and techniques to assist user-centred design of IT systems has been and continues to be a major obstacle to progress in the HF programme. For example, there are no readily available techniques to assist users in understanding IT system proposals, to explore job design implications or to aid communications between users and designers. Users struggle, for example, to discern from static, two-dimensional data flow diagrams how day-to-day working practices will change as a result of implementing the proposed system. Proposals are represented typically in formal language, sometimes in abstract terms, and can only convey little meaning to most of the recipients. What is required is an array of techniques and media which will convey in a realistic and dynamic way how working life will proceed when the proposed IT system is in operation. Applied Psychology has yet to provide users with the tools they urgently require in order to make sense of IT proposals. Rapid prototyping tools offer considerable promise here.

2.9.4 Short term focus of the user organisation

The notion that users should be involved in the development of IT systems which they will eventually use is now widely accepted. In the DHSS it has proved difficult for the user management to address IT issues seriously when delivery of the proposed systems is still several years away. The day to day pressures force out long term considerations, especially where the long term issues are unclear and demand considerable investigation and analysis before they can be adequately addressed. There is a need to create posts with the sole function and responsibility to address human and organisational aspects of the IT systems under development. This will be considered further in Section 3 of this paper.

3. How to develop a Human Factors strategy

3.1 *The need*

3.1.1 Historical evidence

DTI Pilot Studies (DTI, 1986) showed the need for far more application of Human Factors expertise. About one third of the pilots failed and one third were only partly successful; the primary reasons for this were both broader organisational issues and more detailed human-computer interface issues.

The DTI findings reflected some of the results of an American survey conducted a decade earlier (Mowshowitz, 1976). Such research evidence now exists in abundance and supports the premise that many IT applications fail, in varying degrees, for human and organisational reasons. Further, the evidence suggests that the plethora of MMI, HCI and related research projects and almost two decades of exhortations and experiments concerned with user participation have failed to influence significantly most IT developments. As was noted in Section 1, it seems clear that a more integrated and strategic approach to the application of HF is required before any substantive benefit from HF expertise is reflected in the design, development and, especially, the uptake of IT.

3.1.2 Need for a strategic framework

As has already been noted in Section 2 of this paper, a first requirement for successful application of HF to IT would seem to be that HF ceases to be dependent upon a few enthusiasts but is instead integrated into all aspects of organisational life. A further requirement is that the focus of HF must shift from optimisation of isolated elements of the IT system to optimisation of the wider socio-technical system of which IT is one technical sub-system. A Human Factors Strategy for IT provides the framework to enable such a shift to occur. Desirably the HF strategy of an organisation would be a coherent part of a wider National or European HF Strategy for Information Technology. The steps involved in creating a strategic framework are represented in Figure 3.

3.2 *Setting up an HF strategy*

There are four key areas to setting up a HF strategy:

Identifying and educating key people;
Integrating HF with design and decision-making processes;
Integrating HF with feedback processes;
Providing resources for HF.

These are discussed below, and each section is summarised by a number of Action Points, which combine to form a 12-point Action Plan for setting up a HF strategy.

3.2.1. Identifying and educating key people

Starting up. To achieve the transition from a fragmented, piecemeal application of HF to a holistic, strategic approach requires that an Action Group be set up within the organisation to implement the Action Plan. The precise composition of the group will vary with specific circumstances, but it must have the authority to be able to implement the plan whilst receiving acceptance and cooperation within the organisation. The Action Group must include one or more HF Specialists (depending on the scale of the operation) and an influential member of the parent organisation who has some understanding of HF. A first task for the group will be to identify the key people who should be members of the Action Group.

Gaining approval. Given the all-pervasive nature of IT and HF, it is vital for people at Board and Senior Management level to understand and endorse the concept of a Human Factors Strategy in an IT context. Many policies and procedures will need to incorporate HF principles. Senior management will have to authorise these changes and the deployment of resources to achieve them. Their commitment to setting up a HF strategy is therefore crucial. If senior management understanding of HF is limited, HF specialists find themselves fighting a rear-guard action to justify their work, consuming time and effort unproductively. Education of senior people is essential to reduce the ambivalence described in Part 2 and to gain support for the effort required to set up and implement an effective HF strategy.

Staff training. Apart from educating the upper strata of an organisation, staff throughout the organisation will need to understand HF principles and apply them in their work, in order to develop the internal expertise the HF Strategy will require.

Action Points:

1. List relevant key people and negotiate review of their terms of reference to include HF.
2. Initiate short courses in HF for senior people (Shackel, Eason and Pomfrett, 1988).
3. Initiate and develop training in HF for all management grades.
4. Initiate HF training modules for IT analysts and designers.

3.2.2 Integrating HF with design and decision-making processes

To ensure that HF informs the activities and decision-making associated with IT developments such expertise must be available in relevant steering committees, project groups, etc. This will usually be achieved by involving a HF specialist. The

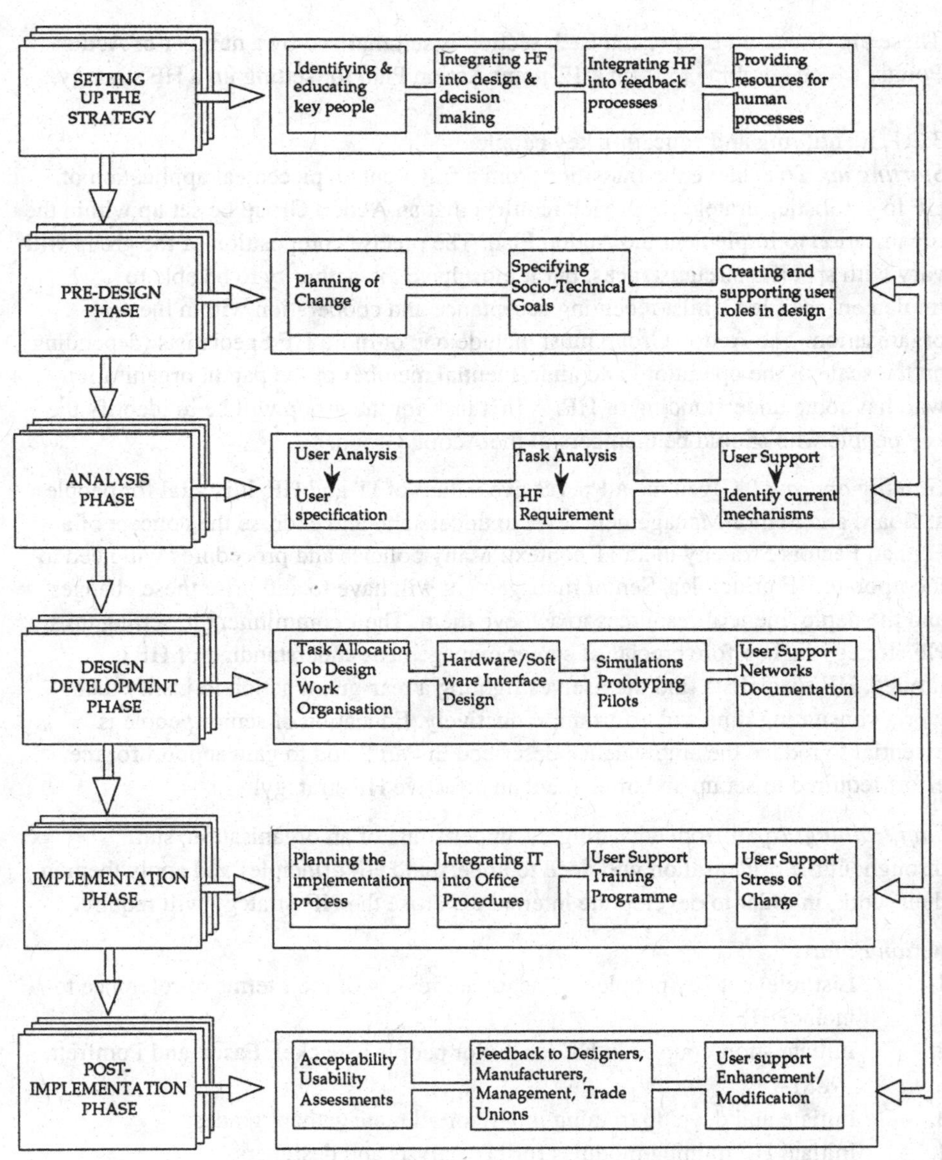

Figure 3: Steps in creating an HF strategy.

design methodology must include application of HF principles (see Figure 4, for example, where the HF strategy is related to SSADM) and it is also important that other experts, particularly external consultants, recognise the need for HF.

Action Points:

5. Review membership of key decision-making bodies to include HF expertise.
6. Integrate HF principles and techniques into system design methods.
7. Review contracts with outside consultants to include HF in terms of reference.

3.2.3 Integrating HF with feedback processes

Appraisal, Assurance and Auditing:- The ability to apply HF principles in the course of normal working must be recognised in any performance appraisal and assessment process. Only by emphasising a positive approach to applying HF will 'in-house' expertise and acceptance of HF develop. Additionally, products (including proposals) from every stage need to be assessed for HF qualities prior to acceptance.

Also, the impact of IT on users requires monitoring to ensure positive effects. Audits provide information to managers and designers on the acceptability of the IT supplied to the users, giving feedback for genuinely useful modifications or organisational changes.

Action Points:

8. Initiate negotiation to include HF aspects in annual assessment/performance appraisals.
9. Include HF design criteria in Quality Assurance.
10. Conduct long-term auditing of job design and work organisation to assess the impact of IT and its acceptability.

3.2.4 Providing resources for HF

Skill support. To support the work, HF specialists are required, at least in the short-term, while expertise develops within the host organisation. These specialists could be external or part of an in-house group.

Budget planning. For a HF strategy to become a reality, adequate resources of skills, time and facilities are required. These need to be costed and given appropriate budget allocations.

Action Points:

11. Consider an in-house unit of HF specialists. If this appears appropriate, decide location (dispersed or localised), staffing, equipment, etc.
12. Review relevant budgets and schedules to see that HF activities are included.

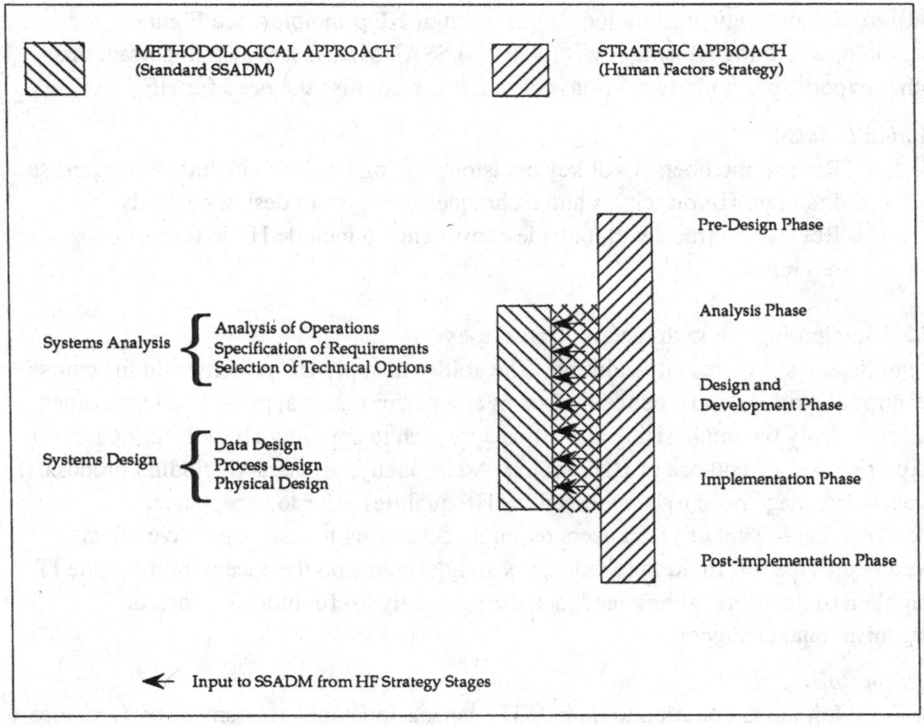

Figure 4: Relationship between design phases in SSADM and the Human Factors Strategy.

3.3 *HF strategy phases*

The many HF contributions required during the IT application cycle can be revealed by the contributions which are relevant to each phase of the HF strategy described below.

3.3.1 Pre-design phase

Before IT design begins it is important that the HF specialist contributes to the four key areas outlined below.

The planning of change

In the early deliberations for exploiting IT it is important that the HF specialist assists the user organisation to consider its future mission and the potential rôle of IT in furthering this mission. Top management seminars which include brainstorming sessions as well as formal presentations and group discussions have been used successfully to raise relevant issues and promote understanding (Bennis, Benne and Chin, 1969).

Specifying socio-technical goals
There is a crucial need to consider the forms of work organisation and job design which future IT systems might support or preclude. Such an exploration is fundamental to identifying and specifying the human and organisational criteria to be fulfilled by the new IT system.

Creating mechanisms
To enable IT design to take adequate account of HF requires appropriate mechanisms and media, as described in the Action Plan (Section 3.2). An infrastructure must be created to facilitate the setting up and application of a strategy such that HF training, user involvement, quality assurance and IT enhancement can proceed as required.

User support
In this early stage of planning, users require considerable support in understanding the User Rôle in IT design, coping with unfamiliar demands (e.g., IT concepts and jargon), and identifying ways of influencing the IT design. The process of educating managers in HF needs to begin to ensure managers are sufficiently well-informed to play a constructive, pro-active role in the planning, design and implementation of IT.

Designer training in HF
Training in Human Factors principles for designers should be made available as soon as possible. Such training is essential if the HF standards and guidelines under development are to be of any practical utility. Workshops on key topics such as dialogue design are urgently required. Use of a VDU as a key medium for presenting options in dialogue style could well prove advantageous. Use of a familiar tool and a relevant medium may well be more successful than paper-based materials in persuading designers to apply Human Factors design criteria in their work. This approach is being pioneered by the HUSAT Research Centre in Loughborough University at the present time with groups of programmers.

A multi-media approach is needed to providing education and training in HF to all ADP staff and to designers of IT equipment, if the design and development process is to receive the support it requires from HF.

3.3.2 User specification
In this phase it is essential to conduct a number of analyses which will complement those carried out in conventional system analysis. For instance, typically there is a need to:

1. Analyse the general work context in terms of the priorities, pressures,

communication patterns, etc.

2. Identify the users.
3. Establish crucial task demands which will continue to exist once the new office system is in place, e.g., the continued need to respond to customer queries.
4. Analyse the work rôles.
5. Establish the extent to which each user is prepared for the introduction of the new system.

These user analyses generate useful data to explain and expand the information collected to identify work flows; moreover, such analyses ensure that job design and work organisation issues are taken into account from the earliest stage in the life-cycle of the office system. The typical products of the user analysis process are the:

- Identification of Main User Groups
- Description of Users' Tasks
- Skill Profile of Users
- Sources of Job Satisfaction/Dissatisfaction
- Work Load Variations
- Career Structures
- Variability in Forms of Work Organisation
- Identification of Informal Control Processes

Thus user analysis greatly enhances the validity of the user specification since it highlights problem areas requiring further investigation, provides data on non-computer related tasks, and defines job design criteria for a given user group or population.

It is critical that the HF specialist ensures the products of the analysis phase are adequately represented in the specification document for the system to be designed. The HF specialist can assist the users in establishing criteria both for producing and for evaluating the user specification. For example the user should be encouraged to ensure that the user specification includes three main sections:

1. Functional/operational requirements — to support business strategy.
2. System/technical requirements — e.g., reliability, volume of traffic, etc.
3. User acceptability/usability requirements (see Shackel, Chapter 2; Damodaran, 1984).

The first two sections are usually included in a user specification while the third is not. The user acceptability/usability requirement needs to include task match, ease of use, user support, job design and work organisation criteria.

3.3.3 Design and development phase

Job design and work organisation

Crucial HF decisions are made throughout the early stages in the design life-cycle, determining many aspects of job design and work organisation. For example, deciding which functions should be performed by the IT system and which by people is profoundly important for the resulting quality of jobs. Specialised HF techniques such as task allocation procedures used with job design criteria are required to identify options in job design and work organisation. Data from user analysis are used to specify job design and work organisation requirements in the User Specification document, also providing the basis for assessing the acceptability of the design options which emerge. Thus in this phase the HF specialist must consider the likely impact of the planned IT development and influence design decisions to ensure a satisfactory quality of working life.

Hardware/software interface design

This design rôle is the traditional HF rôle in the design of the human machine interface — both on hardware and software attributes.

In this stage the HF specialist should contribute knowledge of two types:

i) Knowledge of universal human characteristics

This type of knowledge relates to the limitations of short term memory, the impact of fatigue on performance and the nature of learning curves. Such knowledge is relevant to the use of information technology. Other research findings and everyday experience permit identification of a number of rules relating to acceptable interactive dialogues. For example, there is a need for consistency in the construction of codes and abbreviations, avoidance of ambiguity, and compatibility in format and language used on screens and documents.

ii) Knowledge of specific characteristics of a given user population

This is made available through Human Factors methods of user analysis, user trials, pilots and simulations. Investigation of user views and experiences can provide knowledge relating to sources of job satisfaction, degree of autonomy in the job, task demands, appropriate dialogue styles, help facilities, error messages, training needs, etc.

A range of guidance documents and standards now exist relating to the design of hardware, work stations and work place design. Similarly, much guidance has been written about dialogue design and the design of 'user friendly' interfaces. However, it has become clear that in order to make real use of guidance the designers need to understand the reasons behind it. As a member of the design team the Human Factors specialist has a key rôle to play in interpreting guidance for the designers and in developing specific design solutions to problems posed by users and designers.

Simulations, prototyping, pilots
Powerful tools such as user trials, pilots, prototypes and simulations are available to assist in user-centred design. These tools serve a number of purposes, providing a medium for communicating ideas between users and designers as well as being a vehicle for testing tentative design ideas. Prototypes and simulations also offer a medium for conveying the user specification to the IT designers. HF guidance on planning and conducting prototyping exercises and simulations is essential to ensure validity of findings and to interpret results.

User support
During the analysis phase support mechanisms in the current system must be identified. In planning the support function efforts should be made to perpetuate and enhance in the new system those mechanisms which work well in everyday use. For example, in organisations where guidance is sought primarily from colleagues, human support should be seen as an important part of the support for the IT system and the evolution of 'local experts' encouraged.

Designing effective IT systems requires careful design of user support (Damodaran, 1986). The HF specialist can contribute to this process by showing the need for a user network of documentation and human support mechanisms. In particular it will be important to identify the within-system aids such as prompts and error messages to be designed. Appropriate decisions on within-system aids can only be made when the amount of training and continuing human support is decided for the rest of the user support network.

3.3.4 Implementation phase
In this phase the HF specialist has two distinct contributions to make:
Planning the implementation process, e.g., to provide guidance on how to phase implementation (where appropriate).

In phased implementation, key Human Factors include the need to ensure that the first part of the system implemented provides immediate utility, requiring a minimum of learning effort on the part of the user. As incremental implementation proceeds other Human Factors criteria will need to be met. For instance the phasing should not require substantial unlearning of one way of working and re-learning of another, and should avoid procedures which must be learned for one stage and unlearned for subsequent stages.

In relation to job design, the phasing should not produce tasks which result in duplication of effort (either clerk/clerk or clerk/computer). Such duplication increases workload and frustration.

Essentially the choice of implementation steps should facilitate the full integration of Information Technology into office procedures.

Phased implementation should also channel useful feedback from end-users to the designers and to user management as implementation proceeds.

User support, e.g., guidance on strategies for coping with disruption.

With regard to User Support, it is clear that problems dismissed as 'resistance to change' arise when the disruption caused by the new system becomes too stressful. HF guidance here includes analysis of all the demands placed upon users during implementation and post-implementation phase, e.g., testing, take-on of static and dynamic data, going 'live', learning new skills and operating procedures, practising new procedures, carrying out the business of the office. Clear identification of these demands ahead of time adequate steps taken to ensure that disruption and pressure on the user are reduced to tolerable limits.

3.3.5 Post-implementation phase

Finally the HF specialist has three important functions to carry out after implementation is complete:

Acceptability/usability assessments

A core concept in HF is concerned with evaluation and feedback. In order to ensure that IT systems are meeting the needs of the users it is important to gain feedback on user experience with any given system on a regular basis after implementation. To do this, a set of user acceptability measures have been developed, as mentioned earlier. The precise form of the measures varies with the nature of the evaluation. For example, measurement of usability is discussed in Chapters 2 and 16 of this book.

Feedback (to designers, manufacturers, management and Trades Unions)

Gaining evaluations of an IT system is clearly not worthwhile in itself. The findings of any user acceptability audit need to be fed back to appropriate bodies for modifications and enhancements to be made. User-designer liaison groups are one forum for achieving this.

User experience is an important input to design. Too often users' reactions are disregarded as capricious or based upon whim. User evaluations or audits based upon acceptability or usability criteria help to counteract this view. Properly conducted by personnel trained in HF techniques the results will show not just that users are dissatisfied or having problems but also the reasons — and often useful suggestions from users for solving problems they experience.

User support

Post implementation support to users will continue to influence the acceptability and viability of the system. The service provided by help desks, by prompts, menus and error messages will continue to be important. With any well-received system users are likely to want to expand the utility of the system for their purposes. Mechanisms for receiving suggested enhancements will be needed. New entrant training will be required to cope with inevitable staff turnover. Providing assistance to established users when they wish to make use of unfamiliar operating procedures is a further support requirement to meet.

3.4 *HF specialist rôles in a HF strategy*

Effective contribution to each of the phases of the HF strategy outlined in Section 3.3 requires HF specialists to fulfil a number of rôles including:

- Strategic/Planning Rôle
- Design Rôle (e.g., Direct Input of HF Expertise to Screen Formats, Dialogue Design, etc.)
- Training/Support Rôle
- Review Rôle (Formal, e.g., QA, and Informal, e.g., Walk-throughs).

The demands of the multiple HF rôles described in this paper cannot be fulfilled by any single specialist, however competent or highly skilled he/she might be. The diversity of work (see Section 2.6) required to implement an effective HF strategy requires specialists to work in parallel at several levels throughout the hierarchy of the IT user organisation. HF specialists may need, for example, to be working 'off-line' carrying out laboratory experiments, conducting a literature search to inform the HF work in progress and carrying out user analysis to assess IT training needs. This requires cognitive psychologists, social psychologists, educational psychologists, ergonomists, etc., to blur the boundaries between their specialisms and to contribute together to ensure that IT can be successfully implemented. Further, psychologists must work with computer scientists and with users if this end is to be achieved.

It is beyond the scope of this paper to provide detailed guidance on the *modus operandi* for achieving effective HF input to IT project work. Work is underway in HUSAT to codify the complex processes which are involved in the utilisation of HF expertise in IT planning design and development. It should however be noted that the critical features of the HF contribution, which have been touched upon here and which are the cornerstone of a HF strategy, are that it operates at a *multiple level, spans the organisational hierarchy, demands team working*, and *crosses organisational boundaries.*

4. Conclusions

The past four years of working to formulate and to implement a Human Factors Strategy have shown that Human Factors expertise can now be used effectively outside the laboratory and in a civilian context. The success achieved so far has required the political will in the client organisation, commitment of key individuals in influential positions and allocation of modest resources. These factors appear to be critical prerequisites for providing an environment in which HF specialists can operate productively.

Some essential groundwork has been done towards institutionalising Human Factors in the DHSS. In particular, a knowledge base on local office work organisation and job design now exists which can be used to inform many significant design decisions, HF design criteria are now incorporated into standards for hardware and software procurement and design, and HF principles have been integrated into the structured design methodology used by the design teams. Training in HF aspects of dialogue design is also underway for designers.

There is still much to be done, particularly in the management education sphere, before the Human Factors strategy is understood and endorsed sufficiently widely. Without managerial support the embryonic HF strategy cannot become a robust and lasting reality since HF principles need to be reflected in all key management functions such as planning, resource allocation, training, supervision, and performance appraisal. Until such support exists the notion of an HF strategy will remain tenuous and vulnerable to extinction.

Practical experience of supporting users and designers in their use of DIADEM with the newly-added HF activities is also urgently required to endorse the HF strategy. While the integration of HF principles into the methodology has been a major advance, the next challenge is to ensure the concepts are understood and applied appropriately by people who have no formal training in HF. Provision of HF training and direct consultancy support will be a priority in the next stage of implementing the strategy.

It has been a major objective of this paper to provide first a descriptive statement of the need and evolution of a Human Factors strategy and second to provide a synthesis of the learning which has emerged through the DHSS case study, so that practitioners faced with these problems will have a rudimentary template with which to guide their own intervention. In the longer term it is our goal to see the material developed and its scope widened so that ultimately HF will be integrated into design and project management as normal practice.

5. Acknowledgements

In commissioning an initial HF project and then supporting the formulation of a Human Factors Strategy and related work the DHSS has shown pioneering spirit and vision. We appreciate greatly this unique opportunity to apply Human Factors expertise to a major IT application and look forward to successful implementation of the Operational Strategy.

Contributors, past and present, to the Human Factors Programme from the HUSAT Research Centre are too numerous to list exhaustively. Especial thanks must however go to Mr Simon Richardson as co-worker on the initial contract for his important contributions to the formulation of the Human Factors Strategy and subsequent work on the programme, to Dr Lisl Klein and Mrs Susan Harker for their crucial professional contributions and continuing support and to my colleagues in the HUSAT Directorate. Throughout the HF programme many members of the Centre devoted long months of committed team effort to progress the exceedingly demanding work often in difficult and frustrating circumstances. My grateful thanks go to all my colleagues past and present for their invaluable contributions and continuing support.

PART 5

Design and Evaluation — Some Specific Methods

CHAPTER FOURTEEN

A TAXONOMY AND RULE BASE FOR THE SELECTION OF INTERACTION STYLES

BEN SHNEIDERMAN

1. Introduction

Recent empirical research has shed much light on the design of interactive systems. As researchers, we now understand more precisely the strengths and weaknesses of system variants. As system developers we now have substantially improved evaluation techniques. Academic and industrial researchers have begun to develop predictive and descriptive theories, while thoughtful professionals have compiled useful guidelines documents for practitioners. In spite of all this progress, designers who confront a new application are often reduced to mimicking familiar examples or extrapolating intuitively from experience.

This attempt at a set of design guidelines is intended to aid designers in choosing among the primary interaction styles and in refining their design to suit specific user communities performing specific tasks. The first step is an understanding of the five primary interaction styles: menu selection, form fill-in, command language, natural language, and direct manipulation. Variants and combinations are possible, but these basic styles are a useful taxonomy (Shneiderman, 1987). The second step is an understanding of the factors that guide designers in choosing among the five primary interaction styles. A formal decision procedure would be attractive, but for the moment we must rely on informal rules which although they often stem from extrapolations of experiments need to be validated and refined.

2. Taxonomy of interaction styles

There are many ways of interacting with a computer. The variations result from differences in tasks, computer concepts, and interface devices. The five primary interaction styles described in this paper could each accomplish the full range of interactions, although some would be awkward in certain situations (see Table 1 for an overview). The remainder of this section reviews each style, shows an example, and offers guidelines for improving the design.

Menu selection
- Advantages: shortens training, reduces keystrokes, structures decision-making, permits use of dialog management tools, easy to support error handling
- Disadvantages: danger of many menus, may slow frequent users, requires screen space, requires rapid display rate

Form fill-in
- Advantages: simplifies data entry, requires modest training, assistance is convenient, shows context for activity, permits use of form management tools
- Disadvantages: consumes screen space, requires typing skills

Command language
- Advantages: flexibility, supports user initiative, appeals to 'power' users, potentially rapid for complex tasks, supports macro capability
- Disadvantages: requires substantial training and memorisation, difficult to retain, poor error handling

Natural language
- Advantages: relieves burden of learning syntax
- Disadvantages: requires clarification dialog, may require more keystrokes, may not show context, unpredictable

Direct manipulation
- Advantages: visually presents task, easy to learn, easy to retain, errors can be avoided, encourages exploration, high subjective satisfaction
- Disadvantages: may require graphics display/pointing devices, more programming effort until tools improve, may be hard to record history or write macros

Table 1: Overview of interaction styles with their advantages and disadvantages.

2.1 *Menu selection*

In menu selection systems the computer displays a list of items from which the user selects. If the items are meaningful to the user then menu selection can be a rapid, accurate, and satisfactory approach. If the items are hard to understand or appear similar to each other, users can become confused and make errors. Menu selection is advantageous because it decomposes a complex interaction into a series of smaller steps and because it provides structure for decision-making. On the other hand this same decomposition process can be too rigid for some users and it may slow down the knowledgeable frequent user.

For many situations menu selection can substantially reduce the number of keystrokes necessary and thereby reduce error rates and performance times. Menu selection mechanisms can be the familiar numbered menus, lettered menus, mnemonic lettered menus, or unlabelled menus. Unlabelled menus operate by movement of a highlight bar over the items, under the control of arrow keys, a mouse, a joystick, a graphics tablet, etc. Table 2 provides a brief set of guidelines while Smith and Mosier (1987) offer extensive guidelines for menu selection systems. Shneiderman (1987) reviews empirical studies and suggests practical design rules.

- Use task semantics to organise menus (single, linear sequence, tree structure, acyclic and cyclic networks)
- Prefer broad/shallow trees
- Show position by graphics, numbers, or titles
- Items become titles for trees
- Meaningful groupings of items
- Meaningful sequencing of items
- Brief items, begin with keyword
- Consistent grammar, layout, terminology
- Type-ahead, jump-ahead, or other short-cuts
- Jumps to previous and main menu
- Consider: online help, novel selection mechanisms, response time, display rate, screen size

Table 2: Menu selection guidelines.

Figure 1 is.an example of menu selection as applied to airline reservation systems when the users are air travellers making reservations from a hotel or airport lobby. This hypothetical example for Boswash Airlines will be used to illustrate all five interaction styles. Each version is merely a sketch for a system, meant to encourage discussion and to emphasize differences. A full system might have more instructional material, online help, a mixture of interaction styles for different parts of the task, special hardware, greater provision for reversibility of action, more informative feedback, etc.

In Figure 1 the user is confronted with a rigid sequence of menus that force the user to make decisions in a system-defined order. Users who would be willing to change their departure time or date to find a cheaper flight would become frustrated with this design. The numbered menus do help structure the users' work, but more knowledgeable users might be annoyed that items such as the date were broken into

```
BOSWASH AIRLINES RESERVATIONS MENU SYSTEM

What month do you want to take your trip?

1  January      4  April     7  July         10  October
2  February     5  May       8  August       11  November
3  March        6  June      9  September    12  December

Type the number of your choice and press RETURN: __
```

---------- New screen ----------

```
Type the date in the month you want to take your trip: __
```

---------- New screen ----------

```
What is your departure city?

1  Albany, NY                    5  Philadelphia, PA
2  Boston, MA                    6  Washington, DC
3  Hartford, CT                  7  White Plains, NY
4  New York, La Guardia

Type the number of your choice and press RETURN: __
```

---------- New screen ----------

```
What is your arrival city?

1  Albany, NY                    5  Philadelphia, PA
2  Boston, MA                    6  Washington, DC
3  Hartford, CT                  7  White Plains, NY
4  New York, La Guardia

Type the number of your choice and press RETURN: __
```

---------- New screen ----------

```
What time of day do you wish to take your trip?

1    7:00 AM  to  10:30 AM
2   10:01 AM  to   3:00 PM
3    3:01 PM  to   6:00 PM
4    6:01 PM  to  10:00 PM

Type the number of your choice and press RETURN: __
```

Figure 1: Menu selection approach, with occasional form fill-in for fields such as names, phone numbers or charge numbers.

two separate items. They might prefer a form fill-in approach. Also the layout, wording of items, instructions, and error handling might all be improved. On the other hand, some form of menu selection system is likely to be the most successful in a public waiting room environment where computer and typing skills are not uniformly high.

2.2 *Form fill-in*

In a form fill-in interaction the users' main task is to provide data in labelled fields clustered on one or more screens. Sometimes the data items are merely binary choices (Yes/No or Male/Female) or selections from short lists (days of the week or a set of colours), but they can also be taken from large domains (personal names or chemical formulae) or may be essentially unbounded (explanatory paragraphs or meteorological data). Of course, it is possible to replace form fill-in with a series of menu choices, but this strategy can become extremely tedious. Keyboards or other input devices are effective ways of inputting lengthy data fields. The keyboard may be seen as a continuously displayed menu that permits rapid selection using a well-learned skill. Increasingly data entry is handled more automatically as is done in reading magnetic stripes on charge cards to get names and account numbers or grocery packages with bar codes.

Form fill-in requires that users learn to use the keyboard with tab, cursor control, and backspace keys. If the users are competent keyboard operators and field labels are meaningful then form fill-in is an effective approach that produces a quite rapid rate of data entry, a moderate level of errors, and good user satisfaction. There has been very little research in the design of form fill-in systems but there are several sources of design guidelines (Galitz, 1980, 1981; Smith and Mosier, 1987) (see also Table 3 for a brief list).

The Boswash Airlines example as a form fill-in (Figure 2) demonstrates the increased density of information that can be supplied on a single screen when compared with menu selection. Presumably the user can press arrow or tab keys to move around the form and perform error correction. The keyboard usage might reduce the number of potential users when compared to menu selection, but might increase the willingness of more knowledgeable and frequent users to work with the system.

Research issues include very basic questions of appropriate layout, justification, spacing, grouping, sequencing, handling of optional fields, and online help. A combination of form fill-in with menu selection might help the novice user. For example, the list of departure cities might be made available when the cursor is moved to that field; then the user could select a city instead of typing it and it would be displayed in the field. A useful conjecture, that needs validation, is that as user

- Meaningful title
- Comprehensible instructions
- Logical grouping and sequencing of fields
- Visually appealing layout of the form
- Familiar field labels
- Consistent terminology and abbreviations
- Visible space and boundaries for data entry fields
- Convenient cursor movement
- Error correction for individual characters and entire fields
- Error messages for unacceptable values
- Optional fields should be marked
- Explanatory messages for fields

Table 3: Form fill-in guidelines

BOSWASH AIRLINES RESERVATIONS FORM

Type the information required and press RETURN:

Departure date: __/__/__ (09/08/87 indicates September 8, 1987)
Departure city: ____________
Arrival city: ____________
Departure time: __:__ _ (8:30 P indicates 8:30 in the evening)
Number of seats: _
Last Name: ____________ First Name: ____________
Phone Number: (___) ___-____
Charge Card: __ (MC=MasterCard, AE=American Express, or VI=Visa)
Charge Number: ____ ____ ____ __

Figure 2: Form fill-in provides guidance, but requires knowledge of field labels, permissible values, and typing.

experience increases, the density of fields on a single screen can be increased while the field labels can be shortened.

2.3 *Command language*

Knowledgeable frequent users do not want to be distracted by having to locate an item in a list, nor do they want to have to view and move a cursor over a form. They can manipulate the possibilities in their mind and want concise notations for issuing commands with modest informative feedback. These 'power' users want to be able to put several commands on a single line and even create new commands that encapsulate the work of several frequently used command sequences. The learning time may be days or weeks, but since usage is frequent the benefits of concision are great.

Often command languages emerge from familiar notations such as mathematics, boolean logic, or music, but many command languages have been created to deal with novel task domains such as text and string manipulation, hotel reservations, or information retrieval. There has been much research in command language design for text editors and other applications. Consistency in structure, meaningfulness, orderly abbreviations, small number of commands, and congruent pairs of commands have been shown to be important determinants of rapid learning, rapid use, low error rates, high satisfaction, and easy retention over time (see Table 4 for a brief set of guidelines).

- Create explicit model of objects and actions
- Choose meaningful, specific, distinctive names
- Try for hierarchical structure
- Provide consistent structure
  (hierarchy, argument order, action-object)
- Support consistent abbreviation rules
  (prefer truncation to one letter)
- Offer frequent users the capability to create macros
- Consider command menus on high-speed displays
- Limit number of commands and ways of accomplishing a task

Table 4: Command language guidelines.

Airlines reservations systems used by travel agents and airlines employees use a very concise and cryptic command language strategy. The Boswash Airlines command language (Figure 3) is modelled after the American Airlines SABRE system that has been in use for approximately 25 years. The information is packed in a coded form without delimiters and the feedback is also quite dense, but these are advantages to the frequent user.

2.4 *Natural language*

Many computer scientists and computer users propose that the "ultimately desirable" way of using a computer is through natural language interaction. They argue that people already know their own natural language and therefore learning to use the computer would be simplified if the computer accepted natural language input. This vision has propelled many researchers over the years as they tried to make natural language interaction systems for programming, database retrieval, or expert systems usage. There are commercial products such as INTELLECT (Artificial Intelligence

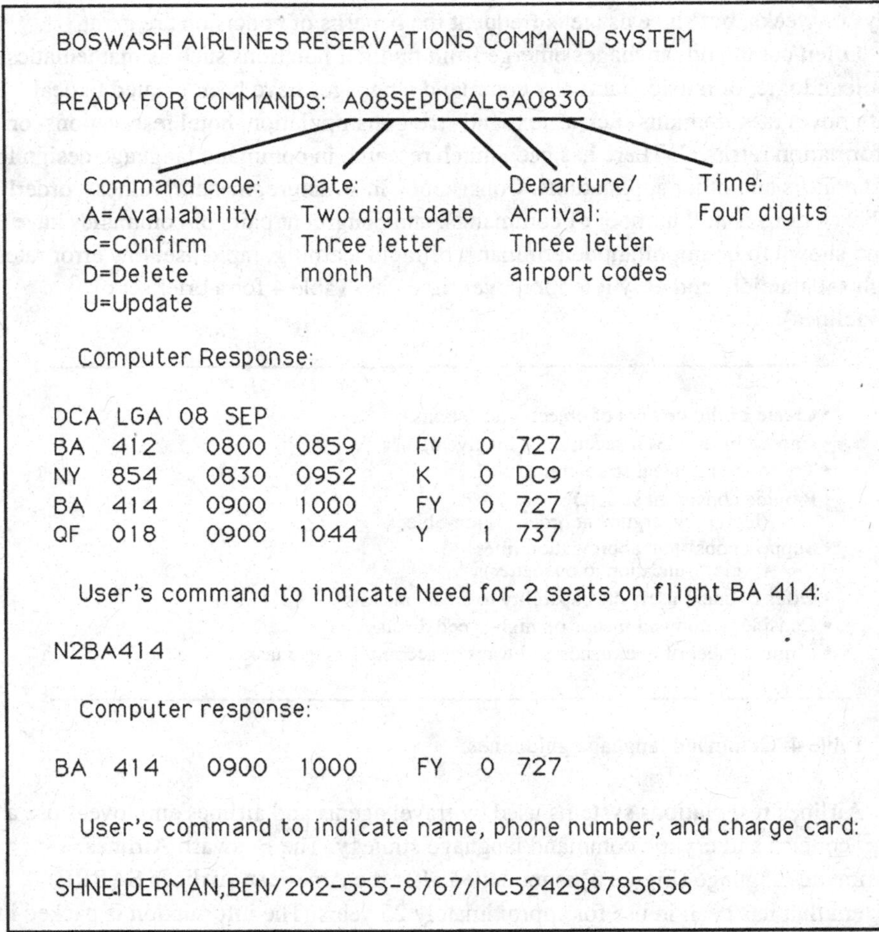

Figure 3: Command language style requires special knowledge of fields and permissible field values. Command language style requires few keystrokes but potentially substantial training.

Corporation) or Q & A (Symantec) but the success could only be considered to be modest. Relieving the user of the burdens of syntax is only a small part of the problem in using a computer and is of benefit only to novice and intermittent users. The much more complex part is understanding the computer concepts and the task domain. Relief from syntactic details does not ensure that the users will know that files must be saved before quitting or that stock market purchases must be in blocks of 100 shares.

Furthermore, natural language interaction systems constantly confront the user with the problem of uncertainty about whether a particular input will be acceptable to the machine. This inhibits planning ahead since users must always be ready to engage in clarification dialogue. Improved designs will mitigate this problem and speech input might reduce the penalty of typing, but the users will still be struggling to discover the syntactic and semantic scope of the system. Therefore, this author is sceptical that natural language interaction will become widely used. The reader should be cautioned that there are still many people who hold a more optimistic view. Natural language generation and natural language parsing of textual databases are likely to be more successful applications of the technology of computational linguistics. Finally, the special case of interactive fiction and adventure games should be cited as a highly successful application of natural language interaction. The success stems from the fact that in this situation part of the challenge and fun is to discover the syntactic and semantic bounds of the program. Table 5 summarizes some of the issues concerning natural language interaction.

- Reducing syntactic load is not enough
- Computer and task semantics should be represented
  predicate calculus, boolean algebra, set theory, normalisation theory, database entities and values, permissible operations and constraints
- Make syntactic and semantic scopes visible
- Therefore, NLI might work best for:
  - Users who are knowledgeable about task domain
  - Intermittent users who cannot retain syntax
  - Users with moderate computer skills
  - Good typists (until speech I/O improves)

Table 5: Natural language interaction guidelines.

The scenario for Boswash Airlines (Figure 4) is meant to be positive and attractive. It is not clear that such a system could be built or that it would be sufficiently successful to be commercially viable. It might be improved by more instructional information and some display of the previously made decisions.

2.5 *Direct manipulation*

The first four interaction styles emerged from a 'teletype mentality' or at best a text-oriented view of the task. However, many designers are breaking away from the constraints of teletype and keyboard designs and employing screen-oriented, form-oriented, visual and graphic approaches with pointing devices such as arrow keys, a

```
BOSWASH AIRLINES RESERVATIONS SERVICE

WHAT DAY DO YOU WANT TO TRAVEL?

September 8, 1987.

WHERE DO YOU WANT TO FLY FROM?

I want to fly from New York.

ASSUMING YOU MEAN LAGUARDIA AIRPORT IN NEW YORK CITY.
IS THIS CORRECT?

Yes.

WHERE DO YOU WANT TO FLY TO?

Boston.

WHAT TIME DO YOU WANT TO TRAVEL?

Around nine in the morning.

ASSUMING YOU MEAN 9:00 AM THEN THERE IS A FLIGHT:
BOSWASH AIRLINES 414,
DEPARTS LAGUARDIA AT 9:00 AM AND ARRIVES BOSTON AT 10:00 AM.
HOW MANY SEATS DO YOU WANT?

One seat, no smoking, on the aisle.

RESERVATION CONFIRMED.
```

Figure 4: Natural language style could work well in this example because the users are familiar with airline terminology and concepts. However, it requires substantial user input, clarification of possibly ambiguous phrases, and may cause difficulty in situations when unfamiliar terms are used. Also, the users may be uncertain as to what the scope of the semantics and syntax are.

mouse, touchscreens, or a graphics tablet. These new designs often depend on bit-mapped high resolution displays, but the concepts of direct manipulation can be applied with simple text screens and a simple pointing device.

The key to direct manipulation design is to create a visual representation of the 'world of action' that includes selectable displays of the objects and actions of interest. Then with pointing, zooming, and panning the user can rapidly perform operations, see the results immediately and reverse operations if necessary. These ideas have been applied in the Xerox STAR, Apple Macintosh, videogames, many word processors, and other applications (Shneiderman, 1983, 1987). The benefits include relatively rapid learning with high retention over time and high user satisfaction. Errors can often be prevented because the representation shows the users the impossibility of performing a task and because typographic errors are eliminated when the user selects from a set of displayed objects. Exploration is often encouraged in direct manipulation environments, especially when reversibility of actions is ensured. There are disadvantages in current direct manipulation designs. It is often difficult to create programs and recording the history of a session can be troublesome.

Developing direct manipulation systems is difficult with current software tools, but improvements are expected. There is some concern also for visually impaired users. For some tasks, frequent users may prefer command language approaches (unseen manipulation) because they prefer not to be distracted by having to locate objects and actions on the screen and then select them. The definition of direct manipulation with some of the benefits and concerns is in Table 6.

- Create visual representation of the 'world of action'
  - Objects and Actions are shown
  - Tap analogical reasoning
- Rapid, incremental, and reversible actions
- Replace typing with pointing/selecting
- Make results of actions immediately visible

Benefits

Control/display compatibility
Less syntax reduces error rates
Faster learning and higher retention
Encourages exploration

Concerns

Increased system resources, possibly
Some actions may be cumbersome
Macro techniques are often weak
History/tracing may be difficult
Visually impaired have more difficulty

Table 6: Direct manipulation guidelines with benefits and concerns.

The Boswash Airlines example (Figures 5a–e) shows a form that provides the context for the decision process. Users can touch a field to begin the flight selection process. Then with the form still on the screen, they might be presented with a map showing departure cities. After selecting the departure city the screen would show a map with arrival cities accessible from the selected departure city. Then to choose the date, the calendar provides familiar context, avoids the questions of data entry format, and can be very rapid. Finally, the results of each selection are displayed on the form allowing continuous visibility of status and an opportunity to make changes.

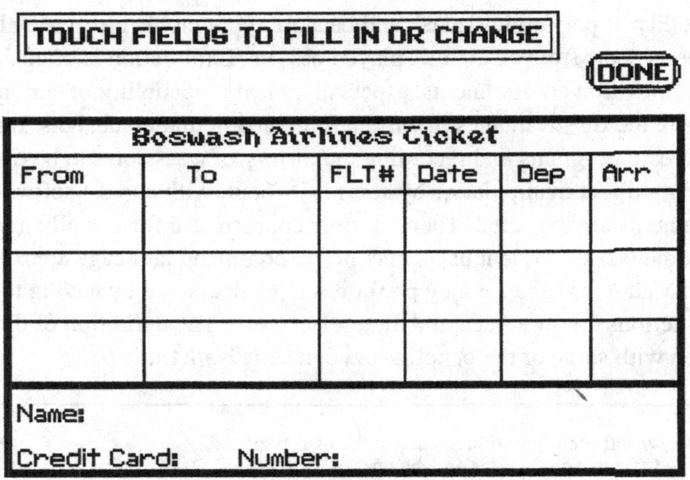

Figure 5a: Form to be filled. The user has some flexibility in order.

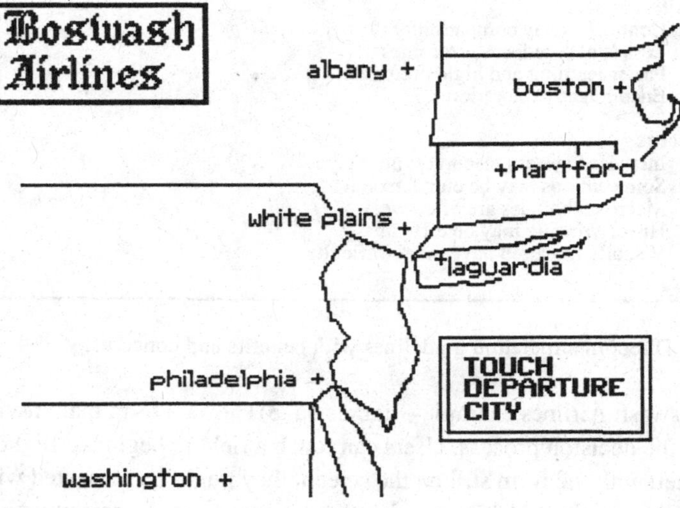

Figure 5b: Map to select departure city shows geographic relationships.

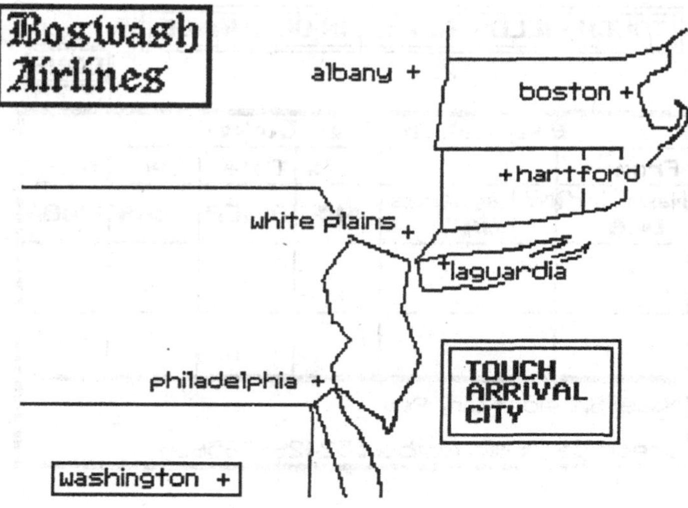

Figure 5c: Map to select arrival city.

Figure 5d: Calendar to select date with indications of past (crossed out), current (boxed in and made bold), and future dates.

TOUCH FIELDS TO FILL IN OR CHANGE

DONE

Boswash Airlines Ticket					
From	To	FLT#	Date	Dep	Arr
Wash. Nat'l DCA	NY Laguardia LGA	414	8 SEP	900A	1000A

Name: Shneiderman, Ben

Credit Card: MC Number: 524298785656

Figure 5e: Form as it looks filled in with cities, times, and date. Name and credit card number are supplied by simply 'dipping' card in reader.

3. Choosing an interaction style

Like good cooking, good user interface design is a blend of measurable aspects (calorie counts, fat percentages, vitamin levels) with subjective issues (smell, texture, colour, taste) and stylistic variations (Szechuan, French, Northern Italian) plus contemporary fashion (nouvelle cuisine, par-boiled vegetables, rare meat). Designers absorb each problem situation thoroughly, then apply reason and intuition combined with experience to produce a solution. Some designers favour menu selection or command language for all situations because they are familiar with the strategies for design and implementation. In other cases the availability of form management software may sway designers to depend heavily on this approach.

As a design field, human-computer interaction is moving beyond depending only on the intuition of designers; empirical evidence is accumulating to guide designers. Still interface design is a new field and much work remains to be done before reliable designs for multiple situations are available.

3.1 *Factors influencing choices*

What follows is the author's attempt to suggest rules for designers to follow in selecting appropriate interaction styles. The rules are presented in an informal rule-based notation that is similar to what is used in expert systems. Much work remains to refine these rules. Undoubtedly there are exceptions, missing criteria, or simply poor decisions. However, this first attempt is meant to be compact, be narrowly focused, and therefore to provide a basis for discussion and improvement.

Table 7 lists some of the aspects of the task domain that influence the selection of interaction style. For example, if the task has a high degree of data entry, then form fill-in is strongly recommended, although command language can be used. If a familiar notation is already available to the users, then that notation should be converted into a compact and hopefully easy to learn command language. If exploration is important, as in circuit or automobile design, then direct manipulation can provide a flexible environment with minimum distraction from the task.

```
IF high degree of data entry
==> ff | cl

IF paper form exists
==> ff

IF familiar notation exists
   (e.g., arithmetic or boolean expressions, chemical formulae)
==> cl

IF natural visual representation exists
 | modest number of objects and actions can represent the task domain
==> dm

IF multiple decisions are required
 | selection from a large unfamiliar state space
==> ms | dm | cl

IF poor keyboard skills
==> ms | dm | (nl with speech input)

IF exploration and intuition are important goals
==> dm
```

Table 7: Task factors are an important determinant of interaction styles. This informal rule based representation expresses the author's opinions in design situations; there will undoubtedly be exceptions and refinements. The notation uses ==> to mean *then*, & for *and*, and | for *or*. The interaction styles are menu selection (ms), form fill-in (ff), command language (cl), natural language (nl), and direct manipulation (dm).

User skill level has a profound influence on the selection of an interaction style (Table 8). With novices, menu selection or some form of direct manipulation present familiar words or visual representations of the task domain. These styles require limited keyboard skills and computer knowledge. More knowledgeable users can work more rapidly with a form fill-in approach. Knowledgeable intermittent users can work with any style. As frequency of use and proficiency increases, users will

```
IF novice
==> ms | dm

IF modest knowledge of task domain with some computer skills
==> ms | dm | ff

IF intermittent knowledgeable
==> ms | dm | ff
  | (cl with online help or pocket guide)
  | nl

IF frequent user
==> (cl with macros)
  | (ms with type-ahead)
  | (dm with adequate shortcuts)
  | (ff with dense display)
```

Table 8: User skill levels are a key determinant of interaction style. These informal rules capture some of the possible combinations. Undoubtedly there are exceptions or a more thoughtful way of forming the rules.

seek more rapid and productive styles with less to look at on the screen. Expert users expect short response time and macro facilities to encapsulate frequent sequences of actions into a single command.

In addition to the interaction style, there are a host of variables that have to be adjusted as a function of the users' knowledge and frequency of use (Table 9). For example, novices need meaningful labels, while knowledgeable intermittent users prefer abbreviations so that more information can be shown in a single display. Expert frequent users may prefer to eliminate some labels and use concise codes, thereby speeding up screen scanning and permitting still denser displays. Similarly, the desire for informative feedback when actions are taken generally decreases with increased expertise and frequency of use. These rules describe some of the design features that vary with the users' profile. There are certainly other features and exceptions to these rules.

3.2 *Blending interaction styles*

The five primary interaction styles are meant for exposition and education. In real systems, designers blend styles where appropriate. For example, in the Boswash Airlines menu selection example, the date was requested as a fill-in item, because menu selection would have been preposterous. Similarly, personal names are usually handled as a form fill-in item. For a short list, say 2 to 12 items, if the display rate is reasonably fast, a menu selection strategy is often the best. As the list gets longer the designer must weigh the users' familiarity with the items, the potential and

IF novice ==> high density of meaningful labels
& high density of informative feedback
& slower pace
& introductory tutorial/demo
& limited subset of actions and functionality

IF knowledgeable intermittent ==> modest use of labels
& modest use of informative feedback
& moderate pace
& online help to explain objects and actions
& chance to move up to more powerful actions, but protection danger

IF frequent user (knowledgeable about task/computer/syntax) ==> short, sparse, or no labels
& short, sparse, or no informative feedback
& faster pace
& online reference with elaborate search mechanisms
& abbreviations, shortcuts, user-defined macros, with access to system internals

Table 9: User skill levels are a key factor in determining a variety of aspects of the interaction design. These rules are an informal representation of the author's opinions that will undoubtedly have exceptions and will need to be refined. It is meant as a first attempt to provoke discussion.

seriousness of an error, the speed of interaction required, and the length of the items. All but the final criteria are difficult to assess quantitatively, leaving the designer with the responsibility for making a tough judgment.

A few versions might be built and subjected to empirical testing. Sometimes a blend of interaction styles can help resolve the problem. For example, maybe the user is presented with a form fill-in for the departure and arrival cities. Those who wish to can type in the city name or the short three letter airport code if they know it. Alternatively, the placement of the cursor in the field may generate a pop-up window with a menu of cities that can be selected by pointing (mouse or arrow keys). Then the selected city name is automatically displayed in the form. Form fill-in can be nicely supplemented by pop-up menus for less knowledgeable users.

Similarly, command language systems can be supplemented by a form fill-in or menu selection strategy for less knowledgeable users. For example, many text editors (e.g., Wordstar or Finalword) start with a command language approach that has a hierarchical structure. After pressing the first key for the first part of the command, the user can immediately type more characters to complete the command, but if they are less familiar with the commands a menu will appear automatically after 4 – 6 seconds.

Some users prefer to make the menus visible all the time, others prevent them from ever appearing. A quite similar approach, that might be called command menus, has been implemented in LOTUS 1-2-3. The top line of the screen shows a menu with items that are selected by arrow keys or typing the first letter. Then another one-line menu appears, or arguments are typed in, going down as many as five levels in the tree structure. Novice users walk slowly through the menus while experts type ahead rapidly enough that the menus appear on the screen for only a fraction of a second.

Another blending approach is to offer a form fill-in and allow the knowledgeable user to type a long sequence of commands in the field. Direct manipulation systems often revert to menu selections approaches when a visual representation cannot be found. Some direct manipulation systems offer a menu of visual items, such as a colour or texture palette. Tennant, Ross and Thompson (1983) offer an imaginative blend of natural language and menu selection. The users select from a menu of syntactically and semantically acceptable sentence fragments. As each choice is made, the permissible sentence fragments change. With a rapid display and pointing device, the user can quickly assemble a syntactically and semantically correct query for a database. These are but a few of the possibilities. Identifying useful and appropriate blends for different users in different situations is an important goal for researchers and system designers.

4. Conclusions

Designers of interactive systems have had to work from their own experience and intuition, validating their designs by costly and time consuming iterative testing. There is some hope that we can more precisely understand when to apply a particular interaction style and how to refine it so that it produces rapid user performance, low error rates, high satisfaction, ease in learning, and ease in retention over time. Blends of interaction styles can be very effective in serving a range of users and in dealing with certain interaction tasks. A massive program of empirical research will be necessary to guide this research, but the payoff in more reliable and effective designs can be enormous. Finally, a useful psychological theory, tied to the interaction styles would be a tremendous benefit.

CHAPTER FIFTEEN

DESIGNING AND EVALUATING DOCUMENTATION FOR I.T. USERS

PATRICIA WRIGHT

1. Varieties of documentation

Many kinds of documentation are associated with computer systems. Programmers document the code they write so that applications can be easily amended and enhanced. Hardware requires information to assist those who maintain and upgrade it. Both kinds of material are very different from the tutorials designed for people learning to use the application. Recent research has shown that it can be beneficial to reduce the amount of printed paper accompanying tutorials and encourage users to explore the functionality of the software in an artificially safe environment (Carroll and Rosson, 1987). Other documentation provided for users is intended for reference, and relies on users knowing how to formulate appropriate questions. Inexperienced users may find this difficult, tending to ask fairly global questions (e.g., "Why won't it work?"). Therefore reference materials need to offer users assistance with trouble shooting and refining their questions.

It will not be possible in the present chapter to consider the problems raised by all these different kinds of documentation. Valuable insights into the design of interactive tutorials will be found in Charney and Reder (1986). There is an overlap between research on the design of tutorial materials for computer users and the broader domain of Interactive Computer Assisted Instruction (ICAI). An introduction to this research literature will be found in Dede (1986), but it is too large a problem to be covered in the present chapter. Here the focus will be on information intended for end users, particularly material used for reference. The reason for this choice is partly that reference materials are important because they are used frequently throughout the life of the application, and partly because they raise a number of more general issues which will apply to other kinds of documentation. Indeed, many of the design factors discussed below, such as the need for legibility and easy readability, will apply to all documentation.

The ten point plan proposed by Chapanis (1988) is a sound approach to most computer documentation. He suggested that writers should first seek to understand fully how the software and its documentation would be used (e.g., for what tasks and in what circumstances) and he pointed out that analysing similar documents could indicate some of the good and bad approaches that others have taken to similar problems. Chapanis emphasized that writers needed three distinct categories of knowledge: about the research literature on documentation, about the characteristics of the user population and about the subject matter. He advises writers to enlist the help of other specialists. His last three points stress the need to create a draft which is then evaluated and revised, this cycle of evaluation and revision continuing as long as is necessary. Similar emphasis on evaluation will be found in others concerned with improving document design procedures (e.g., Duffy, 1981; Redish, Felker and Rose, 1981).

Although I am fully in agreement with these proposals about the constituents of the document design process, rather than repeat them here the present chapter will illustrate how an understanding of the way in which readers interact with technical documentation can offer writers assistance during several stages of the design process. This chapter seeks to bridge the gap between the advice to "Find out about the audience" and the detailed understanding of just what information is needed when documenting a particular product and how to get that information.

1.1 *Online help*

Reference manuals are usually printed, but there is an increasing opportunity for making information available to users in various online forms. This has several advantages (e.g., it does not go missing, can be easily updated, and so forth). It is not inevitable that online information will be more useful than paper-based documentation. Limitations of screen size may cause the material to be abbreviated, sometimes to the point of ambiguity (e.g., a menu with the options 'Copy' and 'Echo'). Space limitations may force the reader to search through hierarchical menus to find the information needed. This can be slower than using hard-copy. Shneiderman (1986) reported that people took almost half as long again to use documentation on the screen as they did to use the same information in hard-copy form.

The way in which information is organised can help users who start with vague questions (e.g., "Is there a quicker way to do this?"). It can be more difficult for readers to grasp this structure in online displays. Reference material on screen is usually less easily browsed than information on paper, for which most readers have well-developed skipping and jumping techniques. Much of the online documentation currently available is difficult to "personalise". Many users seem to find it helpful to create their own crib-sheets which list the subset of commands and procedures they wish to work with. The margins of printed manuals can acquire many kinds of annotations (corrections, translations into plain English, and suggestions to look elsewhere). Customising online documentation is seldom as easy for the novice as would be writing in the margin of a text on paper.

The advantages of online displays will be pointed out in the later discussions of how readers interact with technical documents. However, some of these advantages will be closely tied to the prevailing technology. For example, the use of large bit-mapped screens which are able to display two A4 pages simultaneously undoubtedly increases the potential of online documentation. The higher resolution displays may eliminate the slower reading speeds usually associated with texts on screen (Haas and Hayes, 1985; Gould *et al.*, 1987). The larger display area means that no longer will users have to alternate between viewing their problem and reading the advice given on how to solve it. Haas and Hayes (1985) have shown that some of the reader's search difficulties disappear with larger screen sizes. In time, users' expectations about handling documents online will also become more sophisticated. Nevertheless, the manipulative skills of flicking between two or more sections of a manual are for most users better established than the techniques of having two pages of the same document simultaneously displayed on screen. For those interested in pursuing the design of online documentation, an extremely valuable and comprehensive review of the literature has been compiled by Schriver *et al.* (1986).

1.2 *Economic consequences*

Gradually the computer industry is realising that poor documentation has economic consequences. The costs of user-support can be considerable and are unnecessary if telephone hotlines have to be manned in order to repeat information already given in the manual, or to provide recovery from procedures which have been misinterpreted by readers of the manuals. Poor documentation can detract from product marketability. Reviewers tend to comment on the adequacy of user support in the articles they write; customers often look through the manuals before making a purchase. A survey by Jereb (1986) found that documentation was the second most important factor influencing the decision to purchase, second only to the quality of the product itself.

1.3 *Factors determining success*

The assumption that bad manuals are the product of stupid and careless writing is seldom warranted. Most writers, whether or not they are professional technical authors, do attempt to communicate their ideas as well as they can. However, the products suggest that being a native speaker of the language is not a sufficient qualification to ensure communicative success.

There are at least four clusters of factors which contribute to badly written manuals: one cluster might be described as *organisational factors*. These factors include management decisions about who does the writing (the product developers or specialist technical authors). Organisational factors also include the frequency and nature of the contact between the writers and the product developers. Without such contact there is a risk that the product is modified during development but no-one remembers to tell the writers. Without close contact there is even the risk of functionality being instantiated in a way which is unnecessarily difficult for writers to explain to users.

A second cluster of factors concerns the *time scale* allocated for the writing process. Successful technical writing involves detailed early planning, drafting and considerable revising (Duffy, 1981). Unless adequate time is made available, then the planning and revision processes are likely to be curtailed. Yet one of the safeguards against problems of a mismatch arising between what the product does and what the specifications say it does is empirically to check that correspondence, and revise the draft in the light of this feedback.

It is interesting to note that the monitoring of people using a manual has led in some instances to the manual being drastically pruned (e.g., Carroll *et al.*, 1987). This relates to a third, and rather different, cluster of factors; namely the absence of any clear *theoretical rationale* which might guide decisions about what content should be included in a manual and how this information should be presented. These twin issues have been considered in some detail by Wright (1987). In the absence of theoretical underpinnings, the present chapter will be based around a simple outline of how people interact with documentation.

Conducting empirical evaluations of a draft text highlights a fourth cluster of requirements for good documentation, namely adequate *resources*. These resources may need to include people with differing skills. People good at visual layout and graphic displays tend not to be the people who are good at expressing ideas in words. Neither the visualisers nor the verbalisers necessarily have the skills for devising text-evaluation procedures, knowing what data to collect and how to interpret it. Failure by senior management to recognise this need for multidisciplinary skills within the document design team, or not knowing when and how to obtain the necessary expertise, contributes to poor documentation.

From the multiple reasons for bad documentation, it will be clear that no simple recipe for "good writing" is going to cure all the problems. In the remainder of this chapter we will examine how readers interact with documentation, pointing out the implications that this has for document design. We will consider some of the ways in which computers can offer assistance with the process of document design. Finally, we will turn to the selection and use of various evaluation techniques.

2. How readers interact with documentation

It has been suggested (e.g., Wright, 1981) that there are six stages through which readers interact with documents. These are summarized in Figure 1 where their relationship to the activity normally thought of as "reading" is emphasized.

For expository convenience we will consider these processes under just three headings. Readers faced with documentation must first FIND information they think is relevant to them. Secondly they need to UNDERSTAND what the writer has said. Thirdly they must be able to APPLY that understanding to the current task in order to solve the problem they had that prompted them to turn to the documentation. Writers can help readers achieve each of these goals by the appropriate use of design options.

Synopsis of User-Document Interaction

Before Reading

- Formulate question
- Find potential answer

During Reading

- Comprehend text
- Create action plan

After Reading

- Execute plan
- Evaluate outcome

Figure 1 : An outline characterising how users interact with technical materials such as computer documentation.

2.1 *Finding information*

There are many ways in which writers can help readers find information. The use of index lists and contents pages are among the most obvious. But even here things can go wrong. Contents pages need to be easy to locate, not buried behind prefaces and introductions. Few reference manuals put the contents list on the inside cover, but this is one place where it is extremely easy to locate. Price (1984) has emphasized the need for the information in the contents list to be short enough so that it can be easily scanned by readers. When writers adopt full sentences as chapter headings they make this scanning process much slower. The information in headings also needs to be adequately informative so that users can determine if a section matches their current information needs. Titles such as "For advanced users" do not meet this criterion of informativeness.

The problems of indexes are slightly different from those of contents lists. Some indexes are too sparse to be helpful, while others are so detailed that they present the reader with linguistic hurdles caused by the multiple levels of nesting used for the entries (e.g., colour, use of in multiwindow displays). Indexes need to include not only the jargon terminology chosen by the application's designers (e.g., clone) but also the synonyms that people might have used in formulating their queries (e.g., copy, duplicate). Multiple indexes with the information organised in different ways can often be helpful. For example, one index might be organised around trouble-shooting symptoms, whereas another may reflect the organisation of on-screen menus. These are not substitutes for each other, they serve different purposes, enabling readers with different kinds of queries to find quickly the information they seek.

Research by Sticht (1977) suggests that using indexes and contents lists may not be the preferred search strategy for many readers. He found that people would often thumb through a manual, particularly if they thought that they knew whereabouts the information was likely to be. The design factors which can assist such searchers include the use of informative page headings (i.e., not the product/manufacturer's name on every page) and the provision of clearly visible subheadings on the page itself.

A rather different way in which writers can help readers find/notice information is by using pictures or other symbols to draw the reader's attention to particular categories of information. For example, the Epson manual for the PX-8™ typographically flags warnings by the use of an exclamation mark within a diamond. This symbol is two rows deep and is accompanied by the subheading WARNING; the warning information itself is indented to the right of the diamond. While this might seem like overkill, personal experience suggests that it is a very effective way of gaining people's attention and so dissuading readers from stopping reading too soon, before they get to the critical warning information.

This raises the issue of whether people are always prepared to read the information made available to them. Wright, Creighton and Threlfall (1982) have shown that there are several reasons why readers may not bother to read information. Sometimes people think they already know the information. As an example, consider the print commands in a word processing system such as WordStar™. Many of these commands toggle, with the same command being used to begin an operation (such as underlining or emboldening) as to stop it. Readers who consult the documentation about a new print facility, such as enlarging, may only look for the start command

and assume that it too toggles. Although the culprit is the inconsistency in the design of the interface, the writer needs to be aware of the possibility that readers will be misled, and take steps to correct faulty assumptions that might be held.

Another reason why people are sometimes reluctant to read information is that the cognitive cost of looking may be too high. Whalley and Flemming (1975) showed that an author's reference to a circuit diagram, printed on the same page, was much more likely to be read if it was located immediately under the reference to it rather than (as in the original publication) at the top of an adjacent column. Presumably the need to re-find their place in the text after detouring into other columns deters readers from responding as writers might hope.

To some extent online help facilities can make it easier for users to locate relevant information. The software can monitor the current context in which the user is working and provide information relevant to only that context, and it can do this in response to a simple request from the user such as "?". However, these simple requests are less viable in powerful applications which allow users to do a wide range of things in almost all contexts, because the resulting list of legal actions is too long to be useful. Reading lengthy texts on screen does not seem acceptable to many users (Nielsen, 1984). Moreover the electronic medium offers opportunities for structuring texts which have no counterpart in the printed medium. These two factors taken together strongly imply that online help needs different organisational and access structures from printed documentation. Several research programs are currently exploring ways of configuring electronic books, particularly for use as reference materials (e.g., Brown, 1985).

But the successful use of reference material will always depend in part on the ability of the reader to formulate questions (O'Malley, 1986). It would seem that if online documentation is going to be really helpful it requires the ability of an "intelligent listener" to interpret the reader's questions. In this respect the interaction between the user and the documentation when online may be closer to that of a conversation than to that more usually thought of as "reading".

2.2 *Understanding information*

There are numerous factors which can influence the ease with which readers will understand the text they read. For convenience we will consider some of these factors in three broad groupings: factors which operate at the word level, those having an effect at the sentence level, and factors operating above the sentence level. It may be of interest to note that less able writers tend to concentrate on the "word" level of the text whereas experienced writers are more likely to worry about the higher levels of organising the material and of sequencing the information so that it can be easily used (Sommers, 1980). What makes this interesting is that Redish *et al.* (1985) have pointed out that most of the serious problems in technical materials concern the higher levels of organising the material.

At the word level readers will obviously have difficulties with the unfamiliar terminology and jargon, and probably even more so with familiar words now used in unfamiliar ways (e.g., "handshake"). Unfortunately writers find it very difficult to recognise their own jargon. So too do other experts in the same area (Hayes, 1986). Testing draft documents with members of the target audience may be the only safe way of discovering what is not common knowledge among the readership.

Less obvious sources of difficulty at the word level concern the asymmetric difficulty of words such as "more" and "less". Research has shown that people are more accurate when making decisions involving "more" than the same decisions involving "less" (Barnard and Wright, 1975). Similarly, for many comparative dimensions (size, length, height, temperature) people find it easier to understand the word that would be used to describe having *more* of the quantity denoted by the underlying dimension. For example, the adjectives *larger*, *longer*, *higher*, *hotter* are easier for people to understand than the corresponding terms *smaller*, *shorter*, *lower*, *colder* (Clark and Card, 1969). The explanation lies partly in these more difficult terms being implicitly negative (i.e., *short* denotes an absence of height rather than *long* denoting an absence of "shortness"). Words derived from other words, particularly nouns from verbs (e.g., *reduction* from *reduce*) also tend to increase readers' comprehension difficulties.

At the sentence level, research has shown that it is helpful for the order of mention within the text to correspond to the order of any temporal sequence being described. So rather than writing "Before saving the file check that there is enough file space", it would be better to write, "Check that there is enough file space before saving the file" (Clark and Clark, 1968). As well as maintaining a temporal correspondence it also helps readers if the main clause precedes the subordinate clause. This effect of main and subordinate clauses can be particularly salient with some conditionals (e.g., "unless") where people often find it easier to follow instructions saying "Do X unless Y" rather than "Unless Y, do X" (Wright and Hull, 1988).

Above the sentence level, information must be given in a helpful order. For example, when a sequence of steps is being described, readers prefer these steps to be numbered (Frase, 1981). There may be two contributory reasons for this preference. The numbering may help readers keep their place as they carry out the sequence. These numbers may also help readers segment the task into tractable units, and so provide a framework within which the task can be carried out. The importance of such a framework has been illustrated in studies by Dixon (1987). He gave people instructions such as, "Draw an inverted capital T with a U on top". He varied whether he told people before or after this instruction that their drawing would look like a wine glass. People given the overview first spent less time reading the instruction and produced better drawings than those given the overview after the instruction.

In computer documentation an orienting framework can be provided either by the use of short summaries, or by appropriate topic sentences at the beginnings of paragraphs. It is not yet clear to what extent such orienting frameworks are usefully amplified so that they provide readers with "mental models" of the application. There is certainly evidence that encouraging the formation of such models can improve understanding and the application of that understanding in new contexts (e.g., Kieras and Bovair, 1984), but the details of the model provided can be crucial and not all models have been as successful as their designers had hoped (e.g., Foss, Smith-Kerker and Rosson, 1987). Writers need to be able to draw upon a simple representation that can form the basis of the reader's mental model. Sometimes analogies will serve this function effectively, but on other occasions readers may misunderstand the intended points of correspondence between the analogy and the new situation (Halasz and Moran, 1982). So while it is safe to conclude that a general orienting framework can assist readers' understanding, the use of more detailed frameworks/models needs care.

The problems of giving too much detail were also noted by Carroll *et al.* (1987). They observed that lengthy summaries of procedural information sometimes encouraged people to try executing the procedures before all the necessary information has been made available from the text. Clearly there is a difference between providing an orientation for readers and giving a precis of the subsequent text. More detailed summaries at the ends of chapters or long sections may help readers assess whether they have understood that section, and may also help those searching a manual decide whether this is likely to be a relevant section for their needs.

Not only do mental pictures aid understanding, but so too do real pictures. There are some procedures which are much easier to illustrate than to describe verbally. But where detailed sequences must be remembered, verbal memory can be better than visual memory. In this respect, supplementing an illustration with a textual description is not necessarily providing redundant information.

Redundancy is also important at the higher levels of text organisation, where writers need to bear in mind that readers may not have read preceding sections of the text. While cross-references have the advantage of saving space, this saving needs to be traded against the convenience for readers of repeating information where it is needed. We have already seen that writers who are hoping readers will comply with directives to look elsewhere can sometimes be over-optimistic.

2.3 *Applying information*

Inference and reference are perhaps the two main pitfalls that lie in the path of readers trying to apply what they have understood from the documentation. Writers can help by reducing the number of inferences that readers must draw. For example, it will help if writers make procedures explicit. Instead of writing "Check that you are earthed for static" they can suggest earthing procedures that might be followed.

The problems of reference can be more difficult to solve. On the one hand there are the organisational problems mentioned earlier, where the product actually changes so that textual references to "the blue key" are no longer appropriate. On the other hand there are inadvertent miscommunications. This can be illustrated with reference to an episode described by Tognazzini at the ACM CHI'86 Conference (reported in Nielsen, 1986). The designer of a computer system wished to elicit from each user whether they were using a colour or monochrome display screen. The first attempt was to put a message on the screen asking "Is this picture in colour?" People working with green or amber monochrome displays would reply "Yes". Several iterations, each involving modifying the question and checking what answer it produced, were necessary before a successful form of words was found that differentiated those viewing monochrome and colour screens. The difficulty of this apparently trivial problem emphasises the need for user testing as part of the documentation procedure.

We have already commented on the research that shows readers understand information more easily if it is sequenced appropriately. It is worth mentioning in this connection that there can be a difference between the order which is natural for declarative sentences (e.g., an expository text might say, "There is a terminal emulation facility in the Instal.Com file on the Utilities disk") and the order which would be appropriate for giving procedural instructions (e.g., an instruction manual would say: "1. Load the Utilities disk. 2. Open the Instal.Com file. 3. Access the terminal emulation facility"). In circumstances where carrying out instructions requires users to create detailed action plans involving several steps, it seems particularly important to have the information in the correct temporal sequence; but for short sequences the order of mention that facilitates understanding may not be that which facilitates the application of the new knowledge (Wright and Lickorish, in preparation). This mirrors the earlier discussion when considering how to sequence information so that it could be found easily by readers; the issues surrounding the decision about an appropriate organisational structure for the information in a reference manual are far from simple.

3. Computer assistance with document design

There are a number of claims for "self-documenting" systems (e.g., Glushko and Bianchi, 1982; Walker, 1986). In practice these turn out to be systems which respond to new input from authors by updating the rest of the text, and changing any numbering or cross-references that may be necessary. They do not eliminate the need for writers. The text in such systems resembles a data-base of information, with many explicit links among different sections, rather than a conventional book.

Computers can offer authors a variety of tools for writing and information design. Word processors make revision of the text much easier than it would otherwise be. Computers can also provide various forms of editorial assessment. Let us consider three classes of such support: readability formulae; stylistic advice about syntax and phrasing; graphic representations of the text.

Readability formulae are easily implemented by software. Their major ingredients are word length and sentence length. However, the sheer number of such formulae available (over 100 were reported by Klare, 1979) testifies to the fact that the desire for such a measuring instrument is keenly felt. Nevertheless each version seems to have been found inadequate by its successors. Rye (1985) compared the Flesch, FOG and SMOG indices with teachers' ratings of texts covering the readership range 7 – 15 years and found considerable discrepancy among the formulae. The Flesch index achieved the closest correspondence to the mean of the teachers' assessments of texts intended for readers above the age of 12.

Duffy (1985) has discussed the many limitations of readability formulae. One of the most serious is that they ignore meaning; they would give a text the same score even if it were written backwards. Although formulae are more suitable for use with continuous prose than with other kinds of text they ignore the relations among sentences. Many formulae have difficulty making allowance for readers' prior knowledge or the terminology of specialised domains. The word "computer", because it has three syllables, will be judged to be a hard word which adds to the difficulty of the text. For the domain of computer manuals this seems unlikely to be the case. Short words, like "cache" or "boot", are much more likely sources of confusion. Formulae ignore display characteristics, yet these can be either sources of clarification (e.g., the diagrams or illustrations that accompany the text) or can generate ambiguity and misunderstandings for readers (Waller, 1982, 1985).

Another shortcoming of readability formulae is that they provide only a global assessment of the text as a whole, whereas writers need to know precisely where they have been misunderstood. At best formulae have an asymmetric utility. If they suggest that a text is difficult to understand, then revision will almost certainly be worth while; but a satisfactory readability score for the text as a whole is no guarantee that it is free from disaster spots throughout. There is evidence that revising a text in order to get it to pass some readability criterion does not necessarily make the end product any easier for readers to use (Bruce, Rubin and Starr, 1981).

There are a number of more sophisticated alternatives to readability formulae. Examples include CRES, the Computerised Reading Ease Scale devised for military manuals by Kincaid and Schalow (1985), subsequently extended by Kieras (1985), and EPISTLE devised by Miller (1986). One of the first of these sophisticated authoring tools was the Writers WorkBench™ developed by AT&T Bell Labs (Cherry and Macdonald, 1983). This software provides summary statistics about the text (e.g., the number of short sentences (less than 13 words); the number of long sentences (more than 28 words); the length and location of both the longest and the shortest sentences; the percentage of various sentence types – simple, complex, compound, etc.; the percentage of different parts of speech – verbs, nouns, prepositions, adverbs, etc.). There is evidence that when such software is made available to authors the feedback it provides enhances their writing skills (Frase, Keenan and Dever, 1980; Frase, Macdonald and Keenan, 1985).

Other software provides writers with a more schematic representation of the text structure. For example, outlining software can extract section headings, preserving the section-subsection relations. This can be useful at the early prewriting stages of considering alternative organisations for the information. Later it can be used to give the author an overview of the draft text which can be compared with the intended outline. Yet other software generates "punctuation graphs" in which the sentences are displayed one per line with each word being replaced by an underscore, but retaining the punctuation verbatim. This helps the writer see how much time or space is being given to particular topics. Software programs such as these can obviously be combined to give authors multiple views of their text, but it is too early to know what effects they have on the quality of the writing produced.

There are word processing packages which offer assistance with indexing but this is too complex an activity to be automated entirely. For example, pages may address topics without particular keywords being mentioned. Nevertheless, indexing software offers another means whereby writers can get an overview of the documentation. Authors can check if the intended topics have been covered, if the coverage of topics has been split, and even if some keywords are over-used.

In spite of the advances in the kind of feedback that computers can give authors about their text, Hartley (1984) had one of his own drafts evaluated by both people and software. He observed that there were some important differences between the response from computers and from human editors. People may not be as good as software at catching typos in the text but only people will suggest that particular sections of the text should be omitted completely. Computer critiques of a document are one form of evaluation, but other forms are also necessary.

In summary, software can offer writers useful tools, but this support is mainly at or below the sentence level. Software offers little help for decisions either about what content to include or about the way it is displayed. So computer-based assistance for writers cannot guarantee that documentation is free from serious usability problems.

4. Evaluation techniques

Evaluation can have various objectives. One objective might be to determine whether the draft text is *adequate for release*. Evidence is needed that no major catastrophies are lurking within the text. Techniques such as the editorial comments of other experts, performance measures from members of the target audience and some formalisms will all have something useful to contribute. A different objective is that of determining whether the current version can be *improved*. It is here that guidelines, checklists and other design heuristics play a part. A third objective is to discover what can be *learned for next time* from the preparation of the current document. Here field studies and surveys can be helpful, but even more useful would be the development of theories of documentation. Ideally these could be drawn on to assist design decisions as information is translated across media.

Let us consider the first of these objectives in more detail. How can a writer tell whether a draft is adequate? This question gives rise to two others, one concerning the content included in the draft, the other concerning the way in which this content is presented. Sullivan and Chapanis (1983) have proposed techniques for addressing each of these questions. They suggest that in order to check the accuracy of the information in the manual authors should "walk through" all the procedures described. This enables them to check that the system does respond in the way the manual says. In order to determine whether readers correctly understand the information, Chapanis and Sullivan suggest that authors carry out a "User Edit". Essentially this procedure consists of the author being in the room, willing to answer questions, while a member of the target audience for the product tries to perform designated tasks. Note is kept of the questions asked and the trouble spots encountered. After each "edit" the draft is revised so that the difficulties encountered by the last user will not arise next time. This process is iterated as often as necessary until users are able to work satisfactorily from the documentation. Chapanis and Sullivan reported that after several intensive revisions they were able to withdraw from the room and monitor the user's performance on a linked terminal. By this stage the difficulties remaining may cause readers to pause momentarily, but usually these can be resolved by users for themselves without the need of external help. These difficulties can also be the subject of further revisions.

Knowing at what point to terminate the iterations is not necessarily obvious. The ideal of attaining perfection with no trouble spots encountered by any users may be unrealistic. There is no arbitrary level of adequacy that can be set as universally "good enough". Much depends on the precise nature of the mistakes that are being made, their costs to users and the ease of eliminating the causes of these difficulties. For example, if the last five User Edits produced a total of 10 errors, the authors might decide to live with this if the errors were scattered throughout the documentation. In contrast, if the errors tended to cluster in particular places (e.g., if all five people made mistakes at the same location within the text) then it would seem to verge on the irresponsible not to try improving the text at this point.

Different evaluation procedures can sometimes point in different directions. Wright (1980) reported three different rank orderings from best to worst of a set of design options for a printed form. One order was obtained from performance data (the time taken by people to fill in the printed form/questionnaire in one or other of the design variants being examined). Another order was obtained by asking these form fillers how long they thought it would take to complete the different designs. Yet a third order was obtained by measuring the performance of people transcribing the completed forms onto large record sheets for analysing the data. Which rank ordering should be accorded the most weight? This can only be decided by a careful consideration of where the costs fall if different options are taken up. If people receive the form at home, and think that it is going to be irksome to complete then they are likely to delay returning it and those creating the form may find that they have additional costs in sending reminders. So in these circumstances it may not matter that people were actually mistaken in their impressions. What matters is that they should be willing to complete the form, or to read the online help. That the version they like will take them a little longer than the most efficient design may not be a cost of any significance. In contrast, if the forms are completed (or the documentation read) within some more regimented procedure then procrastination may not be an option, and now saving company time may become more important than user appeal. There are no short and simple answers in the evaluation phase, just as there were none in the earlier stages of design. Careful consideration of the trade-offs inherent in particular design decisions is always needed (Norman, 1983, 1986).

While Walking Through the document and applying User Edits helps writers discover trouble spots, these techniques will not necessarily indicate where alternative design decisions would be preferable. It is here that the opinions of other experts can be helpful. That expertise may be encountered dynamically face to face or it may be captured in some static form such as guidelines (e.g., Felker *et al.*, 1981; Hartley, 1981, 1985). Whichever shape it takes it will be helpful but not infallible. Consulting experts will serve to show that expert opinions differ. Guidelines tend to be either remote from specific procedures (e.g., "Write clearly") or so detailed that they have numerous exceptions which make them both difficult to interpret and to remember, or perhaps even difficult to select which are appropriate (Mosier and Smith, 1986).

Some of the forms of computer assistance described in the previous section offer a viable compromise between these extremes. But even sophisticated computer-based writing aids work well only for verbal materials. Developments in information technology mean that documentation can now be communicated in many ways. The designer is faced with making choices about the modality in which the information should be provided (visual, auditory, mixed). If the information is to be visual then choices must also be made about the form of representation (e.g., words, pictures, numbers, shapes) and the medium to be used for displaying these representations (print on paper, computer screen, keyboard — especially where dedicated soft keys can be made available), or some mixture of all these. Finally there have to be decisions about the style of document interaction with the user. This interaction may be relatively passive on the part of the documentation. Users search for the information they require and then read it. In contrast, the style could be highly interactive, with some form of intelligent support helping users to modify their search in appropriate ways. Once the design space is recognised as being as large as this, then the contribution of guidelines is seen as providing at best only a partial answer to the document designer's needs.

It is an inevitable consequence of the design space being so large that a multiplicity of skills need to be drawn upon. An ideal multidisciplinary design team might contain people with expertise in writing and editorial processes, plus some who have an understanding of human cognitive processes (such as attention, decision making and memory), and others with a background in linguistics and a knowledge of the research literature on language comprehension. Also needed are people who have been trained in instructional science and who can devise tutorial packages; the contribution of experts with a grasp of human factors that enables them to analyse users' tasks could be very beneficial to documentation decisions about content and sequencing information. People with skills in graphic design will know how best to create and deploy illustrations and diagrams, whereas those with an understanding of typography will be able to advise more generally on the display of information on the page/screen. Finally, a multidisciplinary team needs to include people who know about the technical constraints on generating the finished product, and of course someone has to have expertise in the subject matter.

It is not necessary for such multidisciplinary teams to be permanently constituted as an in-house resource, although for large organisations this may well be the economic thing to do. Certainly having all the expertise in-house may be the easiest way of building up a pool of knowledge about the solutions to documentation problems within a particular company. But whether the expertise is in-house or contracted in from outside there will be a problem as to how such a team is co-ordinated. MacDonald-Ross and Waller (1976) have suggested that documentation requires someone to control the operation much as a radio/television producer might, knowing when special skills are needed and where to find them.

5. Conclusion

In conclusion, this chapter has examined some of the reasons for poor documentation and some of the methods by which it can be improved. In the Introduction it was pointed out that producing good documentation requires adequate resources of time, money and organisational support. The richness of the design options available for presenting information to computer users contributes to the large gulf between familiar writing tasks (e.g., a letter to a friend) and the the complexity of producing adequate technical information. The way people interact with computer documentation was briefly characterised so that writing objectives could be sharpened, and design options could be assessed in relation to users' requirements. Discussion of the essential rôle of evaluation procedures highlighted the importance of multidisciplinary design skills. The contributions from this broad band of expertise underlined the difference between casual writing activities and professional document design procedures.

CHAPTER SIXTEEN

EVALUATING USABILITY[1]

ALPHONSE CHAPANIS

1. Introduction

> "Virtually every computer on the market today is advertised as a user-friendly computer, and many programs are sold as user-friendly products...Probably 50 to 80 percent of the programs and computers that claim to be user friendly are not. Many of them are user surly or user hostile...The main problem is that many computer models and programs are not easy to use, no matter what the ads claim." (Willis and Miller, 1984, p. 30).

I start with an assertion that I think is true: no manufacturer or designer deliberately designs computers, computer programs, or manuals so that they are *hard* to use. If that is true, why is it that computers almost invariably turn out to be much harder to use than their designers thought they would be? What is even more difficult to understand is why this often turns out to be the case even when designers and programmers have consciously tried to make their computers easy to use. I think these things happen because designers either (a) make no attempt to evaluate usability, (b) make an attempt to evaluate usability but don't do a good job of it, or (c) evaluate usability but don't think it is important enough to correct features that the evaluation shows are hard to use.

I suppose you could argue that computers are always evaluated for usability. The designer who makes no deliberate attempt to evaluate usability at least has a subjective or intuitive idea about his system. In such cases, the implicit assumption may be, "I can use the system, and if I can use it, it's obviously easy to use." Whether or not you want to call this an evaluation is not of great importance for the general

[1]This is an expanded and updated version of Chapanis (1981)

theme of this paper. The relevant point is that evaluations run the gamut from those in which there has been no formal testing for usability to those that are carried out with rigor and sophistication.

1.1 *The importance of evaluating usability*

Evaluating usability is always, or should always be, important to designers, manufacturers, salesmen and customers. It is important to designers because every new computer system is, in some respects, novel. It may involve new technology or new combinations of old technology and one cannot always find principles and guidelines to cover these situations. Even if designers were to use all the available guidelines for making computers usable, they still need to know how well they succeeded. As I shall elaborate later, we don't have, and I don't think we shall have in the foreseeable future, a set of principles and guidelines that can be used while a computer system is being developed to predict with accuracy how easy it will be to use after it has been designed. That being the case, designers have to evaluate usability empirically. They cannot depend on analytic measures to give them answers. Even if usability evaluations should reveal difficulties or faults that cannot be corrected in the model under development, the information is still important for the designer in planning for the next one.

Evaluating usability is also, or should be, important to manufacturers and salesmen because it is important for them to know whether the new product is better than its predecessors and better than those being sold by competitors. Moreover, most computer systems are being advertised and sold these days on the basis of how easy they are to use. Figure 1 is a composite of excerpts from advertisements that have appeared in trade journals.

The word that keeps appearing over and over again in those advertisements is *easy* — easy to learn, easy to use. If a manufacturer or salesman is going to sell computer systems on that basis, and do it with honesty and integrity, he has to know, or should want to know, whether the claims he makes for his system being easy to use are in fact correct.

Finally, usability evaluations are important to customers because potential buyers need to have some sound basis for deciding whether advertising claims are indeed correct.

1.2 *Good evaluations are hard to find*

However important it may be to evaluate usability as a matter of principle or of good business practice, the reality is that evaluations of this kind do not appear to be done very often, or, if they are done, they are not done well. It is hard to find examples of

Figure 1: Excerpts from advertisements in trade journals.

good evaluations in the published literature (see, for example, Reisner, 1981). In 1980 an entire number (Number 4) of the *IBM Systems Journal* was devoted to software development. Although the nine articles in that issue discuss a wide variety of principles and procedures for software engineering and development, the user, if he is mentioned at all, is mentioned only incidentally. To be sure there is one article that does specifically mention a "human-engineered, user friendly production system" (Mishelevich and Van Slyke, 1980), but the only evidence I could find that that system meets those criteria is the authors' statement that it has been "actually demonstrated by routine, daily use" (p. 502). Although the authors may very well be correct, I, at least, do not find some aspects of their software user-friendly (see Figure 2)!

I don't think the explanation for the lack of substantial literature is that evaluations are done in house, that is, within a corporation, and never published. Our journals, magazines, and newspapers are too full of the problems, difficulties, and frustrations that people have in trying to use the computerized systems that technology is providing them. I think the truth of the matter is that good evaluations are hard to find because (a) there really haven't been very many done, (b) it's hard to measure usability and (c) not many people know how to do it.

In this paper I discuss some problems of, and procedures for, evaluating, or

REF	PASS (See Note 2)	STATUS S1	STATUS S2	STATUS S3	COMMAND OR DATA NAME	OPERAND(S)	EXPLANATIONS *FOR THIS PAPER ONLY* FUNCTIONS IN WHICH LINE ACTIVE (See Note 1 Below) O	V	RCP	RICP	D
						TARGET STATUS →	10	30	38	82	97
1		33		97	$DM	GET=ORDER;			RCP	RICP	D
2		11		30	$DM	GET=ORDER;		V			
3				05	ORPROCED	(See Note 3)					
4				10	ORTYPE	RAD;	O				
5				05	ORCATGY	(See Note 3)					
6			10	32	ORCLNHX	$S=RADCLHX;	O	V			
7			10	32	ORDATE	$PROG=SYSDT;	O	V			
8			10	32	ORTIME	$PROG=SYSTM;	O	V			
9			10	32	ORFREQN	$S=RADFREQ,$EP=FREQEDIT	O	V			
10	P		10	11	ORSIGN	$PROG=SISIGN;	O				
11	P		10	32	ORPERSN	$S=ORDPERSN;	O	V			
12			05	64	ORPRICE	$EP=PRICE,$ERRS=PRICE;	O	V	RCP		
13		10		11	$RS	RREVIEW;	O				
14			38		$RS	RADRCP;			RCP		
15	P		30	32	ORVERIFR	$S=ORVERIFR;		V			
16			30	32	ORVERDT	$PROG=SYSDT;		V			
17			30	32	ORVERTM	$PROG=SYSTM;		V			
18			82		REASON	$S=RICPREAS;				RICP	
19			10		$DM	ISRT=ORDER;	O				
20		11		30	$DM	REPL=ORDER;		V			
21		35		89	$DM	REPL=ORDER;			RCP	RICP	
22		10		82	T-PRIOR	N;	O	V	RCP	RICP	
23		35		89	$ACCT				RCP	RICP	
24		10		32	T-DESTID	HOME;	O	V			
25			10		$PRINT	RORVER,T-PRIOR,T-DESTID:	O				
26	P	64		82	HNURSTA	$PROG=DOGETLOC:				RICP	
27			82		$PRINT	CANREAS,T-PRIOR,HNURSTA:				RICP	
28		30		32	$PRINT	RADADD,T-PRIOR,T-DESTID:		V			
29			97		$RS	RADDISP:					D
30			30	35	T-DESTRR	RADIOL:		V			
31		30		35	$PRINT	RADREQ,T-PRIOR,T-DESTRR:		V			

Figure 2: Sample data collection list for the IBM Health Care Support/DI/I-Patient Care System (from Mishelevich and Van Slyke, 1980).

measuring the usability of computers, programs, procedures, and manuals. To make it easier to write about them, I shall generally use the single word *computers*. to refer to these products collectively.

2. What do we mean by usability?

Before you can evaluate, or measure something you have to know exactly what it is you propose to evaluate. What exactly do we mean by usability? There have been a number of attempts to find a satisfactory answer to that question, many of which have tended to obscure, rather than clarify it. The definition I propose is modified from one by Shackel (1981):

The usability of a computer is measured by how easily and how effectively the computer can be used by a specific set of users, given particular kinds of support, to carry out a fixed set of tasks, in a defined set of environments.

Although that definition is patterned after Shackel's, mine differs from his in several respects — the most important of which is that mine excludes the purely physical arrangements of the computer workplace. These are what Shackel acknowledges are related primarily to anthropometric or biomechanical considerations — the configuration of the computer station, the placement of the keyboard and screen, the user's seating arrangement, and the design of the computer environment to eliminate noise, glare, and other annoyances.

These physical features of a computer workplace are certainly important and I do not mean to ignore them. I would argue, however, that they have to do more with physical comfort and fatigue than with usability. For example, it may be extremely easy to use a certain computer to compose letters or to create spreadsheets, but the computer may be so badly configured that it creates strains, headaches and other physical problems for the user. Conversely a computer workplace may be ideally designed from the standpoint of comfort, but the computer program may be so complex that it is virtually impossible to use. Since the physical features of a computer workplace are easily dealt with, I prefer to confine my definition to the ease with which tasks may be performed from the standpoint of their mental requirements.

My definition may seem to be circular because it uses two other apparently inexact words: *easily* and *effectively*. Actually, there are several possible ways of defining ease of use and effectiveness operationally, that is, in ways that can be observed and measured. Some of them are:

- Ease of start up, that is, the time required to install and get a program "up and running".
- Ease of learning, the time required to learn how to do a set of tasks
- Performance, that is, the time to execute a specific set of tasks
- Error scores, the number of errors committed, or the time taken to correct errors
- Versatility or functionality, that is, the number of different kinds of things the computer or program can do, for example, align decimals, do mathematical operations, permit the creation of footnotes, split screens or windows, send notes to other users, and so on.
- Overall evaluation, some mathematical combination of two or more of the preceding measures.

Although they cannot be directly observed, users' perceptions can be measured indirectly. So another measure of effectiveness is:

- Users' ratings of ease of use

3. Some issues of evaluation

3.1 *Multiple and objective measures*

Although it might appear difficult to choose among these several measures, I think the situation is not as complex as it might seem at first. In the general practice of human factors it is a common finding that well human-engineered machines or systems satisfy several objectives at the same time. Well designed systems often simplify operations, reduce errors, reduce learning time, reduce personnel requirements, reduce maintenance requirements, and sometimes do other good things as well. Examples in which multiple objectives have been achieved through good design are easy to find. Is this also true for computer systems?

Finding data to answer that question is difficult. The data that are available, however, support a positive response. One source of information comes from evaluations conducted by Software Digest. One of their books (Software Digest, 1984) reports evaluations of 30 word processing programs with the seven performance measures listed above. I have computed rank-order correlations among the several measures and show them in Table 1.

	Ease of learning	Ease of use ratings	Error handling	Performance	Versatility	Overall evaluation
Ease of start up	+.65	+.51	+.50	+.24	–.39	+.62
Ease of learning		+.87	+.72	+.67	–.38	+.93
Ease of use ratings			+.79	+.84	–.29	+.95
Error handling				+.64	–.34	+.82
Performance					–.15	+.81
Versatility						–.25

Table 1: Rank order correlations between measures used to evaluate 30 word processing programs (computed from data given in Software Digest, 1984).

Notice that all the measures, except one, are positively correlated with each other. The one exception is versatility, which correlates negatively with all the others. What these findings suggest is that those programs that were well designed were easier to start up, easier to learn to use, judged easier to use, allowed users to deal with errors more easily, and allowed users to perform tasks more quickly. On the other hand, those programs that were more versatile, that is, more complex, were harder to start up, harder to learn to use, and so on. Notice, too, that a single overall evaluation measure consisting of an algebraic combination of all the others correlated highly, and generally very highly, with each of the component measures.

Although they are highly suggestive, the data reported by Software Digest in this and in other publications are flawed from a methodological standpoint. In this case, ten users were tested with each program and we have no indication about the order in which programs were tested. It is well known that there are always transfer effects, sometimes positive and sometimes negative, when the same subjects are tested on different systems or with different procedures. In other words, the experience of working with one system invariably affects performance on the next, depending on, among other things, the number of similar or dissimilar features the two contain. This procedural difficulty contaminates all Software Digest ratings to some unknown extent.

The only other extensive set of data I have been able to find that relate to our question come from Roberts and Moran (1983). These investigators tested nine text editors with four evaluation measures: the average error-free time taken by expert subjects to complete a set of tasks, the average amount of time experts spent in correcting errors[1], the average time it took novices to learn how to do a core set of tasks, and functionality, a measure of the number of different tasks that could be done with the program.

Intercorrelations among these four measures are given in Table 2. Notice again the relatively high positive correlations among the first three measures. Those programs that were well designed permitted expert users to do their work more quickly and with fewer errors, and permitted novice users to learn the program more quickly. On the other hand, functionality, or complexity of the program, correlated not at all with the three performance measures. These findings lead Roberts and Moran to conclude that:

"The conventional wisdom among designers is that there is a tradeoff between

---

[1] Roberts and Moran actually reported the average times experts spent making and correcting errors as percentages of their error-free performance times. From their data I have computed the average times spent in making and correcting errors, because I think it is the more meaningful measure.

	Errors	Learning	Functionality
Time	+.64	+.78	–.12
Errors		+.71	+.08
Learning			–.08

Table 2: Rank order correlations between evaluation scores for nine text editors (computed from data in Figure 6, p. 274, in Roberts and Moran, 1983).

systems that are easy to learn by novices and systems that are efficient to use by experts. However, if we correlate the Learning scores with the Time scores, we see exactly the opposite. The data from our study show a high positive correlation (R = .79...) between the Time and Learning scores...the same factor — procedural complexity — underlies both expert performance (longer methods take longer to execute) and novice learning (longer methods imply that there (is) more to learn)." (p. 282).

Unfortunately, the Roberts and Moran findings are marred by the same methodological difficulty that I pointed out for the Software Digest data. Roberts and Moran tested four expert users for two of their measures and four novice users for the learning measure. They do not, however, say whether the same eight subjects were tested on all nine editors and, if so, in what order they were tested. So we again have the possibility of some contaminating transfer effects of unknown magnitude.

There are, of course, other data, not so extensive, that contribute to our question. For example, Sullivan and I (1983) rewrote a manual for a text editor and then evaluated the two manuals with secretaries who were given identical tasks to do with either the old and new manuals. Our results showed that secretaries who were tested with the rewritten manual turned out better quality work, used more commands successfully, asked fewer questions of the experimenter, and expressed more favourable attitudes than did those tested with the original manual. Although our tests do not suffer from the methodological flaw of those cited above, we compared only two manuals. Still, the results are clear: the rewritten manual was better in several respects.

Essentially the same kind of findings have been reported by Ledgard, Singer and Whiteside (1981), whose experimental design is discussed in greater detail later in this paper. They tested a slightly modified version of a commercially available

Control Data Corporation editor supplied with NOS against a version of the editor which they remodeled with identical power but with its syntax altered so that all commands were based on legitimate English phrases composed of common descriptive words. Their results show that with the remodeled set of commands both experienced and inexperienced users were able to do more work in a given time, with fewer errors, and with greater efficiency than they could with the original language. An attitude questionnaire also showed that users preferred the newer editor over the older one. Once again, these findings were obtained with a sound methodology, but they unfortunately compare only two editors.

Although the empirical evidence is not as good as I would like, the accumulated weight of it is compelling enough to allow me to conclude confidently that, in general, computers, computer programs, and manuals that are well designed will be easier for people to learn to use, easier to use, allow users to do more work with fewer errors, and will be better liked than those that are not well designed. The various ways that we could measure performance correlate positively, and usually correlate highly with each other. If I were to nominate one single performance measure to be used in evaluating usability it would be errors. Errors can be easily observed and counted. If you could design a computer and program that novices could learn to use without a single error you would indeed have a computer that is genuinely easy to use!

3.2 *Subjective measures*

Generally our feelings about something correlate with our performance in using it. We feel that something is easy to use if we don't have a lot of trouble using it. The correlation is far from perfect, however, because our feelings are also determined by some other things — our prior experiences, our perceptions, and our expectations. Appearances may also affect our feelings. If something — a keyboard — looks complicated, many people immediately feel that it is going to be hard to use, no matter what the realities may be. Similarly, if we have been led to expect that something is going to be easy to use, any little difficulty we have in using it may be magnified out of proportion to its real significance.

All of which means that evaluations of usability should take into account how users feel. That in turn means administering an attitude questionnaire or rating scale. Zoltan and I (1982) used a 64-item questionnaire successfully to determine attitudes of professional persons towards computers. Our article lists the items in our questionnaire. Shneiderman (1987, pp. 400–407) gives an example of a short and long form of a questionnaire for evaluating computer systems. Although he does not cite any data obtained with either questionnaire, both appear to have considerable potential.

3.3 *Usability must be measured empirically*

The foregoing lead to my first four guidelines:

RULE 1: Usability has to be defined operationally, that is in terms of the operations that are used to measure it.

RULE 2: An evaluation of usability should include measurements of objective performance and of subjective feelings.

RULE 3: Objective, or performance, measures of usability include learning time, time to perform a set of tasks, or errors.

RULE 4: Subjective measures of ease of use are obtained by ratings on an attitude questionnaire.

Measuring usability means, almost by definition, measuring performance, that is, the behaviour of a person and a system while they are actually doing a job (see also Bennett, 1979). When I say *system* I mean everything related to the computer — the workstation; the input device, for example, the keyboard, light pen, or mouse; the display, for example, the CRT, plasma display, or printer; the computer program; the instructions; the manual; and the environment in which all are used. For that reason, no single analytic criterion, such as readability level, size of manual, or number of keystrokes, can be used to predict with accuracy how easy it will be to use a computer. The concept *usability* implies activity that has to be evaluated by actual behaviour.

4. Alternatives to empirical measurement?

The above are such strong statements that it is worth looking at two other procedures that are sometimes thought to provide alternatives to actual performance testing.

4.1 *Guidelines*

There are now available several excellent sets of guidelines bearing on the design of computers, computer screens, and interactive dialogs (see for example, Galitz, 1985; Smith and Mosier, 1984; Williges and Williges, 1984). Responses to a survey by Mosier and Smith (1985) show that their guidelines are indeed useful. Of 130 respondents, 99, or very nearly three-quarters of them, reported that they had actually used the guidelines to establish design requirements, as an aid during design, to evaluate a proposed design, to evaluate a completed design, to evaluate an operational system or for still other purposes. Still, respondents also had numerous complaints about the guidelines, the most frequent one being that they are too general.

A couple of examples illustrate the problem. Following is a guideline from Smith and Mosier:

> "In text displays and labels, word usage should incorporate familiar terms and the technical jargon of the user, and avoid the unfamiliar jargon of the interface designer and programmer."

and here is one from Williges and Williges:

> "Command languages should be concise, precise, powerful, and flexible." (p.187).

It's difficult to find fault with the aim of either one, but, without any intention of disparaging them, the difficulty is that unless you actually test or measure something you never know whether you have met the guideline. How can you be sure that the words you have used really incorporate "familiar terms and the technical jargon of the user"? Or how can you be sure that the command languages you have devised are really "concise, precise, powerful, and flexible"? As Mosier and Smith point out there is a dilemma here, the balance between generality and specificity. The more specific a guideline is written, the less likely it is to apply to a variety of situations. Unfortunately, computers are not alike. They are all specific and their proper evaluation requires an evaluation of their particular features.

4.2 *Predictive models*

A second possible technique for evaluating usability involves models for predicting user performance. Tullis (1986), for example, describes a procedure for evaluating screen formats. Inputs to the model are (1) overall density of characters on the screen, (2) the local density of other characters near each character, (3) the number of visual groups of characters, (4) the average visual angle subtended by those groups, (5) the number of labels or data values, and (6) a measure of how poorly aligned the screen elements are with each other.

Validation studies seem to show that this is a useful technique for a very limited and specific purpose: evaluating and rearranging items on a screen when everything else is held constant. It does not, however, enable the investigator or designer to evaluate the results of changing typography, colour, highlighting, or legibility of letters. Nor does it enable the designer to evaluate changes in the usability of a format, if, for example, the information content on the screen is changed. Still, the model does serve an important rôle in screen design, even though it cannot possibly substitute for performance evaluations of a computer system, as a system.

Two other models that have received considerable attention are the GOMS (Goals-Operators-Methods-Selection rules) and Keystroke-Level models developed by Card, Moran and Newell (1983). Both are attempts to describe certain kinds of operator behaviour in certain situations. The GOMS model, for example, describes well the behaviour of a computer-user in a text-editing task, and the Keystroke-Level model is a refinement of the GOMS model that will predict the time a user will take to do a number of tasks with a computer. Among other things, both models are predicated on the performance of *expert* users who do their jobs *without* error. These are clearly not the kinds of constraints that are acceptable in evaluating usability. In fairness, however, I should point out that Card *et al.* never intended their models to be used for measuring usability, although some people have assumed them to be appropriate for that purpose.

To sum up, then, guidelines and predictive models are interesting and useful for very restricted purposes. But if your aim is to evaluate usability, then, to quote Dumas and Redish (1986, p. 1209) "the only way to know whether a product is effective is to have users test it," a sentiment echoed by Schell (1986, p. 1213) "...the only method of ensuring good design is a properly conducted usability test," and by Rubinstein and Hersh (1984, p. 190) "You build it, you test it."

5. Factors contributing to usability

From the definition I gave earlier we can identify several components that need to be considered in evaluating usability. Three that I want to elaborate on are:

- the computer
- the user
- the task

5.1 *The computer*

Computers may vary differentially in usability depending on what features you look at. What I mean is that a particular computer may be easy to use in some ways, and difficult to use in others. To take a simple example, compare two functions as they are performed on an IBM Correcting Selectric III Typewriter, and on an IBM Electronic Typewriter 75. The two functions are the erasure of errors made (a) at the end of something that has been typed, and (b) in the middle of something that has been typed.

In the first case, imagine that you have just typed the following material:

Ease of use has many facets, each of which qwerty

Here the letters "qwerty" are in error and need to be erased. On the Selectric you go through the following steps:

1. Depress the correcting key
2. Depress the "y" key

3. Depress the correcting key
4. Depress the "t" key
5. Depress the correcting key
6. Depress the "r" key

and so on.

In other words 12 key presses are required to erase the letters "qwerty" on the Selectric Typewriter. To correct the same letters on the Electronic Typewriter you need to make only one key press. You push the "Backspace" key and hold it down until all the incorrect letters have been erased.

But compare the two machines when you make a typing error in the middle of something that has been typed:

Ease of ude has many facets, each of which ...

Here the letter "d" in the word "ude" needs to be erased. On the Selectric two actions are required:

1. Depress the correcting key until you come to the letter "d". Since the correcting key is typamatic, that is, it has a repeat action, you need only to push it and hold it down.
2. Type the letter "d".

On the Electronic Typewriter 6 actions are required:

1. While you hold the "Code" key down,
2. Depress the "Backspace" key until you come to the letter "d".
3. While you hold the "Code" key down,
4. Push the "NoPrt" key.
5. Push the "d" key.
6. Push the "Backspace" key.

Clearly, correcting this kind of error is harder on the Electronic Typewriter than on the simpler Selectric.

So, if you were to be asked, "On which typewriter is it easier to correct errors?", your answer would have to be "Well it depends". Some kinds of errors are easier to correct on the one, other kinds of errors are easier to correct on the other, and a really good answer would depend on how many errors of various kinds people typically make.

A more sophisticated example comes from a study by Reisner (1977) which, among other things, compared two programming languages, SEQUEL and SQUARE. In one part of her study, Reisner measured the difficulty of different features of each program. Her results for the SEQUEL language are shown in Table 3.

Feature	Programmers	Non-Programmers
Mapping	98	91
Selection	89	87
Projection	100	73
Assignment	94	87
Built-in functions	89	88
And/or	82	77
Set operations	88	70
Composition	74	53
Group by	61	46
Correlation variables	33	12
Computed variables	44	7

Table 3: Mean percentages of "Essentially Correct" scores earned by 18 programmers and 15 non-programmers on a final examination covering basic features of the SEQUEL programming language (from Reisner, 1977).

The various features of this programming language differ greatly in their difficulty, or conversely, in their ease of use. None of the programmers had any difficulty with the projection feature. On the other hand, only a third were able to give correct answers to the questions dealing with correlation variables.Discrepancies are even greater among the scores for the non-programmers.

Still another example comes from a study by Pagerey (1981) on an evaluation of the BASIC programming language. Among other things, subjects were asked to rate the difficulty of learning and using various commands. Although there are some differences between the ratings made by programmers and non-programmers, the correlation between the two is statistically significant and positive (+0.49). Non-programmers, for example, rated the LET, LIST, RUN, SAVE, and STOP commands easiest to use, and the GOTO, IF, INPUT, NEXT, and READ, commands hardest to use.

In these examples we have three different kinds of data pointing to differences in the ease of use of various features. Data such as these are, of course, open to several questions and alternative interpretations. For example, in Reisner's study, one might question whether the amounts of instruction devoted to the several features were equal, whether the questions about the several features on the final examination were equal, and so on. Nonetheless, I think the weight of the evidence clearly supports the assertion that most computers or programs are generally easy to use in some respects, hard to use in others. Thus, usability evaluations may give different results depending on what aspect(s) of the computer or program you evaluate, or what function(s) you want to perform with the computer. That leads to my fifth guideline:

RULE 5: In evaluating usability be sure to sample all the relevant functions or features and weight them according to their frequency of use or importance.

5.2 *The user*

It goes without saying that usability also depends greatly on the user. Software that is easy for a programmer may be difficult or even completely incomprehensible to a novice, or occasional user. Table 4, taken again from the study by Reisner (1977), shows the mean percentages of "essentially correct" scores by programmers and non-programmers on a final examination covering basic features of the SEQUEL and SQUARE programming languages at the end of a training course on the program involved. Programmers, as you might expect, earned higher scores than did the non-programmers.

Programming language	Programmers	Non-Programmers
SEQUEL	78	65
SQUARE	78	55
Mean	78	60

Table 4: Mean percentages of "Essentially Correct" scores by programmers and non-programmers on a final examination covering basic features of two programming languages (from Reisner, 1977).

Figure 3 shows the time taken by two groups of subjects to read ten chapters and to program six sets of problems at the end of certain chapters dealing with the BASIC program. Not only is there a difference between the mean times taken by the two groups, but there isn't even any overlap between them. The programmers took from 3.5 to 5.5 hours to go through the training exercise; the non-programmers took from 5.9 to 9.4 hours to go through the same exercise.

Differences such as these are what one might expect. More important from a methodological standpoint are interactions that occur between level of sophistication of the user and various aspects of user performance. For example, in Reisner's data (Table 4), programmers had exactly the same percentage of correct answers on the examinations for the SEQUEL and SQUARE programs. Non-programmers, on the other hand, earned significantly lower scores on the SQUARE program.

Another example occurs in Pagerey's study of the BASIC language in which users were required to program in BASIC six sets of problems at the end of certain chapters. Table 5 shows the average times taken by the programmers and non-

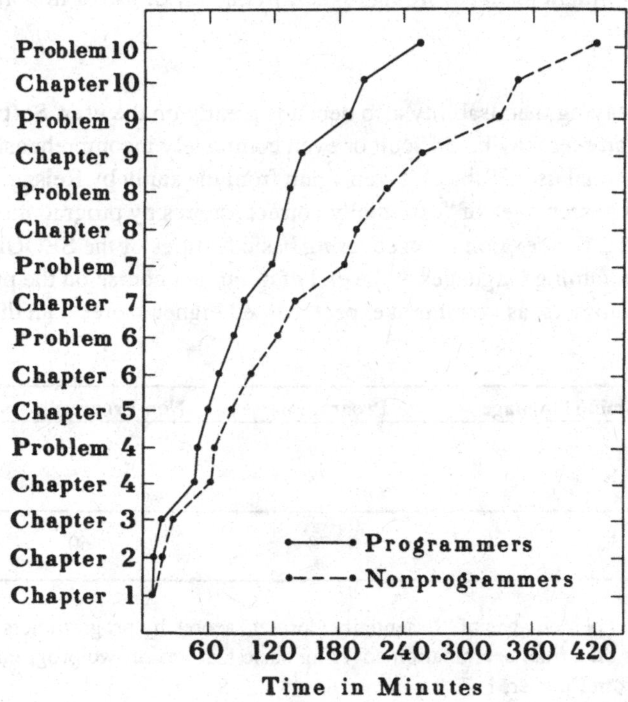

Figure 3: Average learning curves by programmers and non-programmers to complete a course in BASIC (from Pagerey, 1981).

programmers to complete those problems. Note that problem 4 was completed in about the same time by both the programmers and non-programmers. Problem 8, on the other hand, was completed fastest by the programmers, whereas non-programmers took over three times as long to complete it.

Earlier I mentioned ratings made by programmers and non-programmers on the difficulty of 17 BASIC commands. Although the ratings by the programmers and non-programmers were correlated, there were some important differences between the ratings of the two groups. Non-programmers rated the SAVE command among the five easiest, programmers rated it among the five most difficult commands. Conversely, non-programmers rated the GOTO command among the five most difficult whereas programmers rated it among the five easiest. Interactions between the level of sophistication of the user and various aspects of performance need to be considered in usability evaluations.

Problem	Programmers	Non-Programmers
4	12.3	12.5
6	13.7	26.7
7	24.3	46.0
8	9.7	31.8
9	52.0	73.7
10	51.7	73.9

Table 5: Average times taken by six programmers and six non-programmers to program six problems in the BASIC programming language (after Pagerey, 1981).

Some other human characteristics that are important in evaluating usability are:

- Sensory capacities, for example, visual acuity
- Motor abilities, for example, ability to type
- Intellectual capacities, for example, intelligence level
- Learned cognitive skills, for example, familiarity with the English language.
- Experience, for example, experience with computers
- Personality, for example, persistence, compulsiveness
- Attitudes, for example, attitudes towards computers
- Motivation, for example, motivation to work.

The foregoing leads to my sixth and seventh guidelines:

RULE 6: In evaluating usability it is important to know "usability for whom". A complete user description is essential.

RULE 7: Be sure the evaluation is made with a representative sample of the prospective user population.

5.3 *The task*

Next, usability varies with the task. There are well known differences between various computer languages. COBOL is easier than ALGOL in handling many business applications, ALGOL is better for scientific computations. Equally important are the various other subsidiary features of the task that are sometimes easily forgotten or overlooked. A manual that can be consulted while it is lying open on a desk is much easier to use than one that has to be consulted by a maintenance man while he is working inside a console. A keyboard that is similar to a conventional typewriter keyboard is easier to use by people who type than is a keyboard with an unconventional layout. Considerations such as these lead to my eighth guideline:

RULE 8: Be sure to evaluate computers for the same kinds of tasks, and under the same conditions, that the user will have.

6. Numbers, scales, and what they mean

Measurement implies numbers and at this point it is useful to clarify what numbers mean when we measure usability or think we have measured it. In measurement, numbers are assigned to things, and what those numbers mean is determined by the kinds of operations you perform on the things you measure. Those operations in turn define four kinds of scales:

- Nominal
- Ordinal
- Interval
- Ratio.

6.1 *Measurement scales*

(i) Nominal scales. In nominal scales numbers are used only as names for things. So, for example, in his study of the BASIC programming language Pagerey (1981) identified several kinds of errors made on the IBM 5110 Computer System: 500, 502, 503, 550, 551, 556, 606, 634, 668, 670, 671, and 708. A 606 error, for example, meant "unsupported diskette label entries found." A 634 error meant "conversion error detected," and a 668 error meant that "a referenced number cannot be found." When numbers are used in this way the only thing you can do with them is count them. They cannot be added, subtracted, or used in any other arithmetic computations. In fact, you can't even say that the thing represented by any number is more or less than the thing represented by any other number. That is, a 606 error is neither more or less than a 634 error. The numbers 606 and 634 are merely substitutes for names. They have no other meaning.

(ii) Ordinal scales. In ordinal scales numbers are assigned to things according to whether those things have more or less of some characteristic or quality. So, for example, on a rating scale of 1 to 7, where 1 means "very easy to use" and 7 means "very hard to use", the number 4 means harder to use than the number 2. The ordinal scale, however, doesn't allow us to say that 4 is twice as hard as 2. Nor can we say that the difference between a rating of 4 and 3 is the same as the difference between a rating of 3 and 2. In an ordinal scale, equal differences between numbers do not mean equal differences between the things being measured. The numbers only express relative amounts.

(iii) Interval scales. In interval scales equal differences between number represent equal differences between things. The difference between Day 13 and Day 14 is the same amount of time as the difference between Day 22 and Day 23. Try as I could, I couldn't think of any kind of measurement you might make in evaluating usability that would produce only an interval scale.

(iv) Ratio Scales. In ratio scales you not only have equality of units, but you also have an absolute zero. Having an absolute zero means that you can make statements like "twice as much" or "one-quarter as much", or use percentages. Time is the only kind of measurement I could think of that meets these conditions in measuring usability. Time has an absolute zero and units of time are equal to each other. So in measuring the time taken to do something, you can validly say things like "it took twice as long to read Manual A as Manual B" or "task C could be done 75% faster than task D'.

6.2 *Implications*

The implications are that almost without exception the only thing you can do when you measure usability is to make comparative measurements. A particular computer has to be compared against something else. Although those comparisons may yield numbers, the only thing you can legitimately conclude from those numbers is that a particular product is easier or harder than some other, or that it does, or doesn't, meet some standard. You cannot legitimately say anything more exact about "how much harder" or "how much easier." This is true about measurements like:

- Numbers of errors
- Scores on quizzes or examinations
- Ratings from questionnaires

These are severe restrictions on what numbers mean and how they can be interpreted in usability studies. The one exception is time. Measurements of the time taken to do something can be used without restriction and can be interpreted in all the ways that we customarily think numbers can be used.

All that is strictly correct from a theoretical standpoint. As a practical matter, however, we can and do make somewhat more descriptive statements about numbers. For example, if 131 errors were made on Task A, 120 on Task B, and only 10 on Task C, we would probably say that A and B appear to be much harder than C, and that A and B are more nearly alike in difficulty. These are rough statements, to be sure, but they are probably justified in many instances. Nonetheless, the guideline I draw from this discussion is :

RULE 9: Numbers resulting from measurements of usability generally form only ordinal scales. Only comparative conclusions — "easier" or "harder" — can be drawn. Any other more quantitative conclusions must be made cautiously, if at all. The only exception to these cautions is measurement of the time taken to perform tasks or functions. Time measurements can be interpreted in all the ways that we customarily use numbers.

7. Determining the purpose of the evaluation

When you have finally settled on how you plan to measure usability and have accepted what numbers mean when you measure it, the next question you need to answer is: "Why exactly do you want to evaluate a computer product?" The quick answer you are likely to get to that question is a kind of startled, "Why, to find out how easy it is to use the computer, of course." That answer is really not good enough, because there are in fact several different reasons why you might want to evaluate a computer and the methods you would use in your evaluation depend on why you are doing it. Let's look at some purposes and how they may be served by evaluations. In the next three sections, three different types of purpose are considered in turn and some appropriate evaluation procedures are outlined for each.

8. Improving an existing product

The simplest, but not the least important purpose that could be served by an evaluation is to improve some existing product. The product may be under development or it may actually be in use. The point is that you have it, or a prototype of it, and you want to make it better. For this purpose you don't need to conduct an elaborate, carefully controlled experiment with rigorous statistical analysis of data. Much simpler methodologies will work quite well. Direct observations of persons using the computer, activity analyses (including time-lapse photography), questionnaires, and protocol analyses are methods that are appropriate. Combinations of them can also be used.

8.1 *Diagnostic evaluation*

I illustrate one procedure with a study done by Al-Awar, Chapanis, and Ford (1981) to write a tutorial for the IBM 3277 Display Station, Model 2. Our method was to write a program, test it on a sample of the target population, find out what was wrong with the program, and revise it accordingly. This cycle of test-rewrite was repeated over and over until a satisfactory level of performance was reached. In this case, our goal was to write a program that could be completed by 95% of first-time computer users, without any written instructions or documentation except what appeared on the display unit and without any help from an instructor. This tutorial has since been used as an introduction to more sophisticated applications, and the level of performance has exceeded the goal that was set for it.

Evaluations in this study were made in three main ways:

(i) *Performance.* Most important was the performance of the test subjects. Corrected and uncorrected errors, hesitations, help requests, complaints, and long response times were all symptoms of difficulties that needed to be considered seriously. In the beginning there were many of these indications of difficulty. As the program became perfected, these evidences of difficulty decreased in variety and frequency.

(ii) *Attitudes.* A questionnaire was used to evaluate user attitudes toward the tutorial. The questionnaire consisted of two parts. In the first part users were asked to rate such things as the overall clarity of the instructions, the difficulty of the language used, the "friendliness" of the computer, and the interest value of the session.

(iii) *Frame-by-Frame analysis.* The second part of the questionnaire consisted of a frame-by-frame analysis of the program. At this time the user was told that he was an active partner in the effort to perfect the program. An experimenter sat alongside the user and went through the entire program one frame at a time. In each case the user was asked to analyze the frame, particularly in those places where he had made errors or had difficulties. The experimenter probed to find out why the subject thought he did what he did, whether the instructions were unclear, whether the information presented was inadequate, whether the vocabulary was too difficult. When the user identified trouble spots, the experimenter usually asked, "How would you say it?" Probing for the user's own words is useful because users often have a way of saying things that are better than the experimenter's or the programmer's. An important rule to observe here is that the user knows best. His logic or his way of interpreting a frame — and not the programmer's — is the one to follow.

Although this procedure may seem unsystematic and unstructured, experience suggests that there is a surprising amount of consistency in what users report. Difficulties are not random or whimsical. They do form patterns. In the 1981 version of this paper I called this general procedure *diagnostic evaluation* because it is something like what a physician does when he goes about diagnosing a disease. The experimenters in this case, used symptoms — errors, difficulties, complaints — to diagnose problems, that is, things that were wrong with the program.

Sullivan and I (1983) used essentially the same procedure when we rewrote the text editor manual mentioned earlier. A term that is sometimes used to refer to the procedure when it is used in writing manuals is *user editing*. When users are involved in the testing, identification and correction of problems with programs, computer dialogs, or computer systems, the procedure is usually referred to nowadays as *participatory design*, *prototyping*, or *rapid prototyping* (see, for example, Pfauth, Hammer and Fissel, 1985; Shneiderman, 1987). Whatever it is called, the essence of the procedure is that models, prototypes, or trial versions of products are constructed, tested with users, and modified to eliminate whatever difficulties the tests reveal. Although the basic idea is simple enough, participatory design or rapid prototyping may become very involved in the case of large and complex systems (see, for example, Gottschalk, 1986; Percival and Johnson, 1986).

8.2 *Experimental evaluations*

Discovering what's wrong with a computer may also be done with more systematic forms of experimentation. The simplest kind of experimental design that could be used for this purpose is shown in Table 6. Test subjects, or users, are asked to perform a series of tasks with the computer, and the evaluator measures their performance in carrying out these tasks. This kind of design is what is referred to in the statistical literature as a repeated-measurements design (Keppel, 1973; Myers, 1979; Winer, 1962). Since subjects are tested on a number of tasks, or treatments in statistical jargon, measurements are repeated on them, hence the name repeated-measurements.

	Users (or Test Subjects)				
Tasks	S_1	S_2	S_3	...	S_N
T_1					
T_2					
T_3					
.					
.					
.					
T_t					

Table 6: A simple repeated-measurements experimental design for evaluating computers.

Pagerey's study of the BASIC programming language added one more level of complexity to the simple repeated-measurements design in Table 6. A major purpose of his study was to evaluate and, through recommendations, to improve the IBM 5110 Computer System version of BASIC that had been re-coded to run on the IBM system/370. His design (Table 7) is referred to in the statistical literature as a mixed design (Keppel, 1973; Myers, 1979) a between-within design, (Keppel, 1973; Myers, 1979) or a split-plot design (Kirk, 1968). As you can see, Pagerey added a new variable, level of sophistication of the user, to the simple design in Table 6. Since the subjects in each level of sophistication are different subjects, this new variable is a

Tasks	Programmers						Non-programmers					
	S_1	S_2	S_3	S4	S5	S6	S_7	S_8	S_9	S_{10}	S_{11}	S_{12}
Read Chapter 1												
Read Chapter 2												
Read Chapter 3												
Read Chapter 4												
Do Problem 4												
Read Chapter 5												
Read Chapter 6												
Do Problem 6												
Read Chapter 7												
Do Problem 7												
Read Chapter 8												
Do Problem 8												
Read Chapter 9												
Do Problem 9												
Read Chapter 10												
Do Problem 10												

Table 7: The experimental design used by Pagerey (1981) in his evaluation of the BASIC programming language.

between-subjects variable. As in Table 6 each subject performed a series of tasks — in this case, 16 in all. The tasks were to read 10 chapters of a manual on the BASIC programming language and to do 6 problems at the end of some of the chapters. Since each subject did all 16 tasks, tasks are a within-subjects variable. Hence the name between-within design.

Pagerey used six dependent measures in his study:

- The time to read each chapter and complete each problem
- The number and kinds of questions asked of the experimenter
- The number and kind of errors made
- The number of attempts required to complete problems
- Scores earned on a quiz covering the material learned
- Responses to a questionnaire soliciting attitudes towards the programming language.

All these dependent measures turned out to be useful, first, because they all corroborated and supplemented each other. For example, programmers did their work faster, with fewer errors, and asked fewer questions of the experimenter than did non-programmers. At the same time, the different measures each provided information that supplemented what was obtained with the others. So, for example, responses to questionnaire items suggested improvements, a kind of information that could not be deduced from any of the quantitative measures.

8.3 *A comparison of prototyping and experimental evaluations*

These two forms of evaluation — prototyping and experimental — each have advantages and disadvantages. Because they are more highly structured, experimental evaluations yield data that can be easily summarized and portrayed. Refer, for example, to the data in Figure 3 and Table 5. These data can then be used to generalize about particular difficulties with a specific kind of software. Prototyping does not yield data of that kind. Since programs are constantly being modified as difficulties are diagnosed, the nature of the task is constantly changing.

Prototyping usually requires more subjects than do experimental evaluations. In prototyping, a subject is typically used once, but then generally cannot be used again after he has gone through the task. Each new modification of the software requires a new group of user subjects.

On the positive side, however, prototyping does two things at once. It not only helps to identify difficulties, but it also serves as a test bed for eliminating difficulties and testing modifications. Experimental evaluations, on the other hand, are more elegant ways of identifying difficulties with computers, but they provide no answers about ways to eliminate those difficulties. The experimenter still has the job of modifying the product and then conducting another evaluation to find out whether his modifications have in fact done what he hoped they would do.

Another difference between prototyping and experimental evaluations is that the former are generally easier to conduct. They require less advance planning and, because they are conducted on a one-to-one basis, tend to be more personal and informal than experimental evaluations.

Which method is the better? There is no simple answer to that question. Used properly, both are valid and effective. The choice between them is best made on the basis of other considerations — availability of test subjects, laboratory facilities, scheduling problems, and purpose to be served by the evaluation, e.g., does the experimenter want to produce a report for management or for publication, or is the experimenter's primary interest in going directly to the improvement of a product?

9. Comparing two or more products

A somewhat different reason for doing computer evaluations is to compare two or more products, e.g., to find out whether A is easier to use than B, or to find out which of A, B, and C is easiest to use. This purpose requires some sort of systematic experimental plan. Informal prototyping that can be used for improving software is not appropriate for this purpose.

The simplest form of experimental design that can be used for this purpose is illustrated in Table 8. Various products, p in number, are shown along the left-hand

Product	Subjects	Tasks				
		T_1	T_2	T_3	...	T_t
1	S_{11} S_{21} S_{31} . . . S_{n1}					
2	S_{12} S_{22} S_{32} . . . S_{n2}					
	. . .					
p	S_{1p} S_{2p} S_{3p} . . . S_{np}					

Table 8: A simple experimental design that can be used for comparing the usability of several products.

side of the table and *np* users are randomly assigned to the *p* products. Each subject is required to do a series of tasks with the product to which he has been assigned.

The simple design shown in this table can be elaborated by the addition of other variables. In her comparison of two software packages, SEQUEL and SQUARE, Reisner (1977) did as Pagerey did. She ran tests on two groups of subjects, programmers and non-programmers. Her experimental design is shown in Table 9. The advantage of Reisner's experimental design over the simpler one in Table 8 is that hers provides more specific information about an additional variable, user sophistication.

Still more complex variations of the design illustrated in Table 9 are possible. Ledgard, Singer, and Whiteside (1981) used such a design in their study of two editors, a notational and a more English-like editor. Examples of the two kinds of editors are shown in Table 10. Their experimental design (Table 11) differed from

			T_1 T_2 T_3 ... T_t
SEQUEL	Programmers	S_1 S_2 . . . S_{18}	
	Non-programmers	S_{19} S_{20} . . . S_{33}	
SQUARE	Programmers	S_{34} S_{35} . . . S_{44}	
	Non-programmers	S_{45} S_{46} . . . S_{64}	

Table 9: Experimental design used by Reisner (1977) in her study of the SEQUEL and SQUARE query languages.

that used by Reisner first in that they used subjects with three different levels of sophistication.

Their "inexperienced" users were 8 individuals who claimed less than 10 hours of experience with computer terminals. Their "familiar" users claimed between 11 and 100 hours of experience, and their "experienced" users claimed over 100 hours of such experience. The addition of a third class of users is by itself a minor extension of the design used by Reisner. What does constitute a significant change is that Ledgard *et al.* tested every subject on both editors, but half the subjects were tested first with the notational editor and second with the English-like editor (Order 1 in Table 11). The other half of the subjects were tested in the reverse order, first with the English-like editor, second with the notational editor (Order 2 in Table 11).

This is sometimes referred to as a *cross-over* design, or as having each subject serve as his own control. The potential advantage of such a design is that it reduces

Function	Notational editor	English editor
Current line moves back to the nearest line containing TOOTH	FIND: /TOOTH/ ;1	BACKWARD TO "TOOTH"
Erases 7 lines starting with the current line. Next line becomes the current line.	DELETE; 7	DELETE 7 LINES
Displays all lines from current line to the last line of text. The current line becomes the last line displayed.	LIST; *	LIST ALL LINES
Changes every instance of KO to OK in the current and all subsequent lines. The current line becomes the last line to be changed.	RS: /KO/ ,OK/ ;*	CHANGE ALL "KO" TO "OK"

Table 10: Examples of functions as expressed by the notational editor and English editor tested by Ledgard, Singer and Whiteside (1981).

the variability that always characterizes experiments with people because both treatments are tested on the same people. In that way the sensitivity of the experiment is increased in the sense that it is possible to find significant differences between the main variable of interest (the two editors in this case) with fewer subjects.

The disadvantage of the cross-over design is that you often get interference in the second task because of having done the first. An obvious example of such interference would be if subjects learned to type proficiently on a keyboard with a QWERTY layout and then had to learn to type on a keyboard with an alphabetic layout, or *vice versa*. In learning to type on the second keyboard, the subject has to "unlearn" the habits acquired in the first task, and then learn a completely new set of habits in the second. These carry-over effects are sometimes referred to as retroactive inhibition and they result in what are called interaction effects in statistical jargon. But whatever they are called, the net result is that these effects usually complicate the interpretation of data that come out of experiments using such designs.

Ledgard *et al.* were lucky in their experiment. They found only one such interaction due to "carry-over" effects, probably because their learning periods were so short. The entire experimental session — studying each editor and then doing an editing task with each editor — took only about 2 hours.

Three kinds of quantitative results were obtained in the experiment and once again the three kinds of data corroborate each other nicely. As user experience increased, the percentage of the editing task completed and the editing efficiency increased, while the percentage of erroneous commands decreased. Similar consistency was found for the comparisons involving the two editors. The percentage of the editing

			Notational editor	English-based editor
Inexperienced users	Order 1	S1 S2 S3 S4		
	Order 2	S5 S6 S7 S8		
Familiar users	Order 1	S9 S10 S11 S12		
	Order 2	S13 S14 S15 S16		
Experienced users	Order 1	S17 S18 S19 S20		
	Order 2	S21 S22 S23 S24		

Table 11: Experimental design used by Ledgard, Singer and Whiteside (1981) in their study of two interactive languages.

task completed and editing efficiency were higher, and the percentage of erroneous commands lower for the English-like editor than for the notational editor.

10. Evaluating computers against a standard

Although the two kinds of evaluations that I have discussed were useful, they still do not provide the final answer to what many computer designers would like to know. It is useful, for example, to be able to say that A is easier to use than B, but that answer doesn't tell the designer whether A is easy enough. Should he accept A as it is, or should he try to make it even easier to use?

It would be ideal if we had some kind of an absolute standard for usability. If there were such a standard, the job of the evaluator would be to measure a particular product to see whether it does, or does not, meet the standard. Examples of items in such a standard might be:

The manual should be written at reading grade level W.
The manual should not contain more than X pages.
The program should be comprehensible to Y percent of users after Z hours of study.

10.1 *Is the standard valid?*

Evaluations in which computers are compared against a standard raise a new question: How valid is the standard? That is, is the standard really a measure of usability? It is simple enough to write into a standard that a manual should be written at, say, no more than a 10th grade reading level. But measures of readability are themselves not necessarily good indicators of usability. Readability formulas make use of such things as vocabulary words, length of sentences, and number of personal references. Yet a passage that has an acceptable score on a readability formula can be made completely incomprehensible merely be rearranging the words in a random order. Gibberish, made-up words, and acronyms may make a passage completely unintelligible. (Bruce, Rubin and Starr, 1981; Redish, 1981).

Similarly, a standard specifying that a manual should not contain more than X pages of instructions may not take into account the value of graphics. A manual of, say, 10 pages may be made easy or hard by the addition or omission of appropriate graphics.

Considerations such as these lead to:

RULE 10: Do not accept "standards" for usability uncritically. Standards must themselves be evaluated empirically.

10.2 *Testing for compliance with a standard*

Assuming that you have a standard and that you have confidence in its validity, then what? That depends to a considerable extent on the nature of the standard. If the standard consists of statements such as:

The readability should not be greater than the Xth grade level,

or

The manual of instructions should be no longer than Y pages, the evaluator's task is simple. He merely has to compute the readability level in the first instance or count pages in the second. If, however, the standard consists of statements like:

> Ninety-five percent of typical users should be able to read and understand the instructions in less than X minutes,

or

> Eighty percent of users should be able to diagnose and correct their errors in less than Y minutes,

there are special problems in insuring that the product meets the standard.

10.3 *Selection of test subjects*

First, of course, is the problem of defining who typical users are, a problem I have already mentioned. Having defined the population of typical users, the evaluator then has the problem of selecting a representative, or random, sample of them. That's a pretty hard thing to do and one of the most common errors made in conducting evaluations is made at this point. All too often the subjects used in evaluation studies are selected for the convenience of the evaluator. The worst mistake of all, of course, is to use people from the industry or corporation that is developing the product. Selecting subjects for test, and doing it properly, is a tough problem that would take far more time and space than I have to discuss it. Under the circumstances, the best I can do is to repeat my RULES 6 and 7:

> RULE 6: In evaluating usability, it is important to know "usability for whom". A complete user description is essential.
>
> RULE 7: Be sure the evaluation is made with a representative sample of the prospective user population.

10.4 *Dependent measures*

Having selected test users, the next problem is deciding on appropriate dependent measures. How can you be sure that the users have read and understood the instructions, as the standard says. Or, how can you be sure that the users have diagnosed and corrected their errors? Asking subjects whether they understand instructions is not necessarily good enough. Some ways of testing whether readers have understood what they have read is to have them:

Paraphrase what they have read
Answer questions on a test of what they have read
Apply what they have read

The important point I want to extract from this brief discussion of dependent variables is:

RULE 11: Pick dependent measures with care. The dependent measures should relate in a clear and meaningful way to the performance under consideration.

10.5 *On the number of subjects*

By their very nature data obtained in human experiments do not yield absolute statistics. There is always a region of uncertainty around any statistic that you calculate. That region of uncertainty is generally called a confidence interval, and it has associated with it a probability. So, for example, if the average time taken to do a task is 20 minutes, a statistician might express the finding in this way: "The probability is 0.95 that the true average lies between 20 ± 5 minutes." The ± 5 minutes is the confidence interval, or region of uncertainty, and it is related to a couple of things, one of which, the variance, is not under the control of the investigator. One thing that is under his control is the number of subjects he tests. In general, the confidence interval, or region of uncertainty, is inversely related to the square root of the number of subjects. In other words, you can increase the precision of your findings by testing more subjects, but to get twice as much accuracy, you need to test four times as many subjects.

Testing subjects costs money and takes time. Obviously, the experimenter has to make a decision about how much precision he is willing to sacrifice to reduce the cost and effort of testing subjects. Where is the balance point? There really is no simple answer to that question. Although there are statistical formulae that enable you to compute the number of subjects needed to get a certain level of precision, these formulae require an estimate of the variability, technically, the statistical variance, that you are likely to find in the data. Unfortunately, that variability is something that you never really know in advance. The only way you can estimate that variability is on the basis of data obtained from similar studies. The trouble is that there haven't been enough studies done on the evaluation of computers to provide the investigator with even a rough estimate of variability. Under the circumstances, about all I can tell you is that an investigator has to rely on his past experience with experimentation of this or similar kinds and make an intuitive guess about how many subjects he should use. It sounds very unscientific, and it is, but that's the way things stand. As more computer evaluations get done, we will begin to acquire the experience and data needed to serve as more reliable guides.

11. A general evaluation strategy

In this section I discuss a few more matters that apply to all evaluations.

11.1 *Plan ahead*

By now it should be clear that doing a good evaluation involves a lot of fairly technical and interacting decisions. All these things do not just happen. They must be planned for in advance. Here are the steps involved:

- Define what you mean by "usability"
- Define your target population
- Select a random, or representative, sample of test subjects from the target population
- Settle on the purpose of your evaluation
- Select an appropriate methodology or experimental design
- Determine what tasks you will have subjects do
- Decide on appropriate dependent measures
- Set up experimental facilities
- Pilot test the evaluation
- Conduct the evaluation
- Analyze the results

Jumping into an evaluation without any advance planning is almost certain to result in a badly conducted evaluation, data that cannot be interpreted, wasted time and effort, or some combination of them. For a good practical illustration of the reasons why advance planning is so important, read "The diary of a human factors experiment" in Ledgard *et al*. (1981, pp. 105-145). This is the reason for my

RULE 12: To avoid disasters, plan evaluations in advance. Generally speaking, devote as much time to planning as to the actual evaluation.

11.2 *Facilities and equipment*

One thing I have not discussed so far is that the conduct of a good evaluation requires facilities and equipment. The evaluation needs to be conducted somewhere and specially designed or designated areas are best for that purpose. Insofar as possible, the facilities should be away from normal production or work areas to avoid the contaminating effects of extraneous interruptions or influences, unless the normal work environment is something that is of direct relevance to the evaluation. For many evaluations, however, it is more important to keep the working environment constant than it is to conduct the evaluation in the normal work situation.

Evaluations usually require equipment, for example a computer, not only for storing and presenting the software package, but also for capturing data. Neal and Simon (1984) describe an elegant system for doing that. Oftentimes, however, a combined software and hardware system may not be available because it is still being developed. In such cases, the evaluator needs to be able to model the product he is to test. That involves a great deal of work in itself (Curtis, 1980). Generally speaking, the more nearly the test product models or duplicates the final production package, the better the evaluation will be. This makes:

> RULE 13: Be sure to provide appropriate facilities in which to conduct the evaluation, and equipment to support the presentation and capture of information to and from users.

11.3 *Test the system as a whole*

Products should not be tested in pieces. You cannot, for example, just test a manual by itself. Well, you can, but it will not necessarily be a good evaluation. The usefulness of a manual depends to some extent on the hardware and the computer program for which the manual has been written. Here, for example, is the second instruction from the *Basic User Training* manual for a telemail system:

> Make sure that both the terminal and the coupler are in the REMOTE position.

The instruction seems perfectly clear and easy to understand. The only difficulty is that neither the terminal nor the coupler have anything that is labeled a REMOTE position, nor does either have any switch that could be turned to a REMOTE position. This is a case in which the manual by itself seems perfectly readable, but the manual is inadequate when you try to use it with the equipment for which it has been written.

To continue, instruction 7 in the same manual tells you that the system will ask you for your name and that you are supposed to reply by typing in your name. That instruction once again is simple and clear. What the manual does not tell you is that the software is so designed that it will not accept your name if you do what most people do, namely, leave a space between your first initial, or first name, and your last name. If you do leave a space, the system does not tell you what you did wrong. Considerations such as this lead to:

> RULE 14: Evaluate all the ingredients — hardware, software and manuals — as a unit. Remember that you are evaluating a computer system, not a product in isolation.

11.4 *Avoid biasing the evaluation*

One of the most difficult problems the evaluator has to contend with is biasing his findings, that is, inadvertently influencing the findings so that they do not really tell him what he thinks they tell him. Some important sources of bias are:

- The experimenter or evaluator
- The instructions to the test subjects
- The assignment of subjects to experimental conditions
- The way data are recorded.

An experimenter who starts out to "prove that his software package is better than that of his competitor" is already biased. That bias may be conveyed subtly, perhaps unconsciously, by the way the experimenter instructs the subjects, by suggesting that he prefers one software package to another, by inadvertent comments that he might make about one or the other software package, or even by what he identifies and counts as difficulties and errors.

One way of reducing bias from that source is to have the experiment run by a research assistant who tests subjects and collects data according to a set of rigidly defined rules and instructions, without knowing very much about the experiment or its purpose. Automating data collection is another effective way of reducing some kinds of experimenter bias.

Bias can also arise from the way subjects are assigned to software packages, or experimental conditions. The best rule here is to let chance make the decisions about which subjects get assigned to which conditions. Chance, in this case, is a table of random numbers.

To reduce bias from instructions, instructions should be standardized and, where possible, written as opposed to spoken. Or, if spoken instructions are used, they should preferably be tape-recorded so that every subject gets precisely the same instructions.

These considerations are summarized in:

RULE 15: Beware of biasing the evaluation. The experimenter should do the evaluation with the attitude that he is "finding out", not "proving". If possible, the actual tests should be run by a neutral research assistant according to a rigid set of rules and instructions. Automating data collection will remove some sources of bias. Subjects should be assigned at random to experimental conditions. Instructions should be written out and standardised.

11.5 *Pilot testing*

When all the plans have been made, facilities and equipment have been set up, and instructions have been prepared, the experimenter should always run some pilot tests before he begins to collect data in earnest. It seems to be a law of nature that unanticipated difficulties invariably turn up in a prospective evaluation, no matter how carefully it has been planned in advance (see, for example, Ledgard *et al.*, 1981, pp. 105-145). The best way to deal with those difficulties is to run a few pilot tests first. The time spent in pilot testing is almost without exception time well spent. So:

> RULE 16: Always pilot test an evaluation before you start collecting data in earnest.

12. Evaluations by experts

Any discussion of computer usability would not be complete without some mention of the evaluations of computers, computer hardware, and programs that appear daily in newspapers, journals and magazines. Figure 4 is an example of the summary of such an evaluation. Notice that it includes both documentation and ease of use. These summary evaluations are supported by qualitative statements in the text of the article. Examples are:

> Documentation earns a very good rating. The only thing keeping this from being excellent is the lack of quick-reference materials (Satchell, 1986, pp. 55-56)

and

> The Compaq Deskpro 386 is an absolute joy to use. It's quick. It's nimble. It feels right. The keyboard and display are comfortable to use; our chair caused more discomfort than these items. (Satchell, 1986, p. 56).

There are even whole books that rate computers (for example, Willis and Miller, 1984) and computer software (for example, Software Digest, Inc., 1984).

It's hard to judge the accuracy, validity, or usefulness of such evaluations. All clearly try to provide at least an ordinal scale of usability (see Figure 4). The difficulties with them, however, are several. To start with, we can't be sure of the standards or criteria being used by the evaluators. What are their standards or criteria, and are they constant? When reviewers test multiple products, as for example, Willis and Miller and Software Digest did, we have no information about the order in which products were tested. Subjects, or, in the cases we are considering here, evaluators, change during any experiment or study. They learn and their criteria and performance change as they learn. That's why human factors professionals control or randomize the order of presentation of trials and conditions according to carefully prepared schemes.

Another consideration is that we have to assume that many reviews are based on a sample of one — the reviewer. To be sure, Software Digest says that its reviews are based on "10 staff reviewers with varied levels of experience" but that is still scanty information. Nor do we know what tasks the reviewers engaged in to evaluate the

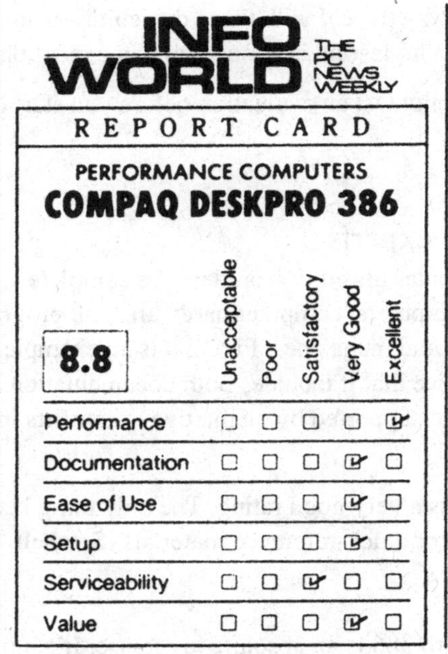

INFO WORLD THE PC NEWS WEEKLY

REPORT CARD

PERFORMANCE COMPUTERS

COMPAQ DESKPRO 386

8.8

	Unacceptable	Poor	Satisfactory	Very Good	Excellent
Performance	☐	☐	☐	☐	☑
Documentation	☐	☐	☐	☑	☐
Ease of Use	☐	☐	☐	☑	☐
Setup	☐	☐	☐	☑	☐
Serviceability	☐	☐	☑	☐	☐
Value	☐	☐	☐	☑	☐

Figure 4: Summary of the evaluation of a computer. (Satchell, 1986).

product, or how representative those tasks are of the kinds of things users might need to, or want to, do with the product.

Finally, these reviewers are almost certainly not representative of the user population, whatever that might be. A note appended to the article by Satchell, for example, says that he has been involved in computing since 1971 as a systems engineer and product programmer. That is clearly a level of sophistication very few people have. Anyone who has done empirical evaluations of usability has almost certainly discovered many instances in which things that seemed simple and obvious to experts were unexpectedly and uncommonly difficult for novices and ordinary users. Even if we were to assume that the 10 reviewers contributing to the Software Digest book were representative of users when they began, they were certainly not so by the time they had gone through 3 or 4 programs, and by the time they had evaluated all 30 programs, they must have been extremely knowledgeable.

The other side of the coin is that expert reviewers have presumably been able to see and to use a variety of computers, and, in so doing, have been able to build up some kind of internal standards and so recognize quickly things that make computers easy or difficult to use.

To sum up, evaluations by experts undoubtedly have some validity and they are probably most useful to prospective customers as rough and approximate indicators of usability. For designers and manufacturers, however, their chief drawback is that they are too late. They are made only after a computer has been designed, manufactured and put on the market. That is much too late to do any good for design, or to promote sales.

13. A final word

The success of any experiment on people depends on a combination of things. Knowledge of the subject matter area in which the experiment will be done is essential. So also is knowledge about technical matters of experimental design and the statistical analyses that are appropriate for each design. Experience helps greatly in suggesting what to look for and what pitfalls to avoid. Good judgement is indispensable in preparing instructions, designing tasks, and picking dependent variables. Perseverance is necessary to do a lot of work involved in setting up an evaluation, running it, and seeing it through to the end. Finally, we cannot overlook the importance of chance, or just plain good luck. To sum up in a nutshell everything I've said in this paper:

> It's hard to measure usability and do it well
> BUT IT CAN BE DONE.

REFERENCES

Abrahamsen, T.C. (1984) Design aspects of the Burroughs ET 1100 ergonomic workstation. *Behaviour and Information Technology*, **3**, 379-380.

Adelson, B., Littman, D., Ehrlich, K., Black, J. and Soloway, E. (1985) Novice-expert differences in software design. In B. Shackel (ed.) *Human-Computer Interaction — Interact '84*. Amsterdam: North-Holland. 473-478.

Al-Awar, J., Chapanis, A. and Ford, W.R. (1981) Tutorials for the first time computer user. *IEEE Transactions on Professional Communication*, **PC-24**, 30-37.

Allen, R.B. and Scerbo, M.W. (1983) Details of command-language keystrokes. *ACM Transactions on Office Information Systems*, **1**, 159-178.

Allen, T.J. (1977) *Managing the Flow of Technology: Technology Transfer and the Dissemination of Technological Information within the R & D Organisation.* Cambridge, MA: MIT Press.

Alty, J.L. (1984) The application of path algebras to interactive dialogue design. *Behaviour and Information Technology*, **13**(2), 119-132.

Alvey (1982) *A Programme for Advanced Information Technology: The Report of the Alvey Committee.* London: HMSO.

Anderson, J.R. (1983) *The Architecture of Cognition.* Cambridge, MA: Harvard University Press.

Anderson, N.S. and Olson, J.R. (1985) *Methods for Designing Software to Fit Human Needs and Capabilities.* Washington, DC: National Academy Press.

Anon. (1983) Getting rid of the bugs: angry systems users are taking their complaints to Court. *Time*, October 3, 68.

Asimow, M. (1962) *Introduction to Design.* Englewood Cliffs, NJ: Prentice-Hall.

Bailey, R.W. (1982) *Human Performance Engineering: A Guide for Systems Designers.* London: Prentice-Hall.

Bainbridge, L. (1979) Verbal reports as evidence of the process operator's knowledge. *International Journal of Man-Machine Studies*, **11**(4), 411-436.

Bainbridge, L. (1986) Asking questions and accessing knowledge. *Future Computing Systems*, **1**(2), 143-149.

Barnard, P.J. (1987) Cognitive resources and the learning of human-computer dialogs. In J.M. Carroll (ed.) *Interfacing Thought: Cognitive Aspects of Human-Computer Interaction.* Cambridge, MA: MIT Press. Ch. 6, 112-158.

Barnard, P.J. and Wright, P. (1975) Effects of "more than" and "less than" decisions on the use of numerical tables. *Journal of Applied Psychology*, **60**, 606-611.

Barnard, P.J., Hammond, N.V., Morton, J., Long, J. and Clark, I.A. (1981) Consistency and compatibility in human-computer dialogue. *International Journal of Man-Machine Studies*, **15**, 87-134.

Barnard, P.J., Wilson, M.W. and MacLean, A. (1986) The elicitation of system knowledge by picture probes. *Proceedings of CHI '86: Human Factors in Computer Systems.* New York: ACM. 235-240.

Barnard, P.J., Wilson, M.W. and MacLean, A. (1987) Approximate modelling of cognitive activity: towards an expert system design aid. *Proceedings of CHI + GI '87: Human Factors in Computing Systems.* New York: ACM. 21-26.

Beevis, D. and Slade, I.M. (1970) Ergonomics — costs and benefits. *Applied Ergonomics*, **1**(2), 79-84.

Bennett, J.L. (1972) The user interface in interactive systems. *Annual Review of Information Science and Technology*, **7**, 159-196.

Bennett, J.L. (1979) The commercial impact of usability in interactive systems. In B. Shackel (ed.) *Man-Computer Communication, Infotech State-of-the-Art Vol.* 2. Maidenhead: Infotech International. 1-17.

Bennett, J.L. (1984) Managing to meet usability requirements. In J.L. Bennett, D. Case, J. Sandelin and M. Smith (eds.) *Visual Display Terminals: Usability Issues and Health Concerns.* Englewood Cliffs, NJ: Prentice-Hall. 161-184.

Bennis, W.G., Benne, K.D. and Chin, R. (eds.)(1969) *The Planning of Change.* New York: Holt, Rinehart and Winston.

Benz, C., Grob, R. and Haubner, P. (1983) *Designing VDU Workplaces.* Rheinland: Verlag TUV.

Berns, T.A.R. (1984) The integration of ergonomics into design — a review. *Behaviour and Information Technology*, **3**, 277-283.

Bird, D.F. (1987) International standards in military communications. In C.J. Harris and I. White (eds.) *Advances in Command, Control and Communication Systems.* London: Peter Peregrinus Ltd.

Bjørn-Andersen, N. (1984) Are human factors human? In N. Bevan and D. Murray (eds.) *Man-Machine Integration.* Pergamon-Infotech State of the Art Report 13:l, Maidenhead: Pergamon-Infotech.

Bjørn-Andersen, N. (1985) Training for subjection or participation. In B. Shackel (ed.) *Human-Computer Interaction — Interact '84.* Amsterdam: North-Holland. 839-846 .

Black, J. and Sebrechts, M. (1981) Facilitating human-computer communication. *Applied Psycholinguistics*, **2**, 146-177.

Bobrow, D.G. and Stefik, M.J. (1983) The LOOPS Manual. Xerox Corporation, Palo Alto Research Center.

Boff, K.R. (1987) The Tower of Babel revisited: on cross-disciplinary chokepoints in systems design. In W.B. Rouse and K.R. Boff (eds.) *Systems Design: Behavioural Perspectives on Designers, Tools and Organisations*. New York: Elsevier.

Boff, K.R. and Lincoln, J.E. (1988) (eds.) *Engineering Data Compendium: Human Perception and Performance.* Human Engineering Division, Armstrong Aerospace Medical Research Laboratory, Wright-Patterson Air Force Base, Ohio, USA.

Boose, J.H. (1985) A knowledge acquisition program for expert systems based on personal construct psychology. *International Journal of Man-Machine Studies*, **20**(1), 21-43.

Boose, J.H. (1986) Rapid acquisition and combination of knowledge from multiple experts in the same domain. *Future Computing Systems*, **1**(2), 191-216.

Boose, J.H. and Bradshaw, J.M. (1987) Expertise transfer and complex problems: using AQUINAS as a knowledge acquisition workbench for knowledge-based systems. *International Journal of Man-Machine Studies*, **26**(1), 3-28.

Boyle, C.D.B. and Clarke, M.R.B. (1985) An intelligent mail filter. In P. Johnson and S. Cook (eds.) *People and Computers: Designing the Interface*. Cambridge: Cambridge University Press. 331-341.

Bradshaw, J.M. and Boose, J.H. (1986) NeoETS. Proceedings of North American Personal Construct Network Second Biennial Conference, University of Calgary, Department of Computer Science, 27-41.

Branscomb, L.M. (1983) The computer's debt to science. *IBM Perspectives in Computing*, **3**(3), 4-19.

British Standards Institution (1975) *Reclosable Pharmaceutical Containers Resistant to Opening by Children*. British Standard BS5321:1975.

British Standards Institution (1987) *Draft British Standard Recommendations for Ergonomic Requirements for Design and Use of Visual Display Terminals (VDTs) in Offices*. Ref: 87/40674-9, British Standards Institution, 2 Park Street, London.

Broadbent, D.E., Fitzgerald, P. and Broadbent, M.H.P (1986) Implicit and explicit knowledge in the control of complex systems. *British Journal of Psychology*, **77**, 33-50.

Brown, P.J. (1985) Making UNIX on-line documentation more effective. *Microprocessors and Microsystems*, **9**, 346-349.

Bruce, B., Rubin, A. and Starr, K. (1981) Why readability formulas fail. *IEEE Transactions on Professional Communication*, **PC-24**, 50-52.

Bullinger, H.-J., Fahnrich, K.-P. and Ziegler, J. (1987) Software-ergonomics: history, state-of-the-art and important trends. In G. Salvendy (ed.) *Cognitive Engineering in the Design of Human-Computer Interaction and Expert Systems, Vol. II*. Amsterdam: North-Holland. 307-316.

Burch, J.L. (1984) *Computers: The Non-Technological (Human) Factors*. Lawrence, KA: The Report Store.

Burchett, R. (1985) Data analysis and the LBMS Structured Development Method (LSDM). *Information Technology Training*, **3**(2), 45-50.

Butler, K.A. (1985) Connecting theory and practice: a case study of achieving usability goals. *Proceedings of ACM CHI '85 Conference*, 85-88.

Cakir, A., Hart, D.J. and Stewart, T.F.M. (1980) *Visual Display Terminals*. Chichester: Wiley.

Card, S.K., Moran, T.P. and Newell, A. (1980) The keystroke-level model for user performance time with interactive systems. *Communications of the ACM*, **23**(7), 396-410.

Card, S.K., Moran, T.P. and Newell, A. (1983) *The Psychology of Human-Computer Interaction*. Hillsdale, NJ: Lawrence Erlbaum Associates.

Carroll, J.M. (1984) Minimalist design for active users. In B. Shackel (ed.) *Human-Computer Interaction — Interact '84*. Amsterdam: North-Holland. 39-44.

Carroll, J.M. (1987) Preface to J.M. Carroll (ed) *Interfacing Thought: Cognitive Aspects of Human-Computer Interaction*. Cambridge, MA: MIT Press. ix-xv.

Carroll, J.M. and Rosson, M.B. (1987) Paradox of the active user. In J.M. Carroll (ed.) *Interfacing Thought: Cognitive Aspects of Human-Computer Interaction*. Cambridge, MA: MIT Press. 80-111.

Carroll, J.M. and Thomas, J.C. (1982) Metaphor and cognitive representation of computing systems*IEEE Transactions on Systems, Man and Cybernetics*, **SMC-12**(2), 107-116.

Carroll, J.M., Smith-Kerker, P.L., Ford, J.R. and Mazur-Rimets, S.A. (1987) The minimal manual. *Human-Computer Interaction*, **3**, 123-153.

Ceri, S. (1986) Requirements collection and analysis in information systems design. In H.-J. Kluger (ed.) *Information Processing '86*. Amsterdam: North-Holland. 205-214.

Chalfen, K. (1986) A knowledge system which integrates heterogeneous software for a design application. *Proceedings of JSST Conference on Recent Advances in Simulation of Complex Systems*. Tokyo: Japan Society for Simulation Technology. 300-304.

Chapanis, A. (1959) *Research Techniques in Human Engineering*. Baltimore: Johns Hopkins Press.

Chapanis, A. (1981) Evaluating ease of use. *Proceedings of IBM Software and Information Usability Symposium*. Poughkeepsie, NY, 15-18 September, 105-120.

Chapanis, A. (1988) "Words, words, words" revisited. *International Reviews of Ergonomics*, **2**, in press.

Charney, D.H. and Reder, L.M. (1986) Designing interactive tutorials for computer users. *Human-Computer Interaction*, **2**, 297-317.

Checkland, P. (1981) *Systems Thinking, Systems Practice*. Chichester: Wiley.

Cherns, A. (1976) The principles of socio-technical design. *Human Relations*, **29**(8), 783-792.

Cherry, L.L. and Macdonald, N.H. (1983) The Unix Writers' Workbench software. *Byte*, **8**, 241-248.

Chi, U.L. (1985) Formal specification of user interfaces: a comparison and evaluation of four axiomatic approaches. *IEEE Transactions on Software Engineering*, SE-11(8), 671-685.

Christensen, J.M. (1971) Human factors engineering considerations in system development. In W.T. Singleton, J.G. Fox and D. Whitfield (eds.) *Measurement of Man at Work*. London: Taylor & Francis. 177-187.

Clark, H.H. and Card, S.K. (1969) Role of semantics in remembering complex sentences. *Journal of Experimental Psychology*, **82**, 545-553.

Clark, H.H. and Clark, E.V. (1968) Semantic distinctions and memory for complex sentences. *Quarterly Journal of Experimental Psychology*, **20**, 56-72.

Clegg, J.M. (1985) Reducing customer difficulties in international dialling. *Behaviour and Information Technology*, **4**, 151-161.

Collins, H.M. (1985) *Changing Order: Replication and Induction in Scientific Practice.* London: Sage.

Cook, S. (1986) Modelling generic user interfaces with functional programs. In M.D. Harrison and A.F. Monk (eds.) *People and Computers: Designing for Usability.* Cambridge: Cambridge University Press. 369-385.

Corlett, E.N. (1988) Cost benefit analyses of ergonomic and work design changes. In D.W. Oborne (ed.) *International Review of Ergonomics*. London: Taylor & Francis.

Corlett, E.N. and Coates, J.B. (1976) Costs and benefits from human resources studies. *International Journal of Production Research*, **14**(1), 135-144.

Cranach, M. v., Kalbermatten, U., Indermuhle, K. and Gugler, B. (1980) *Zielgerichtetes Handeln.* Bern: Huber.

Curtis, B. (1980) Measurement and experimentation in software engineering. General Electric Information Systems Programs, Software Management Research, Arlington, VA, Report Number TR-80-388200-1.

Damodaran, L. (1984) Measures of user acceptability. In B.G. Pearce (ed.) *Health Hazards of VDTs?* Chichester: John Wiley.

Damodaran, L. (1986) User support. In N. Bjørn-Andersen, K.D. Eason and D. Robey (eds.) *Managing Computer Impact*. Norwood, NJ: Ablex. 77-88.

Damodaran, L., Simpson, A. and Wilson, P.A. (1980) *Designing Systems for People.* Manchester: National Computing Centre.

Davis, R. and Lenat, D.B. (1982) *Knowledge-Based Systems in Artificial Intelligence.* New York: McGraw-Hill.

Dede, C. (1986) A review and synthesis of recent research in intelligent computer-assisted instruction. *International Journal of Man-Machine Studies*, **24**, 329-353.

DHSS (1980) *A Strategy for Social Security Operations.* London: HMSO.

DHSS (1982) *Social Security Operational Strategy: A Framework for the Future*. London: HMSO.

DIN 66234 (1981) Deutsche Institut für Normung ev, Bildschirm Arbeitsplatz, Burghgrafenstraße 4-10, D1000 Berlin 30.

Dixon, N. (1981) *Preconscious Processing*. Chichester: Wiley.

Dixon, P. (1987) The processing of organisational and component step information in written directions. *Journal of Memory and Language*, **26**, 129-138.

Drenth, P.J.D. (1984) Personnel appraisal. In P.J.D. Drenth, H. Thierry, P.J. Willems and C.H. de Wolff (eds.) *Handbook of Work and Organizational Psychology Volume 1.* New York: Wiley. 197-234.

DTI (1986) *Profiting from Office Automation; Office Automation Pilots*. London: Department of Trade and Industry.

Duffy, T.M. (1981) Organising and utilising document design options. *Information Design Journal*, **2**, 256-266.

Duffy, T.M. (1985) Readability formulas: what's the use? In T.M. Duffy and R. Waller (eds.) *Designing Usable Texts*. Orlando, FL: Academic Press. 113-143.

Dumas, J.S., and Redish, J. (1986) Using plain English in designing the user interface. *Proceedings of the Human Factors Society 30th Annual Meeting (Vol. 2)*. Santa Monica, CA: The Human Factors Society. 1207-1211.

Duncker, K. (1935) *Zur Psychologie des Produktiven Denkens*. Berlin: Springer (3rd. reprint, 1974).

Dunlop, M.H.S. (1985) Clues to avoiding litigation, arbitration. *Management Information Systems Week*, **6**(13), March 27, 36.

Dzida, M., Langenheder, W., Cornelius, D. and Schardt, L.P. (1984) Auswirkungen des EDV-Einsatzes auf die Arbeitssituation und Moglichkeiten seiner arbeitsorientierten Gestaltung. St Augustin, GMD-Studien No. 82.

Eason, K.D. (1981) A task-tool analysis of the manager-computer interaction. In B. Shackel (ed.) *Man-Computer Interaction*. Amsterdam: Sijthoff and Noordhoff.

Eason, K.D. (1982) The process of introducing information technology. *Behaviour and Information Technology*, **1**, 197-213.

Eason, K.D. (1983) Methodological issues in the study of human factors in teleinformatic systems. *Behaviour and Information Technology*, **2**(4), 357-364.

Eason, K.D. (1983) User centred design for information technology systems. *Physics in Technology*, **14**, 210-224.

Eason, K.D. (1984) Towards the experimental study of usability. *Behaviour and Information Technology*, **3**, 133-144.

Eason, K.D. (1988) *Information Technology and Organisational Change*. London: Taylor & Francis.

Eason, K.D., Harker, S.D.P. and Poulson, D.F. (1986) Preliminary investigations into the use of human factors data in the design process. HUSAT Memo No. 377, Loughborough University of Technology.

Edmonds, E.A. (1981) Adaptive man-computer interfaces. In M.J. Coombs and J.L. Alty (eds.) *Computing Skills and the User Interface*. London: Academic Press. 389-426.

Edmonds, E.A. (1982) The man-computer interface – a note on concepts and design. *International Journal of Man-Machine Studies*, 16, 231-236.

Edwards, J.L. and Mason, J.A. (1987) Evaluating the intelligence in dialogue systems. *International Journal of Man-Machine Studies*, in press.

Egan, D.E. and Gomez, L.M. (1985) Assaying, isolating and accommodating individual differences in learning a complex skill. In R.F. Dillon (ed.) *Individual Differences in Cognition, Volume 2*. London: Academic Press. 174-217.

Eisenstadt, M., Hasemer, T. and Kriwaczek, F. (1985) An improved user interface for Prolog. In B. Shackel (ed.) *Human-Computer Interaction — Interact '84*. Amsterdam: North-Holland. 385-389.

Ellis, S.H. (1977) An investigation of telephone user training methods for a multiservice electronic PBX. *Proceedings of the Eighth International Symposium on Human Factors in Telecommunications*. Harlow, Essex: Standard Telecommunication Laboratories. 393-401.

Ericsson, K. and Simon, H. (1980) Verbal reports as data. *Psychological Review*, **87**, 215-251.

Faehnrich, K.P. and Ziegler, J.E. (1984) Workstations using direct manipulation as interaction mode – aspects of design, application and evaluation. In B. Shackel (ed.) *Human-Computer Interaction—Interact '84*. Amsterdam: North-Holland. 693-698.

Federal Register (1971) US Special Regulation under the Poison Prevention Packaging Act. Federal Register, 26 No. 225, Saturday 20 November, 1971.

Feigenbaum, E.A. (1980) Knowledge engineering: the applied side of artificial intelligence. Report STAN-CS-80-812, Stanford University, Department of Computer Science.

Felker, D.B., Pickering, F., Charrow, V.R., Holland, V.M. and Redish, J.C. (1981) *Guidelines for Document Designers*. Washington, DC: American Institutes for Research.

Fielden, G.B.R. (Chairman) (1963) *Engineering Design*. Report of a committee appointed by the Council for Scientific and Industrial Research. London: HMSO.

Fiske, E.B. (1984) Computers in the groves of academe. *The New York Times Magazine*, May 13, 40-41, 86-67, 90.

Fitts, P.M. (1954) The information capacity of the human motor system in controlling amplitude of motion. *Journal of Experimental Psychology*, **47**, 381-391.

Foley, J.D. and van Dam, A. (1973) *Fundamentals of Interactive Computer Graphics*. Reading, MA: Addison-Wesley.

Foley, J.D. and van Dam, A. (1982) *Fundamentals of Interactive Computer Graphics* (2nd Edition). Reading, MA: Addison-Wesley.

Foss, D.J., Smith-Kerker, P.L. and Rosson, M.B. (1987) On comprehending a computer manual: analysis of variables affecting performance. *International Journal of Man-Machine Studies*, **26**, 277-300.

Frase, L.T. (1981) Writing, text and the reader. In C.H. Frederiksen and J.F. Dominic (eds.) *Writing, Vol. 2: Process, Development and Communication*. Hillsdale, NJ: Lawrence Erlbaum Associates.

Frase, L.T., Keenan, S.A. and Dever, J.J. (1980) Human performance in computer aided writing and documentation. In P.A. Kolers, M.E. Wrolstad and H. Bouma (eds.) *Processing of Visible Language, 2*. New York: Plenum Press.

Frase, L.T., MacDonald, N.H. and Keenan, S.A. (1985) Intuitions, algorithms and a science of text design. In T.M. Duffy and R. Waller (eds.) *Designing Usable Texts*. Orlando, FL: Academic Press. 97-112.

Freeman, P. (1983) Fundamentals of design. In P. Freeman and A.I. Wasserman (eds.) *Software Design Techniques*. Los Alamitos, CA: IEEE Computer Society Press.

Frese, E. (1975). Koordination. In E. Grochla and W. Wittmann (eds.) *Handwörterbuch der Betriebswirtschaft*. Stuttgart: Poeschel. 2263-2273.

Freud, S. (1914) *Psychopathology of Everyday Life*. London: Benn.

Fry, J., Hughes, S. and Mansfield, R. (1986) *1987 Computer Buying Guide*. Pasadena, CA: Mansfield and Associates.

Furnas, G.W., Gomez, L.M., Landauer, T.K. and Dumais, S.M. (1982) Statistical semantics: how can a computer use what people name things to guess what things people mean when they name things? *Proceedings of Human Factors in Computer Systems*. New York: ACM. 251-253.

Furnas, G.W., Landauer, T.K., Gomez, L.M. and Dumais, S.T. (1983) Statistical semantics: analysis of the potential performance of key-word information systems, *The Bell System Technical Journal*, 1753-1806.

Gablenz-Kolakovic, S., Krogoll, T., Oesterreich, R. and Volpert, W. (1981) Subjektive oder objektive Arbeitsanalyse? *Zeitschrift fur Arbeitswissenschaft*, **4**, 217-220.

Gaines, B.R. (1976) Behaviour/structure transformations under uncertainty. *International Journal of Man-Machine Studies*, **8**(3), 337-365.

Gaines, B.R. (1977) System identification, approximation and complexity. *International Journal of General Systems*, **3**, 145-174.

Gaines, B.R. (1984) Perspectives on fifth generation computing. *Oxford Surveys in Information Technology*, **1**, 1-53.

Gaines, B.R. (1985) From ergonomics to the fifth generation: 30 years of human-computer interaction studies. In B. Shackel (ed.) *Human-Computer Interaction — Interact '84*. Amsterdam: North-Holland. 1-5.

Gaines, B.R. (1986a) Sixth generation computing: a conspectus of the Japanese proposals. *ACM SIGART Newsletter*, **95**, 39-44.

Gaines, B.R. (1986b) Socio-economic foundations of knowledge science. *Proceedings of International Conference on Systems, Man and Cybernetics*, Volume IEEE 86CH2364-8, 1035-1039.

Gaines, B.R. (1986c) Foundations of knowledge engineering. In M.A. Bramer (ed.) *Research and Development in Expert Systems III*. Cambridge: Cambridge University Press. 13-24.

Gaines, B.R. (1987a) An overview of knowledge acquisition and transfer. *International Journal of Man-Machine Studies*, **26**(4), 453-472.

Gaines, B.R. (1987b) A systemic analysis of human-computer interaction in complex systems. *International Journal of Man-Machine Studies*, in press.

Gaines, B.R. and Andreae, J.H. (1966) A learning machine in the context of the general control problem. In G.D.S Mclellan (ed.) *Proceedings of the Third Congress of the International Federation for Automatic Control*. London: Institute of Mechanical Engineers. 14B.1-14B.8.

Gaines, B.R. and Shaw, M.L.G. (1984) Principles of dialogue engineering. Paper presented to NATO Workshop on Research Needs in User-Computer Interaction. Loughborough University, September.

Gaines, B.R. and Shaw, M.L.G. (1984) *The Art of Computer Conversation: A New Medium for Communication*. Englewood Cliffs, NJ: Prentice-Hall.

Gaines, B.R. and Shaw, M.L.G. (1985) From fuzzy sets to expert systems. *Information Science*, **36**(1-2), 5-16.

Gaines, B.R. and Shaw, M.L.G. (1986a) Foundations of dialog engineering: the development of human-computer interaction, part II. *International Journal of Man-Machine Studies*, **24**(2), 101-123.

Gaines, B.R. and Shaw, M.L.G. (1986b) Knowledge engineering techniques. *Proceedings of AUTOFACT '86*. Detroit: Society of Manufacturing Engineers. 8-79–8-96.

Gaines, B.R. and Shaw, M.L.G. (1986c) Induction of inference rules for expert systems. *Fuzzy Sets and Systems*, **18**(3), 315-328.

Galitz, W.O. (1980) *Human Factors in Office Automation.* Atlanta, GA: Life Office Management Association.

Galitz, W.O. (1981) *Handbook of Screen Format Design.* Wellesley, MA: Q.E.D. Information Sciences.

Galitz, W.O. (1985) *Handbook of Screen Format Design.* (2nd Edition) Wellesley Hills, MA: QED Information Sciences.

Gardner, A. and McKenzie, J. (1988) Human Factors Guidelines for the Design of Computer-Based Systems (Parts 1-6). Issue 1, HUSAT Research Centre, Loughborough.

Gediga, G., Greif, S., Monecke, U. and Hamborg, K.-C. (1989) Aufgaben- und Tätigkeitsanalysen als Grundlage der Softwaregestaltung. In S. Maaß and H. Oberquelle (eds.) *Software-Ergonomie '89. Aufgabenorientierte Systemgestaltung und Funktionalität.* Gemeinsame Fachtagung des German Chapter der ACM und der Gesellschaft für Information in Hamburg. Stuttgart: Teubner. 80-88.

Gevarter, W.B. (1983) Expert systems: limited but powerful. *IEEE Spectrum*, **18**, 39-45.

Gilb, T. (1988) *Principles of Software Engineering Management.* Wokingham: Addison-Wesley.

Glushko, R.J. and Bianchi, M.H. (1982) On-line documentation: mechanizing development delivery and use. *The Bell System Technical Journal*, **61**, 1313-1323.

Goguen, J.A. and Meseguer, J. (1983) Programming with parametrized abstract objects in OBJ. In D. Ferrari, M. Bolognani and J.A. Goguen (eds.) *Theory and Practice of Software Technology: Proceedings of the First International Seminar on Software Engineering, Capri, Italy, 1980.* Amsterdam: North-Holland. 163-193.

Goldberg, A. (1983) *Smalltalk-80: The Interactive Programming Environment.* Reading, MA: Addison-Wesley.

Gomez, L.M. and Lochbaum, C.C. (1984) People can retrieve more objects with enriched keyword vocabularies. But is there a performance cost? In B. Shackel (ed.) *Human-Computer Interaction — Interact '84.* Amsterdam: North-Holland. 257-261.

Gottschalk, K.D. (1986) The system usability process for network management products. *IBM Systems Journal*, **25**, 83-91.

Gottschall, K., Mickler, O. and Neubert, J. (1985) *Computerunterstützte Verwaltung.* Frankfurt/M: Campus.

Gould, J.D. and Lewis, C. (1983) Designing for usability – key principles and what designers think. *Proceedings of ACM CHI '83 Conference*, 50-53.

Gould, J.D., Alfaro, L., Barnes, V., Finn, R., Grischkowski, N. and Minuto, A. (1987) Reading is slower from CRT displays than from paper: attempts to isolate a single variable explanation. *Human Factors*, **29**, 269-299.

Gower, J.C. and Eason, K.D. (1985) Introduction of new technology: a case study. *Proceedings of the Ergonomics Society Annual Conference*, Exeter.

Grandjean, E. (1987) *Ergonomics of Computerised Offices.* London: Taylor & Francis.

Grandjean, E. (1984)(ed.) *Ergonomics and Health in Modern Offices.* London: Taylor & Francis.

Grandjean, E. and Vigliani, E. (1980)(eds.) *Ergonomic Aspects of Visual Display Terminals.* London: Taylor & Francis.

Green, M. (1985) Design notations and user interface management systems. In G.E. Pfaff (ed.) *User Interface Management Systems*. Berlin: Springer.

Green, M. (1986) Survey of three dialogue models. *ACM Transactions on Graphics*, 5(3), 244-275.

Green, T.R.G., Schiele, F. and Payne, S.J. (1988) Formalisable models of user knowledge in human-computer interaction. In G. van der Veer, T.R.G. Green, J.-M. Hoc and D. Murray (eds.) *Working With Computers: Theory Versus Outcome.* London: Academic Press. 3–41.

Greenwald, J. (1984) How does this %@!/ thing work? *Time*, June 18, 64.

Greif, S. (1978) Entwicklung einer systemtheoretischen Definition des Begriffs der Organisation. *Zeitschrift für Sozialpsychologie*, **9**, 206-221.

Greif, S. (1983) *Konzepte der Organisationspsychologie*. Bern: Huber.

Greif, S. (1989) Exploratorisches Lernen durch Fehler und qualifikationsorientiertes Software-Design. In S. Maaß and H. Oberquelle (eds.) *Software-Ergonomie '89. Aufgabenorientierte Systemgestaltung und Funktionalität.* Gemeinsame Fachtagung des German Chapter der ACM und der Gesellschaft für Information in Hamburg. Stuttgart: Teubner. 204-212.

Greif, S. (1990) The role of German work psychology in the design of artifacts. In J. Carroll (ed.) *Designing Interaction.* Cambridge: Cambridge University Press.

Greif, S. and Gediga, G. (1987) A critique of one-best-way models in human-computer interaction. In M. Frese, E. Ulich and W. Dzida (eds.) *Psychological Issues of Human-Computer Interaction in the Work Place*. Amsterdam: North-Holland. 357-377.

Greif, S., Holling, H. and Nicholson, N. (1989) (eds.) *Arbeits- und Organisationspsychologie. Ein internationales Handbuch in Schlüsselbegriffen.* München: Psychologie Verlags Union.

Greif, S., Monecke, U. and Tolksdorf, M. (1986) Heterarchische Aufgabenanalyse. Paper presented at the 35th Congress of the West-German Psychological Society, Heidelberg, 28 September-2 October.

Grudin, J.T. and MacLean, A. (1984) Adapting a psychophysical method to measure performance and preference tradeoffs in human-computer interaction. In B. Shackel (ed.) (1985) *Human-Computer Interaction – Interact '84*. Amsterdam: North-Holland. 737-741.

Grudin, J.T. and Barnard, P.J. (1984) The cognitive demands of learning command names for text editing. *Human Factors,* **26**, 407-422.

Guest, S.P. (1982) The use of software tools for dialogue design. *International Journal of Man-Machine Studies*, **16**, 263-285.

Gupta, M.M., Kandel, A., Bandler, W. and Kiszka, J.B. (eds.) (1985) *Approximate Reasoning in Expert Systems*. Amsterdam: North-Holland. 271-281.

Haas, C. and Hayes, J.R. (1985) Reading on the computer: a comparison of standard and advanced computer display and hard copy. Technical Report, 7. Pittsburgh, PA: Communications Design Center, Carnegie-Mellon University.

Hacker, W. (1985) Activity: a fruitful concept in industrial psychology. In M. Frese and J. Sabini (eds.) *Goal Directed Behavior: The Concept of Action in Psychology.* Hillsdale, NJ: Lawrence Erlbaum Associates.

Halasz, F.G. and Moran, T.P. (1982) Analogy considered harmful. *Proceedings of the Conference on Human Factors in Computing Systems*. New York: ACM. 383-386.

Halasz, F.G. and Moran, T.P. (1983) Mental models and problem solving in using a calculator. *Proceedings of CHI '83: Human Factors in Computer Systems*. New York: ACM. 212-216.

Hamborg, K.-C. (1989) Task analysis for software design. Unpublished dissertation, University of Osnabrück.

Hammond, N.V. and Barnard, P.J. (1984) Dialogue design: characteristics of user knowledge. In A. Monk (ed.) *Fundamentals of Human-Computer Interaction*. London: Academic Press. Ch. 9, 127-164.

Hammond, N.V., Barnard, P.J., Morton, J., Long, J. and Clark, I.A. (1987) Characterising user performance in command driven dialogue. *Behaviour and Information Technology*, **6**, 159-205.

Hammond, N.V., Christie, B. and Marshall, C. (1987) The rôle of cognitive psychology in user-interface design. In B. Christie and M. Gardiner (eds.) *Applying Cognitive Psychology to User Interface Design*. Chichester: Wiley. Ch. 2, 13-53.

Hammond, N.V., Hinton, G., Barnard, P.J., MacLean, A., Long, J. and Whitefield, A. (1984) Evaluating the interface of a document processor: a comparison of expert judgement and user observation. In B. Shackel (ed.) *Human-Computer Interaction — Interact '84*. Amsterdam: North-Holland. 725-729.

Hammond, N.V., Jorgensen, A.K., MacLean, A., Barnard, P.J. and Long, J. (1983) Design practice and interface usability: evidence from interviews with designers. *Proceedings of CHI '83: Human Factors in Computer Systems*. New York: ACM. 40-44.

Hammond, N.V., Long, J.B., Clark, I.A., Barnard, P.J. and Morton, J. (1980) Documenting human-computer mismatch in interactive systems. *Proceedings of the Ninth International Symposium on Human Factors in Telecommunications*, Red Bank, NJ, 17-24.

Hannigan, S. and Kerswell, B. (1986) Towards user friendly terminals. *Proceedings of the ISSLS Conference*, Japan.

Hansen, W.J. (1971) User engineering principles for interactive systems. *Proceedings of the Fall Joint Computer Conference*. New Jersey: AFIPS Press. 523-532.

Harker, S.D.P. (1986) The rôle of user prototyping in the system design process. *Proceedings of the International Scientific Conference on Work with Display Units*, Stockholm, 808-811.

Harker, S.D.P. and Eason, K.D. (1980) Task analysis in theory and practice. HUSAT Memo № 206, Loughborough University of Technology.

Harker, S.D.P. and Eason, K.D. (1985) Representing the user in the design process. *Design Studies*, **5**, 79-85.

Harker, S.D.P. and Eason, K.D. (1990) Human Factors in Systems Design. Final Report on Alvey/SERC Project № MMI 080, HUSAT Research Institute, Loughborough University of Technology.

Harris, D.H. (1984) Human factors success stories. *Proceedings of the Human Factors Society 28th Annual Meeting (Vol. 1)*. Santa Monica, CA: The Human Factors Society. 1-5.

Hartley, J. (1981) Eighty ways of improving instructional text. *IEEE Transactions on Professional Communication*, **PC-24**, 17-27.

Hartley, J. (1984) The rôle of colleagues and text-editing programs in improving text. *IEEE Transactions on Professional Communication*, **PC-27**, 42-44.

Hartley, J. (1985) *Designing Instructional Text.* (Revised edition) London: Kogan Page.

Hawkins, D. (1983) An analysis of expert thinking. *International Journal of Man-Machine Studies*, **18**(1), 1-47.

Hayes, J.R. (1986) Is this text clear? How knowledge makes it difficult to judge. Paper presented at the convention of the American Educational Research Association (AERA), San Francisco.

Hayes-Roth, B. (1985) A blackboard architecture for control. *Artificial Intelligence*, **26**(3), 251-321.

Hayes-Roth, F. (1984) The industrialization of knowledge engineering. In W. Reitman (ed.) *Artificial Intelligence Applications for Business*. Norwood, NJ: Ablex. 159-177.

Hayes-Roth, F., Waterman, D.A. and Lenat, D.B. (eds.) (1983) *Building Expert Systems*. Reading, MA: Addison-Wesley.

Heckhausen, H. (1980) *Motivation und Handeln*. Berlin: Springer.

Hedberg, B. (1975) Computer systems to support industrial democracy. In E. Mumford and H. Sackman (eds.) *Human Choice and Computers*. Amsterdam: North-Holland.

Helander, M. (1988) (ed.) *Handbook of Human-Computer Interaction*. Amsterdam: Elsevier.

Helmreich, R. (1984) Human aspects of office systems — user acceptance research results. In B. Shackel (ed.) (1985) *Human-Computer Interaction — Interact '84*. Amsterdam: North-Holland. 715-718.

Hill, R.D. (1986) Supporting concurrency, communication and synchronization in human-computer interaction — the Sassafras UIMS. *ACM Transactions on Graphics*, **5**(3), 179-210.

Hirsch, R.S. (1981) Procedures of the Human Factors Center at San Jose. *IBM Systems Journal*, **20**(2), 123-171.

Hirschheim, R.A. (1985) *Office Automation: A Social and Organisational Perspective*. Chichester: Wiley.

Hirschheim, R.A., Land, F.F. and Smithson, S. (1985) Implementing computer-based information systems in organisations: issues and strategies. In B. Shackel (ed.) *Human-Computer Interaction — Interact '84*. Amsterdam: North-Holland. 855-862.

Holling, H. (1987) Systemresponsezeiten. Osnabrück, unpublished Habilitation manuscript.

Holsapple, C.W. and Whinston, A.B. (1987) *Business Expert Systems*. Homewood, IL: Irwin.

Hoppe, H.U. (1987) A grammar-based approach to unifying task-oriented and system-oriented interface descriptions. Workshop on Mental Models and Human Computer Interaction, Schaerding, Austria, June.

Hoppe, H.U., Tauber, M. and Ziegler, J.E.(1986) A survey of models and formal description methods in HCI with example applications. ESPRIT Project 385 HUFIT, Technical Report Fraunhofer Institute IAO, Stuttgart.

Hughes, S. (1986) Question classification in rule-based systems. In M.A. Bramer (ed.) *Research and Development in Expert Systems III*. Cambridge: Cambridge University Press. 123-131.

ISO (1988) *ISO/DIS 9421/2: Ergonomic Principles Applied to the Design of Office Tasks in Visual Information Processing Systems*. Draft International Standard, International Organization for Standardization, Geneva, Switzerland.

ISO: 7498 (1984) *Information Processing Systems: Open Systems Interconnection (OSI) – Basic Reference Model.* Geneva, Switzerland: International Organization for Standardization.

Jackson, M. (1983) *System Development.* Englewood Cliffs, NJ: Prentice-Hall.

Jacobs, R.J.K. (1983) Using formal specifications in the design of a human-computer interface. *Communications of the ACM*, 26(4), 259-264.

Jereb, B. (1986) Plain English on the plant floor. *Visible Language*, **20**, 219-225.

John, B.E. and Newell, A. (1987) Predicting the time to recall computer command abbreviations. *Proceedings of CHI + GI '87: Human Factors in Computing Systems.* New York: ACM. 33-39.

Johnson, P. (1985) Towards a task model of messaging. In P. Johnson and S. Cook (eds.) *People and Computers: Designing the Interface*. Cambridge: Cambridge University Press. 46-62.

Johnson, P., Diaper, D. and Long, J. (1984) Tasks, skills and knowledge: task analysis for knowledge description. In B. Shackel (ed.) *Human-Computer Interaction — Interact '84*. Amsterdam: North-Holland. 499-503.

Kahn, G., Nowlan, S. and McDermott, J. (1985) MORE: an intelligent knowledge acquisition tool. *Proceedings of the Ninth International Joint Conference on Artificial Intelligence*. California: Morgan Kaufmann. 581-584.

Kariya, S. (1984) Seeking a perfect chair. *PC Magazine*, **3**, 139-148.

Karlin, J.E. (1977) The changing and expanding role of human factors in telecommunications engineering at Bell Laboratories. *Proceedings of the Eighth International Symposium on Human Factors in Telecommunications*. Harlow, Essex: Standard Telecommunication Laboratories. 329-333.

Katz, D. and Kahn, R.L. (1978) *The Social Psychology of Organizations*. (Second Edition) New York: Wiley.

Keister, R.S. and Gallaway, G.R. (1983) Making a software user friendly: an assessment of data entry performance. *Proceedings of the Human Factors Society 27th Annual Meeting*. Santa Monica, CA: The Human Factors Society. 1031-1034.

Kelley, D.F. (1984) Skylink self-service ticketing terminal: design and ergonomics. *Behaviour and Information Technology*, **3**, 391-397.

Kelly, G.A. (1955) *The Psychology of Personal Constructs.* New York: Norton.

Keppel, G. (1973) *Design and Analysis: A Researcher's Handbook*. Englewood Cliffs, NJ: Prentice-Hall.

Kern, H. and Schumann, M. (1984) *Das Ende der Arbeitsteilung?* Munchen: Beck.

Kidd, A.L. (1985) What do users ask? — some thoughts on diagnostic advice. In M. Merry (ed.) *Expert Systems 85*. Cambridge: Cambridge University Press. 9-19.

Kidd, A.L. and Cooper, M.B. (1985) Man-machine interface issues in the construction and use of expert systems. *International Journal of Man-Machine Studies*, **22**(1), 91-102.

Kieras, D.E. (1985) An augmented computerized readability editing system: final report. Technical Report 22, University of Michigan.

Kieras, D.E. and Bovair, S. (1984) The role of a mental model in learning to operate a device. *Cognitive Science*, **8**, 255-273.

Kieras, D.E. and Polson, P. (1985) An approach to the formal analysis of user complexity. *International Journal of Man-Machine Studies*, 22, 365-394.

Kieras, D.E. and Polson, P.G. (1984) A generalized transition network representation of interactive systems. In A. Janda (ed.) *CHI '83 Human Factors in Computer Systems*. Proceedings of CHI '83 Conference, Boston. Amsterdam: North-Holland.

Kieras, D.E. and Polson, P.G. (1985) An approach to formal analysis of user complexity. *International Journal of Man-Machine Studies*, **22**, 365-394.

Kieser, A. and Kubicek, H. (1976) *Organisation*. Berlin: Gruyter.

Kiger, J.I. (1984) The depth/breadth trade-off in the design of menu driven user interfaces. *International Journal of Man-Machine Studies*, **20**, 201-213.

Kincaid, J.P. and Schalow, S. (1985) The computer readability editing system. *Proceedings of Human Factors Society 29th Annual Meeting*. Santa Monica, CA: The Human Factors Society. 489-493.

Kirk, R.E. (1968) *Experimental Design: Procedures for the Behavioral Sciences*. Belmont, CA: Brooks/Cole.

Kitto, C.M. and Boose, J.H. (1987) Heuristics for expertise transfer: the automatic management of complex knowledge acquisition dialogs. *International Journal of Man-Machine Studies*, **26**(2), 183-202.

Klare, G. (1979) Writing to inform: making it readable. *Information Design Journal*, **1**, 98-105.

Klein, L. (1986) Institutionalising Human Factors (DIADEM Management Binder). London: Department of Health and Social Security

Kloster, G.V. and Tischer, K. (1985) Man machine interface design process. In B. Shackel (ed.) *Human-Computer Interaction – Interact '84*. Amsterdam: North-Holland. 889-894.

Knuth, D.E. (1979) *TEX and METAFONT: New Directions in Typesetting*. Bedford, MA: Digital Press.

Kubicek, H. and Welter, G. (1985) *Messung der Organisationsstruktur*. Stuttgart: Enke.

Kupka, I., Maass, S. and Oberquelle, H. (1981) Kommunikation – Ein Grundbegriff für die Informatik. IFI-HH-M-91/81, Fachbereich Informatik, Universitaet Hamburg.

Landauer, T.K. (1985) Psychological research as a mother of invention. *Proceedings of CHI '85: Human Factors in Computer Systems*. New York: ACM. 44.

Landauer, T.K. (1987) Relations between cognitive psychology and computer systems design. In J.M. Carroll (ed.) *Interfacing Thought: Cognitive Aspects of Human-Computer Interaction*. Cambridge, MA: MIT Press. Ch. 1, 1-25.

Landauer, T.K. and Nachbar, D.W. (1985) Selection from alphabetic and numeric menu trees using a touch screen: depth, breadth and width. *Proceedings of CHI '85: Human Factors in Computing Systems*. New York: ACM. 73-77.

Landauer, T.K., Galotti, K.M. and Hartwell, S. (1983) Natural command names and initial learning: a study of text editing terms. *Communications of the ACM*, 26, 495-503.

Lansdale, M.W. (1985) Beyond dialogue design guidelines: the rôle of mental models. In B. Christie (ed.) *Human Factors of Information Technology in the Office*. Chichester: Wiley. 242-270.

Ledgard, H., Singer, A. and Whiteside, J. (1981) *Directions in Human Factors for Interactive Systems*. New York: Springer-Verlag.

Ledgard, H., Whiteside, J., Singer, A. and Seymour, W. (1980) The natural language of interactive systems. *Communications of the ACM*, **23**, 556-563.

Lehnert, W.G. (1977) *The Process of Question Answering*. Hillsdale, NJ: Lawrence Erlbaum Associates.

Lenat, D., Prakash, M. and Shepherd, M. (1986) CYC: using common sense knowledge to overcome brittleness and knowledge acquisition bottlenecks. *AI Magazine*, **6**(4), 65-85.

Licklider, J.C.R. (1960) Man-computer symbiosis. *IRE Transactions on Human Factors in Electronics*, **HFE-1**, 4-11.

Lucas, H. (1974) *Toward Creative Systems Design*. New York: Columbia University Press.

Macdonald-Ross, M. and Waller, R.H.W. (1976) The transformer. *Penrose Annual*, **69**, 141-152.

Mack, R.L., Lewis, C.H. and Carroll, J.M. (1983) Learning to use word processors: problems and prospects. *ACM Transactions on Office Information Systems*, **1**, 254-271.

MacLean, A., Barnard, P.J. and Wilson, M.W. (1985) Evaluating the human interface of a data entry system: user choice and performance measures yield different trade-off functions. In P. Johnson and S. Cook (eds.) *People and Computers: Designing the Interface*. Cambridge: Cambridge University Press. 172-185.

Maguire, M.C. (1982) An evaluation of published recommendations on the design of man-computer dialogues. *International Journal of Man-Machine Studies*, **16**(3), 237-262.

Malone, R.B. (1986) The centered high-mounted brake light: a human factors success story. *Human Factors Society Bulletin*, **29**(10), 1-3.

Marcus, S., McDermott, J. and Wang, T. (1985) Knowledge acquisition for constructive systems. *Proceedings of the Ninth International Joint Conference on Artificial Intelligence*. California: Morgan Kaufmann. 637-639.

Margerison, C.J. (1978) The adviser's rôle in organisational change. In P.B. Warr (ed.) *Psychology at Work* (2nd edition.) Harmondsworth: Penguin.

Martin, J. (1973) *Design of Man-Computer Dialogues*. Englewood Cliffs, NJ: Prentice-Hall.

McCormick, E.J. (1976, 1982) *Human Factors in Engineering and Design*. New York: McGraw Hill.

McCosh, A. (1984) Factors common to the successful implementation of twelve decision support systems and how they differ from three failures. *Systems, Objectives, Solutions*, **4**,17-18.

Meisner, D. (1982) The rôle of human factors in system development. *Applied Ergonomics*, **13**(2), 119-124.

Meister, D. and Farr, D.E. (1967) The utilisation of human factors information by designers. *Human Factors*, **9**(1), 71-77.

Meister, D. and Rabideau, G.F. (1965) *Human Factors Evaluation in System Development*. New York: Wiley.

Michalski, R.S. and Chilausky, R.L. (1980) Knowledge acquisition by encoding expert rules versus computer induction from examples — a case study involving soyabean pathology. *International Journal of Man-Machine Studies*, **12**, 63-87.

Michalski, R.S. and Winston, P.H. (1986) Variable precision logic. *Artificial Intelligence*, **29**(2), 121-146.

Michie, D. (ed.) (1979) *Expert Systems in the Micro Electronic Age*. Edinburgh: Edinburgh University Press.

Miller, D.C. and Pew, R.W. (1981) Exploiting user involvement in interactive system development. *Proceedings of Human Factors Society 25th Annual Conference*, 401-405.

Miller, D.P. (1981) The depth/breadth trade-off in hierarchical computer menus. *Proceedings of the Human Factors Society*, 296-300.

Miller, G.A., Galanter, E. and Pribram, K.H. (1960) *Plans and the Structure of Behavior*. New York: Holt, Rinehart and Winston.

Miller, L.A. (1986) Computers for composition: a stage model approach to helping. *Visible Language*, **20**, 188-218.

Miller, R.B. (1962) Task description and analysis. In R.M. Gagné (ed.) *Psychological Principles in System Development*. New York: Holt, Rinehart and Winston. 187-230.

Miller, R.B. (1971) Human ease of use criteria and their tradeoffs. IBM Report TR 00.2185, 12 April. Poughkeepsie, NY: IBM Corporation.

Minsky, M. (1975) A framework for representing knowledge. In P.H. Winston (ed.) *The Psychology of Computer Vision*. New York: McGraw-Hill. 211-277.

Mischelevich, D.J. and Van Slyke, D. (1980) Applications development system: the software architecture of the IBM Health Care Support/DL/I-Patient Care System. *IBM Systems Journal*, **19**, 478-504.

Mitroff, I.I. (1980) Management myth information systems revisited: a strategic approach to asking nasty questions about systems design. In N. Bjørn-Andersen (ed.) *The Human Side of Information Processing*. Amsterdam: North-Holland.

Monecke, U. (1987). Heterarchische Aufgabenanalyse. Eine erste überprufung. Osnabrück, unpublished Diplomarbeit.

Moran, T.P. (1981) The Command Language Grammar: a representation for the user interface of interactive computer systems. *International Journal of Man-Machine Studies*, **15**, 3-50.

Moran, T.P. (1983) Getting into a system: external-internal task mapping analysis. *Proceedings of CHI '83: Human Factors in Computing Systems*. New York: ACM. 45-49.

Morgan, C., Gregg, W. and Lemmons, P. (1983) An interview with Wayne Rosing, Bruce Daniels and Larry Tesler. *Byte*, **8**(2), 90-114.

Morton, J., Barnard, P.J., Hammond, N.V. and Long, J. (1979) Interacting with the computer: a framework. In E.J. Boutmy and A. Danthine (eds.) *Teleinformatics '79*. Amsterdam: North-Holland. 201-208.

Mosier, J.N. and Smith, S.L. (1985) Application of guidelines for designing user interface software. Proceedings of the Human Factors Society 29th Annual Meeting (vol. 2). Santa Monica, CA: The Human Factors Society. 946-949.

Mosier, J.N. and Smith, S.L. (1986) Applications of guidelines for designing user interface software. *Behaviour and Information Technology*, **5**, 39-46.

Mosteller, W. and Rooney, R. (1982) SY-0141A JCL error study (Unnumbered report). Vienna, VA.: Boeing Computer Services Company.

Moto-Oka, T. (1982)(ed.) *Fifth Generation Computer Systems*. Amsterdam: North-Holland.

Mowshowitz, A. (1976) *The Conquest of Will: Information Processing in Human Affairs*. Reading, MA: Addison-Wesley.

Mumford, E. (1981) *Values, Technology and Work*. Alphen aan den Rijn: Martinus Nijhoff.

Mumford, E. (1983a) *Designing Human Systems*. Manchester: Manchester Business School.

Mumford, E. (1983b) *Designing Participatively*. Manchester: Manchester Business School.

Mumford, E. (1986) *Using Computers for Business Success*. Manchester: Manchester Business School.

Mumford, E. and Weir, M. (1979) *Computer Systems in Work Design — The ETHICS Method*. London: Associated Business Press.

Myers, J.L. (1979) *Fundamentals of Experimental Design*. (3rd ed.) Boston: Allyn and Bacon.

National Electronics Council (1983) *Human Factors in Information Technology*. Chichester: John Wiley.

NCC (1985) *STARTS Guide*. Manchester: National Computing Centre.

Neal, A.S. and Simon, R.M. (1983) Playback: a method for evaluating the usability of software and its documentation. *Proceedings of ACM CHI '83 Conference*, 78-82.

Neal, A.S. and Simon, R.M. (1984) Playback: A method for evaluating the usability of software and its documentation. *IBM Systems Journal*, **23**, 82-96.

Neisser, U. (1967) *Cognitive Psychology*. New York: Appleton-Century-Crofts.

Newell, A. (1973) Production systems – models of control structure. In W.G. Chase (ed.) *Visual Information Processing*. New York: Academic Press.

Newell, A. and Card, S.K. (1985) The prospects for psychological science in human-computer interaction. *Human-Computer Interaction*, **1**(3), 209-242.

Newell, A. and Simon, H.A. (1972) *Human Problem Solving*. Englewood Cliffs, NJ: Prentice-Hall.

Newman, W.M. and Mott, T. (1982) Officetalk: an experimental integrated office system. In P. Degano and E. Sandewall (eds.) *Integrated Interactive Computer Systems: Proceedings of European Conference ECICS '82*. Amsterdam: North-Holland.

Newman, W.M. and Sproull, R.F. (1979) *Principles of Interactive Computer Graphics*, Second Edition. New York: McGraw-Hill.

Nicholls, J.E. (1979) Programming the end user. In B. Shackel (ed.) *Man-Computer Communication. Infotech State of the Art Report Vol. 2*. Maidenhead: Infotech International.

Nickerson, R.S. (1969) Man-computer interaction: a challenge for human factors research. *Ergonomics*, **12**(4), 501-517.

Nielsen, J. (1984) How readers annotate textbooks and manuals. DAIMI PB, 182. Aarhus, Denmark: Computer Science Department, Aarhus University.

Nielsen, J. (1986) Trip report from the ACM CHI'86 Conference on Human Factors in Computing Systems, Boston, MA, 13-17 April 1986. Technical Report ID-TR: 1986-12. Lyngby, Copenhagen: Department of Computer Science, Technical University of Denmark.

Nielsen, J. (1986): A virtual protocol model for computer-human interaction. *International Journal of Man-Machine Studies*, 24(3), 301-312.

Nievergelt, J. and Weydert, J. (1979) SITES, MODES and TRAILS: Telling the User of an Interactive System Where he is, What he can do, and How to get to places. Technical Reports. Institute for Informatics, ETH Zürich, 28.

Nisbett, R.E. and Wilson, T.D. (1977) Telling more than we can know: verbal reports on mental processes. *Psychological Review*, **84**, 231-259.

Norman, D.A. (1983) Some observations on mental models. In D. Gentner and L.A. Stevens. (eds.) *Mental Models*. Hillsdale, NJ: Lawrence Erlbaum Associates.

Norman, D.A. (1983). Design principles for human-computer interaction. *Proceedings of CHI '83: Human Factors in Computing Systems*. New York: ACM. 1-10.

Norman, D.A. (1986) Cognitive engineering. In D.A. Norman and S.W. Draper (eds.) *User Centered System Design*. Hillsdale, NJ: Lawrence Erlbaum Associates. 31-62.

Norman, D.A. and Draper, S.W. (1986) Introduction to D.A. Norman and S.W. Draper (eds.) *User Centred System Design*. Hillsdale, NJ: Lawrence Erlbaum Associates. 1-5.

Norman, D.A. and Draper, S.W. (1986) *User Centered System Design*. Hillsdale NJ: Lawrence Erlbaum Associates.

Nygaard, K. and Dahl, O.-J. (1981) The development of the SIMULA languages. In R.L. Wexelblat (ed.) *History of Programming Languages*. New York: Academic Press. 439-480.

O'Malley, C. (1986) Helping users help themselves. In D.A. Norman and S.W. Draper (eds.) *User Centered System Design* . Hillsdale, NJ: Lawrence Erlbaum Associates. Ch.18, 377-398.

O'Malley, C., Draper, S.W. and Riley, M.S. (1984) Constructive interaction: a method for studying human-computer interaction. In B. Shackel (ed.) *Human-Computer Interaction —Interact '84*. Amsterdam: North-Holland. 269-274.

Oborne, D. (1986) *Computers at Work*. London: Wiley.

Olson, J.R. (1985) Expanded design procedures for learnable, usable interfaces. *Proceedings of ACM CHI '85 Conference*, 142-143.

Olson, J.R. (1987) Cognitive analysis of people's use of software. In J.M. Carroll (ed.) *Interfacing Thought: Cognitive Aspects of Human-Computer Interaction*. Cambridge, MA: MIT Press. Ch. 10, 260-293.

Otway, H.J. and Peltu, M. (eds.) (1983) *New Office Technology: Human and Organizational Aspects*. London: Frances Pinter, for the Commission of the European Communities (INSIS-Paper).

Pagerey, P.D. (1981) Empirical evaluation of the BASIC programming language. IBM, Human Factors Department, System Communications Division. Kingston, NY, Report Number TR 21,769.

Parrish, R.N., Gates, J.L., Munger, S.J., Towstopiat, O.M., Grimma, P.R. and Smith, L.T. (1983) Design Guidelines and Criteria for User/Operator Transaction with Battlefield Automated Systems. Arlington, VA: US Army Research Institute for the Behavioural and Social Sciences. WF-28-AD-00.

Parsons, H.M. (1972) *Man-Machine System Experiments*. Baltimore: Johns Hopkins Press.

Pava, C. (1983) *Managing New Office Technology: An Organizational Strategy*. London: Collier MacMillan.

Payne, S.J. (1984) Task action grammars. In B. Shackel (ed.) *Human-Computer Interaction — Interact '84*. Amsterdam: North-Holland. 527-532.

Payne, S.J. and Green, T.R.G. (1983) The user's perception of the interaction language: a two-level model. *Proceedings of CHI '83: Human Factors in Computing Systems*. New York: ACM. 202-206.

Payne, S.J. and Green, T.R.G. (1986) Task-action grammars: a model of the mental representation of task languages. *Human Computer Interaction*, **2**(2), 93-133.

Pearl, J. (1986) Fusion, propagation and structuring in belief networks. *Artificial Intelligence*, **29**(3), 241-288.

Percival, L.C. and Johnson, S.K. (1986) Network management software usability test design and implementation. *IBM Systems Journal*, **25**, 92-104.

Peterson, D.E. and Botterill, J.H. (1982) IBM System/38 — an IBM usability experience. *Proceedings of Human Factors in Computer Systems*. Washington DC: Institute for Computer Sciences and Technology, National Bureau of Standards. 262-267.

Pfaff, G.E. (ed.) (1985) *User Interface Management Systems*. Berlin: Springer-Verlag.

Pfauth, M., Hammer, A. and Fissel, J. (1985) Software prototyping as a human factors tool. *Proceedings of the Human Factors Society 29th Annual Meeting (Vol. 1)*. Santa Monica, CA: The Human Factors Society. 467-469.

Pheasant, S.T. (1986) *Bodyspace*. London: Taylor & Francis.

Pollack, M. (1984) Good answers to bad questions: goal inference in expert advice-giving. *Proceedings of CSCSI/SCEIO*, London,Ontario. 20-24

Polson, P.G. (1987) A quantitative theory of human-computer interaction. In J.M. Carroll (ed.) *Interfacing Thought: Cognitive Aspects of Human-Computer Interaction*. Cambridge, MA: MIT Press. Ch. 8, 184-235.

Polson, P.G. and Kieras, D.E. (1984) A formal description of users' knowledge of how to operate a device and user complexity. *Behavior Research Methods, Instruments and Computers*, **16**, 249-255.

Polson, P.G. and Kieras, D.E. (1985) A quantitative model of the learning and performance of text editing knowledge. In L. Borman and B. Curtis (eds.) *CHI '85 Human Factors in Computer Systems II*. Proceedings of the CHI '85 Conference, San Francisco. Amsterdam: North-Holland. 207-212.

Polson, P.G., Muncher, E. and Engelbeck, G. (1986) A test of a common elements theory of transfer. *Proceedings of CHI '86: Human Factors in Computing Systems*. New York: ACM. 78-83.

Pomfrett, S.M., Olphert, C.W. and Eason, K.D. (1985) Work organisation implications of word processing. In B. Shackel (ed.) *Human-Computer Interaction — Interact '84*. Amsterdam: North-Holland. 847-853.

Price, J. (1984) *How to Write a Computer Manual.* Menlo Park, CA: Benjamin/Cummings.

Rappaport, A. (1986) Task analysis in intelligent systems design. WESTEX-86, IEEE 86CH2332-5, Anaheim. 61-67.

Rappaport, A. (1987) Multiple problem spaces in the knowledge design process. *International Journal of Man-Machine Studies*, **26**(4), 435-452.

Raveden, S. and Johnson, G. (1989) *Evaluating Usability of Human-Computer Interaction: A Practical Method.* Chichester: Ellis Horwood.

Redish, J.C. (1981) Understanding the limitations of readability formulas. *IEEE Transactions on Professional Communication*, **PC-24**, 46-48.

Redish, J.C., Battison, R. and Gold, E.S. (1985) Making information accessible to readers. In L. Odell and D. Goswami (eds.) *Writing in Non-academic Settings.* New York: Guilford Press. 129-153.

Redish, J.C., Felker, D.B. and Rose, A.M. (1981) Evaluating the effects of document design principles. *Information Design Journal*, **2**, 236-243.

Reisner, P. (1977) Use of psychological experimentation as an aid to development of a query language. *IEEE Transactions on Software Engineering*, **SE-3**, 218-229.

Reisner, P. (1981) Formal grammar and human factors design of an interactive graphics system. *IEEE Transactions on Software Engineering*, **SE-7**, 229-240.

Reisner, P. (1981) Human factors studies of database query languages: a survey and assessment. IBM Research Laboratory, Computer Science, San Jose, CA. Report Number RJ3070 (38116).

Reisner, P. (1982) Further developments towards using formal grammar as a design tool. *Proceedings of Human Factors in Computer Systems.* New York: ACM. 304-308.

Reisner, P. (1983) Formal grammars as a tool for analyzing ease of use: some fundamental concepts. In J.C. Thomas and M.L. Schneider (eds.) *Human Factors in Computer Systems.* Norwood, NJ: Ablex.

Reisner, P. (1987) Human-computer interaction: what is it and what research is needed. In J.M. Carroll (ed.) *Interfacing Thought: Cognitive Aspects of Human-Computer Interaction.* Cambridge, MA: MIT Press. 337-352.

Reitman, W. (ed.) (1984) *Artificial Intelligence Applications for Business.* Norwood, NJ: Ablex.

Rissland, E.L. (1984) Ingredients of intelligent user interfaces. *International Journal of Man-Machine Studies*, **21**(4), 377-388.

Roberts, T.L. and Moran, T.P. (1983) The evaluation of text editors: methodology and empirical results. *Communications of the ACM*, **26**, 265-283.

Rogers, C.R. (1967) *On Becoming a Person: A Therapist's View of Psychotherapy.* London: Constable.

Rohr, G. and Tauber, M.J. (1984) Representational frameworks and models for human computer interfaces. In G.C. van der Veer, T.R.G. Green, M.J. Tauber and P. Gorny (eds.) *Readings on Cognitive Ergonomics — Mind and Computers.* Berlin: Springer.

Rosenblatt, F. (1958) The Perceptron: a probabilistic model for information storage and organization in the brain. *Psychological Review*, **65**, 386-407.

Rosson, M.B., Maass, S. and Kellogg, W. (1987) Designing for designers: an analysis of design practice in the real world. *CHI + GI '87: Human Factors in Computing Systems.* New York: ACM.

Rubinstein, R. and Hersh, H. (1984) *The Human Factor: Designing Computer Systems for People.* Burlington, MA: Digital Press.

Runciman, C. and Hammond, N.V. (1986) User programs: a way to match computer systems and human cognition. In M.D. Harrison and A.F. Monk (eds.) *People and Computers: Designing for Usability.* Cambridge: Cambridge University Press. 464-481.

Russell, A.J. (1986) Delivering human factors skills to designers. Presentation to ESPRIT Technical Week, October, Brussels.

Rye, J. (1985) Computing readability. *Reading,* **19**, 110-116.

Sackman, H. (1970) *Man-Computer Problem Solving.* Princeton, NJ: Auerback.

Salmon, W.C. (1984) *Scientific Explanation and the Causal Structure of the World.* New Jersey: Princeton University Press.

Salvendy, G. (1987) (ed.) *Handbook of Human Factors.* Chichester: John Wiley.

Sasso, R. (1984) Personalising the software interface. In B. Shackel (ed.) *Human-Computer Interaction – Interact '84.* Amsterdam: North-Holland. 355-361.

Satchell, S. (1986) Compaq Deskpro 386: 80386 micro is fastest IBM PC compatible. *Info World,* October 20, 54-56.

Scapin, D.L. (1981) Computer commands in restricted natural language: some aspects of memory of experience. *Human Factors,* **23**, 365-375.

Schell, D.A. (1986) Usability testing of screen design: beyond standards, principles, and guidelines. Proceedings of the Human Factors Society 30th Annual Meeting (Vol. 2). Santa Monica, CA: The Human Factors Society. 1212-1215.

Schriver, K.A., Hayes, J.R., Danley, C.C., Wulff, W.A., Davies, L., Cerroni, K., Graham, D., Flood, E. and Bond, E. (1986) Designing computer documentation: a review of the literature. Pittsburgh, PA: Communications Design Center, Carnegie Mellon University.

SDS Ltd. (1985) *CORE - the Method.* Camberley, Surrey: Systems Designers Scientific Ltd. Issue 1.0.

Sengenberger, W. (ed.) (1978) *Der Gespaltene Arbeitsmarkt.* Frankfurt/M: Campus.

Shackel, B. (1959) Ergonomics for a computer. *Design,* **120**, 36-39.

Shackel, B. (1962) Ergonomics in the design of a large digital computer console. *Ergonomics,* **5**, 229-241.

Shackel, B. (1969) Man-computer interaction: the contribution of the human sciences. *Ergonomics,* **12**(4), 485-499.

Shackel, B. (1971) Criteria in relation to large scale systems and design. In W.T. Singleton, J.G. Fox and D. Whitfield (eds.) *Measurement of Man at Work.* London: Taylor & Francis. 223-231.

Shackel, B. (1974)(ed.) *Applied Ergonomics Handbook.* Guildford: Butterworth.

Shackel, B. (1981) The concept of usability. Proceedings of IBM Software and Information Usability Symposium, Poughkeepsie, NY, 15-18 September. 1-30; and in J.L. Bennett, D. Case, J. Sandelin and M. Smith (eds.) (1984) *Visual Display Terminals: Usability Issues and Health Concerns.* Englewood Cliffs, NJ: Prentice-Hall. 45-88.

Shackel, B. (1984) The concept of usability. In J.L. Bennett, D. Case, J. Sandelin and M. Smith (eds.) *Visual Display Terminals: Usability Issues and Health Concerns*. Englewood Cliffs, NJ: Prentice-Hall. 45-88.

Shackel, B. (1985) Ergonomics in information technology in Europe — a review. *Behaviour and Information Technology*, **4**(4), 263-287.

Shackel, B. (1985) Human factors and usability — whence and whither. In H.-J. Bullinger (ed.) *Software-Ergonomie '85*. Stuttgart: Teubner. 13-31.

Shackel, B. (1985)(ed.) *Human-Computer Interaction — Interact '84*. Amsterdam: North-Holland.

Shackel, B. (1986) IBM makes usability as important as functionality. *The Computer Journal*, **29**(3), 475-476.

Shackel, B. (1987) Human factors for usability engineering. In C.E.C. Directorate General of T.I.I. (ed.) *ESPRIT '87 — Achievements and Impact, Part Nº 2*. Amsterdam: Elsevier. 1019-1040.

Shackel, B., Eason, K.D. and Pomfrett, S. (1988) Organisational prototyping — a case study in matching the computer system to the organisation. In S.D.P. Harker and K.D. Eason (eds.) *Application of Information Technology*. London: Taylor & Francis, to be published.

Shaw, M.L.G. and Gaines, B.R. (1986) Interactive elicitation of knowledge from experts. *Future Computing Systems*, **1**(2), 151-190.

Shaw, M.L.G. and Gaines, B.R. (1987) KITTEN: knowledge initiation and transfer tools for experts and novices. *International Journal of Man-Machine Studies*, **27**(3), 251-280.

Shneiderman, B. (1980) *Software Psychology: Human Factors in Computer Information Systems*. Cambridge, MA: Winthrop.

Shneiderman, B. (1983) Direct manipulation: a step beyond programming languages. *Computer*, **16**(8), 57-69.

Shneiderman, B. (1986) Human-computer interaction research at the University of Maryland. *SIGCHI Bulletin*, **17**, 27-32.

Shneiderman, B. (1987) *Designing the User Interface: Strategies for Effective Human-Computer Interaction*. Reading, MA: Addison-Wesley.

Shortliffe, E.H. (1976) *Computer-Based Medical Consultations: MYCIN*. New York: Elsevier.

Silberman, C.E. (1966) *The Myths of Automation*. New York: Harper and Row.

Simon, H.A. (1969) *The Sciences of the Artificial*. Cambridge, MA: M.I.T. Press.

Smith, A. (1786) *An Inquiry into the Nature and Causes of the Wealth of Nations*. (Fourth edition). London: A. Strahan & T. Caddell.

Smith, D.C. (1977) *Pygmalion*. Basel: Birkhauser.

Smith, D.C., Irby, C., Kimball, R. and Harslem, E. (1982) The Star user interface: an overview. *Proceedings of the AFIPS 1982 National Computer Conference*, 50, 515-528.

Smith, D.C., Irby, C., Kimball, R., Verplank, B. and Harslem, E. (1983) Designing the Star user interface. In P. Degano and E. Sandewall (eds.) *Integrated Interactive Computing Systems*. Amsterdam: North-Holland. 297-313.

Smith, H.T. and Green, T.R. (1980)(eds.) *Human Interaction with Computers*. London: Academic Press.

Smith, S.L. and Mosier, J.N. (1984) Design guidelines for user-system interface software (Tech. Rep. No. EST-TR-84-190). Hanscom Air Force Base, Massachusetts: USAF Electronic Systems Division.

Smith, S.L. and Mosier, J.N. (1987) *Design Guidelines for User-System Interface Software.* Bedford, MA: The MITRE Corporation.

Snowberry, K., Parkinson, S.R. and Sisson, N. (1983) Computer display menus. *Ergonomics*, **26**, 699-712.

Software Digest, Inc. (1984) *The Ratings Book™ 1984/85 edition: IBM PC Word Processing Programs (Volume 1).* Wynnewood, PA: Software Digest, Inc.

Soloway, E. and Iyengar, S. (eds.) (1986) *Empirical Studies of Programmers.* Norwood, NJ: Ablex.

Sommers, N.I. (1980) Revision strategies of student writers and experienced adult writers. *College Composition and Communication*, **31**, 378-388.

Spackman, J.W.C. (1987) Towards an integrated network for DHSS. *Computer Bulletin*, **3**(1), 11-14.

Sproull, R.F., Sutherland, W.R. and Ullman, M.K. (1985) *Device Independent Graphics.* New York: McGraw-Hill.

STA (1985) *Promotion of R&D on Electronics and Information Systems That May Complement or Substitute for Human Intelligence.* Tokyo: Science and Technology Agency.

Stachowiak, H. (1973) *Allgemeine Modelltheorie.* Wien: Springer.

Staehle, W.H. (1985) *Management.* (Second edition) München: Vahlen.

Stewart, T.F.M. (1985) Ergonomics of the office. *Ergonomics*, **28**(8), 1165-1177.

Sticht, T. (1977) Learning by listening. In M.A. Just and P.A. Carpenter (eds.) *Cognitive Processes in Comprehension.* Hillsdale, NJ: Lawrence Erlbaum Associates. Ch. 8, 221-246.

Sufrin, B. (1986) Formal methods and the design of effective user interfaces. In M.D. Harrison and A.F. Monk (eds.) *People and Computers: Designing for Usability.* Cambridge: Cambridge University Press. 24-43.

Sugaya, H., Stelovsky, J., Nievergelt, J. and Biagioni, E.S. (1984) XS-2: An Integrated Interactive System. BBC Forschungsbericht KLR 84-73C. Baden (Switzerland).

Sullivan, M.A. and Chapanis, A. (1983) Human factoring a text editor manual. *Behaviour and Information Technology*, **2**, 113-125.

Swartout, W. and Balzer, R.M. (1982) On the inevitable intertwining of specification and implementation. *Communications of the ACM*, **25**(7), 438-440.

Swartout, W.R. (1986) Knowledge needed for expert system explanation. *Future Computing Systems*, **1**(2), 99-114.

Tauber, M.J. (1985) Top Down Design of Human-Computer Systems from the Demands of Human Cognition to the Virtual Machine — An Interdisciplinary Approach to Model Interfaces. Proc. IEEE Workshop on Languages for Automation. Palma de Mallorca, June 1985. 132-140.

Tauber, M.J. (1988). On modelling human-computer interfaces. In T.R.G Green, J.-M. Hoc, D. Murray and G.C. van der Veer (eds.) *Theory and Outcomes in Human-Computer Interaction.* London: Academic Press.

Taylor, B. and Harker, S.D.P. (1985) Developing human factors standards for dialogue design: a case study. In I.D. Brown, R. Goldsmith, K. Coombes and M.A. Sinclair (eds.) *Ergonomics International '85*. London: Taylor & Francis.

Tennant, H.R., Ross, K.M. and Thompson, C.W. (1983) Usable natural language interfaces through menu-based natural language understanding. *Proceedings of CHI '83 Conference on Human Factors in Computing Systems*, available from ACM Order Dept., P.O. Box 64145, Baltimore, MD.

Thomas, J.C. (1984) Organising for human factors. In Y. Vassiliou (ed.) *Human Factors and Interactive Computer Systems*. Norwood, NJ: Ablex. 29-46.

Thompson, D.A., McEvers, D.C. and Olson, C.H. (1986) Case study in data entry system design. *Proceedings of the Human Factors Society 30th Annual Meeting (Vol. 2)*. Santa Monica, CA: The Human Factors Society. 744-748.

Thorndike, E.L. and Woodworth, R.S. (1901) The influence of improvement in one mental function upon the efficiency of other functions. *Psychological Review*, 8, 247-261.

Totterdell, P. and Cooper, P. (1986) Design and evaluation of the AID adaptive front-end to Telecomm Gold. In M.D. Harrison and A.F. Monk (eds.) *People and Computers: Designing for Usability*. Cambridge: Cambridge University Press. 281-295.

Trist, E. (1981) *The Evolution of Socio-Technical Systems*. Ontario: Quality of Working Life Centre.

Trist, E.L., Higgin, G.W., Murray, H. and Pollock, A.B. (1963) *Organisational Choice*. London: Tavistock.

Tullis, T.S. (1986) A system for evaluating screen formats. *Proceedings of the Human Factors Society 30th Annual Meeting (Vol. 2)*. Santa Monica, CA: The Human Factors Society. 1216-1220.

Tyler, M. (1982) New life for voice mail (Editorial). *Datamation*, **28**(13), 53-55.

U.S. General Accounting Office (1985) Effectiveness of U.S. Federal Software Projects. Report available from the U.S. General Accounting Office, Washington, DC.

Ulich, E. (1978) Über das Prinzip der differentiellen Arbeitsgestaltung. *Industrielle Organisation*, **47**, 566-568.

Ulich, E., Baitsch, C., Katz, C., Ruch, L., Spinas, P. and Troy, N. (1986) Computer-aided office work — concepts and research findings. Zürich, unpublished paper presented to the ILO.

Van Cott, H.P. and Kincade, R.G. (eds.) (1972) *Human Engineering Guide to Equipment Design*. Washington, DC: US Government Printing Office.

Vandor, S. (1983) The Starburst user interface. *Byte*, **8**(12), 189-194.

Veer, van der G.C., Tauber, M.J., Waern, Y. and Muylwijk, B. (1985) On the interaction between system and user characteristics. *Behaviour and Information Technology*, 4(4), 289-308.

Volpert, W. (1982) Das modell der hierarchisch-sequentiellen Handlungsorganisation. In W. Hacker, W. Volpert and M.v. Cranach (eds.) *Kognitive und Motivationale Aspekte der Handlung*. Bern: Huber. 38-58.

Walker, J. (1986) On-line documentation: design and implementation issues. Paper presented at Workshop on HELP systems, Syracuse University, New York.

Wall, T.D. and Clegg, C.W. (1981) A longitudinal study of group work redesign. *Journal of Occupational Behaviour*, **2**, 31-49.

Waller, R.H.W. (1982) Text as diagram: using typography to improve access and understanding. In D.H. Jonassen (ed.) *The Technology of Text, 1*. Englewood Cliffs, NJ: Educational Technology Publications. 137-166.

Waller, R.H.W. (1985) Using typography to structure arguments: a critical analysis of some examples. In D.H. Jonassen (ed.) *The Technology of Text, 2*. Englewood Cliffs, NJ: Educational Technology Publications. 105-125.

Wasserman, A.I. (1986) Software tools in the user software engineering environment. In D.R. Barstow, H.E. Schrobe and E. Sanderwall (eds.) *Interactive Programming Environments*. New York: McGraw-Hill. 370-386.

Wasserman, A.I. and Shewmake, D.T. (1984) A RAPID/USE Tutorial. Medical Information Science, University of California, San Francisco.

Waterman, D.A. (1986) *A Guide to Expert Systems*. Reading, MA: Addison-Wesley.

Weinberg, G.M. (1971) *The Psychology of Computer Programming*. New York: Van Nostrand Rheinhold.

Welbank, M. (1983) *A Review of Knowledge Acquisition Techniques for Expert Systems*. BTRL, Ipswich: Martlesham Consultancy Services.

Whalley, P.C. and Flemming, R.W. (1975) An experiment with a simple recorder of reading behaviour. *Programmed Learning and Educational Technology*, **12**, 120-124.

Whitefield, A. (1985) A model of the engineering design process derived from Hearsay-II. In B. Shackel (ed.) *Human-Computer Interaction — Interact '84*. Amsterdam: North-Holland. 555-559.

Whiteside, J. and Wixon, D. (1987) Improving human-computer interaction: a quest for cognitive science. In J.M. Carroll (ed.) *Interfacing Thought: Cognitive Aspects of Human-Computer Interaction*. Cambridge, MA: MIT Press. 353-365.

Wilkerson, W. (1985) *Guide to Expert Systems Program Management*. Burlington, MA: Digital Publications.

Williges, B.H. and Williges, R.C. (1984) Dialogue design considerations for interactive computer systems. In F.A. Muckler (ed.) *Human Factors Review: 1984*. Santa Monica, CA: The Human Factors Society. 167-208.

Willis, J. and Miller, M. (1984) *Computers for Everybody: 1984 Buyer's Guide*. Beaverton, OR: Dilithium Press.

Wilson, B. (1984) *Systems: Concepts, Methodologies and Applications*. Chichester: Wiley.

Wilson, D. and Whiteside, J. (1985) Engineering for usability: lessons from the user-derived interface. *Proceedings of ACM CHI '85 Conference*, 144-147.

Wilson, M., Barnard, P. and MacLean, A. (1986) Using an expert system to convey HCI information. In M.D. Harrison and A.F. Monk (eds.) *People and Computers: Designing for Usability*. Cambridge: Cambridge University Press. 482-497.

Winer, B.J., (1962) *Statistical Principles in Experimental Design*. New York: McGraw-Hill.

Winograd, T. (1972) *Understanding Natural Language*. Edinburgh: The University Press.

Winston, P.H. (1984) *LISP*. Reading, MA: Addison-Wesley.

Woodmansee, G.H. (1985) The Visi On™ experience — from concept to marketplace. In B. Shackel (ed.) *Human-Computer Interaction — Interact '84*. Amsterdam: North-Holland. 871-875.

Woodward, J. (1958) *Management and Technology*. London: HMSO.

Woodward, J. (1965) *Industrial Organization: Theory and Practice*. London: Oxford University Press.

Wright, P. (1980) Strategy and tactics in the design of forms. *Visible Language*, **14**, 151-193.

Wright, P. (1981) Problems to be solved when creating usable documents. Paper presented at IBM symposium on Software and Information Usability. Available as HF077 from IBM Hursley, Winchester, UK.

Wright, P. (1987) Issues of content and presentation in document design. In M. Helander (ed.) *Handbook of Human-Computer Interaction.* Amsterdam: North Holland. 629-652.

Wright, P. and Hull, A.J. (1988) Reading to do: creating contingent action plans. *British Journal of Psychology*, **79**, 187-211.

Wright, P., Creighton, P. and Threlfall, S.M. (1982) Some factors determining when instructions will be read. *Ergonomics*, **25**, 225-237.

Young, R.M. (1981) The machine inside the machine: users' models of pocket calculators. *International Journal of Man-Machine Studies*, **15**, 51-85.

Young, R.M. (1983) Surrogates and mappings: two kinds of conceptual models for interactive devices. In D. Gentner and A.L. Stevens (eds.) *Mental Models*. Hillsdale, NJ: Lawrence Erlbaum Associates. 35-52.

Young, R.M. and Barnard, P.J. (1987) The use of scenarios in human-computer interaction research: turbocharging the tortoise of cumulative science. *Proceedings of CHI + GI '87: Human Factors in Computing Systems*. New York: ACM. 291-296.

Young, R.M. and Green, T.R.G. (1986) Towards programmable user models. *Alvey Programme Annual Report 1986 Poster Supplement*. London: Alvey Directorate. Project MMI/112, p. 319.

Ziegler, J.E., Hoppe, H.U. and Faehnrich, K.-P. (1986) Learning and transfer for text and graphics editing with a direct manipulation interface. In M. Mantei and P. Orbeton (eds.) *Human Factors in Computing Systems – III*. Proceedings of CHI '86 Conference, Boston. Amsterdam: North-Holland. 72-77.

Ziegler, J.E.; Vossen, P.H. and Hoppe, H.U. (1986) On using production systems for cognitive task analysis. Proceedings of 3rd European Conference on Cognitive Ergonomics, Paris. Le Chesnay: Institut National de Recherche en Informatique et en Automatique. 115 -128.

Zipf, G.F. (1965) *Human Behavior and the Principle of Least Effort* . (2nd edition) New York: Hafner.

Zoltan, E. and Chapanis, A. (1982) What do professional persons think about computers? *Behaviour and Information Technology*, **1**, 55-58.

AUTHOR INDEX

SUBJECT INDEX